ANA REGINA NOGUEIRA

FRATERNITY
INTERNATIONAL HUMANITARIAN MISSIONS

Shasti Association

IRDIN

Copyright © 2020 by Ana Regina Nogueira da Costa

Irdin is a nonprofit publishing house

Photos
By the author and by anonymous volunteers

Graphic project
Ana Regina Nogueira, in collaboration with Pedro Crown

Cover
Camarinha Comunicação

Cover photo
Feliciano Henrique Machado Coelho

Proofreading
Volunteer team of Irdin Editora Association

International Cataloging in Publication Data (CIP)

Nogueira, Ana Regina

Fraternity — international humanitarian missions /
Ana Regina Nogueira — Carmo da Cachoeira : Irdin, 2020.

484p. : il.

ISBN 978-65-990510-7-4

1. Humanitarian Aid. 2. Missionaries. 3. Refugees.
4. Natural catastrophes. 5. Spiritual Life. I. Title

CDD: 361.7

The book was written in Portuguese and translated into English
All rights reserved by
SHASTI ASSOCIATION
P.O. Box 318 – Mt Shasta, CA
96067-0318
www.shasti.org
ASSOCIAÇÃO IRDIN EDITORA
Cx. Postal 2, Carmo da Cachoeira—MG, Brasil, CEP 372225-000
Phones: (55 35) 3225-2252 | (55 35) 3225-2616
www.irdin.org.br

I thank my spiritual instructor, the philosopher and writer José Triguei-rinho Netto, who taught me treasures, told me to write this book and read it line by line, offering me precious suggestions.

I thank the volunteers listed below, who work for free for the sake of universal Good and Peace.

To the primary missionaries, protagonists who gave me support in the course of interviews: Ana Maria Moreira Bruzzi (Shen) – also content editor, Gaston Capdeville (Imer), Ricardo Rinaldi Baumgartner, Vânia Fátima dos Santos (Clara).

To those who shared experiences and reflections: Anastasia Ioannidis, Anderson Pereira Santiago, André Luís Esteves Pinto (Frei Thomas), Angelica Del Lujan Baglivo, Arthur Francisco dos Santos Gonçalves, Augusto dos Reis Vieira e Silva (Frei Zeferias de Tarso), Camila Ribeiro Quaresma (Irmã María de la Alegría), Celina Estela Santos, Claudia Sanches Machado, Cristiane de Oliveira Ferreira Soares, David Marinho e Silva (Iesus), Débora Caldeira Murta, Denise Mendes Gomes, Eliana Coelho Ramos, Elizane Gonçalves Pires (Madre Maria Glória), Fernando Esteves Pinto, Flora Agni Teresa Lima, Florencia Biancalana, Gabriel da Cunha Nunes de Araujo Reis, Helentiana de Paiva Gonçalves, Juan Jose Correa Franco (Elamed), Juliana Oliveira Maurício da Silva Mangaba (Irmã Maria Auxiliadora), Juliana Pacifico Cabral (Esther), Lilia Ramona Cabral Sánches (Faustina), Luiz Fernando Perez de Moraes, Mabel Teresa Jozami, Luzia Serdano (Mariandja), Maria Alexandrina Fonseca Magalhães, Maria Alice de Miranda Carvalho, Maria Cairamir Arruda Braga, Mauricio Gonçalves de Oliveira Guidetti, Mauro Cristiano Cavalcanti, Mene Abdo Meni, Pedro Bambini Vasconcellos (Vitório), Míriam Blos, Olga Elena di Lorenzo Cedeño, Patricia Sánchez, Rosimar Cordeiro da Silva (Madre Teresa), Rosineide Lima Pereira de Freitas (Rosi), Samanta Mary Martins Singh, Silvio José de Campos, Stella Giok Hoa Sih, Tenente J. Lima, Valéria Nogueira Alves Meni (Hayla), Viviana Walsh, Wanderley Américo de Freitas.

To the proofreader in the Portuguese language, Teresinha Pires, for her support to the author in each step of the writing, Beatriz Beleza and Maria de Lourdes Tavares Costa (Ave Isis). To the content editor Josué Nogueira dos Santos (Friar Sebastian). To the audio transcribers Dilma Villela, Evânia Oliveira, Iara Gomes de Bulhões (Sister María de la Compasión), Marilda Cerri, Regina Célia Frederico.

To the translator into English, Eliza Graça and Mauro Rotenberg, and their proofreaders, John David Cutrell, Linda Rae Summer, Luis Gonzaga Fragoso and Terry Lee. To the translator and proofreaders into Spanish.

To the anonymous missionaries who recorded most of the missions photographic collection, and to the photographers Feliciano Henrique Machado Coelho and Murilo Gomide Machado Coelho. To my son Pedro Crown, who drew the maps of the book and helped me create its graphic design.

To the team of volunteers of Irdin Editora, especially to its director Jose Luis Lopez Cortes and to its designer Alice Keiko Taira.

To the members of the Council of Permanent Guidance of Fraternidade— Humanitarian International Federation: Carmem Cecilia Correa Guedim (Mother María del Salvador), Elisabeth Cesar Blanco (Mother María Shimani), Francesco Gullo (Friar Luciano), Samuel Berkman Mendonça Santos (Friar Supremo).

To thousands of personages from diverse nations, who are present in this book. Finally, to all human and non-human beings who give themselves to missionary care, the *raison-d'être* of the fraternal encounter.

And last, to Eryannis Maria Flores Torres, the Venezuelan girl on the cover, photographed in the shelter of Boa Vista for displaced indigenous people, whose story is on the last page of this book.

To all, our deep gratitude.

Dedicated to Trigueirinho,
our patient instructor.

Table of Contents

PART VIII   PULSING CHRONICLES

PART IX   INSPIRING LIVES

EPILOGUE

ARGENTINA 1 Capilla del Monte, 2 Cordoba, 3 Buenos Aires,
4 Surroundings of Resistencia, 5 Tartagal

BRAZIL 6 Belo Horizonte, 7 Boa Vista, 8 Carmo da Cachoeira and surroundings,
9 Pacaraima, 10 Palmeira dos Índios and vicinity, 11 São Carlos,
12 São Paulo, 13 Vista Alegre

CHILE 14 Doñihue, 15 San Javier de Loncomilla, 16 Santa Olga

COLÔMBIA 17 Cúcuta

NICARÁGUA 18 Managua

PARAGUAY 19 Ciudad del Leste e Presidente Franco

URUGUAY 20 Ciudad de la Costa and surroundings, 21 Dolores, 22 Paysandu

Fraternidade Humanitarian Missions

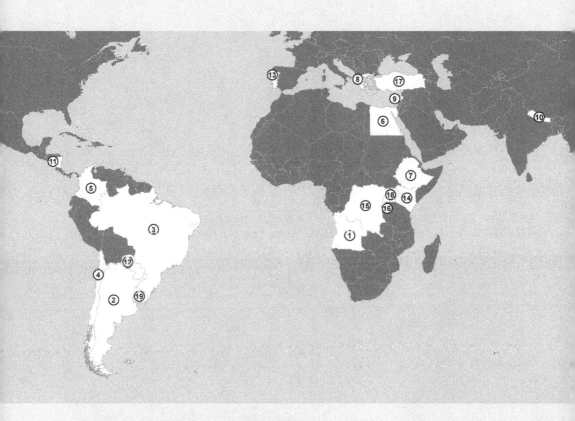

1 Angola   2 Argentina   3 Brazil   4 Chile   5 Colombia
6 Egypt   7 Ethiopia   8 Greece   9 Lebanon
10 Nepal   11 Nicaragua   12 Paraguay   13 Portugal
143 Kenya   15 Democratic Republic of the Congo
16 Rwanda   17 Turkey   18 Uganda   19 Uruguay

List of acronyms and abbreviations

ANVISA   National Health Surveillance Agency, Brazil

APAC   Association for the Protection and Assistance to Convicted Persons, Brazil

APAE   Association of Parents and Friends of Disabled Persons, Brazil

ASAM   Association for Solidarity to Asylum Seekers and Migrants, Turkey

AURORA   Light-Community of Fraternity, Aurora, Paysandu, Uruguay

CÉU AZUL   Light-Nucleus of Sacred Heaven, Belo Horizonte, Brazil

CLC   House of Light on the Hill Association, Minas Gerais, Brazil

CRER-SENDO   Light-Community of the New Earth, Rio de Janeiro, Brazil

ERKS   Light-Community of Brotherhood, Cordoba, Argentina

FAB   Brazilian Air Force, Brazil

FIHF   Fraternidade—International Humanitarian Federation

FIHM   Fraternidade—International Humanitarian Missions

FIGUEIRA   Light-Community of Figueira, Minas Gerais, Brazil

FUNAI   National Foundation of the Indigenous People, Brazil

GM   General Meeting in the Light-Communities of Figueira and Aurora

GRANJA VIANA   Light-Nucleus of Figueira in São Paulo, Brazil

IOHR   International Organization of Human Rights

NGO   Non-Governmental Organization

GMO   Grace Mercy Order

PADF   Pan American Development Foundation

PAHO   Pan-American Health Organization

SESAI   Special Secretariat for Indigenous Health, Brazil

SETRABES   Roraima Labor and Social Welfare Secretariat, Brazil

UFRR   Federal University of Roraima, Brazil

UN   United Nations

UNESCO   United Nations Educational, Scientific and Cultural Organization

UNFPA   United Nations Population Fund

UNHCR   United Nations High Commissioner for Refugees

UNICEF   United Nations Children's Fund

USAID   United States Agency for International Development

Introduction

If a fruit tree is bursting into bloom, it is because its roots are very deep and have overcome many obstacles that allow them to share the best they can express.

In this context, Humanitarian Missions emerge as a result of the work of over thirty years of a group of volunteers. During the cycles of maturing, these volunteers went through storms, faced the aridity of deserts, survived hard lessons of altruistic life. Despite the imperfection of the human condition, the missionaries are willing to bear fruit, whose flavor they will not taste because the role of a leafy tree is to yield fruits to travelers, to give shade to those who need to pause, to give aromas to those who need harmony and to give the colors of their flowers to those who have become accustomed to the monotony of the monochromatic life of current human society.

Through the Humanitarian Missions, Fraternidade—Humanitarian International Federation aims to promote its best values—equality, fraternity, cooperation, the spirit of common good and neutrality, values that are developed for the sake of evolution. This is reflected in the evolution of the other Kingdoms of Nature, whose positive coexistence with humanity leads them to growth.

The Humanitarian Missions described in this book were undertaken with the spirit of reflecting values through activities that foster the uplifting of people, environments and other beings of Nature.

Missionaries who participate in actions that benefit the balance of specific regions, communities, and countries may awaken to the profound meaning of existence. By giving less importance to their own needs and giving priority to the needs of others, they are bound to find the fundamental key for rescuing the archetypes of human consciousness: the common good.

In this book, Ana Regina Nogueira fascinates us through her language, she charms the reader with her authenticity and broadens horizons within each sensible human being who is willing to rediscover 'something else' to give meaning to their life and to that of other beings.

May this book take us beyond the author's reports, far beyond them... and make us realize that whenever we decide to serve the planet and humankind, we will find that 'something' right there, within us.

I hope you enjoy reading it, and may you have a good re-encounter with the missionary spirit itself.

Frei Luciano
General manager and member of the Council of Permanent
Guidance of Fraternidade—International Humanitarian Federation

PROLOGUE

*A missionary does not propagate
any religious creed, but their duty
is to activate the inner potential
of the souls they attend to.*

Trigueirinho

What is it to be a missionary?

*The main thing is to look at the other
and tell them, "I'm here for you".*
A missionary consideration

The intriguing question is: *What does being a missionary mean, after all?*

Without formulas found in books, the group gradually grasps the archetype. A missionary's life is about defending, raising, supporting people, it is about simply being. Before leaving for one of their first trips, they were given the instruction: *A missionary should not indoctrinate anyone, just be peace.*

There are words that, besides having body and history, have a mind, a soul and a non-material spirit to be unveiled. Such is the case for the word **missionary**.

Dictionaries partially explain it. The Houaiss Dictionary of the Portuguese Language defines the word's **body** as: *the one who has received or assumed the duty of conducting certain tasks or carrying out their fulfillment.* In the mind of the word is embedded the Portuguese verb *missionar: to propagate, to disseminate an idea.* The **soul** of the word missionary designates: *a living expression of Universal Love.* What about the **spirit** of the word? It is: *one of the paths of consecration to the Evolutionary Plan.*

Missionaries of Fraternidade have served in nineteen countries in Africa, WWAmerica, Asia, Europe and the Middle East between 2011 and 2018. Without resorting to proselytism, they share daily lives, talk, play and pay attention to strengthening bonds with those they serve. At the same time, they adhere to the essential task of raising consciousness. Therefore, changes happen naturally.

Like flocks of birds, they practice flapping their wings restlessly to conquer heights and their goal. The leader goes ahead, setting the tone, and in charge of making contacts and the overall organization of each mission. He finds support from the most committed ones, who fly on his right and left sides. These represent both the masculine and the feminine polarity. In harmony and with mutual respect, they make decisions and statements to the press and deal with official bodies. With eagle eyes, they indicate courses of action, curves, and shortcuts to those who follow them. They also protect the general harmony.

The missionaries core activity is made up of four **primary missionaries**, who are entirely dedicated to meeting the standards set by superior commanders. They donate their life for the Purpose of Love to be fulfilled. They may be in Northern Brazil today, in Europe next week, engaged for a few months in a permanent mission or coordinating a temporary, national or international mission. They are called and sent to the most difficult, most distant, most conflictive places, which require a higher degree of preparation and maturity.

They are role models for **auxiliary missionaries**, who dedicate themselves partially to the task. Remaining for periods on permanent missions, they gain experience and expand their knowledge. They are committed with every day life, jobs and families. Most of them are appointed for missions not too far away from the headquarters, considered as having a medium degree of difficulty and danger. They are also fundamental in supporting the most complex missions, conducted by primary missionaries.

With the expansion of the missionary activity, new volunteers help weave the **Planetary Mission Network**. Even if they participate in only one mission, some of them say it was a turning point in their life. Upon returning to their hometown, they transmit the peace and strength gained in their experience. The most important thing is not the size of the work done, but the amount of love put into doing it.

After all, what is a mission?

Shaped by each member's will, technical knowledge, maturity, fraternal and collaborative attitude, it brings together missionary energy—whether there are thirty, fourteen, ten, seven or even four members—to fulfill the proposed goal. Internal issues are gradually dissolved during compassionate help, and souls can be rescued from social chaos.

Simplicity is the life proposed by the primary and auxiliary missionaries. They practice not having individual privileges: *If we are given a piece of chocolate, we must share it in equal parts with the group. Anyone who drinks coffee at the airport pays for all.*

Instructions received through lectures over the years guides them: *Practice being empty, having no desires, no complaints, and do not oppose whatever life brings you. Practice giving whatever you can give and then leaving without any attachment. Practice prayer combined with service.*

A primary missionary says: *In Africa, we embraced the liturgies proposed by the Missionaries of Charity of Mother Teresa of Calcutta. Prayer plus service is a perfect formula for moving lightly amidst chaos, to keep balance in the face of what we witness. It reduces feelings of hopelessness and doubts that arise in the contact with people's needs. It helps us to endure horrors and conflicts without being disheartened by the weight of circumstances.*

The missionaries know that serving others is one of the most powerful ways to transform themselves and their surroundings and awakens their hidden potentials. Each situation calls for a certain type of assistance. They adapt quickly and learn from each encounter. As they commune with the pain of those who were struck by a catastrophic event and meet the needs of the deprived, they are being trained.

Overcoming ourselves is the most difficult challenge, says a primary missionary. *I am my greatest adversary and my greatest sister. It is not easy, because I carry myself wherever I go, bearing my own good and not so good things. But I love quite a few aspects of mine. If it were not so, how could I love my neighbor as Christ taught us: "Love your neighbor as yourself"? I had to learn how to love myself not egoistically, without hero worship.*

At first, the missionary is filled with impulses. The passing of time is the big problem to be overcome. Surrendering completely brings with it some suffering, some uneasiness, some anguish. However, joy emerges again as positive outcome arise from their actions.

It delights them to observe values and virtues blossoming within themselves and in others, realizing how much they are served while they serve. Also, they count on strong bonds that little by little are strengthened among the members of the team: *If we begin to feel bad, we seek support in one another to raise our vibratory level and accomplish the mission.*

Fraternidade Missionary. Pacaraima, Roraima, Brazil, 2018

Joy is one of the characteristics of the group: it dissolves hopelessness, it unblocks sorrows wherever it goes, it relieves disbelief, it trains hearts. In order to clear the air, the soldiers of peace laugh together. During pauses of relaxation to renew energies between battles, they adopted the good-humored theory that classifies missionaries in three types: Nutella, the trademark of a hazelnut butter, Root and Legendary.

The one who only drinks light tea is a Nutella. A Root faces tough black tea and hard, sugar-free coffee. Well, a missionary asking for hibiscus tea does not remain on the mission. The Nutellas like to live the good life. The Roots will always accept anything they find, whether they sleep on the floor or in a bed. Another class of people arose unexpectedly. When someone put salt instead of sugar in the coffee and drank it without making a face, the group of the Legendary was born, who revels in newly steeped boldo tea. They say: *A Legendary is a rarity, a Root is the rustic, a Nutella is the one who likes amenities, taking a hot bath every day.* When they go pick up a missionary at the airport, the jokes begin: the Nutella arrive with a suitcase on wheels, and the Roots with a heavy-equipment backpack. But, as everyone needs a break, every now and then, the Roots and the Legendary adopt Nutellist comforts.

What keeps them fresh? Supported by subtle vibrations, even when feeling tired after an intense day, they wake up restored. Still, from time to time they leave the front for a period and return to Figueira, the mother-house community of all. They need phases of reflection, recovery, retreat, and deeper inner contacts. Being a missionary is taking a path of consecration to Love that shapes character and forges serving souls.

Humanitarian Missions

Triumph or defeat, this is in the hands of God.
So let's celebrate the battle!
From the movie: Lorenzo's Oil, by George Miller

It was 2011. A new life was beginning between endless valleys and hills. On the summit of an illuminated hill, the first stars saw hundreds of people praying for peace. In the distance, a forest began to burn. Smoke billowed, fire spread, getting redder and more visible at nightfall. Towards the end of the prayer meeting, the Immediate Action Team, which later became the Solar Group, were summoned to deal with it. For 30 years it has been putting out fires and assisting people in accidents on BR-381 highway, near the town of Carmo da Cachoeira. The members left at once. After hours of battle into the night, they defeated the flames from the arson attack.

Prompt obedience to the call for help from distressed trees, technical training, and group unity were observed. Since the incident took place, the group was considered mature enough to take a bigger step. A few days later, those who were at the Light-Community of Figueira heard a surprising proposal: the announcement of a mission to Nepal.

That year, in September, the missionary group Fraternidade was born, a branch of the neutral and independent Fraternidade—International Humanitarian Federation, FIHF, which takes on broad tasks to disseminate universal peace. Ready to embrace the foreigners' pain, the missionaries served the Nepalese for two weeks. Since this mission, the first of many others around the world, they have been rekindling the passion of enthusiasm in lukewarm consciousnesses.

Exactly six years later, a new missionary activity cycle was born. Thanks to the remarkable effectiveness in the support to indigenous and non-indigenous Venezuelan refugees in Roraima, a state in the north of Brazil, the Fraternidade was invited to be a partner of the United Nations, UN. Thus, in September 2017, FIHF formalized a mutual cooperation with the United Nations High Commissioner for Refugees—UNHCR, in order to support the Brazilian government and other entities in the management of an increasing number of shelters. At first, two shelters for Venezuelan indigenous people came and later, some others for non-indigenous people, who are called *criollos*.

Volunteers discover the joy of giving themselves without asking anything in return. This is one of the goals of the Humanitarian Missions, which are a role model for a missionary approach that emerged in response to the trauma caused to humanity by World War II. They impose nothing on people and communities, instead they help them to remember universal values that are pressing to be restored in humanity. They do not carry religious or cultural messages to people: they only radiate inner healing so that reconciliation among men may expand throughout the Earth.

Humanitarian missions have brought new colors and nuances to the old proselytical model that had taken place over centuries. Until 1945, proselytical missions were working all over the planet. Their immovable purpose was to convert, catechize and attract followers or supporters for certain causes, doctrines, religions, ideologies, and philosophies.

The Fraternidade missionaries do not indoctrinate. On the contrary, they encourage the cultural manifestation of the people, their faith, and the talent of each individual. They welcome neighbors of any creed, nation or tribe listening to the most diverse dialects and languages they don't know. They enjoy the multiplicity of expressions, without sticking to the old disagreement and boundaries established by men.

Missionaries do not find it difficult to communicate with foreigners. They understand them from their heart, without linguistic limitations. A primary missionary explains: *We use other resources in order to have a dialogue. We look closely at the person who is pleading for something, until we are able to identify their needs. If they ask us for medicine, it is not only the remedy itself that they need, above all they need to make a connection and receive an affectionate touch. Can I supply their simple demand? Sure, I can. I give them the medicine and, more than that, I offer them my attentive presence. When we accept the other, this calms them down, it reassures them, it brings a glow to their sore eyes.*

Willing to go to the remotest parts of the Earth, the humanitarian pilgrims bring together selfless actions, and a sense of responsibility. They feel a profound union with their fellow beings and with the Kingdoms of Nature—mineral, plant and animal. The focus of the missionary model is on seeking the other, by reaching out to someone, to an animal, to a tree, or to the waters.

The humanitarian pilgrims get transported by the winds. In Uruguay a hurricane passes, and they move southward. In Africa, they cross oceans to comfort Ethiopian street dwellers in their agony. In Turkey, they smile to children in exile. In Brazil, they play the flute with Brazilian countryside men, rescue a cat, or plant trees. They come face-to-face with the inexplicable pain of the orphaned boy from Syria or the Congo, to the Afghan or indigenous refugee, to the Chilean artist whose house disappeared in the flames of a forest fire, to the donkey covered by the toxic mud of Mariana, in the state of Minas Gerais, Brazil, to locations and debris to be cleaned up.

Now they clear a stream silted by dry leaves and twigs, harvest avocados, load a truck with fruits, separating the green ones from the ripe, and even distribute them in the farms of Light-Communities. They may be looking after babies in Egypt or take an indigenous grandmother to a hospital.

They work for love, not for money. They live on the food, clothing, and under the roof they are given. They prefer challenges and sacrifices to comfort and consumption. They take a vow of poverty when they devote themselves to the service. What is a vow of poverty? *Indeed, we have no possessions, not even our own room. If, by the time we come back to Figueira, one of the communities where we live, our previous room is occupied, and we are given a different bed, we adapt to it. The moment we devote ourselves to this task, we have three or four changes of clothing. That's our outfit, and two backpacks, one of which is used for the trips. Personal belongings, such as study material, are essentially a couple of boxes and a second backpack, which are stored in the community while we are traveling. These are our possessions. Thank God, that's enough. Of course, it's not always easy, because bodies have their needs. However, if these needs are real, by spiritual law eventually they will be fulfilled.*

Their physical exertion is immense, but the effort to transform themselves is even greater. In order to have a better vision, a better intuition, they rely on mysterious inner fires, which build their strength. They give themselves to the visible life, but they belong to non-material life and to distant radiant galaxies.

A number of personal attributes are their supporting pillars. Naturally super-dynamic, missionaries should inspire confidence, be willing to help, be practical and organized, be calm and self-assured in their speech and actions, be agile in movements and able to respond in a second.

Having packed and ready to begin a journey towards a sunny Brazilian countryside, all of a sudden the eternal traveler receives a quick notice of a change in location and deviates his route towards European winter. A missionary obeys: *This is a constant reality in our lives. This teaches us the dynamics of constructing and deconstructing.*

In quick steps, but not rushing, they gradually evolve, mature, and climb the mountain without a peak. Ricardo, the coordinator of the Missionaries, explains: *We work as a group and move in a single line through the metropolises or in the woods. If we walked side by side, we would occupy the whole width of the sidewalk or the road. By walking this way, we don't disperse, take better care of each other, and no one gets lost or lags behind.*

They enter the most diverse places, trusting that they are being protected and under a Higher guidance. United to the Eternal, they linger over distressed eyes. A missionary does not hesitate, they softly come closer to the person who is suffering and tell them quietly: *I also fell, I was wounded, I had doubts and fears, but I got up and I'm here to give you a hand.* Out of a close bond established in respectful contact with the misfortune of others, they sow harmony.

Besides what is visible, what else do they offer? Everything, including their own life , which, added to those of the participants in each mission, creates an inner urge for rescuing people.

They get strengthened by morning and afternoon group prayers. The love they feel for creation builds pathways through which the Divine

Missionaries of Fraternidade move about
in single lines in Nepal, Ethiopia and Turkey.

sends energy currents that release records of pain from the human consciousness. The One and Only observes the Law of Free Will and just needs a sincere human 'yes' in order to fully collaborate with us. The missionaries offer It their permission. Their selfless presence helps to dissolve inner conflicts and to open pathways so that healing may flow at deeper levels. This is the biggest job, which lasts even after they leave.

They say: *Fulfilling material needs is not our main function. Still, sometimes we try to settle issues related to housing, food, health, hygiene, employment, which are under the responsibility of governmental organizations.*

After meeting members of national and international entities, a missionary says: *In the planet, there is a multinational group dedicated to the general good. In fact, UN officials and representatives of various religions are also missionaries. We make soul contacts with them, and also with people we assisted and labored for.*

She throws light on the meaning of a 'soul contact': *It does not depend on what a person believes, on which religion or political party they have chosen, or on their social view of the world. It does not depend on this person's degree, or level of education. It's something totally different. There are groups of world servers scattered across many countries, who contact the soul of another human being by giving them unconditional love. It's magical to find one of them! But sometimes we only realize the feeling of communion at our departure. We have to leave! Now what? We become One, and we want this union to last forever.*

The missionaries maintain a close relationship with their instructors, who guide and supervise them. Members from several countries working in other branches of the same organization, follow their activities through the trilingual website www.fraterinternacional.org.

The server devoted to the spheres of Truth takes into account the threefold physical, emotional and mental nature of man. He knows the worst evil is beyond it, in consciousnesses that fade. His tiny but transcendental actions open doors to the future, which are recorded in spheres that assist us from some point in the universe.

Going beyond the material horizon

In this world, aspirants may find
enlightenment through two different paths.
For the one who is contemplative: the
path of knowledge. For the active one:
the path of selfless actions.
Bhagavad Gita

The future is immersed in mysteries. In truth, the future is a great strategist. Gradually it shows us that which would be frightening if it had been completely known before.

In the 80's, José Trigueirinho Netto has created two expressions of community life. In 1984, the Céu Azul was inaugurated in Belo Horizonte, followed by the implementation of Figueira Community, in 1987. The dizzying and unusual developments arising from the newly manifested global current of good could never have been imagined. It never stopped growing. An international project has flourished and it gives fruits.

In order to include all its branches of voluntary services, Fraternidade—Humanitarian International Federation, FIHF, was created in 2010. Immediately, some members arrived from various Brazilian states in order to turn the organization into a legal entity. Strongly motivated, some came alone while others brought their families. They invested generous effort until FIHF gained the status of an institutional entity with its headquarters in Carmo da Cachoeira, Minas Gerais, Brazil.

As mentioned in its statutes: *The FIHF aims to promote the cooperation that leads to universal peace and love, in their most varied aspects.*

All support provided to the non-profit entity comes from donations of collaborators of different ages, backgrounds, countries, and experiences. Their aim is to help others. They all consider themselves as brothers and sisters of the great human family and of the Kingdoms of Nature.

These affiliate branches are under the protection of the FIHF: five Light-Communities—two in Brazil and the others in Argentina, Portugal and Uruguay. There are three Light-Nucleus and also Service or Religious Associations and Marian Centers.

These sectors work on seven fronts: Humanitarian help—charity in action; Assistance to Animals—love in action; Preservation of the Environment—compassion in action; Education—light in action; Culture and Art—harmony in action; Group Life—brotherhood in action; Philosophical and Ecumenical Activities—consciousness in action.

The institution also organizes, protects and intermediates the emergence of new branches of service, such as its two pillars: the Missionaries of Fraternidade and the Planetary Light-Network.

In order to compose a mission, in addition to the missionaries themselves, members of the Planetary Light-Network can be summoned, as well as monastics of Grace Mercy Order—GMO. This ecumenical religious association aspires to reconnect life to the sacred and unite one being to another, one culture to another, and one nation to another. At a distance, are those who have the fundamental role of providing financial support, of collaborating with the diffusion sector and of supporting missions by praying from their own homes.

Operating in twenty-three countries, the Planetary Light-Network is, according to the instructor Trigueirinho, a spiritual heritage of mankind. It has around 300 groups with more than 2000 members who, among other activities, help the permanent missions, two of them established in the Brazilian states of Minas Gerais and Roraima.

The Light-Network is also a provider for the Regional Missions. One of them is in Alagoas, Brazil. The Mission in Argentina, in the province of Chaco, supports indigenous Qom communities. The one in Paraguay assists indigenous people who make a living from the collection of recyclables in Ciudad del Este dumps

Each of these servers aims to eventually cross a bridge which will lead them beyond material horizon.

Conversations with missionaries

Each man bears a secret within himself.
Rarely does the curtain of the past roll back,
only when subtle energy abounds during one's
earthly life. The memory suddenly illuminates,
and the past stands out in all justice
Aum, by Helena Roerich

In order to write this book, I had a long introductory talk via Skype with Ricardo, the general coordinator of the missionaries, who was then serving in Greece. He gave me a general overview of the evolution of the mission's task and its two fundamental principles: love for all and the practice of charity.

I devoted hours to vibrant, real-time talks with each of the primary missionaries, along with a few secondary ones and members of the Light-Network. These conversations took place in a relaxed atmosphere, full of smiles and laughter.

Good-humored and showing a spiritual vision of life, they freely express themselves telling their traveling experiences with radiant faces and occasional tears. They would expose facts and feelings mingled with reflections, and glimpses of stories about characters that inhabited their memories.

Their voices unraveled threads of luminous or miserable experiences. With my eyes fixed on theirs, I followed them through the sands of the human desert. I wandered through landscapes of the world, and I witnessed pain turning into relief, hunger into a banquet. I drank coffee made by Muslims and I listened to mosque bells. I was in the wild paths of weeping, and I felt the meaning of mercy, I entered houses and temples, visible places and invisible feelings.

As the dialogue created bonds between us, I was infused with by the passion of each missionary, which invariably potentialized my inner voltage. Those whom they serve are bound to enjoy the fullness and gratitude I felt.

اتمنى ان يعم السلام في العراق
love forever
I wish SILENCE for world.
MIHYAR
Mohamadreza
Mohamadhosin
somaye
السلام عليكم ورحمة الله وبركاته
بسم الله الرحمن الرحيم
10.02.16
I want Peace And Love

Lively writings began to fill the pages of this book, whose backbone is supported by the four oldest primary missionaries, whose biographies are further on in this book.

The graphic design was inspired by a room at the headquarters of FIHF. In it are exposed handicrafts, objects and printed material received as gifts during travels, as well as drawings made in workshops held during the missions. On the wall, there is a glass-protected symbolic frame, a collage of colorful cards with messages written by Middle Eastern refugees in Arabic, Turkish, English, and French, as well as messages in Portuguese or Spanish, written by the missionaries.

In a small light blue piece of paper, one sees three crosses: the Muslim, the Jewish and the Christian. In others, there are sentences like: *I wish peace for everyone. No more conflicts among people. In the end, all is one. Who cares whether you are a Jew, a Muslim, a Christian, a black, a white, an Asian? I hope I will learn how to play the Dance of Eternity.*

Arab immigrants are not the only ones who yearn for peace, but also the victims of environmental disasters, the secular or religious sufferers, the indigenous people, the slaves descendants, called *quilombolas* in Portuguese. Although the obstacles and torments seem invincible, it is everyone's wish that the people unite to play the Dance of Eternity.

Deep down, they know that, although planetary consciousness is still in monstrous shards, one day these will be restored. They know that in the future, life on this little blue planet, a jewel on the periphery of the Milky Way, will be ruled by wonder.

A bulletin board with messages of peace written in Arabic, Spanish, French, English, Portuguese and Turkish, during missionary work with Arabian refugees in Turkey. Carmo da Cachoeira, Minas Gerais, Brazil, 2016

Young learners

Since the first mission in Nepal, young people have always been welcomed to missionary service. Filled with hope, they aim to expand peace and love around the world. Among those who have awakened for fraternal actions, Anderson has been making great strides. At present, he coordinates the project The Common Good, developed in partnership with UNICEF, whose goal is to educate and protect around 1700 children in the ten shelters for Venezuelans in the Brazilian state of Roraima.

Everything takes place in due time. Twenty years after the primary missionary Imer was engaged in his first volunteer work, in his youth, he realized it was time to call young candidates for missionary life. As soon

A young missionary serves indigenous children.
Permanent Roraima Mission, Brazil, August 2018

as his proposal was approved by the four members of the Regency Council of FIHF, the new cycle flourished: the Missionary Youth for Peace, coordinated by him.

The youthful force responded with readiness, and vibrant hearts. Since May 2018, they have been gathering in cities of Brazil, Uruguay and Argentina one weekend a month for intense two or three day – meetings.

These events take place simultaneously with another event of the Fraternidade: the Youth Campaign for Peace, which aims to raise human consciousness. Festivals are held every three months. In them, prayer, art, music and service are combined to promote peace.

The first Missionary Youth for Peace event was confronted with the challenge of a truck drivers' strike in Brazil, which resulted in a fuel shortage. Imer and three younger people would have to drive 186 miles to Belo Horizonte, the host city, for the Youth Campaign for Peace. They were in doubt: *Shall we go or not*? They went! Confronted with difficulty and doubts, they gave a thorough *yes* revealing the youth's eagerness and values imbued in the emergent missionary action.

No one was discouraged. On the contrary, thirty young people took a lively interest in the event. Whenever there was a bus service, they went by bus. With enthusiasm and backpacks, they walked and biked to the Casa da Criança, The Children's House, the meeting place, which had

First Missionary Event for Peace.
Belo Horizonte, Minas Gerais, Brazil, May 2018

become the headquarters for the youth. It also hosts a choir for the needy children of the region and provides free dental and psychological care.

From there, they left to paint a mural, restore a poor house in a slum and help to organize a small animal farm. Besides providing service, they experienced fraternal coexistence and the feeling of belonging to a group. The youth tend to be sociable: they seek company, they need to exchange and learn from one another. In order to discover their place in society, participating in group life is essential for their education and development in the transition from childhood to adulthood.

When they are filled with the joy of being useful—to a home, a hospital, an institution, a poor settlement, animal sanctuaries—principles of common good are activated in their hearts. During selfless exercise, they find spirituality in the form of kindness. Some of them understand that, when they give something of themselves, they do not only offer something material, but a certain non-material aspect that fosters healing.

The events continued in the Centers of Figueira in the cities of São Paulo and São Carlos, São Paulo. The youth choose their favorite destination to attend the event; Brasília, Florianópolis, Rio de Janeiro, Recife, Salvador. Imer explains: *I give them the initial boost by telling them my own experiences and talk to them on the phone. Then they decide where to go—each day to a different place, traveling up to two to three hours round trip. They organize the activities, their tools, transportation, and meals.*

Each program includes talks on missionary life, on assisting people or even helping animals, or plants. In nature, the sensitive youth find love and God. *Sometimes we arrive in environments with a chaotic organization, where anonymous servers offer their lives for animals in great need,* reports Imer. *They weep, visibly moved while welcoming about thirty young people in blue T-shirts of the Planetary Mission Network. Again and again they have asked for support to the Universe and even visualized, in dreams or in a vision, help on its way: the group is the answer.*

Meetings have been held in Buenos Aires and Cordoba, Argentina. Similarly, in Uruguay—Ciudad de la Costa, Canelones, Maldonado, Solimar, Refúgio de Vida Marina, Marine Life Refuge, home to sea animals

Young missionaries in action.
São Paulo, Belo Horizonte and Roraima, Brazil, 2018

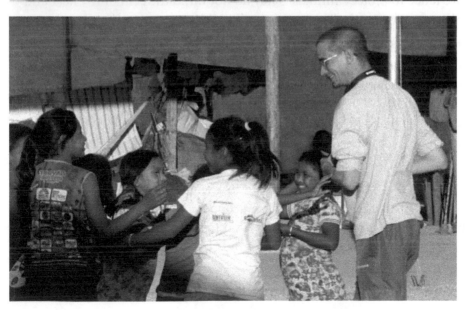

rescued from the ocean. Members of the Missionary Youth for Peace Event are planning to participate in Regional Missions in the Sertão, backwoods of Brazil, in Paraguay and in the Argentine Chaco. They are encouraged to record the experiences in writing, with photos or filming, and then present them at round tables during the festivals. In addition, they are invited to join the Humanitarian Mission for Peace in Roraima.

The basic idea is to nurture a group of generous young people. Anyone with a fraternal spirit may join and invite their friends, classmates, acquaintances, and relatives. At first, the idea was to call people from 18 to 35 years old. However, this age group was extended, because parents started asking about bringing their children and young people also brought older relatives.

Imer says: *May this service continue where the young people live, so that it may expand the Planetary Mission Network. May they live up to the blue T-shirt that identifies them and serves as a protection for them.*

The work done by the volunteers made the people ponder: *Why does this group spend time and money, without asking for anything in return?* They do things no one else wants to do. They handle heavy chores, such as tidying up huge stuffy warehouse with three hundred disorderly stacked pallets. Slipping in mud where they could barely stand up, they built a wire fence to protect animals. They do not mind the cold or the heat and only pause for meals. They transcend it all by extending their hands.

At the opening and closing of the events, each participant introduces him or herself telling stories about their own lives and backgrounds. Many are facing a crisis because they glimpse illusions and rudeness in their daily lives. They are no longer content exclusively with their family's protection, and seek to establish bonds and other references away from home. They need to discover themselves as individuals and learn to express their hearts.

A young Argentine woman moving to Uruguay described a traumatic moment disturbing her. When the group went to visit a home for disabled people with mental and physical problems, she listened to their report on how discriminated they felt because of their limitations.

Missionary Youth for Peace.
Uruguay, 2018

And still, that did not discourage them. At a given moment, servers and those being served began to sing enthusiastically. The young woman was receiving lessons of strength. Experiencing fraternal joy, the Argentine woman underwent a soul healing.

During the talking circle of the last day, she and others expressed how much their afflictions had dissolved during the experiences. A young immigrant from Venezuela was visibly moved, feeling grateful for the opportunity to serve others. He talked about the difficulties he had on the route between his country and Uruguay. For the first time, instead of receiving, he was offering help, and was filled with altruistic hope!

By the end of the meeting, on Sunday evening, they felt exhausted, but exultant. Strengthened by the love they gave and were given, they realized how much they were benefited. Latent capabilities within each of them began to come to the fore. At the departure time, they were planning the next meeting.

A week later, the group went back to the ranch clay house called Together for a Dream, where twenty disabled youths live. They began to rehearse in a choir for a performance to be given at the Uruguay Youth Festival. Alongside music, they went on painting and tidying up the place.

Imer wraps it up: *On this path, we have discovered beautiful volunteers who serve and live united by the purpose of cooperation. They are the beings of goodwill mentioned by the Instruction conveyed to mankind a century ago through Alice Bailey. She predicted the arrival of men and women of pure intent, of all ages, scattered in scientific, cultural, financial, and religious institutions. She said that at some point, a new group of world servers would meet one another. Working for the same purpose—the uplifting of the human race and of Nature—these brothers and sisters would be attracted by affinity and would transcend boundaries, physical appearance, age, skin color. I feel we are silently reaching that point.*

The missions are the opportunity for the youth to put into practice their inner aspiration for justice, for love, and for unity. Often this is the first channel they find to express Good and Beauty. They cannot translate into words or in a way of life their eagerness for concrete experiences. However, they mature as they practice giving something of themselves and, as they advance on the path of service, they become a bearer of peace.

PART I
The first missions

Learning and union with
the Missionaries of Charity of
Mother Teresa of Calcutta and
international secular organizations
that promote peace, justice
and equity among people.

NEPAL MISSION

The first crossing

Go to places where joy makes moods subtle,
go to places where hearts are oppressed by suffering.
Do not fail to sow good seeds wherever you are,
do not fail to herald the Law wherever you are.
The Trajectory of Fire, by Trigueirinho

An earthquake hit a rural area of Nepal in the Himalayans. The devastation was not huge: a few damaged houses, five deaths. However, a missionary group had to go to the area as soon as possible. In the country where Siddhartha Gautama, the Buddha, was born, they would learn more about compassion.

Who would go? A selection of those who, touched by the call, felt an inner summons. Among them was Ricardo Baumgartner, the new coordinator of the Missionaries of Fraternidade. The secretariat of the newly established International Humanitarian Organization had less than a month to interview, select and train the pioneering team as well as to plan the logistics of the trip and get donations to buy plane tickets, clothes, and equipment.

No one knew what would be in store for them. Of course, they thought they would work as rescuers, removing debris in the 'hot zone' of the distant region. The volunteers began the first-aid training, but life paths are not traced by a person's mind but drawn from subtle planes of existence.

Trigueirinho, the community instructor, suggested they make contact with the Missionaries of Charity, a Catholic order founded by Mother Teresa of Calcutta. A call was made to their house in Kathmandu, the capital of Nepal. The Sisters gave them their address, without clearly understanding who was coming from a distant country.

Finally, eighteen people who barely knew one another embarked with rescue equipment and even the first-aid teacher himself. Eagerly looking forward to living altruism and unveiling the unknown, they crossed the

45

Atlantic. They had a fifty-hour layover in the airport lounge in Qatar, Africa, where they became closer to one another, learned to be more patient, fine-tuned their emotional bodies and rehearsed inspiring chants.

The day after arriving in Kathmandu, before traveling to the area of the disaster, they went to meet the Missionaries of Charity. They walked in single line crossing slums of the poor country, filled with exuberant saris.

When they introduced themselves, the Sisters warned them: *Government authorization is mandatory if you want to enter the restricted area. It's hard to get a permit. But we have a lot of work here.* They looked at one another. For the time being, there was no alternative, and the coordinator mumbled: *All right, we'll be here until we can travel.*

That trip to the restricted zone never happened. Their time was spent in the capital of the exotic Federal Democratic Republic of Nepal, which had formerly been a Hindu kingdom. After a decade of civil war between government armies and guerrillas, it became secular in 2007, which was one year after the abolition of the monarchy.

One by one, daily decisions built a group of warriors. They traveled almost 10,000 miles to find masters of love who belonged to the religious order that has 710 houses in 133 countries.

In Kathmandu, only eight sisters provide assistance to people in two buildings: Santibaba, a mental institution housing 40 people with mental disability, and Pashupathi, an asylum nursing home within an ancient Buddhist monastery. The sisters also give shelter and comfort to about 250 people taken off the streets, including 33 with walking impairment.

The Missionaries of Charity welcomed the group unconditionally, without questions. Besides opening the field of service to them, they protected them as maternally as they do to everyone else that approaches them.

As for the missionaries, they showed their willingness to do whatever was needed. The Sisters split the group in two. One to give support to the mental institution, the other to work in the nursing home.

Indeed, there was hard work to be done there. What was the first task? Washing clothes dirty with feces and urine. Accustomed as they were to abundant running water and to wearing plastic gloves, they began working

Kathmandu, Nepal, 2011

over three buckets. There was no clean water to replace the dirty one. Stunned by the precarious conditions, they first wore the orange gloves they had brought but those were eventually torn apart. As they saw the Sisters wearing sandals and washing with bare hands, they did the same.

They observed the Missionaries of Charity, and were also observed by them while they followed their routine: cleaning up rooms and bathrooms, changing bed linens and personal clothing, bathing patients with atrophy and helping them to eat, guiding fork or spoon to their mouths.

After overcoming one challenge, they were faced with others. Two painters were busy painting the sanatorium walls. During the weekend break, the Sisters asked the missionaries to continue with the task. The painters did not come back to work on Monday, neither on Tuesday or Wednesday. They noticed that the professional painters had been dismissed, and now, they were in charge of painting the whole building including the windows, walls, gates, railings, and the little chapel.

Wrapped in colorful fabrics and speaking Nepali, the short slant-eyed patients from the nursing home, as well as from the mental institution cheered up by the Latinos vibration.

Their contact with the Sisters became really close when an old lady was bitten by one of the several 20 inch tall monkeys who moved among temples, squares, town houses, and slept on walls. At once, the therapist of the humanitarian mission volunteered to make the bandage. *Do you know how to give a shot?* the Sisters asked. When he replied affirmative, they set up a stretcher in front of the Prayer Room. He and an assistant injected anti-tetanus vaccine to people who stood in a long line.

This triggered other processes. The therapist and his assistant began examining the inmates and treating their bedsores. As they presented alternative therapies to the Sisters, they would just be told: *Do it! Do it!* Acupuncture, chromotherapy, auriculotherapy, massage, *Vertebralis Praxis*—they accepted all practices, which were applied both on the patients and on themselves.

Objective, precise, but cautious, the Sisters gradually offered them their best. First, they called the group to the 6 a.m. daily Mass, which the eighteen attended punctually, with devotion. After the Masses, they were led to a room with a table set with bread, butter, cheese, coffee with milk, and fruits. Listening to the visitors singing with gratitude before breakfast, they invited them to sing songs at the beginning of the Mass. Later, to do it during the mass, and later on, at the end.

Days passed by. As the Sisters noticed how dynamic but focused and silent the missionaries were, they were invited to pray together in the afternoon and added baskets of boiled eggs to the breakfast menu. A few days later, they included the contemplation of the Blessed Sacrament in their daily ritual. Simultaneously to the invisible task, an extra item was added to the lavish breakfast table: pasta.

A collaborator associated with the Sisters, invited the workforce to be with children hospitalized at a Children's Cancer Hospital. The travelers promptly went to ease the children's loneliness, buying them toys, paper and colored pencils for playful activities and entertaining the children with the language of music. More than that, they took on the tireless task of cleaning of a hospital ward with infants' feces in filthy corridors and clogged bathrooms, while bringing buckets of water from other floors.

The same collaborator requested help for forty children and twenty elderly people from an orphanage-nursing home in deplorable and fetid conditions. Located in a three-story building, it was grimy and corroded

The only outdoor area available for the children to play had been turned into a garbage dump. There was a rusty slide in it. They decided to clean the area. During three days, they separated the reusable material from the pile of objects and burned the rest.

Each missionary cried out to the heavens, in their own way, while the fire disinfected not only germs of matter, but also of negative feelings and thoughts. When the group task was completed, they cheerfully cemented part of the yard, while kids and old people watched from the balconies and windows of the building.

In the intervals of the vigorous cleaning, volunteers inspired by goodness climbed up to the roof of the building. Still with smoke masks hanging from their necks, they filled up white balloons, played the flute, and sang along with little boys and old women dancing with their little eyes closed. Revitalized, they all clapped hands and smiled.

Four to six times a day, the group walked back and forth between the hotel and the nursing home. They elbowed their way through streets laden with motorbikes, people, dust and dirt. Walking in line, in an altruistic way, the one leading pointed the steps to be taken just like migratory birds in the sky and lines of camels on desert dunes.

They would leave at five in the morning for a forty-minute walk. In that country of so many beliefs, bells from belfries rang, devotees played little bells, lit candles, and entered temples. On the way, they also invoked powerful universal rays to pour over Asia.

During a morning walk, one of the eighteen missionaries was given a vision for the group. She saw a shimmering trail of celestial light flow through where they were passing. It looked like a large transparent shroud floating in the wind.

The group considers itself to be cosmic-ecumenical. Why? Just as it seeks unity, service, and dialogue with religious or lay individuals, it raises its consciousness to the mysteries of Stellar Universal Life. They never forget that they are beings of the cosmos who are currently passing through the Earth to deepen their learning about love and forgiveness.

Before saying farewell to the pulsating Nepalese world made up of twelve ethnic groups, they were given two splendid gifts from the Sisters and the chaplain of the nursing home: attending a Sunday mass at the capital's only Catholic church and visiting the Buddhist Temple of the Apes where priests and Lamas welcomed them with tenderness and gratitude.

Located on a hill visible from anywhere in the city is the ancient center of pilgrimage with countless paintings of Buddha's eyes: the one who sees everything. In the temple they listened to a lecture on compassion, the main teaching brought from the Universe by the spiritual teacher. From that geographical region, it spread throughout the world. Next, they were invited to attend a lengthy purification ceremony.

It is said no one remains the same after visiting Nepal. They arrived in the country flying above the Everest, but flew back on even higher flights, beyond the darkness that infests places of this legendary country, praised for its extraordinary natural beauties. After practicing the ability to serve selflessly, some members of the group passed the test in the first course of the Missionary School, that of unconditional love.

In Brazil they had imagined themselves in heroic missions, rescuing living beings buried by rubble. Instead, they had to face a different type of earthquake, an invisible one, hidden in the core of one's own ego. Confronted with what was found, some had strong inner shocks: *A whirlwind came to me, and I could see the worst of me,* confesses a missionary girl.

The eighteen survived, expanded. They learned lessons, not just from the Nepalese, but from one another. The intense co-existence revealed the group's heterogeneity. Only one has consecrated himself and still remains in the missionary task. The others have chosen different directions, however, invariably the experience left its mark on all of them.

Upon returning to the Light-Community, the group had a wonderful reception. Hundreds of people who had built the prayer base that had supported them along the route gathered to listen to their experiences. They all communed with the opening of the humanitarian service.

They went to the Far East, gave something of themselves and left the scene leaving behind joyful footprints in streets, hearts, and memories. But results do not belong to the servers.

Kathmandu, Nepal, 2011

Testimony of a young missionary

Creatures praise altruistic giving as supreme,
for nothing is more difficult to perform than
giving oneself altruistically. Therefore, it is said
that giving is the supreme means.
Upanishads

At the age of 26, I spent two weeks in Kathmandu, Nepal, as a volunteer for a humanitarian mission coming from South America. I left every day comfort without knowing what I would experience, and just opened myself to whatever might happen. Actions like that put us in the vortex of real life and do not show us the best scenes.

For the first time, I took a long trip not as a tourist. I soon realized something beyond the beauty of appearances—because Nepal is a beautiful country, with colorful ancestral monuments and majestic snowy mountains. I started getting annoyed by the attitude of the tourists. They invade the reality of those people without really taking an interest in them, without wanting to do anything to help alleviate so much hunger, disease, and poverty, caused by political conflicts and serious attacks.

While working with the Missionaries of Charity, I learned a lesson for the rest of my life. The one who gives the most to others receives the most. Imagine a person who lives only to take care of the needs of those who have nothing. Well, now imagine people who give a thousand times more than the one you thought of. These are the Sisters. Always light-hearted, always cheerful, they assist dozens of elderly people and children and still have time to pray and wash their white saris.

I am neither a Catholic nor baptized. But what most touched me was a mass at the church of Kathmandu, the same one where a few years before had a bomb attack triggered by religious and political prejudices. Until that day, I had only seen the negative side of this religion, I had never had any contact with the essence of Christian teachings. People ask me: "You were in a country whose Buddhist and Hindu presence is super-strong, but you prefer to report the experience you had at a Catholic church?" Yes. Each person is where they are supposed to be to learn what they need most.

On the eve of the Mass, I dreamed that I was flying among clouds lit by the rising sun. I rose higher and higher towards the sky, and the higher I rose, the more intense was the sense of peace. Then I heard: "That's not the place where they need you". I began to fall at a very high speed, I entered a dark well, but there was light around me, and I could see the walls, despite the darkness.

"Then I understood I am not supposed to be in the world only to benefit from it, but to give my contribution," says the volunteer Flora Agni.

Sometime later, I listened to a story in which a disciple had a vision of Buddha in hell. Baffled, he asked his master how Buddha could be in hell. The answer was: "That's where they need him".

From the moment we entered the flowery and well-kept garden that leads to that church, we felt peace. From a balcony, a life-size sculpture of Jesus Christ with Hindu features greeted us with his right, and left hand on his heart. We left our shoes outside the front door, like everyone else, and were stunned by the beauty and blend of Hindu and Buddhist decorations. Most of the Nepalese population is Hindu, but Buddhists attend Hindu temples and there is a mutual architectural influence of both religions.

The cross-shaped building was extremely high. We sat on maroon-colored cushions well aligned along the decorated floor. On the walls, paintings illustrated Biblical stories with characters and even Oriental-looking angels. In the Holy Supper, the Apostles wore typical hats.

In the Holy Supper, apostles with typical hats. Kathmandu, Nepal, 2011

Members of the small Catholic community of Kathmandu gradually entered the temple. African, European, Asian, and American believers gathered under the same roof to reflect, feel and experience something special and inexplicable, a common aspect of each member of the heterogeneous crowd.

The choir began to sing in English. I never go to Masses nor hear gospel music, but I felt a lump in my throat. My eyes watered. A rock broke inside me: the rock of religious prejudice.

I literally felt on my skin what it is like to be in prayer close to the humanity of which we are a part. I realized how important is each representative of each nation. The word 'humanity' has changed its meaning. Now I aspire to 'serve on behalf of mankind!'

Four priests celebrated the Mass; one Nepali and the others looked Indian or Chinese. The celebrants thanked the group for our presence, showing once again how welcoming the Nepalese are. The line of people receiving Communion was symbolic: it seemed to be climbing the stairway to Paradise, a huge painting behind the altar, which portrayed humanity climbing into paradise.

So many things differentiate us as human beings. Although there are brutish human beings bound to material life, what mostly unites us is the quest for something greater, which transcends our every day life. This is the most important yearning of mankind.

Flying back home, I felt grateful during the ascent of the airplane as Kathmandu faded into clouds. I still do remember moments spent with certain consciousnesses who cry out in that unknown country. The meaning of many things changed, mostly the feeling of being integrated with the needy human family.

To think, to pray, and to ask God for those who suffer took on another dimension. Doing something good "on behalf of humanity" is now truer. I will never forget what I felt inside the cathedral with brothers and sisters from all continents, immersed in a search of the invisible. We are one. We really are!

NICARAGUA MISSION

Music to relieve pain

When the sun sets, my Lord,
my heart, my heart aches.
The sun does not live,
the fire of the day has died.
I want you, I want you, fire of the day,
Fire, don't go, don't go,...
The sun is gone. My heart cries.
Song of the Sun, an oral poem in Nahuatl

There was an old man who could not speak and could not walk. Always in bed, the missionaries would carry him to his wheelchair and go for a walk in the garden. They noticed the elderly man talked through his glowing gaze emanating such purity that, in that silent and almost inert body, they did find a human being at service.

Drawn by the mysterious, each missionary spontaneously approached him. One with a flower. The old man's eyes lit up to contemplate it. His arms, which barely moved, tried to pick it up. Smiling, the missionary brought the flower closer to his wrinkled face. He felt its fragrance with such a delight that feathers touch the sensitive hearts surrounding him. He answered to tender words by the eloquence of silence, exchanging glances which mirrored unnamed feelings of the sacred fraternity language.

They were in Central America for the event Campaign for Peace, at Managua. Once it was over, six missionaries and four monks from GOM, Grace Mercy Order, rendered service for three days at a women's prison, at a house of the Missionaries of Charity, and at a large public hospital. The local Light-Network group had organized and guided the journey.

On the first day, they went to a prison that held about 300 female inmates. Most of them had been convicted for excessive violence and sexual deviation crimes linked to lesbianism, quite usual in the local youth. A missionary said: *There was raw sewage throughout the jail. It was chaotic. It didn't even look like a third-world place, but a fourth-world one. Still, we were able to give the employees a new sense of cleanliness and order.*

55

Half of the incarcerated population is Protestant, the other half Catholic. The weekly Mass was celebrated to the Catholic prisoners while, in another hall, a Protestant service was being held

The missionaries were invited to attend the Mass. Soon the priest asked a monk with a guitar to perform the songs. The power of his music was overwhelming. He remembers: *What a challenge! At the time, I knew nothing about the structure of a Catholic Mass. The priest looked at me and said: "Introit", "Glory". Extremely anxious, I had to make up the songs right there. It was incredible how quickly and joyously the 150 women attending the Mass learned the lyrics and the melodies. The priest went: "Hallelujah", "Offertory". And on top of everything, he allowed me to drink from the chalice.*

The prisoners were touched by the priest's sermon, when he said that they were being given an opportunity similar to that of the Saints of the past who, seeking to be alone with God, lived in the solitude of caves, deserts, cloisters. The prison could then become a place of prayer. They would be closer to Christ if they repented of the past and seek Him out.

On the following day, the group worked directly with the elderly and the children of a house of the Missionaries of Charity, just as they had done in Nepal. The local architecture was exquisite. The square-shaped construction has a chapel in the center, around which are the monastery, the hospital for the elderly, the mental institution for psychiatric cases and the nursery for 40 children, most of whom return home in the late afternoon. The others live and sleep in the house.

Overtired by the years spent in fieldwork all over the world, nuns head for this monastery. Although they spend most of their time in retreat, they do not lose touch with their mission of serving. They pick up sick people off the streets and take them home to be treated by staff paid for by the people or by themselves.

The missionaries joined a group of young Catholic volunteers and seminarians. They watched a surprising musical play produced by the head of the nursery. She managed to make some troublesome five and six year old kids follow the choreography rhythm in perfect synchrony.

Edi, a six year old boy, liked to get in the way of the children's fun and to beat them. A missionary became responsible for him. Being the son to an absent father, he had a two year old mind. When he was given a baby

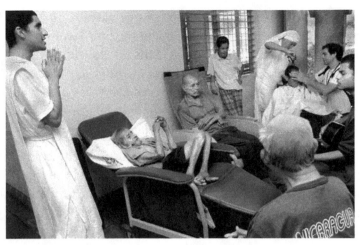

Music and haircuts at the Cancer Hospital, Managua, Nicaragua, in 2011

bottle, he laid down on the floor like a baby. Treating him like a baby was the magical trick to soften him. He missed people's touch and affection.

In the girls' ward, Juanita was extremely violent. She would brutally beat the big and the small ones, fight using karate, and be aggressive with the boys. She was not a mean girl, though. This was her way of showing affection, like she saw at home. A missionary tried to teach her another way of expressing love, to which Juanita responded for a while, but, in secret, she would hit somebody again. Who knows whether a seed of peace was sown in those children?

The missionaries sang, bathed and fed the elderly. They dealt with chronic problems and with people who had completely lost their mind. They separated two psychopathic patients, who had clinched themselves in a fight. To prevent a sufferer of self-harm from hurting himself, a missionary would hold his arms or embraced him.

The doctor treated 39 elderly people. *He's an angel,* they said. *He attends all patients almost on his own, since the volunteers don't dare bathing them or provide physiotherapist help. Once in a while, he can count on two assistants. To his relief, there was specialized support among us; a doctor, a physiotherapist, and a repairman.*

During our first days, there was no wind and with the humid tropical heat, swarms of insects were suffocating in the capital city of Nicaragua, hit so many times by political violence and by major natural disasters, fires, and earthquakes. However, in the morning of the last day, the temperature cooled down. The missionaries put socks on the elderly, gave haircuts and talked to them: *A man had lost his memory. He'd ask my name, where I was from and told me the lake's legend. It was created out of the tears an Indian woman shed for her son. One minute later, he'd ask my name and begin retelling the legend again and again.*

That afternoon, the mission ended. At the Cancer Hospital, the coordinator split the group in two. One group made repairs and did the maintenance of the outside and parts of the inside of the building, which were astonishingly chaotic. As a metamorphosis underwent at surreal speed, enthusiastic passers-by gazed in awe at how order was being quickly installed.

Meanwhile, the second group visited recovery wards for those recently operated on. They entered quietly into eight rooms with about ten terminal cancer patients in each. Someone would start playing the violin, the guitar followed it, and delicate voices sang deep chants, uplifting people's energy. The gentle sounds filled the corridors, attracting doctors, nurses, and directors. The breath of the spirit struck hearts and some cried.

In one room, a young mother in extreme pain screamed. Her family was there. Feeling devastated, the daughter surrendered to the consoling embrace of a missionary monk, who whispered in her ear: Death does not exist, your mother is being released from suffering to proceed toward light. Cancer can be a way of purifying the past. The girl calmed down, stood next to a woman missionary, and both watched the mother take her last breath. Her mother's body had been sick, but perhaps her soul was not injured.

The girl's pain was profound, but there are infinite forms of healing. A loving gesture may relief a sufferer and pacifies those who practice it. People being served and those with hearts wide open are both discovering the right path to be cured.

As they left the hospital, doctors and nurses gently repeated: We are in the clouds. During those days, the good fought a hidden battle, which the Fraternidade surrenders to the hands of the One who creates everything and is in everything.

Service to love in the heart of Africa

*...in ancient communities, service to mankind was
considered to be a tough and difficult test. The person
being tested did not have to change their activity,
but its essence was to be dedicated not to themselves,
to their city, nor to their country, but to the entire
mankind. Thus, the scope of their activity broadened
and resulted in good for all.*
Supermundane, The Inner Life IV, by Helena Roerich

Smiles and glances can remove boundaries between human beings. The
Missionaries of Fraternidade flew over the blue vastness of the Atlantic
Ocean five times to serve six African countries. Deep down, they kept
a constant aspiration to bring peace and unity to people: attributes that
raise human consciousness. They had three missions in Ethiopia and
others in Kenya, Rwanda, Uganda and Congo. Three years later they arrived in Egypt.

A museum of the ancestral history of man, the black continent has now
more than 1.2 billion inhabitants. Living in hectic metropolises, inland
farms, tribes, they have curious customs, unique styles of life and complex ways of seeing and interpreting the world.

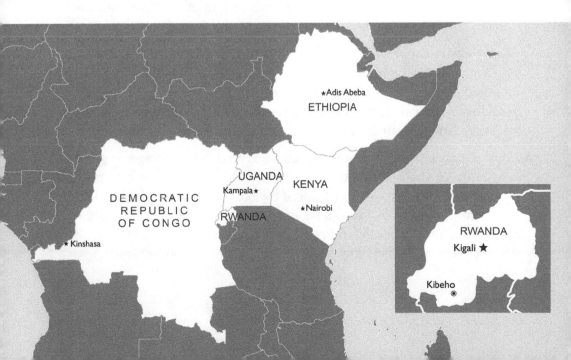

The Earth survived holocausts and continents disappearing, while others emerged. Its spiritual history tells us the first human beings with physical bodies emerged in Africa. Having an ego and a sex, the dark-skinned strong people believed in the illusion of being separate from other beings.

As humankind, we are so unstable that now we evolve, then we go backwards. However, since time immemorial, some people open themselves humbly. They desire to see peace and love emerging from their inner world pouring themselves onto concrete life.

Long before Europeans landed in African countries, natives enslaved fellow natives. From the fifteenth century onwards, the slave trade brutality went on in transatlantic trips taking Africans to other countries.

Slavery still exists in Africa and in other continents, even if in clandestine ways. According to Trigueirinho: *Slaves can only exist in a slaved mankind. People who do forced labor are not the only slaves. Men deceive themselves believing that being free means doing whatever they want, without thinking about the others, and following their own impulses. This makes enslavement even more intense. Only after liberating themselves from these illusions, overcoming their free will, men will perceive what liberation is.*

In the nineteenth century, Portugal conceived the division of Africa. Seven countries held a Berlin conference between 1884 and 1885—Germany, Belgium, Spain, France, Italy, the United Kingdom and Portugal. They subdivided the continent between themselves by defining arbitrary boundaries, which still causes serious problems among peoples and nations today. Only Ethiopia and Liberia remained politically independent.

The extensive exploitation of African colonies practiced by these seven countries was increasingly reduced after the end of World War II, when nationalist movements and fighting for independence began. However, in all the 54 African countries there are still conflicts, social and political injustice, as well as other cruelties

Continental multilingualism is impressive. Over 2,000 languages are spoken, plus 8,000 native dialects, and 35 nations have at least one European or Arabic official language. Influenced by local dialects, they are no longer "pure" European or Arabian languages, just as African pronunciation and vocabulary interfered in Brazilian Portuguese during 400 years of slavery, when six million Africans were forcibly taken to other lands.

What is the inner truth of this continent? How do you find and bring to the forefront the perfect serenity immanent to each expression of life? How can Africa liberate itself?

As the Africa Missions were announced, missionaries felt an inner call. A yes to the invitation rang inside them. Miraculously, obstacles to the trip were removed. Some volunteers felt self-summoned. Others felt a silent aspiration and nevertheless received a letter to join the group.

Wearing a gray T-shirt with the new humanity cross and the lettering Fraternidade—International Humanitarian Missions, they put the black backpacks on their shoulders and left to continue the work begun in Asia and Central America with the Missionaries of Charity.

Mother Teresa of Calcutta chose to "serve the poorest of the poor and to live among them and like them". Her teaching remains alive in the hearts of almost 5,000 Sisters of the Order all over the world. They live in the school of giving of self: altruism, unconditional service, boundless love, readiness, joy.

The Fraternidade was in eight of their African homes. They relentlessly served the poorest of the poor and lived among them in the countries visited between 2012 and 2015. In 2018, they returned to the continent, to Egypt. The daily contact with people taught them to master their own minds, feelings, instincts and to recognize the guidance of the intuitive voice, in order to see and better understand their fellow beings.

The missionary Imer says: *From dawn to nightfall, our daily tasks boiled down to serving and helping, to serving, and working, and praying, and being thankful, and keeping vigil, and then serving again. Our first years were intense. We gradually imbued ourselves with the task. The physical movement and the contact with terrible needs is not easy. Being a missionary is a path that implies renunciation, external and inner offering, sacrifice. Our life has become that. To sustain surrender, we must overcome our weaknesses, surpass our own limitations to work as souls and for souls.*

The bonds of kinship between them and the Sisters were strengthened. The Sisters treated them as equals. Always including them in meetings with other religious orders, even though they knew they belonged to an independent organization. Under their maternal guidance, the group learned more about the secrets of being a missionary.

ETHIOPIA

Bringing peace with joy

To all those who suffer and are alone,
always give them a smile of joy.
Do not just provide them with
your care, but also offer them your heart.
Mother Teresa of Calcutta

3rd Mission
ADIS ABABA
November 2 to 18, 2012

Before landing in the unknown African world for their first Humanitarian Mission on the continent, fifteen missionaries were trained in the spirit of unity and flexibility. To prepare themselves, they attended intense physical trainings and spiritual retreats in four Light-Communities, two in Brazil, one in Uruguay, another in Argentina.

Living by the motto *Let go of your ego to become a channel of the Divine*, they left to extend their compassion to the suffering people from the high plateaus of Ethiopia, where the source of the Blue Nile is. Its waters emerge from Lake Tana, whose islands are home to old monasteries of the Ethiopian Christian Church. From there, they gush down cliffs, join the waters of the White Nile and go down into valleys until they flow into the Mediterranean Sea.

In Addis Ababa, the cold-weather capital surrounded by eucalyptus-covered hills, twenty Sisters attend to one thousand of the poorest among the poor. That house, a mix of hospital, nursing home, orphanage and mental institution, is the second largest of the religious order on the planet. The largest one is the headquarters of Calcutta.

They had just arrived when a symbolic task emerged. A missionary of Fraternidade donated blood to a missionary of the Charity. There was hardly any chance of finding someone with the O-negative blood type for the Sister's surgery. Their last hope was in the volunteers, who were seen as a balm by the Sisters. That communion of people blood was a clear sign that life, energies, and the work of the two groups of love were united both physically and spiritually.

The facts of life speak, and so does a gesture, a noise, or an aroma. Sometimes, a word thrown to the wind is heard: here's a sign. A dream is recalled: here's another sign. Guided by messages sent by instructors, the missionaries remain attentive to the meaning of those subtle daily signs.

We have all been traveling among civilizations of the cosmos until a current of life brought our essences to the Earth. Here, we descended from a primary human race, which enabled multiple evolutions. At any given moment, we will proceed to other spheres towards infinity.

Ethiopia, one of the world's oldest regions, is a country where discoveries of fossils have indicated it is home to the earliest *Homo Sapiens*. It has become one of the poorest countries in the world after the fall of the monarchy along with tragic periods of drought and famine in the 1980's resulting in millions of deaths.

Having had *coups d'état*, rebellions and a huge problem involving refugees, this fascinating country of ancestral culture and exotic tribes with different traditions, is slowly recovering.

Serious illnesses get exposed in the house of the Sisters: infectious diseases, countless physical and mental handicaps. The missionaries of Fraternidade had to deal with patients with tuberculosis, cerebral palsy, typhoid and tropical fever, traumatized, burned, HIV-positive patients, psychiatric cases, leprosy, among countless other cases.

They bandaged people and took care of their personal hygiene, including baths, tooth brushing and nail trimming. They helped prepare food and did laundry. They treated patients with physiotherapy and alternative therapies, such as nourishing baths, urine therapy, and music therapy. They also gave herbal preparations to the disabled, malnourished, single mothers and children of all ages.

In addition, there is at the Hospital of Charity an average of ten to fifteen deaths per week. Every dying person is closely accompanied with tenderness and respect, in a ritualistic way. The opening of a soul may occur when they receive attention, even if only for an instant before death. A lifetime thirst for affection can be finally quenched with a caress, with some care, or by a loving gaze. When leaving the body, a soul may not

Having fun in the house of the Franciscan sisters, and a chart in Amharic, one of the official languages of the country. Ethiopia, 2012

አበጹ ወይን እፍለሰክ እምዓጠጹ
ሰጸደክ እህ፟ሃበ ወተከልክ ከዳሃ
ወጸነክ ፍኖተ ቅድሜሃ።

feel as though it has never been loved. The missionary Imer says: *With the Sisters, we have learned to give full attention to each person who goes through the process of dying. We do our best until the person passes on clean sheets, carrying the love recently received.*

When a patient was about to die, the Sisters called the Missionaries to pray by the bed during the liberation process. After taking part in the funeral mass for the intention of the deceased, they followed the coffin to the burial ceremony. Each person threw shovelfuls of dirt into the grave, following a local tradition. In Kenya, they also collaborated in similar rituals. The van used by the group carried coffins to the cemetery.

Most of the Sisters were Europeans. At first they were disturbed by the working pace of the Missionaries, naturally more accelerated than the majority. *Slowly, slowly,* they said. Gradually they accepted it, exclaiming in surprise: *You are so organized and prepared!*

International organizations—USAID, the UN, Doctors Without Borders—collaborate with the Hospital of Charity. It receives substantial material assistance from Europe, a way these countries found to compensate for the great material and spiritual debt created during colonization. However, not many volunteers come to work. And they do not arrive in organized groups, but come alone. The missionaries only met a Spanish man, a French woman, an English woman, and, later on, a Lebanese woman.

Striving to become better servers, the missionaries decided to take vows during their journey. The vow of letting ego go away in order to devote themselves completely to the needs of others. The vow to give up specific things, such as hours of sleep, in order to dedicate themselves to prayer. The vow to never complain but be grateful for everything they receive: food, the type of accommodation, a cold bath. The vow of austerity: a commitment to restrict consumption during the trip and to turn the money saved into a donation for the Sisters. For this reason, they traveled by car at its fullest capacity, without overnight lodging or buying food on the road. The vow to obey what was previously determined and to criticize nothing, not even mentally. The vow of silence, which the group strained to keep.

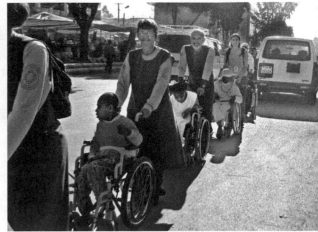

Missionaries take disabled children to the Zoo. Addis Ababa, Ethiopia, 2013

4th mission
ADIS ABABA
February 4 to 22, 2013

Three months after returning to Brazil, sixteen missionaries took the same route back to Ethiopia. They kept on spreading seeds of fraternity on the 8,000 feet high lands of Addis Ababa.

Besides activities similar to those of the first trip, their relationship with the patients deepened. The Sisters gave them new opportunities to help the suffering people. They visited together wretched houses and distributed food to the undernourished homeless. It was a joy to take mentally and physically handicapped children to the zoo pushing wheelchairs through crowded streets in the middle of the traffic. It had only one animal species: lions. Of diverse populations, they had great morphological varieties in size, color, thickness of their coat, texture of the mane. Hunting in African countries is both legal and illegal. At least at the zoo they were safe from the cowardly shooting of the so-called big five—lions, buffaloes, rhinoceros, leopards and elephants— which continue to live in vast wildlife reserves.

On the day before the flight back to Brazil, they went to a school for children with HIV, a scourge that derives from the degeneration of sexual energy, which has affected millions of young Africans. The boys challenged the missionaries to play a soccer match. What a success! The boys drubbed them, four to one. The field was then opened for all to celebrate, sing and pray in several languages.

They traveled once again two months later, this time in a group of ten, to conclude the work in Ethiopia and then go to Kenya, a bordering country to the South.

Ethiopia follows the Julian calendar, a little different from the Gregorian one. Whereas this event had already taken place in South America, they found preparations for the Easter festivities in progress at their arrival. Therefore, besides the same routine chores with the internees, the Sisters gave them the celebration tasks: clean the church, get the outdoor and the chapel altar Mass ready, keep vigil until midnight and be at the ceremonies.

At a time when most of Europe was still polytheistic, Ethiopia was the second country to adopt the Christian faith in the world, which has been the official religion of the nation since the fourth century. The first great emigration of Islamic history and the oldest Muslim settlement in Africa also took place at that time.

Today, a third of the inhabitants follows principles of Islam and pray facing the direction of Mecca, but most remain faithful to Christianity, despite the siege and invasions of hostile neighbors. By living in an enclosed world, Ethiopia has preserved ancient Christian customs. Quaint and curious in their outward aspects, they follow original rituals of one and a half millenniums ago without losing their Christian essence.

On Easter Saturday, they saw people bringing an ox to be deboned and chopped up with axes, a strange ritual for the vegetarian group. From 5 p.m., the Eucharistic liturgy unfolded amidst incense smoke and multiple musical rhythms. An immense camp fire was lit. Chants broke the air as believers adorned in bright colors followed in a procession to the richly ornate church. At the tinkling of bells, they shook branches of plants.

The Mass was celebrated in Amharic, the official language of the country whose people communicate in ninety dialects, English being the most spoken and studied foreign language in their schools. The human faith was crying out, palpitating as much as the flame of the great paschal candle.

Home for the needy, sick and dying people. Ethiopia, 2012

In most areas of Africa, important events are celebrated with songs and dances. Following the vows of Happy Easter and the snack with Easter bread, enthusiastic Christians clapped their hands and had traditional dances around the campfire, to the sound of percussion instruments of different sizes and timbres, used in the continent as a positive or negative transcendental bond. On the tops of the hills that surround the city, thousands of campfires gleamed, while the black thin faces of stylized saints on sacred paintings contemplated the Divine.

Explosions were heard. Cannon shots sounded at 3 a.m. At six, 21 gun salutes announced the Mass. Since the local tradition is to eat a goat on Easter Sunday, three were sacrificed. These animals lived for a few days along the path the Missionaries took regularly, they gave compassionate glances to the goats and whispered affectionate words to them. On sidewalks where they passed, piles of goat heads and goat meat exposed in pieces indicated the future of those animals.

That week the missionaries' efforts strengthened them and transformed them into better human beings. They replaced the regular workers on the Good Friday holiday and also on Easter Sunday. Charged with changing dozens of bandages from a men's ward, they pushed the cart with the materials down the hall, where a long line soon formed. A disease commonly found in that place resembled leprosy and degenerates the skin until it exposes the living flesh. There was pus dripping, a fetid smell... and as they removed the old bandage, part of the skin tissue came with it.

A missionary recalls: *At first, I was cautious and attentive, but the man was impatient and pulled off the bandage with one finger almost falling, and cleaned the wound. With the next patient I did it his way, more quickly. We gradually lost our fear. It was very, very difficult. One had a necrotic foot, another had lost an ear, another, part of his nose, another, his eye.*

We worked in pairs and took turns. While one changed the bandage, the other was handing the gauze and the materials to the other, and vice versa. After working on a couple of bandages, we would leave the room to recover. We would pray with faith for the angels' support. It was like raising your head out of the water to fill the lungs before plunging back into the task.

The soldiers of peace did not give up the fight. On that Good Friday, they were the most benefited. In the wounded men they found great teachers of faith. When the work on the bandages was over, they knew a *Via Crucis* would be waiting for them in the ward. There, at the end of the corridor, a large gate was opened for the procession to pass through to the church door.

Clara says with emotion: *I imagined that in the Via Crucis the Sisters, some employees, maybe another patient would be the only ones present. What a mistake! Present were the same men we had just carefully bandaged: all those people were in deep physical and internal suffering, a pain we couldn't even imagine. There were many. The patient who could cope with the pain would push the wheelchair of the one who could not walk. At every station of the Via Crucis, I looked around. In the midday sun, mutilated people prayed in full devotion, knelt on the hard cement, and touched their heads on the ground. I started calling on my higher levels: the soul, the spirit, to come an witness this. All I could think was: these are the people of God, shattered.*

During this third and last mission in the country, they also made home visits with the Sisters. Two or three of them would walk along very narrow alleys, amidst open-air sewers and filth. The cold was intense in the wattle and daub houses with raffia sack walls and rooms divided by a curtain. In the house of a mother with two children, the bunk in which they slept had been broken by the children's jumping.

The Missionaries of Charity opened raffia bags of sugar and covered the floor with plastic to keep the icy wind out. They left them food, medicine, a little money, and the Sister scolded one child, for playing truant from school. But here life offers no prospect for improvement... that is all they have, a precarious, subhuman, miserably poor life.

On the way back, they asked a Sister why there were so few dogs on the streets. They were told that these animals are used as food by Chinese who do the maintenance of the highways in the country.

Before embarking to the capital of Kenya, the missionaries finished painting the outside garden fences, organized warehouses and made the rooms where they stayed look impeccable. They said goodbye to Ethiopian life which keeps biblical precepts, from which the citizens extract goodness, the hospitality that foreigners are supposed to be given, and generosity toward the poor.

Every day, before getting inside the infirmary, the ten slowed down their quick march as they passed the gardens between three gates contemplating the perfectly trimmed grass, the tidiness, and the vegetation which looked similar to the Brazilian one, with flowering roses, geraniums and creepers.

On the last day, they were filled with joy but also sadness. In a flowerbed, a bouquet of freshly opened white lilies awaited them. Ten lilies. Ten missionaries stood still in front of the symbol. Touched by the white petal's beauty, more than ever, they loved one another, loved life. In that fleeting instant, they glimpsed the soul of the nation. Beyond chaos and pain, was the pure, white, innocent and virgin soul like lilies from Ethiopia.

A baby waiting for adoption receives care from a nun of Grace Mercy Order. House of lodging of the Franciscan sisters. Addis Ababa, Ethiopia, 2012

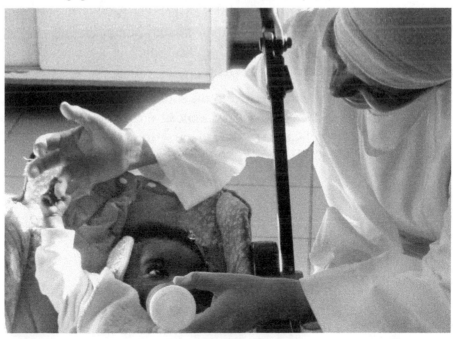

KENYA

You could be one of us

*Our lives are a battlefield on which is fought a continuous war
between the forces that are pledged to confirm our humanity
and those determined to dismantle it; those who strive to build
a protective wall around it, and those who wish to pull it down;
those who seek to mould it and those committed to breaking it up;
those who aim to open our eyes, to make us see the light and look
to tomorrow... and those who wish to lull us into closing our eyes.*
Ngũgĩ wa Thiong'o, a Kenyan writer

From Ethiopia, the ten pilgrims traveled to Kenya's capital. Under British rule, Nairobi had fierce tensions between blacks and whites, between the African and the European culture. Their independence in 1962 was followed by authoritarian regimes, protests, boycotts, and violence.

As they moved away from the airport into the outskirts, the beautiful arrival, the freeways and the fancy cars gradually vanished. During the one-hour taxi ride, driving through chaotic traffic on left-side British-style streets, another reality presented itself: bumpy streets, people arguing in the traffic jam of carts, crowds walking, lots of trash scattered and vendors trading in improvised tents.

Unfortunate Kenya, what happened to the soul of your people? Mothers are forced to kill children who, born disabled because of the nutritional deficiency of the people, are considered cursed, and mothers are supposed to be punished for their sins.

Finally arriving at the lodge, they realized they were inside one of Nairobi's largest slums, with 400,000 inhabitants. Every day they came and went between their lodging and the Sisters' house. White people are rarely seen here. In vain, the group tested the strategy of passing quickly to go unnoticed, but kids wandering everywhere ran alongside the queue amusing themselves, *How are you, how are you, how are you?*

Along the street there were small houses with aluminum roofs and shacks on stilts. In the commerce area were mats on the sidewalks filled

Daily crossing of one of the largest slums in the country. Nairobi, Kenya, 2013

with trinkets, sofas and large objects. A tailor turns the sewing machine wheel, a barber cuts a customer's hair. Hasty people walk among the cars, motorcycles honk: everyone is rushing and looks for a way to make a living. Speaking loudly, they hug one another, give roaring laughs. The scenes were all over the noisy streets.

A missionary remembers: *We were crossing small bridges over open sewage. Goats were being taken to be slaughtered, since the area is home to the largest number of slaughter houses in the city. The traders sell non-refrigerated meat and everything else on filthy sidewalks: clothing, electronic appliances, dried fish, art books, coal, necklaces, fabrics. On the way, a police station building just had the opening to one day install windows and doors.*

In Ethiopia, the pilgrims could walk back to their lodging through roads and avenues at night, worry-free, but in Kenya, this was dangerous. They would leave the Sisters' house no later than 5 p.m., watching out for their cameras and cell phones. Their strategy: whoever was filming should stay in the middle of them and act quickly, that's why the video footage was shaky. In their daily walks, always at the same time, they started recognizing merchants and passers-by and they waved at one another.

On the day of arrival, the Superior Sister of the Missionaries of Charity was late for their introduction meeting. She apologized: *Good morning, sorry to keep you waiting, but I was taking people from the slum to get acquainted with the House. We were robbed here at gunpoint four times because they thought we had material possessions. But, when they arrive*

An urban scene, missionaries serve lunch. Nairobi, Kenya, 2013

for a visit, as we show them our work and our conditions, they realize we have nothing. Most of them weep at seeing what happens inside our walls.

She welcomed them with enthusiasm and was especially glad to learn that they would participate in the consecration of eight novices—since that place is a training center for them—scheduled for the day before the group's departure. Soon, they were taken to attend a Mass in Swahili: the language of thousands of people here. They were enchanted by the sight of one hundred young devotees in white saris kneeling side by side.

The Fathers—the fifth branch of the congregation created by Mother Teresa—devote themselves to the education of priests and assistance to the poor in a slum bigger than their lodging area. The Missionaries of Fraternidade were there to help them serve lunch to 180 male youths and adults. Many of them are born, live and die on the sidewalks, without ever knowing a different life. Before being offered the meal, they read a passage from the Gospel, made comments on it, and chanted.

At the Sisters' request, the missionaries act. Ricardo gives details: *We went without preconceived ideas, ready for whatever might come up.*

They launched us into a range of tasks, from bottle-feeding newborns to more energetic work with firewood chopping. In the meantime, paintings, repairs without tools... there was a bit of everything, wheelchairs, doors, windows. We even restored the sculpture of a saint. In the kitchen, we spent mornings peeling potatoes, chopping cabbage, and on Saturdays we made the "mandazi", a kind of typical cookie—we prepared the dough, fried, and distributed it. Then came an arduous test: we spent two days chopping lambs.

It was as if the missionaries had been living with the Sisters for years... The Missionaries were surprised by a new proposal: *You know,... three days a year we manage to go on a picnic. Since you and the Sister responsible for Africa are here, we will do it! They got on the bus early in the morning living us keys, the patients, everything, and waved us goodbye: Take care of our house!*

Finally, the day came when the eight young novices would be consecrated. The Sisters are an example of boundless dedication. They dressed the patients, woman by woman, with their best clothes embellishing each one with necklaces. The Missionaries were responsible for the transportation of the eighty patients. The bus was overloaded: children, adults, the elderly and the Missionaries, all packed together. As they arrived, all of them were accommodated in the crowded church, chairs were passed from hand to hand through windows.

In the country with a Catholic majority, a flow of people arrived for the event: beautiful and ornate African mamas, the priests, the bishop, the Superior Mother of the Order, a European who is now substituting Mother Teresa of Calcutta.

Swahilis with hearts on fire celebrated for three hours, interspersed by the clear singing of the hundred novices. Ardor burned in the souls. At the Offertory moment, the Missionaries were invited to participate. Next, the bishop blessed the 12-inch crucifixes, which the Superior Mother placed in the waist cordon of each consecrated woman. All under the loud singing of Hallelu-uuujj-jahs.

The next day, they left. The bonds of trust between the Sisters and them had become so strong that they were allowed to take pictures when they mentioned their wish to show the work back home in Figueira. Since the

Sisters wanted to know more about the community where the Missionaries lived, they decided to show them a video. They were told that some Sisters, the patients, children and adults, would attend the presentation. Feeling self-conscious, two missionaries commented between themselves: *But some are mentally handicapped... What are we going to tell them?*

They were about to be given one more precious lesson on love. The Sisters never spared a single moment just for themselves, ignoring their patients. Altruistically, they live for the patients and always give them the best and most beautiful things.

The children laughed at the picture of the bus: *Bus, bus, bus.* The Sisters identified with the indigenous hut: a place for vigil among eucalyptus trees. There are similar constructions in Kenya. They said: *You live in paradise!* At the end, the Sister Superior asked: *Tell your superiors that we are very grateful for you being here and showing us all that you have.*

The Missionaries grew in gratitude, when comparing the poverty over there, where there is hardly a banana, or an orange, with the paradisaical abundance of fruit-filled orchards back home. Compared to the tiny houses of Nairobi, the pictures of immense buildings of the Figueira community left them embarrassed.

The Sisters work in silence, always affectionate and attentive. They speak only what is necessary among them. They say that an example is the best testimony, for it teaches the right attitude in a life of work and prayer. In a dialogue with the Contemplative Sisters of the Order, one of the ten commented on their immense humility and simplicity, to which they replied: *Let us pray that this praise will not be a reason for us to feel proud.* The Missionaries were moved by those words.

Back in Brazil, a young missionary remembers: *The Sisters were amazed at the predominance of male beings in the group and at the fact that they do all the housework so well: cleaning, washing, cooking. They were very touched by the boys' attitudes. In the end, one Sister told them: "You could be one of us, couldn't you?"*

Crossing of the slum and transportation
of internees for consecration of novices.
Nairobi, Kenya, 2013

RWANDA

Outer Africa and inner Africa

The brutal number of murders, tortures and rapes that swept
our country in the spring of 1994 would not have taken place
if ethnic hatred had not been hidden in the hearts of the people.
Twelve years before, in Kibeho, 20,000 people witnessed in dismay
a visionary crying and shuddering at the grotesque vision of human
destruction, torture and carnage that the Virgin Mary prophesied
and unveiled in front of her: "I can see a river of blood!"
Imaculée Ilibagiza, Rwandan writer

In the fourth and final mission to Africa, the missionaries would fraternize with three countries overwhelmed by suffering and indignation: Rwanda, Uganda and the Democratic Republic of the Congo. Summoned on one day and by the next 14 missionaries were chosen. In one month, through donations, the resources were collected to cover all the expenses for the trip, including those for administrative procedures, passport and visa requests.

On the eve of their trip they received a message via Skype: *Many people are asking: "Why go to Africa?" To meet the history of mankind, to touch ones feet on a suffering soil, and to reach spaces of planetary consciousness where love and mercy are lacking. The missionaries will sow a seed there that will grow in the spirit of the nations and will generate merits so that those who suffer unjustly may receive an opportunity of redemption.*

Their first test came at the airport. An official said one of the missionaries could not board because of a typo on their visa. There was tension in the air, since 80% of the group had already checked in. Ricardo was adamant. If that young man could not travel, no one would, and asked them to take their bags off the plane.

Facing the deadlock, the group remained at a distance, in silence, and began a strong movement of silent prayer and surrendering the obstacle to the Divine. In a few minutes, the man's boarding was authorized. The instructions received for years in lectures in the community had been put into practice: *Unity is the truth that builds bridges into infinity.*

After a 19-hour flight, including a stopover, peace-oriented conscious-nesses softly landed in Kigali, the capital of Rwanda. They advanced the clock 5 hours due to the time zone and set off in order to provide assis-tance to social outcasts.

Given the bloody genocide of 1994, the missionaries were surprised by the country's ability to overcome the past and by the great social recov-ery of the mountainous homeland with just under twelve million inhab-itants. Wherever they went, Kigali was rebuilt; clean, quiet, and very si-lent. Citizens, including the president, are seen participating in monthly cleanups of neighborhoods and highways. Rwanda, a nation among the oldest on the planet, is probably the cleanest in Africa.

They stayed at a simple hotel with a tidy environment and polite staff members, ready to meet their needs, including vegetarian food. Early on the next day, as they made their way to the house of the Missionaries of Charity, they entered the Holy Family Church. This was a temple where, at the time of the massacre, more than 2,000 people were murdered, in-cluding the Belgian priest.

Unknowingly, they had arrived in Kigali in the very week the population was in mourning for victims of the war between the ethnic Hutu and Tutsi militias. On the dreadful night of April 7, 1994, the 100-day geno-cide of about 800,000 people began. Those who witnessed the savagery avoid talking about it, but a priest told them that at one point he thought the demons had come out of hell to ramble around the streets of the city.

In 2000, after so many political and social mistakes, the tribal division in Rwanda came to an end, and its inhabitants started regarding themselves as Rwandans, instead of Hutus or Tutsis. Today talking about ethnicity is illegal. The government say this prohibition prevents the country from another bloodshed. Some believe that hate will boil again while others think the veto symbolizes the hope for ethnic groups to reconcile and possibly forgive the other. One of the missionaries asked the chauffeur who was driving them if he was Hutu or Tutsi. The man was silent for a moment and then said: *Neither, I am Rwandan.*

French, the language of the settlers, was abolished. English is spoken by almost everyone, having been adopted as the second official language, after Kinyarwanda. Since 70% of the survivors were women, they had to leave their homes for their sustenance, and were encouraged to take

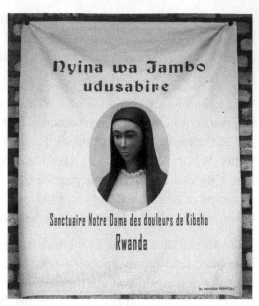

Our Lady of Sorrows. Kibeho, Rwanda

on leadership roles in the communities. Thus, Rwanda became the first nation in the world to have a female majority elected in their parliament. Consequently, it is now the leading African country in health, education, and gender equality. This small country was the first to abolish plastic bags—including biodegradable ones, which take two years to decompose. Since 2008, this bag, one of the worst enemies of the environment, marine and terrestrial life, is forbidden by law.

Not only material life, but diseased bodies and spirits yearning for the evolution to higher planes of consciousness are in a process of restoration in this country. The group received a new message from Brazil: *History left a mark in the streets and highways of Rwanda. May maternal love and the angels of God liberate the imprisoned souls. Dear children, unite with these angels.*

After visiting the church, they introduced themselves to the Missionaries of Charity. Cheerfully greeted as usual, for three days they practiced the exercise of selfless service: they did laundry, cleaning, participated in people's recreation, prepared food and cared for seventy elderly patients, children and disabled people. Four missionaries accompanied two Sisters in their contact with peasants, going up and down hills in a rural region.

Visit to the Marian Shrine. Kibeho, Rwanda, April 2015

As they closed the house at 11.30 a.m., the Missionaries of Fraternidade decided to spend the afternoons at the hotel starting the prayer list requested when they left Brazil. These moments of introspection gave them inner strength to transcend the continuous challenges. At a given point during their three-week journey, they felt that they had opened and consolidated a prayer channel through which the higher energies that truly guide the missions flowed.

From Kigali, they moved on. But before traveling the 100-mile dusty dirt road to Kibeho village, they made two stops. One, at the Genocide Memorial. Another, at the five-star Des Milles Collines Hotel, the setting for the movie Hotel Rwanda, where, its manager provided shelter for Tutsis for several weeks. He himself was a Hutu married to a Tutsi. He managed to save his family and five hundred Tutsis before the building was invaded. Over 1,200 people were hunted down and murdered with machete strokes on the staircases, in the corridors and in the swimming pool.

Denis, the Rwandan driver and guide of the Missionaries, and his wife, toured the hotel with them. Shen recalls: *At the end of our meeting the couple recited a prayer, a request for forgiveness for all the terrible events that had happened there.*

They saw picturesque scenes along the road on the four-hour drive among hills and valleys to Kibeho. When they arrived, they were greeted by a short and delicate rain, just as it had happened in Kigali. From then on, they noticed that during the whole trip to Africa, when entering or leaving each city, heavens welcomed them or said goodbye with drizzles or downpours, depending on the service that was being carried out.

Embraced by the silence and by the intense energy vibration of the retreat house of the Marian Shrine of Kibeho, the group surrendered its prayer channel for the spiritual healing of the nation. When the lights of the Marian center were turned off, at 8 pm, the missionaries were on their way to a night vigil in the chapel. They walked slowly, contacting the vast dark starry mantle, imagining evolved worlds between mini-focuses of bluish light, which travel millions of years, millions of miles, coming from divine spiral galaxies.

On the next day, a priest took them to the dormitory of the three clairvoyants for whom the Virgin of Kibeho first appeared, sending prophetic messages to both the Rwandans and mankind. Before continuing their route, they waited for the passage of the tropical rain. In reference to the arrival of the group, the priest pondered: *Whenever the Sanctuary receives a grace, we get such rains.*

They went down a hill towards the three springs of healing water that the Virgin Mary made emerge at the time of the apparitions, each one dedicated to a clairvoyant. They drank from the blessed water and soaked in it. They also went to visit the church where, during the war, the Tutsis naively took refuge, believing they would be spared. Inside the church five thousand of them were killed at once, amid grenades and fires.

In the end, the priest invited them to participate in the centuries-old custom of Rwanda, the *Igitaramo*. After dinner, the families gather around a large communal fire to sing, dance, make announcements from other villages, tell old stories, settle disputes. Nowadays, the meeting is regarded all over the country as a way to reconcile hearts. There was great joy during the meeting, which fostered mutual strengthening and the union of American and African consciousnesses.

Since the vast dense and subtle worlds are inseparable, while external Africa and America exchanged knowledge, old karmas were being paid, inner wounds were healed.

UGANDA

To serve and to love

We left Kampala... the mess caused by semi-urban
development had destroyed the land's nature and
almost destroyed the systems of the community.
...a red dust road: the old Uganda again, the
green forest acting as a screen; a surprise what
is founding the end of these extraordinary roads.
The Mask of Africa, by V. S. Naipaul

The missionaries could hardly envision what they would find when landing in Entebe after traveling ten hours with a stopover in the crowded and chaotic airport of Addis Ababa. As the plane landed, they saw the magnificent Lake Victoria, the largest in Africa, dotted with islands. The sight of the source of the White Nile, a river that follows northwards until it flows into the Mediterranean, allowed them to imagine a green city. They were mistaken.

The 20-mile trip to Kampala, the capital city where they would render service, took them almost 3 hours due to the traffic congestion. After the old administrative colonial Entebe buildings, the hills were covered by fragile constructions of bright tin roofs and walls painted with advertisements. They crossed path with bicycle and motorcycle *boda-bodas* offering fast and inexpensive rides. Filth, lack of basic resources, chaos, and extreme poverty were a regrettable sight, given that 150 years ago, the hygiene and the order of Ugandans were praised by historians.

Religious conflicts and a six-year war in the late nineteenth century between two international religions, Islam and Christianity, intensified the anarchy and decadence of Ugandan society. Today, in Kampala, we perceive common scenes in cities of the continent: mosques on top of hills, hundreds of Pentecostal and Catholic churches, followers of the traditional African religion with its myths, amulets and gods mingled with voodoo.

Ruled and exploited as a British colony for 160 years, since it gained independence in 1962, Uganda has had corrupt and fierce governments, conflicts, civil war, bloodshed, displacement of one and a half million people in the North of the country and an HIV epidemic. However, centuries ago, an orderly civilization flourished there, ruled by dozens of generations of royal families, kings, queens, princes, courts and palaces.

There are still descendants of this ancient kingdom as well as smaller tribal kingdoms that survived in the interior of the country. Since they did not know writing and only counted on oral memory, there are gaps in the history of the country. Yet, there are written accounts of the travel of European visitors. Ugandans excelled at building boats for navigation on Lake Victoria, and majestic straw huts that endure heavy tropical storms without leaking, and highways as straight as those of the Romans, even though they did not know about the wheel.

Godofredo, a young Ugandan man who arrived at the airport in a micro bus to work as the guide for the group, was eager to schedule wonderful sightseeing tours. He wouldn't stop talking. They were exhausted and wanted some silence. When they got out of the vehicle, they were met by the local police, who inspected each backpack. At the hotel, they found, to their dismay, that double-bed rooms had been reserved. It was not easy to reverse the situation, but the accommodations were finally changed.

A strong atmosphere of celebration prevailed, with a wedding being celebrated that night! People walked everywhere, the restaurant was crowded with men drinking, watching soccer on TV, laughing. There were very strong odors in the air, fierce drumming went on until dawn... Prayer was needed to be able to survive the wild night! Having worked late hours, the employees did not show up the next morning to serve breakfast. There were remains of the party everywhere.

The food, the air, the energy were so unusual that they went through highs and lows. What kept them in high spirits was to close their eyes and turn to the Higher Self.

Two members of the group had flu symptoms. Exhausted, they stayed at the hotel trying to recover. The others took a 30-minute walk to the house of the Missionaries of Charity. Received by the Superior Sister, a Portuguese woman, they were thrilled to follow her recommendation to lodge nearby at the Foyer de Charité. The catholic community sustained by consecrated lay people welcomes religious people for courses and retreats.

Back at the hotel while checking out, they watched a tribal discussion between the manager and the talkative guide, about the reduced cost of the

Kampala, Uganda, April 2015

room rate, as the group was supposed to stay the whole week. Their heated argument prevented them from listening to what a missionary was trying to say: *We will would pay the whole rate. Please just let us leave in peace!* Watching the astounding scene, they found out how well-trained both were in that aggressive performance, commonplace in the nation. Finally, they managed to be listened to and were liberated.

Later on, they got an encouraging message: *Get ready to go deep into the reality of Uganda, which is subject to the deterioration caused by illness and hunger among minors and the innocents. Missionary, your presence in Uganda will be a turning point for the lives of the souls you will serve and love as you have never loved. Because, behind all this poverty, is the most sacred glow that the Heavenly Father has placed in every heart.*

They stayed in the poor neighborhood where Catholic congregations assemble. There, a hundred years ago, a king ordered the torture and burning of the first to preach Christianity in Uganda. Their martyrdom is exhibited in stained glass, pictures, and books. It is said none of the forty-five martyrs resisted nor stopped praying during the execution.

The house of the Missionaries of Charity in Kampala was different from others they had been to. The Sisters, usually joyous, seemed to be reserved. Here, daily activities were the same as in the other ones they had known, but were coordinated by employees and, sometimes, the residents themselves, about fifty people.

They found another painful situation. The Sisters hire professionals from the Congo: business administrators, teachers, a biologist to work with the children. They give them food and a subsistence allowance. Some of them live in the neighborhood, others in the outskirts of town. As the hired professionals learned that the newcomers were Brazilians, that stirred up in them a desire to live the professional dream in a developing country. They had been deluded as they sought better living conditions in Uganda and were almost desperate to leave.

One morning, the missionaries of Fraternidade blew a breeze of life into that house. They took everyone to the yard and started singing in different languages, round-dancing, and playing until they saw the participants eyes glow. Drops of love were deposited in those unfortunate children and professionals.

When they returned the next day, they realized that a weight had been released, the atmosphere was softer.

At Foyer de Charité, there were palm trees and a chapel next to a vast green lawn. The priest asked them to conduct the daily rosary at 6 p.m., praying the Hail Mary in the African languages learned in the countries they had visited. These representatives from South America joined Ugandans to pray in Amharic, Swahili, Kiniarwanda, Zulu and Luganda. In those late afternoons, faith was so great that waves of love poured into the consciousness of the country that wanders aimlessly.

In the middle of the night, when entering the airport of Entebe on the way to the Congo, a quick and powerful downpour fell, sending them goodbye.

DEMOCRATIC REPUBLIC OF THE CONGO

Les Catorze

Justice is everyone's responsibility.
Denis Mukwege, Congolese doctor
and Nobel-Prize winner

They got off the plane under low laden dark gray clouds to face a maddened world that soon showed up in the Kinshasa airport. Queues! There were queues everywhere, the missionaries were completely lost. There was screaming everywhere, in dialects or in French. In vain, they tried to leave the airport but this had been hindered by passport controls, inspections, upheavals... people talking all around them. Outside, rumbling thunder and pouring rain.

A Federal police officer found a problem in one of the visas and prevented them from going ahead. The missionary Luiz spoke with him in French, when the man suddenly stopped speaking in French—the official language of the country—and started speaking Quicongo, the language of one of the 200 ethnicities of the Democratic Republic of the Congo. Being ironic, the officer laughed at the missionary. People nearby were amused. The agent laughed louder in a crescendo.

Luiz was puzzled. There was no reason for laughing, nothing funny, nothing irregular. He became quiet, in peace, and began to pray mentally, observing the unusual scene.

Suddenly he heard a female voice calling: Luiz! He knew no-one in Congo... *My name is Josie, I've come to help you.* The lady ordered the official: *Let them go, they are "Les Catorze"*, the fourteen, in French. She knew the rules, and everyone was suddenly courteous. Talking with the authorities, Josie coordinated all the steps: *Come here, do this, do that.*

And then, *voilà!*, they barely looked at the group's luggage. From that day on, they were known as *Les Catorze*.

Chaos in traffic. Kinshasa, Democratic Republic of the Congo, 2015

The priest of the Foyer de Charité of Uganda had not only reserved lodging for them in Kinshasa but, being aware of the confusion involving the entry of foreigners into Congo, he had also asked for the intercession of Josie, who also accompanied them at the time of departure.

We can hardly think of a more chaotic nation than Uganda. They visited Congo, a land of poor people and rare arch-millionaires. The country has lost inner peace, morals, values. This is reflected in the dizzying streets, the hellish traffic in which passengers ride with half a body out of the vehicles which takes twice the maximum capacity allowed. Sometimes fancy latest-model automobiles pass by, all of them with dents in their bodywork. People drive as they please, on the right or wrong side.

The chauffeur who took them from the airport to the lodging warned that the city was having a wave of protests. Cars around were coming from a collective burial of victims of the bloody local political situation. The fourteen felt trapped in the center of a crazy calamity, an impression that did not change on the following days.

Thanks to the Ugandan priest, they stayed in the austere Centrum Terezianum. Quiet and simple, it had an exquisite garden. The meals, served by the affectionate kitchen staff and religious personnel, were frugal, even though they were paid for. There was no abundance. In one meal four bananas arrived to be shared by *Les Catorze*. Daily meals included rice, creamed corn, green banana and a stew made with manioc leaves.

Sometimes there was one piece of fruit for each, and that was it. During their journey through Africa, the missionaries fed on what was offered them. The only product they bought was bottled water, following the advice given by the Sisters, who claim to have antibodies which allowed them to drink unfiltered water.

In that male Carmelite monastery, they stopped to contemplate a large Teresa of Avila banner. They placed their fatigue in the gentle hands of the saint, who continues to work, from other plans, in behalf of mankind, and also in cosmic tasks.

Near the Equator, the tropical heat of Kinshasa is oppressive, humid. In the low altitude city burns a dim light, which, in the foggy horizon, mixes with the silhouette of the ten-million-inhabitant of the capital, cradled by the rumble of the drums.

Generation after generation, the Congolese have suffered injustices and threats. Over more than three centuries they were among the 11 million men, women and children forcibly taken to the Americas as slaves to supply the continent's labor force. Besides them, countless people perished during long marches to the coast after being captured by black compatriots who sold the survivors to European traders. Representatives of various ethnic groups were crammed into tiny, smelly compartments of slave ships, where they traveled fettered by chains.

Brazil received about 46% of these slaves and was the last nation to abolish mercantile slavery in the 1888's Golden Law (Aurea Law).

Once official slavery was abolished, the ruined Congolese started suffering the most absurd brutalities when their rich territory became the property of a king of Belgium and later a colony of that country.

Having become independent in 1960, the DR Congo remains in the hands of dictators, rebels and foreigners. In nearly twenty years of the bloodiest civil conflict in the world after WWII, six million Congolese have been killed or have disappeared in clashes. Many citizens, while attempting to flee, were murdered at the borders, a common situation in authoritarian regimes, which force them to stay within their own countries.

The genocide in Rwanda, with two million fugitives who were stranded or died of cholera in obscure Congolese rain forests, also had direct implications on their local imbalance.

The Rwandan Hutu militia, escapees since the 1994 genocide, are still present in the border area, where it has joined a local group to sow terror among the civilian population in the region, which is rich in minerals and natural resources.

Statistical data indicate that the DR Congo is the second poorest country in the world, and its area is the second largest in Africa. It is considered second in world biodiversity, second only to Brazil. But its mineral and plant riches are smuggled or used for sponsoring teenager militias trained to be horrendously cruel. The children of this land are exploited from birth by prostitution and heavy labor in mines. Rebels also confiscate part of the agricultural production. Victims of centuries of injustice and evil, the people have lost hope and just try to survive. They have become spiritually impoverished.

By the end of the trip, the flu had spread throughout the group. They were using toilet paper to blow their noses, but all the rolls were suddenly gone. When they tried to find out why they had disappeared, a friar warned them: *Please do not do this. I'll bring you other paper, because every roll like this one costs ten dollars. Nothing is made here. Everything is imported, thus extremely expensive.*

The day after their arrival, *Les Catorze* were crammed into the van, which fit just nine, and proceeded to the usual introductions. The journey became a daily adventure. All drivers honk at the same time. Some cars have the steering wheel on the right side, some others on the left side... in some roads you drive on the right, and others on the left!

The priest driver was driving with one hand on the steering wheel, the other at the horn, and stepped on the brakes only when he turned off the vehicle. Through the windows, they watched the birds pecking the garbage, which causes disfiguring lumps on the forehead and around the beaks. The villagers nicknamed the town *poubelle*, the French word for trash can. There is raw sewage in the streets, mud, heavy odor, traders on the sidewalks and noisy crowds in the middle of it all.

In Kinshasa the Sisters have two houses, one for men, another for women. The former had been going through a renovation for months, so some of its rooms were packed with children, teenagers and men.

People looking for donations. Kinshasa, DR Congo, 2015

The house for women was the counterpoint to everything they had seen so far. It was the cleanest and tidiest they had visited in Africa, with girls and teenagers learning various crafts, such as sewing. Impeccable!

Les Catorze subdivided into two groups. About the women's house, Clara says: *We would sing, take the children here and there, carry the little ones on our arms, rock them, push wheel chairs, with the children smiling. We had lots of fun!*

In the second house they put on bandages on shocking wounds, which totally deformed the limbs. The Sisters also asked them to improvise a chapel and to play at the Mass celebrating the international day of Saint Joseph, the Worker. Once the ceremony was over, they spent the rest of the morning sharing games and plays and helped serve the chicken at lunch. Next, they cleaned everything up.

How could such deep bonds have been created in just one week? On the last morning, *Les Catorze* went to say goodbye to the women's house, and the girls offered them sprigs of flowers. The Sister Superior thanked them for the revolution of love, for having relieved people's suffering, for their affectionate presence, their willingness to work and their careful use of aprons and gloves. *Les Catorze* had lit the sun within each soul.

In the men's house, the boys stopped watching a movie and came running to hug them. The Sister in charge said the kids asked about them every five minutes. As it was the end of the trip, they left donations of clothing and food collected among the group itself, as well as financial aid.

As for the priests of the lodging house, they emphasized their praying rhythm, discipline, silence, unconditional service, and blessed them.

Laughing, Shen brings back a last memory: *The morning of farewells was long, the Van coming in and out, the tension caused by intrepid confrontations of our chauffeur, the indomitable priest driving on the wrong side of the expressway. He learned how to sing protective mantras that we sang along the way. Exhausted, crammed in the van, suffocated by the 104°F temperatures, all we wanted was to take a good shower before eating lunch, pack, and start the last prayer session in Africa.*

With a radiant smile, she remembers other details: *A big surprise! We had run out of water and had no idea of when we would have it again! It was the climax of the trip... No one complained. The most determined ones filled buckets in the laundry area and had a shower... The unusual scene became comical. To complete the scene, we had to immediately vacate the rooms, because another group was coming. Before leaving for the airport early in the evening, the water had not yet returned. Without another option, the least detached also decided to relieve the heat with mug showers.*

Les cartoze had made it! A breath of love relieved the heart of Africa. How many children of that land beg for help from Maternal Love, far beyond the wicked deeds of men? That event opened subtle channels and allowed the Lord's Angels to continue pouring peace into the innermost levels of the continent.

They received a last message from Brazil: *The peace mission in three African nations was a victory of the Light. So many pains were alleviated by the power of charity! So many souls found spiritual healing! So many graces were poured into forgotten and succumbed hearts! So many smiles emerged from the missionaries' inner selves!*

The group was learning the subtle art of moving through chaos, hunger, hatred, tormented bodies. They developed the purest artistic expression:

A farewell portrait. Kinshasa, Democratic Republic of the Congo, 2015

to build resplendent spheres amidst darkness. From their pores escapes the surrender of those who sow light in suffering soil. Slowly, the Africans reap the fruits.

They closed the doors before crossing the ocean back to Brazil, from Kinshasa to the Community of Figueira in Carmo da Cachoeira, in the south of Minas Gerais. Full of ardor, they would continue the work for the regeneration of human consciousness.

A cycle finished. The anonymous service with transcendental consequences was completed, whose memories nourish dry and impoverished hearts.

Painting of the mural of peace at the office of ASAM.
Ankara, Turkey, February 2016

TURKEY MISSION

Only love can heal the pain

Some people have eyes in their heart.
They see the world through these eyes.
May God always lead them toward generous people.
Turkish film: Mucize, by director Mahsun Kirmizigűl

Always moving forward, the missionaries of Fraternidade enthusiastically set off on a new humanitarian journey. They immediate said yes to take mutual love and peace to Arabian refugees sheltered in seven cities of Turkey.

The Eurasian country is in Asia Minor peninsula, or Anatolia, which means "the lands of the sunrise". Surrounded by four seas, it is a bridge between Asia and Europe. It has changed its name and geographic dimension several times. Since the Neolithic period, it has received migratory waves in its semiarid plateaus crowned by hills and mountains, as well as in the coastal areas, which are densely populated. Tribes, kingdoms and empires have left their mark in the history, character and national spirit.

It is currently home to millions of neighboring foreigners, with more migrants than any other nation. These people live under temporary protection, since Turkey grants official refugee status only to those who come from the European continent, although new laws allow Syrians to apply for a work permit.

Fourteen of the most experienced missionaries left the tropical summer, and after hours of flight over oceanic and continental areas, they faced a temperature of 10°F. Given the heavy snow, it was difficult to drive along the white streets of Ankara. In order to continue the physical training for the missionaries to cope with the tasks in the refugee camps, they walked all morning in line towards the Brazilian Embassy. As they entered the building, they wiped snowflakes off their boots and black anoraks.

They were cautious enough to take along tents, sleeping bags, clothing, dietary supplements for the demanding material restrictions in refugee camps. However, other challenges awaited them.

The Turkish Government would not authorize the group's entry into the camps, on the grounds of three reasons. The first: the language barrier, as none of them spoke Turkish, Arabic, or Kurdish, and therefore they would need constant interpreters. The second: there was no infrastructure to accommodate them. The third: their short stay in the country. It was a shock, but they knew: *The right thing will happen.* That was the beginning of the Turkey mission.

For three days, their faith was tested. The Brazilian Embassy committed fully to helping them find another form of service. They made contact with the United Nations agency for refugees, the UNHCR, which referred them to their partner, the Turkish NGO Association for Solidarity of Asylum Seekers and Migrants—ASAM. At once, the coordinator of this entity outlined a detailed program for the missionaries, in which they would make contact with the work of the organization in seven Turkish cities, each presenting a different face of the reality of the refugees.

From Ankara they would go to Gaziantep, gateway of Syrian refugees. From there they moved on to Nigde, Adana, Mugla, Izmir and Istanbul, on highways close to the Mediterranean and Aegean seas. Next, they would return for the final two weeks in Ankara, the departure point. The coordinator defined how many days they would spend in each city. Also, he made arrangements for the hotels , as well as transportation for the group in a 16-seat van with a driver who spoke only Turkish.

The next day, the fourteen, seven women and seven men, traveled to clear a path of kinship in the inner selves of those who emigrated from Arab countries, especially from Syria. The temperature was still below 32°F when they descended 430 miles to the Southeast through silent icy steppes and grandiose snowy mountains in the background. Gaziantep, one of the oldest cities in the world, receives hundreds of thousands of fleeing neighbors as it is less than 75 miles from Aleppo, the ruined Syrian capital.

The armed confrontation, the oppression and the religious intolerance in Syria involve the government itself, as well as a number of rebellious and radical groups, both local and foreign. Leaders of other countries,

terrorists and even criminal gangs meddle in the confusion. It is a powder keg. Since 2011, nearly 500,000 people have been killed. People pray for Allah to stop the war, and many believe that the prophesied Final Judgment has come.

Land troops march through city streets and country roads. Just before chemical and fragmentation bombs are dumped over the city blocks, birds stop singing and time stands still. The air is engulfed by a sepulchral calm until it is torn by dread. Terrifying jolts of jets launching lethal missiles. Shootings and artillery fire replace the beauty of silence. Dogs start barking, freaked out. Children cry. Buildings shake. Century-old buildings are set ablaze. Columns of dark smoke roll over from buildings where entire families die, buried under debris.

A sea of people who love life look for ways to leave in order to save it. *Let's go!* In an ultimate gesture of love, housewives' water their little plants. Husbands lock their houses or hammer metal plates on doors to protect them from looters. They leave and don't look back.

Those who have money, passports, and helpful contacts escape by plane. Others venture by land towards the home of relatives or neighboring nations. They cross snowy mountains, some may die on the way, some are imprisoned while crossing borders. They all come to their destination: the father without the child, the wife without the husband, teenagers, and crowds of orphans.

More than five million people are estimated to have left Syria, half of them are minors. All of them have invariably been affected.

Imer explains: *Migration is a solution to preserve life, but migrants come out of one conflict and enter another. They have many children and live in small crowded places, which often lacks hygiene. Unemployed and having no school for the children, some feel so uprooted that they end up returning. Because in their homeland at least they know the language and the people, they believe they will find means for survival there. But the dream is soon over. They can barely satisfy basic food needs, and some of them are murdered for no reason.*

According to the Turkish Ministry of Interior, over 3 million Syrian refugees have been registered in the country. Nearly 10% are living in community centers, usually made up of prefabricated structures and food supplied by the State. The rest survive on their own.

The missionaries set out for the country of the red flag with the white star and the crescent moon, the Islamic symbol that appeared in a dream of the first Ottoman ruler. They visited the seven cities now offering health services, playing with children, organizing warehouses and making material donations, and participating in home visits accompanied by ASAM servers. In its offices, this humanitarian NGO promotes activities such as medical and psychological care, social assistance, music classes, handicrafts and Turkish, Arabic and English lessons for children.

Their first contact in Gaziantep was a surprise. Boys and girls were celebrating an end of classes with dances, songs and games. Childhood is more resilient. Their little eyes began to peek at visitors, strange and funny men and women dressed alike, with police-like uniforms. Curiosity keeps them alive. The beautiful little children truly smiled, despite the burden of being orphans or traveling alone for having been separated from their parents. They didn't even seem to live in such an unfair world. And the missionaries, touched, reciprocated with kindness.

That was the solution! Those who have lost so much must be in close touch with their childhood and the possibility of playing. The missionaries opened boxes with donations from their luggage and removed colored balloons, ink, paper, handicraft material, and toys. On the following day, part of the group drew and painted along with the little ones. The greatest success was a puppet theater, accompanied by songs, on the topic

Puppet theater on oral hygiene for Arab refugee children. Gaziantep, Turkey, 2016

of oral hygiene. The dialogs were simultaneously translated into Arabic and Persian. The puppet Maria Chiquinha, a girl who loves candies, is talkative and cheerful. She fills her mouth with candy until she breaks a tooth in a bite. As her tooth starts aching, the animals, always trying to warn her to take care of her teeth, give her a huge colored toothbrush. With gestures and silliness, they begin to make fun of themselves. The onomatopoeias were the most amusing part.

Shen remembers: *It was very funny. In fact, the funniest part was us laughing at ourselves. We hid behind a tiny table or a short curtain from where our feet could be seen, and gradually fell down. We rehearsed the dialogue and, in the nick of time, the results were totally different. Luiz was the lion and every time he opened his big mouth, he began with a wwuuaaahhh. As he can't speak English well, the translator, incapable of understanding him, just made up something right there, and everyone laughed all the same. Sometimes Luiz forgot the memorized sentences and improvised: "wwuuaaahhh".*

After the presentation, the kids lined up to receive dental care and were given toothbrushes. One by one, each little tooth was examined by Imer, the missionary-dentist. To wrap up the meeting, a short and cheerful video of Brazilian children and youths from the Community of the New Earth in Rio de Janeiro was shown to them. They sent greetings and messages of peace, simultaneously translated into Arabic.

Since Shen plays the guitar, she was assigned to help a Kurdish music teacher. ASAM hires some refugees to teach. She remembers: *The teacher seemed quite suspicious of our presence there. Since they are victims of attacks and constant political persecution, they may imagine that foreigners may have hidden motives concerning them. Then, when I realized he was not interested in talking, I just stayed and watched the wonderful lesson that he gave to the beautiful kids. A children's choir! The little ones, very obedient and attuned students, sang angelic songs in Kurdish. How beautiful! They had in themselves the archetype of Syrian innocence.*

Meanwhile, in another office, the missionary health team, after a period of adjustment to the ASAM medical and nursing work program, assisted both refugees and staff. They mainly used Eastern medicine techniques, being aware that the exercise of kinship is the greatest instrument for rescuing beings.

In Gaziantep, Nidge, Adana and Izmir, they participated in home visits to refugees. Throughout the country, people usually live in old run-down abandoned houses. One of these was occupied by eleven children with the smaller ones cared for by the older ones, since their parents had left for work. The group then moved to another address where four families resided, and invited them to the Syrian coffee ritual in a room that was a living-room during the day and, at night, became a bedroom for several people.

An ancient cultural element of the Arabs is Bedouin hospitality. Although they are regarded as aloof, these people give foreigners and guests even more than their own possessions. One of the honors they offer is the preparation and the offering of coffee. People sit in a circle on a rug to discuss various subjects, whether with the members of the tribe or with the ones coming from outside. Shen says: *We were blessed by that surreal and picturesque scene. Those who greeted us have a very difficult financial situation. In a very poor household, we tasted coffee in beautiful, small and delicate cups of fine porcelain. At the end of the fraternal conversation, we learned they were owing two months' rent and would be evicted in a few days. So we offered to settle their debts and another month in advance in order to give them time to better organize themselves. Their gratitude was indescribable! They said they will always pray for us.*

Arabian refugees wait at the door of the ASAM office. Izmir, Turkey, 2016

Refugees yearn for a dignified life, to work, study and actively participate in local life, but few manage this. They try to survive on informal work, being at the mercy of Turkish bosses, who take advantage of the situation to force them to ways of working similar to that of slavery, toiling 12 hours a day. They are underpaid, or not paid at all. There had been similar episodes in the past: the Turk have invaded and taken possession of the riches of Syria, and also exported Syrians as slaves.

Children are not spared from cruelty: the ones from eight to nine years of age help in the sustenance of the family. Mothers also suffer for having to send their children to factories to work for a little money.

The group went to visit refugees who live in dark abandoned hidden damp, little shops. At least in this place bombs are not dropped in the neighborhood, as it used to happen in their homeland. Feeling edgy, they freak out at the slightest noise, such as a car exhaust, or of an object that was dropped. At least no one forces them to convert to their own radical version of Islam if they do not want to be beheaded.

Traveling 250 miles further, they arrived in Nidge, where the missionaries spent the afternoon in a house managed by ASAM, which welcomes twenty men in a situation of extreme stress. This NGO assists refugees with both economic and psychological difficulties. Having come from

Iran, Iraq, Sudan, Somalia, Syria and Afghanistan, they were all intensely traumatized by the wrath of authoritarian regimes and the evils suffered in their countries of origin.

The missionaries of health provided them with medical care, while others talked or played with two boys who lived there. How can one ignore offenses and rebuild oneself?

Given that the people assisted had several different faiths, the missionaries prayed with the Christians and, united by the loving vibration, praised Life singing a song of Saint Francis of Assisi at the end of the day. At the end of the meeting the men gently offered the group a tasty vegetarian snack, and hugged them, grateful for the visit.

The servers gave them their full attention and then left. They believe in miracles: those men are in the hands of the Love that moves mountains. Their spirits would be healed! Such simple actions have inner repercussions that harmonize those who try to escape the shadow of hatred and unimaginable cruelties. The missionaries came to remind their brothers and sisters that love exists.

In Adana, the next stop, the two ASAM offices had become warehouses for donations coming from the UNHCR, UNICEF and others. In the sheds the donations for 15,000 people, mostly refugees living in rural areas, are kept orderly. Before distributing them, they pay home visits to update registries and find out about people's material needs. While twelve missionaries left to assist children, two others spent the morning with a staff member of ASAM, delivering grocery cards worth 300 Turkish lira, for families to obtain food supplies at markets.

They followed the coastline to Mugla, contemplating the mystery of shimmering waters and stone islets of the Aegean Sea: a break to enrich the senses with beauty. Fifty miles further they reached Bodrum, one of the most important tourist resorts of Turkey, destination of thousands of refugees from the sudden upwelling of Syrian escapees in the summer of 2015. Although they are not allowed to remain there, some hide among rocks and sleep in icy olive groves, waiting for the coast guard to leave.

Turkey, January and February 2016

Then they launch into the sea in old inflatable boats, on a risky adventure towards the Greek island of Kos, about three nautical miles away.

Hoping to arrive in Europe, those who are deprived of nearly everything pay the little money they still have to middlemen. Then the displaced people watch a basic course on YouTube and pilot second-hand boats with low-power engines and twice their maximum loading capacity. They breathe deeply, pray, and in extreme anxiety confront the waves taking the elderly, babies and orphans to Greece.

Turkish and Greek coastguards watch the sea round-the-clock to prevent people from crossing and to mitigate the risk of drowning. The passengers they catch are sent back to Turkey. When caught, the middleman, often a fisherman eager to exploit refugees, is arrested and prosecuted.

The well-trained rescue team at Mugla's office greeted the missionaries with utmost attention. Unexpected paths led them to meet those admirable and very experienced voluntary divers. Some were former Coast Guard military. They visited the facilities of the association at the marina, the boats used, the equipment room, the control tower. As the missionaries watched videos of marine rescues of family-packed ferry boats, they rejoiced at the kindness and tenderness of the divers, who voluntarily devote themselves to the good of the human community. Their mission is to save as many lives as possible.

On their way to Izmir, Turkey's third largest city, they stopped at Ephesus, a city famous for the Greek-Roman Empire ruins. Their intention was to visit the house where Mary, the Mother of Jesus, lived her last years before ascending to heaven. They felt the profound peace of the Eternal left by the one who gave birth to the Divine Son, saw Him grow, suffered with the death of He whose unfathomable transcendence saved and forever transformed planetary life. Inspired by that atmosphere, they renewed their vows of service and requested for the mission to be fulfilled according to the Greater Plan. They wished love to be the ruler of human hearts, and went on.

Izmir was the main crossing point of refugees towards Lesbos, the Greek island twenty minutes away. ASAM tries to discourage them from traveling through the Aegean Sea and provides them the best means to survive in Turkey.

Distribution of clothing to refugees. Izmir, Turkey, 2016

At that time, 90,000 people were registered in the association. The real figure was estimated to be twice that many, most of them living in the surrounding areas.

In Izmir, there were three offices: a general treatment center and another specifically for children. The third is located in the strategic place where refugees try to escape. In addition to being with the children, in those days the missionaries also loaded a truck with boxes of donations and distributed clothing with members of ASAM. The little ones circled around them like little bees, playing, and giving and receiving hugs. Under the pressure to survive, families toil in the countryside as peasants in exchange for housing, sometimes living in tents. Most women have always been housewives in their home country, so having to work outside is difficult for them.

During the trip, the missionaries handed out winter clothes, thermal blankets and toys, besides using the school supplies and handicrafts sent from Brazil by collaborators of Fraternidade. However, only on the last day in Izmir were they allowed to deliver the dehydrated fruits and vegetables they had brought along.

Here the group had their greatest collective test of a paradigm shift in the pace of activities. Accustomed to readiness for any type of action, as if they were in a small but effective factory, they realized that overemphasizing their willingness to help was bringing inconvenience.

Visit to a refugee camp. Izmir, Turkey, February, 2016

Shen explains: *We found out in a timely manner not to complicate things even more. In fact, we were overloading the employees with extra work and extra responsibility. They did want us to be in contact with the refugees, but within the system of ASAM, in which they would continuously keep us company. As soon as it dawned on us, we would interrupt our practical service on weekends to dedicate ourselves to group restoration and prayers.*

Although Turkey has secular political forces and is a secular state with no official religion, Islam is the predominant religion, adopted by about 98% of the inhabitants, most of whom are practicing believers. From the towers of the beautiful mosques come the calls to believers to do their five daily prayers. On little mats on the floor, they bow toward Mecca, the sacred city where non-Muslims are not allowed to enter. In every hotel where they stayed, arrows indicate the direction towards the most sacred city of the religion.

A symbol of Islam, women's clothing reflects the openness or conservatism of its countless branches. Despite being worn by most Muslims who live in Islamic countries, the *hijab*, a garment with a veil prescribed by the doctrine, has little acceptance elsewhere. In Turkey, for example, the *hijab* is forbidden at universities. In Syria, one of the most liberal-thought Islamic countries, women wear head scarves, but they are colored. As for the *burqa*, a garment that covers women's bodies and faces, with a net covering their eyes, it is mandatory in the strictest Arab nations, such as Saudi Arabia and Afghanistan.

The Catholic community in Turkey is extremely small and consists only of foreigners. Churches are rare. The group visited two of them. In Ankara, they attended a Mass in English. Everyone knew one another, and the missionaries were introduced to them, and told them what group they belonged to, their origin, and the purpose of their stay in the country. On Sunday morning in Izmir, the Mass was celebrated in French, Turkish and Italian. There, a musician showed them the lyrics of Hail Mary in Turkish, and taped it, so that the pronunciation of the words could be registered.

They finally arrived in the fourth largest city in the world. Cosmopolitan Istanbul, former Byzantium or Constantinople, is home to most of the refugees since it is one of the escape routes to Europe.

Much to the driver's relief, increasingly impatient, tired and who was arriving almost two hours late to pick them up, they were about to return to Ankara, the starting point. But beforehand, the missionaries had organized clothing and hygiene items for the ASAM warehouse. Then, they made crafts, played with children, and showed them a video in which Brazilian youths perform a small play, and send hugs to Middle East children. Thrilled, the thirty small children wanted to reciprocate. They recorded Arabian greetings in response, sending kisses and peace to the Latinos. It was sheer joy!

Informed about unimaginable movements and repercussions of cosmic existence on the live of planet, the missionaries learn to be instruments of peace, so the environment around them may be recreated. The workers of empathy know that, beyond the visible tasks, their crystal clear intentions of helping fellow beings heals inner traumas.

TURKEY MISSION

Refugees wait

Kind words open iron doors.
Turkish proverb

Each mission leaves unforgettable marks. At the peak of the refugee crisis, for two weeks members of Fraternidade joined those who passed through the central office of ASAM in Ankara. The agency registers and issues an official identity document to non-Syrian refugees, mostly Iraqis, Iranians and Afghans, besides including them in social programs. The Turkish Government itself is in charge of the registration of Syrians.

At that point of the journey, the proactive missionaries felt in tune with the simplicity of their peaceful routine. They had prepared to go through great material constraints. However, Life had forced them to have a serene working routine.

On the first morning, the coordinator at the ASAM office provided them with a small room where they could be with children. At first, they had the impression fourteen adults plus lots of kids would not fit in the cubicle with a table... but they did. In the little corner a nest of tenderness was woven, interspersed with a thousand and one adventures.

The initial barrier was gradually broken as they made handcrafts and sang. Not only the kids got involved, but also the parents. Over the days, the staff and security personnel also joined in. As a relationship of trust was built, the missionary health team came to be permanently requested for the most diverse services.

Children are spontaneous and straightforward, so the relationship with them was simple and transparent. Stories happened among drawings, windmills, pompoms, divine eyes, modeling clay and clay sculptures. A missionary says: *Muslim children are affectionate, pure, bright-eyed, and always ready to play. They would remain in complete silence and created peace while we wove arrangements with colored wool yarns. I thought, "I'm here to collaborate, and they're the ones who change me. I need to regain their childlike nature".*

Cristiane, a young missionary says: *I felt indescribable love for those little ones. At first, I thought they only needed scissors, glue, paint, paper, and they thought I just wanted them to make drawings, cutouts, things like that... As days went by, we established a curious dialogue. I began to understand the history of each one, how they got there, if they had a father, a mother, siblings. They spoke Arabic, Persian, and I don't even know how I managed to understand them. I found the living language of Love.*

She goes on: *While some of us painted a large panel, others played with the children. At a certain point, I was alone with ten of them. How to interact in a way that they did not leave? I looked at them, all in expectation, as we held hands in a circle. One of them soon started communicating through gestures and began to teach me a game similar to tisket a tasket. They sang a rhyme in Arabic, which I managed to learn! Radiantly, we were spinning in a circle, and feeling great! A foreigner wearing a serious uniform was also playing like that! Parents and even the guards, were infected by joy. Human warmth disconnected them from their misfortunes.*

The missionaries also met children who, having been abused, reacted in fear of being mistreated once again. They would shrink back, and strike at whoever came close to them. Shen remembers: *You could only notice the war trauma in a few children. One of them was very difficult, quite naughty. He had suffered so much that he wouldn't accept anyone around, any kind of affection. There was also another. We tried and tried. We attempted to get closer to him, but he pushes us away aggressively. But most of them are needy, they want to be hugged, given attention, to be together.*

For four mornings, they amused themselves making a mural for Peace on the office entrance corridor walls. There were fourteen missionaries and exactly fourteen yellow, purple, green, blue, and orange panels. Each got in charge of one. Painted in a childlike style, the visual language was coherent. The people's creativity was boosted by someone's playing the guitar, children dipped brushes in paint, smiling parents dared to try brush strokes, and even officials and security guards participated in the playful activity. Each panel represented a specific topic, and the corridor walls were gradually wrapped by sliding waters, fish, bubbles and sea bottom algae, lake, city and countryside landscape, flowers, the Tree of Peace, a garland of flowers around the enormous pink heart of the Virgin Mary, beetles, birds, butterflies, the Angel of Love, a rainbow, the Universe.

In an orange panel, were stamped turquoise, rosy and lunar-green hand palms of various sizes and shapes. Employees of the ASAM agency laughed, took photos, delighted to offer joy to thousands of refugees who passed through the place every week, before entering the lobby.

A missionary says: *The clan entered—the grandparents, the father, the mother, the children—and all were frisked by police officers. A sad situation to look for guns among whole families. Painting panels, we broke the ice. Unable to speak Farsi or any of the languages spoken in Syria or Afghanistan, we communicated through mimics and eye to eye language. We pointed to the brush and ask: "Do you want to paint?" The children laughed, their parents told them to go ahead and they obeyed. Tremendous tensions were released!*

With a skill to make people feel free to express themselves, share their pains and use their imagination, each missionary gives full attention to one person at a time, making them perceive how extremely important and unique they are.

The fourteen were there only to love, not to solve material issues. Some of them stayed with children, while others slowly migrated into the waiting room where adults waited to be attended to. They sat next to each other, tried to communicate through gestures and facial expressions, since most refugees did not speak English, only Arabic.

They found the pain of writers, musicians, choral conductors, artists, peaceful beings forbidden to express themselves in their country of origin. Some had arrived in Ankara the day before, fleeing death and harassment from extremist totalitarian regimes.

Painting of panels at the entrance hall of ASAM.
Ankara, Turkey, February, 2016

Arab refugees wait to retrieve documentation at the ASAM office.
Ankara, Turkey, 2016

Imer clarifies: *When someone finally makes the decision, they have waited and endured a lot, sought alternatives until, after a more violent and traumatic fact, they flee from their home country to the unknown. Of the millions who emigrate, few can achieve a stable life, and that takes years. What initially was hope turns into a nightmare; the financial situation does not improve. They feel rejection, hunger, cold. Europe, the main focus of migrants, is saturated; it says it has no resources...*

In the face of impressive biographies transmitted to the missionaries with descriptions of abandonment, physical and moral cruelty, we can uncover horizons of courage, inner strength capacity for overcoming the pain.

Rosi talked to a few fugitives. She met a young Iranian who believed in Christ and wanted to be a Christian, or even a catholic nun. She felt called, and to profess her faith she took the risk to come by herself to Turkey.

Countless came from rich and structured countries, in reference to health, housing, educational system. They were entrepreneurs, doctors, people who had high financial power and social stability. Misery had never knocked on their door. They did not know what it is to spend the

ASAM office. Ankara, 2016

day looking for a loaf of bread, what it is to not be able to give even a sock to their child in that extreme cold of 5° F. They had left before terrorist groups invaded their homes, abused their families, lured their children. They walked days, months, crossing the desert on ice, and they were there, they and their children with gangrene in the fingers and toes.

Rosi began to enter the soul of a woman who had a very sad look and a child on her lap. She remembers: *I got closer and closer... then asked to hold the baby. She allowed me. My heart began to ache. Without anyone saying anything, she began to cry. She cried and, in the few English words she knew, we established a dialogue. I told her not to lose faith, that God would lead her journey.*

The young lady gave her testimony: *Yes, Allah is helping me!* Her husband had been beheaded, her children became religious fanatic, and that brought her so much pain! One day, before she could escape with the baby and another child, she had nothing to feed them and they were crying. She was pleading with them to be quiet because, if terrorist groups appeared, their lives would be at risk. She begged Allah for protection. At a certain moment, somebody insistently knocked on the door. She opened it. There was nobody, just a huge box. She looked to both sides, there was no one. She took the box into the house and found bread, flour, milk in it. She fell on her knees with her six year old son and thanked Allah, who had listened to them, gave them hope and the strength to go on.

Fraternal listening encourages those who are falling into despair. What is sown may not be visible today, but will eventually flourish in human beings. In silence, the missionaries say: *Life is great and beautiful, it should not be lost. Follow the path of learning, you can do it, inner transformation is what matters most!*

Through the corridor of imaginative panels, Ricardo saw a father come in with an eleven year old boy, both well-dressed, the father with a ponytail. Later he could listen to the kid playing a borrowed guitar. He was frightened, but the notes expressed deep feelings and beauty.

Ricardo says: *The father was a conductor. His two children were also musicians, that boy and a seventeen year old. For this reason, they had been arrested and tortured in Iran. Killing is something common in that country... a family flees its house with three or four members, and only two cross the border. His wife had been murdered. They broke the father's fingers because he was an artist. With tremendous effort, he managed to escape with that son. However, the other remained there, imprisoned.*

Each experience, small or devastating, brings a lesson. Ricardo looked down thoughtfully: *I tried to understand the father's feelings. How difficult it is to relieve his child's anguish, while he himself felt unbearable pain, ignoring whether his other son had been released or killed. For some reason, that struck me. Knowing all this, traveling for tourism loses its meaning.*

No matter how long the volunteers stay with someone, the most important thing is to open up to welcoming them, to let oneself be touched by that person and hold them in a loving place of themselves. Through these stories is woven in the missionaries' hearts a network of peace that invisibly unites creatures, peoples, nations.

The missionaries carry along a black suitcase laden with colorful material. Out of it came the paper with which they set up a small cardboard box. But the box was empty. They asked the youths: *What shall we do now?* One suggested putting their desires and requests in it. And they invited some refugees and officials to do so. Some joined. They filled out the little yellow, turquoise, pink, orange pieces of paper with messages of peace in various languages—Persian, English, Farsi,

Spanish, Portuguese, and Turkish—which were placed in the fragile box that would travel to Brazil.

However, on the way back to the hotel, the little box was forgotten at a bus stop... *Well, that's gone*, they thought. However, the next day, it was returned to them at the office! They did not even send it with their luggage. The treasure box took to the air as carry-on luggage. Later, the messages of peace were framed, and the chart is now at the entrance room of the headquarters of the Fraternidade, in Brazil.

Every single day brought something unique and symbolic. ASAM was visited by a United States senator who, in the little corner of joy, was given gifts. On that day, the daily chants sung by the missionaries before the office closed at 5 p.m. attracted more employees, security personnel and refugees. Shen, who always played the guitar, recalls: *Our musical performance was liberating. We could perceive a channel of light being opened.*

That night, at the hotel, at the beginning of the daily session of prayers, they heard a loud boom. The building shook. Later they learned a bomb dropped by terrorists half a mile from there killed over forty people and injured dozens. The trained group remained calm, but alert to meet any needs. Amid incessant sirens, each one had time to analyze their own reaction in face of danger.

Their journey was coming to an end. Three representatives of the missionaries went to say goodbye and thank the Brazilian Embassy. The staff and the Ambassador were very interested in the reports of the experience and recommended procedures to fully support the future missions.

The missionaries increased their admiration for young ASAM officials. Carrying out activities with commitment, they were good teachers during their time together. On the last day, they received a surprise farewell!

Smiling, Shen says: *On the last day, we were about to pack when, suddenly... employees and security personnel appeared out of nowhere to make handcrafts. Right then, the musicians of the ASAM appeared! One, more experienced, played a popular string instrument called "Baglama", a kind of lute. Then they were followed by the percussionists. For an hour they played and sang to us songs from various regions of Turkey. What a beauty, it was awesome! The Turkish singing conveys a feeling of power but also a lament. At the end of the party, we were invited to typical dances, in which we joined rather shyly!*

They took souvenir photos, some said they would visit Brazil on vacation. After thanking the group for the joy brought to the daily routine of ASAM, the coordinator said that she hoped to see them again as soon as possible. Shen goes on: *It was lovely to hear her say that, she was initially quite serious with us until we reached such complete fraternal feelings. We distributed handmade souvenirs to various employees. While the last refugees were given their records and said goodbye, we sang the last song enthusiastically, "Sacred Mother, establish Your Door of Peace". The Middle East Mission was finished with a golden key.*

They closed the circle by receiving at the hotel the visit of the ASAM's coordinator general, who invited them to return. He said that, at first, they thought it would be hard work to welcome and accompany the missionaries, but after meeting them they were happy to have been together. As a souvenir, they were given samples of various types of handicrafts made with the children. Next, they drove to the airport.

As soon as they arrived at Figueira, the missionaries went "into quarantine", keeping complete silence and receiving countless medical and spiritual services. Later, they were invited to attend the Campaign for Peace, an event that was taking place in another farm of the community. They were supposed to arrive a few seconds before the start and return to the van as soon as the meeting was over.

As they entered the great hall, the fourteen volunteers were surprised by a triumphant homage. Stepping onto the stage, both the instructors and the audience of hundreds of people stood in complete silence and reverence in a touching gesture of recognition for the work done with representatives of Arab nations.

During that sublime celebration, to each of the fourteen was given a white rose as a symbol of fourteen Arabian souls raised to the heart of God by the Maternal Love. Next they were anointed with oil. They also learned they would join a Permanent Mission to be established in Greece in the near future. Shen concludes: *We were flabbergasted.* They were convinced, mysterious streams of peace had really been opened in the inner world of the Middle-East.

PART II
Missions in South America

BACKCOUNTRY MISSION, ALAGOAS, BRAZIL

Crossing borders towards people's hearts

We need to dive into the underground society
to evaluate actions... Giving something to drink
to the one who is thirsty. Well. But how can one
do this work of mercy in everyday life?... Right
there a truly merciful soul had appeared to me.
A free deed, no payment, no expectation
Memoirs of Prison, by Graciliano Ramos

The northeastern drought rips the land, kills the cattle, breaks families apart, casts out husbands and children to humid distant places. The missionaries stepped on the hard soil with the most resolute love: crossing boundaries that separate their hearts from the backcountry's men native to the whitish landscape of Alagoas´s wilderness.

Two months earlier, when the humanitarian mission in Brazil's northeastern hinterland was announced, members of Brazilian North and Northeast Light-Network agreed to take up the shepard's crook of the eternal pilgrim. The hearsay in the wind suggested the work should be developed in places indicated by the Catholic entity Brazilian Caritas. Fifteen days before the mission began, they went with Ricardo to six communities surrounding Palmeira dos Índios and another two, about 125 miles away. On the way their plan of action was outlined.

They would cooperate with Portuguese descendants who have been in livestock farming since the enslaving colonialism period. Also, they would cooperate with descendants from a *quilombo*—the afro refuge camp during slavery times—in Poço das Trincheiras, one of Brazil's poorest municipalities. They would work for the sake of Xucuru and Cariri ethnic indigenous groups in two communities. One is in the vicinity of Palmeira dos Índios; the other on Geripancó, in the Ouricuri Mountain range of Pariconhas municipality. The village is home to Indians fleeing persecution and lacking land to work.

The cosmic-ecumenical group embracing the sixth mission of Fraternidade landed in Maceió: eight missionaries, four Light-Network collaborators and seven nuns of the Monastery of Christic Charity, of Grace Mercy Order, who brought by plane almost 400 pounds of donations to be added to those delivered by other groups directly to Alagoa's capital.

Next day, they left for Palmeira dos Índios, in four rented cars. The fourth most populous city in the state occupies former indigenous lands. For two hours, they crossed a rural landscape occupied by nations and tribes thousands of years before the Portuguese colonization.

The native people's customs and traditions have been disappearing since the eighteenth century. Following the expulsion of the Jesuits from the country, the local government abolished indigenous rituals, prohibited the use of their languages, ordered the huts be replaced by Portuguese colonial style houses and imposed severe control on those who would take refuge in the woods.

Once at the lodging, where they would stay the week, the missionaries settled in with their luggage and donations and headed to the Caritas headquarters for the latest arrangements. As the Bishop wanted to meet them, they went to the Episcopal House. After a warm welcome, he asked them about the origin of the group and their community life, and blessed them.

Invited to participate in the mass celebrated by him in the cathedral, at twilight they listened to the Bishop's sermon. He mentioned the servers who, as Christ asked, left comfort and daily tasks behind in order to devote themselves to those in most need. The respectful attitude should be an example to be imitated. Once again, the Bishop blessed the work. At the end of the mass, he invited a representative to the pulpit to introduce Fraternidade and describe the activities to be carried out—health consultations, puppet educational plays, workshops, activities with children and youths, among others.

Listening to the birds, early the following day they drove 6 miles to Lajes. There and in another eight communities they were warmly greeted. Members of Caritas accompanied the visits, actively participating in the tasks.

Who are those people who joyfully arrived from so far away? The vehicles had hardly been parked, and they were surrounded by local residents and taken to a chapel for a brief introduction. A crowd of curious children and dogs followed the group to the school where healing action would soon occur—medical, dental, psychological and emergency care. At the same time, other missionaries ran workshops—sewing, crocheting, making bamboo flutes.

The solar cooker is a device that particularly drew men's attention. A saucepan with raw pumpkin was left under the sun, surrounded by cardboard covered with sheets of aluminum foil. Nearly four hours later, they took the lid off, and the country women tasted it: *It is squashy, delicious!* The efficiency of the process had been demonstrated.

After Lajes, they ran the same harmonic activities with hundreds of families in Lagoa Nova, Ariado, Baixa Fria, Xucuru-Cariri and also made recyclable collectors from irregular dump sites in Algodãozinho. Wherever the missionaries went, the local residents fixed their daily lunch with the food supplied by Caritas.

Everyone was grateful for the treatment and gifts received—tools, clothes, baby layettes. The most talented children were given two guitars and five wood flutes and began to play melodies taught by a musician-missionary.

The power of charity builds peace among human beings. The missionaries also devoted themselves to listening to mothers and teenagers. A tender language that involves protection and understanding was spoken. Sitting in small circles, they took care of psychological issues, aware that misfortunes are useful impulses for inner transformations. One mother mentioned the way she soothes her own heart: *My son had anemia and nearly died. If he's still with us, I thank God. God is my warrior, my Father, my life.* The peaceful people constantly call to the Invisible, never getting discouraged.

Their simple attitudes, without conflicts or pressures of any kind, made true fraternal encounters flourish. Secret commitments were made between the women served and servers: to evolve through love. As if by magic, life distributed graces and made lightness overcome whatever obstacle arose.

During the 90-mile trip to the Jacu-Mocó, they felt as though they were moving decades, centuries backwards. All seemed fixed in timeless immobility, the tragic hunger and poverty, the countryside scenery. The *quilombola* community did not have drinking water, basic sanitation,

a health clinic, a school. Research carried out there revealed high rates of infant mortality and illiteracy. Nutritional deficiencies bring stunted growth in children. Associated to tobacco consumption, it causes an irrational number of abortion cases.

The huge income inequality of Brazil, the lack of rain, and its long history of bloodshed and contempt are reflected in the desolate faces of elderly *quilombolas*. The missionary Celina describes: *In the upper backcountry, the lack of water is visible in the Plant, Animal, Human Kingdoms. People lack everything, including hygiene, resources. The only thing they never lack is the faith that God looks after them.*

One hundred families live in wattle and dub houses, between *mandacaru* and *xique-xique* cacti and twisted branches, which during drought loses its leaves to avoid evaporation. Just as it had been in previous communities, the health team monitored the blood pressure of the Afro-descendants of Jacu-Mocó and offered them alternative medicinal treatments: neural therapy, nutritive baths, massage, medical dressings, water-suction cups.

From there, the group traveled to the Geripankó indigenous community. A small sign on the front window of the vehicle that had a line: *Mary, passes in the front!*

The missionaries came across people's inertia caused by malnutrition. One hundred families plant corn and cassava and produce flour for family consumption and to sell at the Pariconhas Fair. Their current customs still include feasts and dances inherited from ancestors, but most have forgotten the Tupi, their mother tongue, and only speak Portuguese.

After the dentist Imer did cleanings and tooth extractions, they distributed toothbrushes and toothpaste as part of their donations. Finally, they put on a performance of the puppet theater with a focus on oral hygiene, care for animals and for the elderly. That afternoon, the group radiated compassion for those suffering from the shortage of water, the treasure of treasures.

Workshops on tooth-brushing;
construction of bamboo flutes;
missionaries on their way to provide
assistance and distribute pure seeds.
Alagoas, Brazil, 2014

Alagoas, Brazil, November 2014

The missionaries exchanged glances, words, silences, hugs with 400 families, without discriminating social, religious, cultural differences, traditions. It was time to leave. As they said good-bye to the dry land, the earth's crying was burning within them.

In the farewell lunch at the Caritas' coordinator house, they praised the material and the non-material food that renews and nourishes. While there, the missionary light generated an impulse to carry on with that service. Because of the delightful cooperation with the Caritas entity, the North and Northeast Light-Network decided to open the Alagoas Recurrent Regional Missions, under Celina Estela's coordination. To end the journey they went to say goodbye to the Bishop, who stretched out the conversation to over an hour.

Ricardo says: *In previous missions, we would spend ten, fifteen or more days attending the same people, strengthening our relationship. In this one, we had to be fully devoted to each community for a single day or only for a few hours. It was a process of synthesis, making the most out of every minute available. But when we were about to leave, we were under the impression of having stayed much longer. We developed an intense relationship with so many people in such very little time.*

Dance *toré* in the indigenous village of Geripancó.
Surroundings of Palmeira dos Índios, Alagoas, Brazil, November 2014

In the countryside's desolated landscape, two throbbing worlds had been in contact. The chants still resonated in the inner ears of a country side-man gazing at the cars disappearing around a bend in the road, the dust falling. He had sung with the visitors, lulled by guitar chords and flute notes. Beating the rhythm with his hands on a plastic bucket, he created a musical pulsation: *Where Love reigns, fraternal love, God is there.*

Now the people watch children in new shoes, babies with scented clothes, repaired roofs, water flowing through newly recovered plumbing, and remember the group as if it were a dream.

The time of drought passes. The drizzles soaks the stony arid soil reviving the green of the leaves. Pure seeds brought from Minas Gerais—pumpkins, corn, beans—begin to sprout.

Holding a hoe, the backcountry man has a silent nature. He talks with the triumphant blue celestial sky behind the clouds. He remembers the last farewell given to those who taught how to carve a bamboo flute and then left. He places his lips over the blowing hole, his rough fingers in position, and plays enchanted sounds to attract a rain of graces.

CHACO MISSION, ARGENTINA

The rescue of indigenous people

The Grand Chaco is a living organism.
Population, water courses, climate, sky...
like a person... a being, a very delicate being...
let us listen to him... the Chaco is a master,
it not only teaches us to be with him,
but offers us the opportunity to learn.
Benno Glausser, philosopher

Just as sure as the sun rises for everyone, as certain as the air and the stars are for all, in the future the pieces of the currently shattered human heart will be gathered into a single immense diamond. This is the faith of those guided by the flight of the white dove.

Following the wings of this bird, a line of twenty-one missionaries climbed miles along steep slopes towards the luminous summit of Mount Pajarillo. Looking beyond the afternoon clouds, they contemplated the splendor of the rippling landscape of hills as far as the eyes could see. They asked the wind: *Make us divine, with fruitful hands and souls of gold, to help people in desperate situations.* They brought together the loving strength of each one, lowered their eyes to the valleys covered by people's wounds and went down to offer the wonders they found in silence. During the seven hours between the climbing and descending, the souls in celebration became ready.

In parallel to the Turkey Mission, Fraternidade went to the Province of Chaco, Argentina, to help alleviate the suffering of the poorest indigenous South American communities. The Grand Chaco, the Quechua word *chaku*, that means hunting place, spreads over more than half of Paraguayan and Bolivian territories, extending itself through northern Argentina and a stretch of the Brazilian Midwest.

Beings need protection worldwide. Among them, indigenous people are marginalized and live in extreme poverty, without water, light, hospitals or highways. Among the serious inequalities, child malnutrition and affective, psychological deprivation stand out. And, most of all, the indigenous people have lost their deep alliance with nature's crystalline voice. They used to live in harmony with the natural world, but the shattering of their cultures made most of them forget the soul of the land, the spirit of the waterfalls, the songs of the wind, the buzzing of silence, the speech of the trees, the gaze of a panther, a hug given by the marmoset, how to communicate with animals, how to talk with the stars.

A wave of negativity tries to enslave human beings, destroy their self-esteem, ridicule their cultures. Part of the program of domination is making the oppressed believe they are inferior. To impose themselves, the oppressor depreciates the color of their skin, their knowledge. Through this intentionally malevolent strategy, the settlers made indigenous and black people believe that they are inferior to white people.

Native people have never been understood or respected by white people, who invade their villages, expel them from ancestral and sacred territories, destroy their ways of life and have practically massacred all of them.

Persecuted by the immense human prejudice, which regards these native people as not highly evolved, they have become lost and without place or reference. Everything is unbalanced. Many of them are forced to live in cities and streets without access to the basics, and a huge percentage of them have become alcoholic.

An Argentine Qom indigenous woman tells us a serious and sad story: *Unfortunately, today children do not want to learn Qom, so this language is being lost. A language no longer spoken by children nor by the next generations, get lost: When I was a child, my ancestors taught me the white man was superior to the indigenous people. As time went by, I gradually understood it was not so. This belief has remained in our blood, in our hearts. I'll never deny what I am. One day I wanted to know why there is so much prejudice against me. Talking alone with God, He told me His love is enough. I began to sing in my dialect and felt immense peace. When I sing in Qom, I feel God closer to me.*

Chaco is the Argentine region that has the most native groups: Mapuches, Aymaras, Qom, Quéchuas, Wichi, Colas and others. With peculiar languages and ways of life, in pre-Columbian times, about 4,000 BC, dozens of ethnic groups lived amidst the rich flora and fauna of the pampas, forests, arid and semi-arid climates. Here the climate is harsh, temperatures ranges from 19° F in winter to a thermal sensation that

Chaco, Argentina, 2016

may reach over 122° F in summer. The peoples are renowned warriors. Since Spanish colonization, they have relentlessly fought to survive in their own land, where they used to fish and hunt. Today they fight for the recognition of their own culture. They demand their history and dialects to be studied at school. But governments and private enterprises are still responsible for the violence inflicted on them and the tragedies to which they have fallen victim. The police are sent to dislodge families, tractors enter the lands, destroying communities.

Meanwhile, workings of love try to broaden our understanding of them. This work meets demands and spreads seeds of good, which will surely bear fruit, helping them to reconnect with their original nature.

Twenty-one volunteers worked at the Chaco Mission in five indigenous communities in northeast Argentina: thirteen members of Argentina, Brazil and Uruguay Light-Network, a Light-Community of Brotherhood resident and seven monastics of Grace Mercy Order. Although they had different backgrounds and professions—doctors, dentists, builders, among others—they made up a single service network to benefit 120 families.

Before meeting in the city of Resistencia, some of them came together for an exercise in the Light-Community of Brotherhood, in Capilla del Monte, region of Cordoba. Their intention was to enter the spirit of fraternity during practical training. Mauricio says: *We participated in group activities to find a common rhythm and synchronization among us. We painted walls, we took care of gardens. To protect the community from floods, we built a wall with large round white stones carried from the dry bottom of a river, which were passed from person to person in a pulsating beat.*

However, their last move would be even more arduous. They would climb a mountain for hours, up to the top. Exhausted, a young missionary decided not to go on, until someone gave her some wise advice: *In a task of service, we should only be in tune with the Divine.* She confessed: *I was shaken by that phrase. I went. I learned about the importance of being with the group, ignoring my own needs. When one no longer has much strength, the one by their side impels them to go on. Despite my fatigue, I returned from the walk with great joy, connected to the strength of the group.*

While the missionaries trained, the Light-Network organized the trip logistics—making contacts, food, lodging, conveyance of donations. From Resistencia, they would head to the indigenous communities. There were forty Light-Network members waiting for the twenty-one missionaries when they arrived. They joined forces from the beginning to the very end. They prayed together and departed with a fluttering spirit for the Mapic community.

They were sixty that filled the small community center. As soon as they arrived a torrential rain fell. The earth became clay like. Children soon started throwing mud at each other, and the adults tried to escape being hit. The rain-waters purified the air and the energy, baptizing those present and making joy overflow. The group rolled up their sleeves, passing out material goods. And then went to visit precarious homes made of cardboard shingles.

They were given another blessing in the Tirol district. Bernardino, his pregnant wife and four children live in one room. His little boy was taking a shower in a dripping rain gutter. There was a guitar hanging on the wall. The dripping, the rain, the guitar. A missionary nun asked: *Can we come in? Can we sing? Do you play?* Bernardino: *Yes!* And he gave a lesson. Despite all that precariousness, love for God radiated from him. He took

Visit to Bernadino. Chaco. Argentina, 2016

the guitar and sang, and praised, and the missionaries sang along: *"Love is the precious flame of God. I give you a new commandment: that you love one another. By doing so, you will recognize that you are My disciples, if you have love for one another".* The group applauded, and he added: *Religions or creeds does not matter. What matters is when some people realize the need of others and value them mostly for their human condition. When He surrendered on the cross, Jesus did not do it for the rich, the poor, the junkie. He simply surrendered for mankind. Now we are in charge of communicating this. I rejoice and thank you for coming here today.*

The group felt embraced by the simplicity and humbleness of the Costa Iné community indigenous people who told them, with the purity of a flower-filled garden, about their crying out: *For days, we prayed for God to come and help us. You are the help sent by God.*

There and in four other communities, the missionaries attended to basic personal and oral hygiene needs: nail-trimming, haircutting, lice-removal, hand-washing of the little ones, giving showers. They transmitted peace during artistic activities—painting people's faces, choir singing, games, dances. They donated food, medicine, clothes and toys. Always thanking them, because the donor is given more than the one who receives.

Painting made at the request of the Chief, Chaco, Argentina, February, 2016

They helped to refurbish and paint buildings. At the request of a tribal leader, they painted a mural with a dove and the tree of life with a large open Bible on its trunk. They planted seeds in a vegetable garden and created its irrigation system. They cooked and sang together with indigenous people. They entered people's homes to share stories with them. They dewormed and vaccinated about seventy sick dogs.

Most of the diseases—such as skin and breath pathologies found in the Fontana Community, of descendants of Toba or Qom indigenous people result from hygiene issues, overcrowding, habit changes, a diet without nutrients. The health team provided medical, dental, and nursing services to 120 families, putting on bandages, donating medicines.

In the flow of practical activities, they exchanged kind words with those oppressed by destitution. They served very young mothers with a great expression of sadness in their eyes as well as in their countenance, and also children affected by modernity, less silent and who no longer express the same respect found in other communities.

There was a lot going on in each of the meetings. The bonds between indigenous people and whites needed to be forged anew, and during the contacts, sparks of mutual understanding were ignited. The coordinator

Doctor and missionary group on the way to render service.
Chaco, Argentina, February, 2016

Mother Teresa says: *The mission was nourished by the invisible, which created something that went beyond our human will.*

The doctor says: *When interacting with young patients and their mothers, our hearts were intertwining with theirs. Our consultations were not limited to medical procedures, we tried to grasp the teachings of the indigenous consciousness. The best thing to do was listen to them. The power is in listening, in order to know what they need, to listen to what they have to say about their infirmities.* Another member of the team said: *They sometimes had painful illnesses. Still, they remained in great calm, the resignation typical of the indigenous race.* The dentist adds: *As dentists, we had no difficulty in attending to them, not even the children. They are serene, patient, peaceful. Not in the sense of passivity, but in being calm, in being in a state of acceptance. This is embedded into their consciousness.*

Even in the midst of chaos, sewage, lice, mud, animal scabies, uncertainty, sadness, pain and abandonment, the indigenous people emanate a glow which goes beyond appearances. Although they have withdrawn from their own outer and inner worlds, they conceal the roots of original wisdom in the depths of themselves: purity, meekness, an understanding of coexistence with one another and with Nature.

Chaco, Argentina, 2016

Just as it has been happening in the Middle East, the greatest evils of this people result from the absence of a homeland, from the loss of mores. However, feelings of hope and faith are still alive among the indigenous people, whereas in the Middle East these are often lost.

Music was part of the daily routine. In the Mapic community, singers deeply touched by the fraternal group presence, came to play the guitars and thank them. As for the missionaries, they always played and sang, as in the Mass they were invited to attend by the Saint Joseph Church priest.

There they also prayed Hail Mary in indigenous languages. In Mapuche: *Mari Mari Maria*. *Maitei María* in Guarani, a language spoken by more than seven million people and an official language in Paraguay, along with Spanish. In Xavante, the language of the Brazilian Midwest: *Atsawi di Maria*. In Quéchua, spoken by about ten million people in Andean countries: *Llum'pa Mariya Napayuy*.

Finally, they prayed Hail Mary in the beautiful Nahuatl language, *Ximopakilti Teonantzin María*. In this language were written poems, chronicles and grammar books, after Nahuatl was transcribed to the Latin alphabet following the arrival of the Spaniards in Mexico.

Chaco, Argentina, 2016

The meeting in the Tirol Community was closed. Members of the Light-Network joined the missionaries once again. Each one brought their knowledge and the delicacy of gestures that relief. There was now a larger number of dentists, cooks, and those who were willing to listen to the others. There were more material goods being distributed, more visits to families. The heavens were rejoicing.

After getting in touch with indigenous living conditions, the group grew in maturity: *When we left the Mission, we felt eager to love any populace. Fraternity is implanted in the depth of the human heart, an eagerness to reach out to the other and meet their need, listen to them. Empathy and altruism are in our basic code. We need to leave our homes, not to do great things, but little things with great love. If we do it for one person, one thousand will get the benefit. That was the legacy left to us by Mother Teresa of Calcutta. May we be simple. You don't have to be a doctor or even a scholar: just be willing to love in your own special way.*

MISSÃO
PARAGUAI
Despertando Sementes

21/06 A 4/07 • 2016

PARAGUAY MISSION

All things pass,
the indigenous consciousness observes

The heart is yours, it may suffer.
The face belongs to others, it must smile.
Poster in an essences shop

They play the guitar, sing lullabies to babies. Smiling, they feed children's tiny mouths. They take care of people's teeth, treat wounds, keep them company in hospital for hours, fix roofs and walls and devices, clean whatever is needed, pulling the mud from a porch with a hoe. They remain in silence, look deeply, distribute donations. If they are called to dance, they dance. If someone is cold, they give them warm clothes. If someone is hungry, they provide food. They follow in line on trails in the woods to visit the shaman, a patient, a family.

Surely these movements are symbolic, very little in face of the atrocities perpetrated by the white man and the critical state in which numerous indigenous people find themselves. Virgin land and crystalline water have been stolen from them. Astonished, they see burnt jungles converted into monocultures and pastures. Looking at the stars, indigenous people and sensible white people wonder: *Where does such luck of love come from?* Looking deep inside, it dawns on them, pioneers of the race: *From our innermost core comes the request for forgiveness for all that the white man has inflicted on indigenous people.* Looking at Nature, natives say: *You don't know what you are doing.*

A few people get together to help the native people. Friar Thomas, a member of the Paraguay Mission, ponders: *Five hundred years ago, the Divine Consciousness prepared the meeting between two cultures, the white and the indigenous people in America. Something special was supposed to happen between these two projects for mankind. They would have to exchange the fruit of their own development with one another. This encounter resulted in disaster, in extermination, and prejudice. Extreme hatred perpetuates nowadays, creating a great wound in the heart of the divinity, as well as in the hearts of the indigenous and the white people.*

To define which Guarani people the missionaries would serve in Paraguay, Ricardo and some Light-Network members made early evaluation visits to three locations around the country. First, they went to Chaco and then to the vicinities of the capital, Asunción.

Long before the Spaniards arrived, the Guarani had abundant agricultural production and distributed their surplus. In Chaco, visitors saw preserved traditions. Ricardo describes: *The village is well structured, they make croplands in a large area and are concerned with nature and with water treatment. They have a well-functioning nursery school and a house for artisans. When I asked the tribe leader how they provided heath assistance for his people, he asked us to follow him to the Sacred House and said: "Our attention begins in the opy, the name we call to our Sacred House. The shaman, a spiritual guide, evaluates whether the patient's issue can be solved here or if he needs to seek a physician". He showed us the wind instruments, rattles, rain stick, percussion and explained about the Guarani ceremonies and spirituality.*

In the end, they decided to help communities surrounding Ciudad del Este, capital of the Alto Paraná Department, and also its neighboring town some 12 miles away, Presidente Franco. Both are near Foz do Iguaçu.

The indigenous people have been living on narrow strips of land and degrading conditions since 1982, when thirty-two communities with about 42,000 members were expelled from their territories with contempt by the Itaipú Binational Hydroelectric Power Plant construction.

Under threat, just a few villages were warned about the Paraná River rise for the reservoir formation. Others knew nothing. Its inhabitants, frightened at the sight of waters rising in their direction, fled hastily with relatives who were nearby. The indigenous people cherish family relationship, and many lost contacts with parents and siblings. Since then, they live scattered around the river taking shelter wherever they can.

Over eight thousand indigenous people were exterminated during the expulsion. Others were arrested and tortured. Yet their memories have not been eliminated. The oldest ones say: *You either ran away or died*. An indigenous tribal leader says: *The white man does all this in the name of "progress". But this progress takes lives away and kills cultures.*

Forty years later, they still have not received an indemnity neither reserved lands in recompense. Several groups still wander and lay claim to a sacred ground, called *tekoha*, where they can settle along with the same ethnic group. To live in fullness, they need to interact with Nature, with the spiritual beings of the forest and of the waters. Having none of those or health assistance, they are debilitated, with wounds, tooth decay, diseases. The Humanitarian Mission would bring them some relief.

The missionary group made contact with the Department of Indigenous Health of Alto Paraná Ministry to pool their efforts for medical and dental assistance. Immediately, the organization made a commitment to donate medicines and to send a doctor to help the group.

A Light-Network member was put in charge of subsequent contacts during the mission. She also contacted a private university, through which dentistry students offered support, along with a teacher. At the end of the mission, they committed to continue the consultations, besides promoting educational lectures on oral hygiene for children.

Sixteen missionaries and four monastics arrived in Ciudad del Este and were hosted in a simple lodging of Franciscan nuns. Members of the Light-Network groups from the three countries of the Triple Frontier region joined them: Brazilian representatives of Ciudad del Este, from the State of Paraná, from Foz Iguaçu and Santa Teresinha; and Argentinians from Porto Iguaçu and Posadas, Province of Missiones.

Knowing mankind can be redeemed through service to others and to the Kingdoms of Nature, the Fraternidade members prayed and sang. Opening to the sacred, they set out on a vital humanitarian mission with indigenous groups of recyclers.

During sixteen days, they were in contact with six Mbya and Ava Guarani groups. None of them have the ownership of land nor the recognition by the government as an indigenous community.

Paraguay is one of the only genuinely bilingual countries in the world. Its official languages are Castilian, inherited from the Spanish settlers, and also Guarani, a pre-Columbian language widely spoken in South America. It belongs to the Tupi-Guarani linguistic branch, from which twenty-one languages derive. Taught in schools, it is spoken by 60% of the population, especially in the rural area.

Indigenous families try to preserve their love for the sacred, for the earth, for the water, for the sun, for the wind and respect the spiritual leaders. They use medicinal plants for healing, they protect singing and dance, weave baskets, carve animals and musical instruments out of wood. They wear traditional clothing at parties. All that despite the degrading condition of those who wander without territory, even though white men's fads such as being continuously glued to cell phone screens, have become part of their lives.

Due to the low prices in its shops, Ciudad del Este is greatly sought after by foreigners, especially Brazilians and Koreans. Shopkeepers and tourists daily get rid of packaging in streets and vacant urban areas where tons of trash accumulate. The unhealthy urban landscape is degrading, especially when it rains. And on those days, it rained a lot.

The missionaries were entering the periphery of a slum-like setting, atypical for vulnerable indigenous people who no longer tread on sacred territories but on hills of trash. The community rituals under the moon and starry nights are gone. In the Yvú Porã Rendá community, of the Avá-Guarani ethnic group, they live as a family, supporting one another. For ten years they have been occupying a plot of land leased by the city hall behind a wall that is the municipal dump site, from which they make a living.

It was very cold. The heavy rain made the mud sticky. Appalled at the dishonored way of living, the compassionate missionaries began to participate in the harsh reality of children who were dirty, had no shoes and little clothing. Beginning early, the residents pull heavy carts, slipping in the ocher clay. They pick up plastic and cardboard, which they stack within the community, to select and tie pieces before taking them to sell.

Heartbroken, they watched the little girls picking up broken toys and dragging bags with pieces of colored plastic. Despite their poor condition, the children do not quarrel among themselves, they respect one another, the elders, the tribal leader, the newcomers.

Playing games in the Yvú Porã Rendá indigenous community,
Ciudad del Este, Paraguay, 2016

This ethnic group use to have abundant harvest, to hunt and collect palm hearts in virgin forests, fish in the river. Now without a place even for a vegetable garden, they never know when they will eat. Out of pots placed on stones over a small fire: *They cook beans floating with something else we couldn't identify*, says a missionary.

The Mission Coordinator Clara would ask the tribal leader, Carlos, for advice before releasing each activity: *As soon as we arrived, Carlos introduced us to the members of the community, whom he asked for permission to work with them. They said yes. This was the first lesson for us. They honor collective life and make all decisions together. Then, while we gradually identified the needs of those twenty-two families, we informed Carlos about what we could offer them.*

They asked, for example, if they could protect with lids three wells to collect water, which the leader accepted. A nun looked around, and saw satellite dishes that had been found in the trash, hanging on trees as if they were decoration. She came up with an idea. As they were of the exact size of the mouth of the wells, and not heavy, they improvised them as lids. To top it all, and to everyone's joy, a collaborator paid for the repair of the water pump.

Families dwell in fragile houses furnished with objects found in the garbage dump. In front of the houses, there are piles of old cans and cardboard. There was a shack in worse conditions than the others, leaking through the cover of cloths and plastic bags. It belonged to a mother with two daughters. As the renovation proposal was accepted by the mother and the leader, the missionaries covered the structure—four sticks on the soil, one in each corner—with newly acquired black plastic. There was room for one mattress that a collaborator donated.

Clara describes: *There is a lot of unity among natives, which always make group decisions. We began to understand the way they express themselves. Waiting for a general opinion trained our patience. We were learning to love our fellow beings unconditionally. The leader, concerned with the health of a hundred community members, kept up with the medical care and dental support given at the school. He himself would call those who would have appointments, especially children and pregnant women.*

The physician gave a general diagnosis: *We have seen all sorts of skin lesions. Also, pathologies of the respiratory tract. Their environment facilitates the spread of these diseases. We taught mothers how to treat their children with the medications obtained through the Health Ministry, which also collaborated in the hospital admission of a two-month-old baby with a severe infectious disease on the skin.*

The spiritual strength of the community was shaken since the Sacred House, called *opy*, had fallen to the ground. There the shaman communicates with creative spirits and those of animals, trees, and waters to treat patients with medicinal plants. He only prescribes traditional medicine in extreme cases. The Guarani, called the great people, believe they were created by the supreme god Ñamandú, who has always existed and will always exist.

The tribal leader said many health problems are solved by the shaman in the Sacred House. He was absolutely certain the village would return to a healthy state when it was raised again. Immediately the Fraternity rolled up their sleeves. They constructed the foundations and paid for the transportation costs of some sacred wood collected at the forests, with which the natives raised the walls and covered the roof.

Their farewell was celebrated with lunch, traditional dances, and chants about crossing the *Land without Evils* and birds singing. Clara recalls:

They set up the loudspeaker and the sound device, saying they couldn't play instruments, as they would have to remain silent until the "opy" was erected. Music is a living prayer for them. This was an additional lesson learned about indigenous reverence for the spiritual world and for singing. We ended up dancing with the kids, sheer laughter!

Filled with gratitude, white and indigenous people sealed the triumph of the universal union. Slowly, the understanding between them increased. Both bring within themselves metaphysical ideas and the simplest faith.

The native people value family, Nature, conversations, storytelling and playing music around the campfire rather than material comfort. The Fraternidade members felt enriched at the end of the meeting. Mother Tereza reiterates: *We had a lesson of humbleness and spiritual wisdom. They have a deep relationship with the Sacred, which does not depend on external circumstances.*

Six miles further they set foot on Presidente Franco, the port city on the shores of the large Paraná River, to give assistance to five communities of the Mbya ethnic group. The distance between one another varies from 500 yards to about 5 miles. They are small refuge-villages on farms surrounded by genetically modified soy monocultures, which disturbs biodiversity. Large area farmers have replaced what was left of the virgin forest, shrubby areas and fields for extensive plantations in which they use agrochemicals, poisons that spread severe diseases in the air, affecting people's lungs and skin. Only one of those communities is located within a luxuriant jungle, the ecological reserve Moisés Bertoni.

Forced to leave vast lands, the Indians fight a continuous struggle to resist and have only achieved small victories, such as the building of primary schools by the government.

Clara says: *We focused on health care and other activities in and around schools. The leader who represents the five communities took us to visit them. He gave us details about each one and introduced us to the leaders. The villages have a weekly schedule for the work done in the dump site. We went there on a Sunday. It was shocking to see children picking up plastic and cardboard. The trucks arrive with leftovers from the urban trash because the best of it is picked up beforehand in the city itself. Without getting paid for it, indigenous people themselves unload the trucks,*

The Yvú Porã Rendá indigenous community survives on recyclables.
Ciudad del Este, Paraguay, 2016

as no other worker is sent besides the driver. They earn a ridiculous sum. In exchange for this grueling work, families earn about 15,000 guaranis a day, about 2.5 US dollars.

Food supplies sent to schools to cook children's meals—milk powder, pasta, rice, beans—take up to five months to arrive. A schoolteacher said sometimes he interrupts his work for a day or two to go to urban center to ask the authorities for food donations. The kids wait for his return, but he does not bring even a sack of salt. Gripped by grief for having so much to teach them—mathematics, Guarani and Spanish languages, History, Geography—he says students cannot learn if they are hungry.

When the missionaries went to the shrine Moisés Bertoni, with water springs, they hoped to find Indians in better conditions of life. A century ago, a Swiss scientist purchased the property from the Paraguayan government, although the forest belongs to the Mbya territory. Today, Brazilian and Argentinian agencies take tourists who visit the Iguassu Falls to this place, through the winding Paraná River.

They anchor the boats on the river beach where the Mbya perform dances and try to trade handicrafts. Next the tourists walk six hundred yards uphill to the Bertoni Scientific Museum to visit the laboratory,

Missionaries renovate the shack of an elderly couple.
Sanctuary Moisés Bertoni, Presidente Franco, Paraguay, 2016

the library, the legacy left in areas like botany, zoology, meteorology, anthropology. In a small shop, they find more handicrafts.

The net income from sales is not enough for natives' sustenance. They are undernourished, sick, and explain about the cycle of waiting for food: *Today I'm hungry, tomorrow I'll eat, and then I'll wait for the day when food comes again. I eat, I wait, feeling hungry.*

Dogs with scabies roam around between straw and wood-covered huts with a cockroach infestation. By a trail into the woods, the leader took them to a clearing where a wise and friendly elderly *xeramõi*, Mr. Júlio, lives. A Mentor and spiritual healer of the five communities, he holds indigenous knowledge and wisdom. He used to work with the scholar Bertoni who, passionate about ancient Guarani culture, deepened his knowledge about this people and came to protect them with dedication.

When faced with the shack of the *nhaneramõi*, Guarani name for the elders, the group made the proposal to renovate the roof covered with broken tiles. Also the walls lined with pierced plastic sheets remains and tarps collected in the dump. Mr. Júlio readily accepted. They bought the material and renewed the hovel. The leader himself had said: *No one deserves such a life.*

In the next settlement, Puerto Barreto, a female shaman asked the group to collect wood from a nearby grove, to be used in the construction of the opy destined for sacred rituals. Taking advantage of the enterprising impulse, they then made improvements in the shaman's house.

Besides the consultations given in the communities, the health team attended to thirty-two families of Puerto Flores who had severe skin diseases caused by a pesticide contaminating the air and a nearby creek. They live in a land which belongs to an evangelical church, and provides them with educational and religious assistance. They depend on community well water, which was about to run dry. In the face of the urgency, the group dug it to increase its depth.

Wherever they went, the Fraternity members made home visits, encouraged children to sing and to participate in playful activities, washed and cut hair and trimmed nails. They offered supplies, medications, clothing and work tools, toothbrushes and school supplies. They renovated houses and carried out a task-force for general cleaning of settlements. They showed a solar cooker to those interested. When they came across cultivable land, they donated pure seeds of corn, beans, lettuce, arugula, carrot, and tomato to the tribal leaders.

A Light-Network server recalls: *The greatest beauty was the trust and the communion developed between natives and missionaries, the joy experienced in each encounter. Despite the surrounding trash and their pain, the Indian people maintain solidarity and sharing. They don't complain and remain silent. That was a lesson for us, "whites".*

Shocked by the extreme poverty, they were eager to love more, to love better, to discover ways to offer quality of life to those meek people. The members of Fraternity could not keep watching passively. Thus, the overwhelming abandonment of those people had consequences: from then on the Paraguayan Mission emerged.

The Indian consciousness is resilient. Filled with wonder, the indigenous soul loves the Divinity and keeps its innocent beauty, the natural existence that expresses truth, purity and contemplative values. Resigned, they waits for better times. Touched by the zeal and material relief offered, they felt comforted by the goodness of the missionaries.

PART III
Environmental Disasters in South America

The planet beats consecutive records.

Geophysical records; earthquakes, tsunamis, volcanoes.

Meteorological records; storms and hurricanes.

Hydrological records; floods and the rise of the sea.

Climatological records; droughts, forest fires,

extreme temperatures.

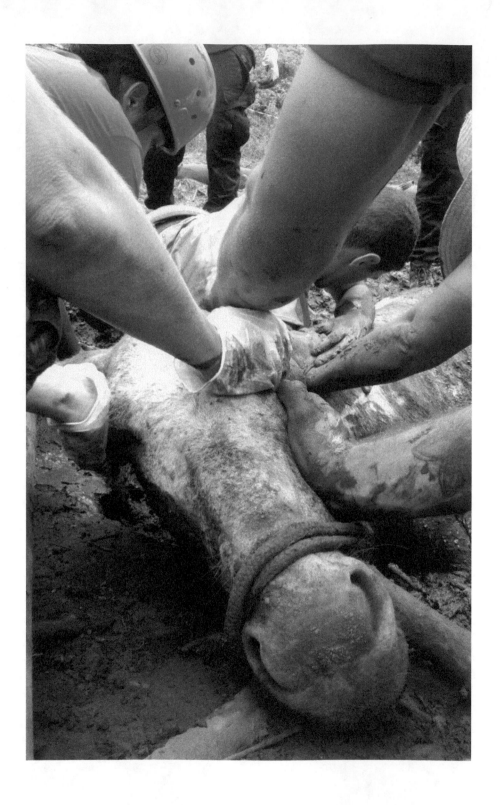

MARIANA MISSION, BRAZIL

The earth: animals in toxic mud

In huge catastrophes, in significant losses,
love cannot die. Love must persist,
it must reign. We must sustain
the torch of love, the fire of love
A missionary consideration

The Mineral Kingdom seems passive and inert. But, when it moves, its tremendous power is revealed. The volcano explodes, the earth trembles, the force of water gives dramatic responses to human abuse.

A dam of iron ore waste and another one of water yielded at the same time. One dragged the other, throwing an avalanche of orange killer gel from the mountainous interior of southeastern Brazil to the Atlantic Ocean. Like a giant serpent, the wave meandered 435 miles down the Doce River and, seventeen days later, it spread into the sea. It altered the color, chemistry, and health of water, animals, plants, and humans.

The unscrupulousness of mining activity caused the worst socio-environmental disaster in Brazil and the planets largest involving tailings deposits. The working miners heard a thundering noise announcing the crash caused by old cracks of the walls. Those who were on its path sought desperately for a safe place. Nineteen people were swallowed up by the flood of mud, some of them inside vehicles.

People, donkeys, ducks, gardens, walls and trucks vanished in the slimy cold mud. A lady witnessed it all from the top of the village. She was in the kitchen when her sister screamed. A shower of dust entered the window. The kindergarten, the church, the farm, Ms. Maria's house disappeared under the toxic clay, sliding, descending, thickening, rising, spreading itself. In a crescendo, the calamity invaded valleys between hills out of sight. People fled hastily. A young woman ran for twenty minutes dragging her nephews and nieces to escape the dread. Dogs howled; chickens, pigs, horses, cows were being devoured.

The lady's house has become a support center for victims. In the small community, everyone knew one another. Into the night, without electricity, she and her brothers carried elderly people, released trapped animals. They received news about the agony of those who took refuge in the shrub or were isolated, because access was blocked and the rescue helicopter could not fly at night. Wounded people were taken to hospitals. Searches for missing people began. They knew of a little girl who let go of her father's hand and was sucked by the treacherous mud before her grandfather's eyes. Bodies emerged to the surface and were soon swallowed, reappearing 60 miles farther along and up to four months later. Residents of the nearby villages were warned to abandon them with urgency. The principal of a school received a phone call and got away in time with students and teachers in an accelerated minibus.

The flood of highly toxic content in the Mariana municipality, a central region of Minas Gerais, followed a cruel path. It invaded towns and affected more than forty cities of two states. It buried springs, killed the life of streams and of the Doce River, whose waters remained without light for six months. The green of the shores dried up, tons of fish were suffocated due to lack of oxygen and gills obstruction. Along with human tragedies came the environmental suffering. The children became orphans, with more than one thousand people directly hit, and 250,000 residents without drinking water. The pain is perennial. Four years later, the area still faces economic stagnation, and people still suffer from severe diseases and allergies. Human beings and animals are shaken by depression. The affected families and the natural environment receive little responses from the authorities.

Greed and extreme indifference from entrepreneurs and politicians regarding people's lives is responsible for the accident. In Brazil, there are 23,000 dams, and the risks they present are unknown. Many companies, giving profit a top priority, reduce security measures, interrupt monitoring and in-depth environmental impact studies. Not only do they operate at the lowest possible cost, but they bribe politicians by donating millions to fund their election campaigns.

The current corrupted legislation protects the entrepreneur. An engineer says the mining company was aware of the risks. He was called upon to remedy cracks in the retaining walls and refused to involve himself with something that could not be repaired.

Since the worst times of the invasion of mud, the powerful mining companies have repeatedly stated it is not toxic. They demonstrate institutionalized selfish behavior by giving interviews that deny and conceal the damaging effects of waste on humans and environmental health. Remaining indifferent to people's needs, these companies deliberately leave the population in a state of confusion.

Serious scholars disagree, the damage generated by the disaster will go through indeterminate decades. Environmentalists and biologists believe that tailings will be increasing toxicity in the sea for at least one hundred years. In several stretches of watercourses, a group of independent scientists found the presence of heavy metals carried by the torrent of mud. Studies have shown that the level of iron, aluminum, and chromium in water has soared. The disappearance of terrestrial and marine ecosystems is added to the violent environmental pollution on the seabed produced by trillions of pieces of plastic and the death of coral colonies caused by rising water temperatures.

Large animals still get bogged down in the devastated areas, so specialized teams mobilized to rescue them. In a shed, cats, cows, pigs, geese, and about three hundred stranded dogs were cared for until they returned to their owners when they were recognized by them.

Days after the tragedy, the Fraternidade received requests for help from collaborators who closely monitored the affected region. The human population in the area was rescued but there was a lack of emergency support to relieve the suffering of small and large animals.

For the first time, missionaries would work along side humanitarian aid groups who were also helping with the rescue work. Until then, they had only supported religious entities. The Marian Mission was also the first to provide assistance to the Animal Kingdom, which expanded the missionary consciousness. Volunteers from two other sectors related to Figueira also joined the mission: experts in animal care at the Service Association Casa Luz da Colina, House of Light on the Hill, CLC, and also the Solar Group, with experts in dealing with socio-environmental emergency services, large-scale disasters, related to individual or collective risks.

Seventeen servers took to the road in two cars and a truck loaded with donations sent by members of Fraternidade: tons of food for dogs, cats and horses. Also, drinking water, boxes of cleaning products and canine accessories such as dog leashes. Surrounded by pure brotherly love, they fraternized on the journey with a smile on their faces, or through silence filled with truth, or during the group prayers. They knew that altruistic service has invisible helpers, and that, in parallel to material actions, a ritual took place in the inner planes.

At the end of the afternoon, they arrived at the huge open shed. Subdivided into sectors, it had a good infrastructure to deal with emergencies. A tent had been assembled inside, where veterinarians attended and performed surgeries until 11 p.m. After being introduced to two groups in the local command—the NGO Veterinários na Estrada (Veterinarians on the Road) and the volunteers of the Red Cross—they were immediately included in the activities and worked nonstop for the next 5 hours.

They sought to align themselves with the new energy as they entered that universe. It was a shock to come across the gazes of the animals. Trauma dwelt in them. Their agony was similar to a human being's, or even worse since they did not understand what was happening to them: *What's going on, why are we in stalls with iron doors?* They were well taken care of. However, there was a greater calamity than the material, psychic disorder. An ecological tragedy creates tensions in physical, emotional and mental bodies of people an animals, and all of these were in turmoil.

The missionaries have logistics. Well trained in group action, they serenely split. Some joined a rescue team to remove a bull from the mud. Others unloaded hay and feed trucks or began to organize stacked objects.

An animal specialist was asked to walk dogs. Hayla reports: *I put a leash on a black and white dog. At once I felt his confusion. He was in a state of shock. He used to have a house, references. That is why he was so afraid. He didn't even want to walk. At last we went out to see the sky. He walked behind me, not by my side or in front of me, as dogs usually do. Slowly we were relearning to walk. I was trying to understand the true meaning of a mission. He was trying to figure out what was happening around him.*

Step by step she would say sweet words to the dog, and he would walk more freely. She was recovering from the journey and the sense of shock she had coming across so much pain. They ran into other volunteers who also walked dogs. She then learned that those people, struck by human neglect, although having lost family members and property, they still did

Unloading fodder. Mariana, MG, Brazil, 2015

not blame the mining company because they were economically dependent on the exploitation and trade of iron ore. The population forgets the
fact that destruction affects small producers and traders and that economic dependence of large corporations prevents them from seeking
greater creative autonomy to sustain themselves without attacking nature.

When he returned to the shed, the puppy was more self-confident. Hayla
also took a stroll with another dog, but the third one took three little
steps shaking, and did not dare going ahead. She started talking to him,
giving him affection until, finally, the dog accepted to take a little walk.

In the meantime, night had fallen. The missionaries had finished unloading the heavy sacks of rations from the full truck. Luiz recalls: *We
had just unloaded the whole thing when the coordinator told us, "Look,
you're going to have to redo the job. The rations was not supposed to be
taken there." We started to laugh. We were exhausted. What else could
we do? Sit down and say, "We won't do that because we're exhausted?" Or
laugh at ourselves, for our human confusion?*

Being told about the mistake, they were astounded, but soon afterwards
they started doing it all over again. Since each daily event has multiple
meanings, that test brought them a lesson. As they worked to reloaded
the truck they had just unloaded, they learned to be more attentive to
what they are told to do. Reflecting in depth, they realized how bewil-
dered they were by the colossal calamity, and to what extent the mineral

Organizing donations. Mariana, MG, Brazil, 2015

contaminations degenerates the subtle and mental threads that joins consciousness to matter.

The population sent generous donations that arrived continuously, creating a chaotic jumble in their facilities. Attracted by the news, all sorts of volunteers came, mostly out of curiosity.

Meanwhile, the young general coordinator, a rescuer, worked so hard that she had no time even for a change of clothes in three days. A missionary got closer to her and said: *We are here to do whatever you need.* As she pointed to the urgency of tidying up the place, stacks of medicines mixed with cleaning material, clothing, and equipment of every kind began to be sorted out and placed in an orderly way on pallets and shelves.

The day of a missionary is intense, with heavy demands. Everyone has to be attentive, obedient, observing one another and everything that happens around them. It was late, they had only had lunch, and then someone brought them tea, fruit, and bread. Someone invited them: *Come on!* Together, the missionaries headed towards a young man who played the guitar. Amidst such acute service, a veterinarian sang, volunteers arrived, welcoming one another tenderly. So many worlds within our world.

They were exhausted. They had been instructed to spend the night at a big house, rented for the storage of sacks of rations. Before leaving the shed, someone came up with the excellent idea: *Shall we take some*

Animals rescued after the breaking of the dam wait for their owners. Mariana, MG, Brazil, 2015

cardboard from here? As they arrived, all they wanted was to take a shower, but as the bathrooms were dirty, they first cleaned them, mopped and swept the floor. Then they divided the rooms in two sections, for men and women. The cardboard was put over the ration sacks and their sleeping bags on top. Finally, they gathered in the entrance hall to close the day with intense prayers.

In minutes, most of them were sound asleep. Yet in one room, four missionaries could not fall asleep. Whispering, they wondered about the vast wound of mud beyond sight, about people's agony, the suffering of Nature. They grew in unity, asked for forgiveness to the Creator, and, grateful for doing their utmost to alleviate this colossal misfortune, they soon dreamed of the Great Hope.

The seventeen awoke refreshed, the fire of their essence sparkling because they were attentive to the rising sun lessons. They were there to bring light and order to a dark abyss, a reflection of devious choices drawn by mankind. Filled with enthusiasm, they departed for heroic actions after praying, because they begin and close each day talking to the Eternal.

For hours, they tidied up every corner of the shed. Focused, they lined every single product on shelves. At the end of the afternoon, the place was unrecognizable and had lightened up. Jumping over sacks to move around was no longer necessary. There were corridors between separate stacks of rations for cats, horses and dogs. Now, veterinarians had quick access to medicines, needles, serum, bandage kits.

The place had now been put into an archetypal pattern of greater order, which helped to organize the mind and feelings of everyone who commented on the quietude around. There is direct correspondence between what goes on in the visible and the invisible, and vice-versa. The release of chaotic energy had repercussions on the animals, who are sensitive to harmonic waves coming from the higher worlds. Ricardo says: *This group works from heart to heart.* A veterinarian who greeted them adds: *They have a complete team. You don't even have to ask them, they do what needs to be done. That's what we need here: volunteers who are willing to work.*

In another part of the shed, there were horses, oxen, pigs. Chickens and other mud-covered animals were washed. They were face to face with the issue of animal flesh being eaten by human beings, but they were there to help, to love, not to judge the others. If judgment had set in, they would have felt a blockage.

A twelve year old volunteer fed a baby foal with a baby bottle, one young being looking after another. A youth who volunteers to respond to any national catastrophe had come to look after orphaned and traumatized children by bringing them toys. As he found them well looked after at the hotel, he headed to the animal ward.

Families arrived looking for their animals: *We've lost everything, and we're at a hotel awaiting a temporary house.* One of them gave the volunteers the name of the dog. No dogs had names there. The person in charge pointed out the stalls to the family. *It is that one!* They found him. They explained to the dog: *We still can't take you home, we'll come back and get you.* And he understood. Realizing the puppy had a blanket, water, food, shelter and, to some extent, the protectors' attention, they felt more comforted. Now the volunteers understood the dog, who was known for always trying to escape. Of course, feeling loved, he wanted to find the family that was connected to him.

Learning is a continuous process. As each human being has his unique light, missionaries, locals and volunteers became teachers of one another. Human diversity holds within itself the science of flexibility. In that shed, mutual respect contributed to the group harmony.

Animal rescue. Mariana, MG, Brazil, 2015

On that overcast day, thirty people made an enormous effort on the rescue of four horses that had gotten stuck in the mud. The missionaries were invited to take part in the action. For three hours, they drove down a dirty road, seeing a little house here and there, and surreal traces of the tragedy along the riverbed. They crossed streams in their pickups. Surrounded by metallic odor, cautiously and in line, they walked over a semi-solid slippery, terracotta brown mud.

Firefighters and veterinarians began the first rescue. At first, the missionaries stood back, silently, to learn. After a while, they joined the group and labored incessantly for more than four hours. The bodies of two donkeys and two mules were buried almost to their necks. They comforted the animals with their presence, calmed them down, brought fresh water to their mouths, whispered to their ears, or just remained silent, looking at them directly in their eyes. To release those docile mammals, they had to dig around them, removing countless shovelfuls of mud. The animals' legs and necks were tied with ropes and, when it was possible, protected by cloth so that they wouldn't get hurt even more.

A donkey weighs almost eleven hundred pounds. Arms and strong hands came together to pull them out of the excavations. Using ropes, all of them supported and protected the aching bodies. When necessary, round sticks were inserted under the chests to carry them. Shen says: *It was distressing, we could feel their pain. We continuously had to sedate*

Donkeys and mules rescued from the toxic mud. Mariana, MG, Brazil, 2015

them. At the time of the rescue, they got hurt, and groaned. It was a torture for them and for us too. Shen adds: *They had been too long buried in the sand, paralyzed, and when they were taken out, they could not stand on their numb legs. They needed time for the blood to circulate so that they could walk again.* Humans felt reinvigorated to see them take their first steps. Other animals were not lucky enough and were swallowed by the vast mud cover, apparently solid and dry on the surface, but sticky and deep underneath—a constant threat.

In the sad scenario of the largest Brazilian environmental tragedy, the missionaries left behind buried dramas and arid stories. Ruins of ghost towns remain there, skeletons of dry trees, 20-feet-high marks on church walls are witnesses to the passage of the sandy tailings, which now accumulate on the margin and at the bottom of the river, apparently clean for those who fly over the area.

The dry earth flies if the wind is strong and, if it rains, it drips and dyes the waters orange. At the mouth of Doce River, in the state of Espírito Santo, surfers no longer surf, shrimp and fish are contaminated with arsenic, lead and cadmium; marine currents carry micro-particles that threaten fragile ecosystems such as corals and mangroves.

Mud covers the edge of the river with a kind of infertile cement, which prevents vegetation from recovering. During the drought, residents feel their eyes burn and breathe the fine dust of the ore, which penetrates through cracks in house doors and windows, covering everything and causing respiratory and skin problems.

Fresh water and salt water, the fauna, the flora, human and animal life continue to cry out for help and are increasingly forgotten. The web of life has been broken, and the wounds need urgent healing. In order to heal matter and the affected subtle worlds, men and angels need to weave together a new history.

A disaster of this proportion and gravity could be an opportunity for us to realize abnormalities on our ways, but the collective consciousness becomes silent, anesthetized. Economic profit is more important than shattered lives. Oh, human blindness!

Mene Habdo, the coordinator of the Kingdoms Sector of Casa Luz da Colina, declares: *People are allowed to use whatever Nature offers them, but out of ambition, they end up exploiting much more than necessary. Driven by greed, they destroy what took millions of years to form. And they don't even realize the evil they create. We have no idea what happens when we penetrate deep layers of soil. This causes shocks on the material levels and on the subtle levels when the ground is disrupted by the abusive use of ore, oil and even water. We need to grow in our respect for the mighty Mineral Kingdom.*

To deal with extreme events, such as rescue of animals in the field, the volunteer must always be in the process of emptying himself of concepts of loss, of feelings of fear, states Hayla. *What's more, emptying oneself of the sense of indifference towards the others. As they empty themselves, they allow the Intangible to fill them with humbleness. One can now see how a droplet in the sea of material life little by little learns to join other droplets, together attaining the joy of bringing relief to the Kingdoms of Nature.*

From Mariana's experience—a small sample of unjust suffering of innocent beings—onwards, new codes of love have been imprinted in missionary cells.

DOLORES MISSION, URUGUAY

The air: a four-minute tornado

I think the practice of solidarity, when truly present
in everyday life, is also a humbleness exercise
that teaches you to recognize yourself in others and
to recognize the greatness hidden in small things.
This implies denouncing the false greatness
in 'grandiose' things.
Live Without Fear, by Eduardo Galeano

A tremendous roar and a tornado came from the field penetrating the diagonal of Dolores, in Uruguay. *What is this, my God?* It crossed the city zigzagging for four minutes. The destruction caused by the howling fury did not reach large tracts, but left behind a trail of debris in its pathway. Horror, confusion, and, after a little while, a great silence hung over the people in pain.

Connected to everything that exists, to the Universe, fifteen days later the Fraternity members left for Uruguay. Without any idea of nationalism, sectarianism or separatism, eight missionaries drove 1,500 miles in order to collaborate with the collective catastrophe victims.

After a three-day-trip, they arrived at the city hall of the typical interior regional town, where each corner has particular stories. Warmly received, they were led by the mayor in a tour through the neighborhoods to learn about the extent of the disaster. Renovation work had started. The streets were relatively clean, but one could still see fallen trees, piles of bricks and doors, twisted metal.

They learned more about the tragedy. A strong storm was coming down on much of the Uruguayan land. It was cold that afternoon when the residents of Dolores, in the Department of Soriano, began to hear a crescendo of tremendous whistles, howls and roars, a herald of brutal danger. With a thundering sound, the gray cloud, spinning at 150 miles per hour, began to smash shop fronts, entering houses, throwing vehicles in all directions. Wherever the angry eye of the tornado twisted, roofs were torn away, walls shook before falling, glass shattered, branches and trees were broken, objects thrown about. The power of the rotary funnel swallowing the earth's surface sucked and displaced devices for 40 miles until the whirlwind disintegrated.

In the aftermath of the tornado, there were five dead, 200 injured, and 17,000 residents in shock. Uncertainty and dread had set in. The name of the city, Dolores, Spanish for "pains", reflected the general community feelings. Those whose houses remained intact faced the devastation in their neighbor's house, the firefighters in search of acquaintances and relatives under the rubble. In only four minutes, the quiet routine of the residents was violated, and the most fragile inhabitants were in sudden torment, traumatized on the psychic level.

The City Reconstruction Committee, created by the mayor and delegates, entrusted the missionaries with the task of tidying up a large shed, which was packed with tons of donations coming from Uruguay and also from Brazil and Argentina. Populations go through evolutionary stages. The country awoke to humanitarian aid by sending material things, but few volunteers came to help. Rescue was left in the hands of political and military forces.

The missionaries worked for six days. Without prior planning to organize the donations, food, mixed with all kinds of objects, were scattered throughout the shed. They began sorting out and bagging clothes distributed on the spot to those affected, a task shared with volunteers in service since the post-tragedy.

From the second day on, realizing the team's ability for organization, the Operational Base coordinating group asked them to deal with non-perishable food and then with the cleaning products. There was a lot to do before storing and sorting out, in order to facilitate the location of each item: sweeping, placing pallets to prevent water damage, sorting products logically, checking expiration dates, separating products according to those dates of expiration.

Despite their different individual histories, nationalities, genders, and ages, the missionaries were joined in a single flow, a coming and going in a constant, rigorous rhythm. A missionary recalls: *We learned the strategy of organizing the incredible amount of donations that arrive in an emergency. It was an exhausting week, but I felt the group as one body acting in silence. One single body moved objects from here to there. For me, this was the practice of unity, the expression of a conscious group service.*

One could hardly recognize the place. Members of the Army unit standing guard in front of the shed, were impressed. The coordinators started showing this shed to visitors as a business card, to be photographed and documented by them.

Each one tries to get the most out of the tasks, a missionary says. In places that lack order and cleanliness, dust grows, cobwebs appear, an undesirable vibration is felt. Ugly, involutionary devas disharmonize the whole. Aware of this, in daily life we try to be attentive to perfect ourselves, to improve the logic in conducting each action, a more practical, more benevolent way for all. At a certain point, the task itself becomes our teacher.

They work like bees, and create a ceremony that generates new visual and energetic order and brings beauty to the environment. Since life is one and as this becomes evident, a subtle vortex is generated, interconnecting visible worlds to invisible worlds.

Then they visited the gymnasium sheltering families that lost homes and had nowhere to go. In the beginning there were many, but when missionaries passed there, only three families were left.

Stories about the tornado's passage were continuously told. Shen recalls the memorable ones: *Although half of the city had been destroyed, there were few deaths. Some residents attributed this to the action of the angels. They said God had protected them with His hands. In a supermarket, people ran back and forth as walls and shelves collapsed, and no one died. In another episode, as the tornado grew more violent, a mother rushed out to fetch her son. On a street corner, a person dressed in black stopped her. The calm and harmonious figure told her, "Don't worry, your son is all right. Go back and remain in silence". She began to walk back. Looking back, she did not see him again. And her son was well, he had no problems.*

They found perplexity with each step they took. People who had been injured or had lost beloved relatives, or material possessions, or means of subsistence acted as if nothing had happened to them. In a state of shock and with a blank expression, they were nearly lethargic. How could they recover and adapt wisely to changes? How to transcend the loss?

Ordering a warehouse with donations sent from all over the country and abroad.
Dolores, Uruguay, 2016

The residents were in a hiatus between two eras, before and after the event, in search of the natural disaster effects in themselves. Human consciousness lacks elements and resources to cope with an event that breaks down and changes everything. They did not understand why nature had subjected them to such a situation.

How could they connect this event to the life process itself? How could they help victims to accept an experience of that magnitude? How could they heal the memory of such a big wound?

Studies on reactions to sudden natural tragedies indicate that, over time, reality dawns on them, and one's attitude of denial can lead to anxieties and post-traumatic stress disorders. When a person cannot establish a relationship between the external world and the inner world, they become even more fragile and vulnerable, which may lead to depression, frustrations, abuse of chemical substances, such as alcohol and other drugs. This is why there is an increase in cases of suicide after accidents.

A man said the tornado had swept away all five stores of a shopkeeper who was regarded as one who took undue advantage of people. He was being judgmental. Considering himself as a victim, he would defend himself: *My house was completely ruined, and my next-door neighbor's house is intact. I do not deserve it.* Feeling life had treated him unfairly, it was hard for him to regain hope.

If people do not go deeper in self-knowledge, it costs them the ability to realize essential facts and to interact with life in a broad, universal way.

A human being who is involved in altruistic service or connected to spiritual groups has a greater capacity to withstand trauma and psychological pain. Associations and churches need to learn to support one another to attentively take care of each person in the community.

The economy of Dolores is based on agricultural activity and it is known as the Capital of Wheat of Uruguay. In the fertile area, genetically modified wheat is planted and beef cattle are raised. Those affected by the tornado began to reflect on this. They felt both these activities are not under Spiritual Laws. They wondered whether they had to go through that because they were so attached to material life, progress, and ambition. Faith, so weak in so many, emerged with vigor.

During their stay, the missionaries collaborated with the Government Operational Base Committee, the Army, the Catholic Church, an institute for children, and the construction union of Uruguay. They establish quick, friendly relationships with other groups as they are harmonized with one another and have a good-humored nature, qualities that break through people's resistance.

They were in two meetings with the institution that gives assistance to special children, whose coordinator had intermediated Fraternidade's contact with the mayor. They attended a presentation of children's songs and presented their own songs to them.

The Army took care of the daily emergency dinner in a tornado-stricken neighborhood. It was served in the parish of the Sacred Heart, which became a center of donation of food and clothing. The missionaries helped, preparing the vegetable stew. But they also organized the place. As the victims gradually arrived, they helped to serve them. It was quite cold, and they made a circle of chanting and guitar-playing around a campfire. On that blessed night, people left carrying a portion of soup in their hands. How much their lives had changed!

Invited to participate in a group service by the construction union of Uruguay, which has a strong presence in the country, the missionaries helped them to build a concrete slab. For four uninterrupted hours, they

Emergency dinner for tornado victims. Dolores, Uruguay, 2016

filled buckets of sand, cement, stone, climbed, emptied, descended, filled again, etc. The task flowed in a coordinated way. And for lunch, the masons roasted them whole vegetables on the fire.

They got an enthusiastic farewell of the volunteers with whom they had worked and the mayor gave them a souvenir from Dolores, a handmade coat of arms, carved in wood.

Before leaving, they went to visit the Mother Church of Our Lady of Sorrows. Running into the priest, he led them on the visit. Much of the cathedral had been destroyed. However, the altar remained intact, as it sometimes happens in tragedies. The parish priest talked about the tragedies and miracles of those saved. In the end, as a gift he gave them an image of the Virgin of the 33, Uruguay patron saint.

In major catastrophes, aid gradually becomes scarce as life goes back to normal. The victims must find ways to accept destiny. Could they find new patterns of behavior, change themselves and the future, or do they make of it just a copy of the past? Each inhabitant would have to find answers, take care of their wounds, take their eyes off the little soup bowl and lift them to the immensity of starry skies. They should go through the curtain of the now and enter a subtler golden horizon.

Life brought a collective test to Dolores population. Ever present, it also blew an extra swirl of graces over the city in pain.

On their way back to Brazil, the missionaries went to northern Uruguay for a few days to give support to the Light Community of Fraternity, located in Paysandu. They installed a HF radio antenna and set up a big tent where events, musical presentations, and lectures take place. They also collected and chopped firewood with a group of youths and visited a nursing home in the city.

They traveled to Light-Community of Brotherhood, in Argentina, where they were in charge of tasks such as sanding and varnishing the structure of a belfry; painting a prayer house; rebuilding a damaged fence; removing debris and rubble from the last flood of a stream; assembling a book stand for an event; tidying and cleaning warehouses, workshops, and outdoor areas.

Taking on the heavy work while passing through Light-Communities they strengthened their soul and spirit, which received subtle codes. They radiate in unpredictable paths through which destiny leads them.

EMERGENCY CHILE MISSION

Forests on fire

At the foothills of the volcanoes, among great lakes,
the tangled Chilean thicket... It's a vertical world:
a nation of birds... In a trembling of leaves,
the speed of a fox crosses the silence,
silence is the law of this foliage.
I Confess I Lived, by Pablo Neruda

The swift wind, years of drought, a scorching summer, and mankind, the primary cause, have provoked the greatest forest fire in Chile's history. The large country between the Pacific and the Andes knows the power of Nature. Decade after decade, the earth trembles, one of its ninety volcanoes awakens, tsunamis drag residents on the coast. The people learn, react with strength in face of constant disasters and each time rise again.

The torrid sun rose and lay on the horizon every day of January and February. These months saw flames flying from tree to tree and licking low herbs, devouring the forests of the center of the country. Noisy birds left eggs and chicks with begging beaks in the nests. Animals ran away, jumping over embers. Blood and high red and orange flames colored ridges and cities, burned houses and factories, burned vineyards and araucarias, burned living hares and foxes, and butterflies, snakes, squirrels. Fate also demanded the death of eleven humans. A mass extinction. The nation receives hard lessons.

Experienced in natural disasters, Chile has become a reference on the subject for the rest of the world. Upon declaring a state of emergency and calling for international aid in fighting 100 fire outbreaks, they were helped by a 600-person brigade, including disaster specialists. The brigade represented Germany, Argentina, Brazil, Canada, China, Colombia, South Korea, Spain, the United Arab Emirates, the USA, France, Japan, Mexico, Peru, Russia, Ukraine, Uruguay, and Venezuela. United to these political forces, multinational fire fighters donated themselves with scientific precision and ardor.

The Chilean people stand in solidary. When a region is affected, the rest of the country mobilizes itself. Over 11,000 civilian volunteers, including doctors, psychologists, and veterinarians, set out to the crusade to help families and animals. Others gave monetary support. In previous experiences, hundreds of trucks transported untrained volunteers to affected regions. This caused even more problems, as these people needed to be fed, vaccinated against tetanus and receive drinking water. This is how the group *Desafío Levantemos Chile*, Let us Raise Chile to the Challenge, began. Working in natural disasters since the great 2010 earthquake, they organize the movements of those who offer humanitarian aid and also the flow of donations to those who lose everything.

Before leaving for Santiago, the fourteen members of Fraternidade team, made up of missionaries, monastics of Grace Mercy Order and members of the Planetary Light-Network, underwent trainings of rescue and first-aid, transportation of wounded, control and fire extinguishment.

The encounter united them with the spirits of joy and readiness. When they arrived, the fires had been extinguished. They followed the law of necessity, whose secret is to be objective and lucid: *If something needs to be done, do it. If it doesn't, don't do it.*

The first week, the group served on a farm 60 miles away from the capital. The Emergency Shelter for Large Animals in Doñihue, commune of the province of Cachapoal, region of O'Higgins, gave shelter to the rescued animals because the owners could no longer take care of them. There were forty horses and dogs. Another eighty horses were being brought. Veterinarians examined the burns on the faces and bodies of those who came and referred severe cases to the clinic of the University of Chile.

Following a ceremonial rhythm, and protected by gloves, boots, aprons, and hats, the missionaries helped to build stalls for foals and horses and to fight a fire outbreak. They set up a tent for veterinary care. They spent days organizing the kitchen and the outpatient clinic, and cleaning corrals. In order to give way to pedestrians and vehicles, they removed stakes and trunks of trees, old tires, wood, stones, bottles and two cars with flat tires. They also started building a place for children and a large compost site for organic garbage. They released a great amount of undesirable energy.

To help vegetation return, they created a greenhouse for native seedlings—Seeds of Light. The idea was to offer a little seedling for each visitor, giving them the chance to plant a tree. For containers, they reused bottles scattered around the area.

Using a tractor, the missionaries accompanied the rescue of a horse trapped in the mud of a ditch. They had a lesson on hoof cleaning and on the importance of this procedure for the health of the animal. They bathed all the dogs of the refuge, fifteen of them of all sizes. Animals are extremely sensitive, suffer too much and go into post-traumatic depression. A dog wouldn't eat for days when a veterinarian devoted herself to him until he was strong enough to eat. A llama, though physically healed, wouldn't stand: the shock had been excessive for its delicacy.

The servers try to reinvigorate themselves from the everyday tasks in the moments in which they sing and did group prayers. They sat in a circle and while chanting, attracted young volunteers and employees. In a circle, thirty-five people sang enthusiastically, accompanied by the guitar: *Burn me in Your flame of love.* With increasing fervor and musical enjoyment, they gradually penetrated unimaginable levels of consciousness, which soothed and united them. The singing lit the subtle fire, an invisible counterpart of the red and smoky orange fire that had destroyed Chilean lives. Burnt souls blazed in joyful love for water, stones, plants, animals, crying out for the One Without Beginning Nor End to save the Kingdoms of Nature.

In the refuge of Doñihue, they learned more about the situation at the epicenter of the disaster. Since the shelters for the burnt animals were overcrowded, animals were being released before fully recovered. Fraternidade headed there, to San Javier de Loncomilla, in the Maule region.

They were received by the group *Desafío Levantemos Chile* and were housed in a school. They initially split into three work groups. One of them unloaded donations from vehicles, transported them and separated those destined for animals or for humans. Another one cooked lunch, and a third one went to help residents of Pangalillo, 38 miles away, who had still not received assistance.

On the following day, the fourteen traveled to help the residents of Pangalillo. The population lived in remote, hard-to-reach houses. They walked

on steep trails and rough terrain covered by a carpet of ashes. Each footstep lifted the very fine powder, the remains of wood and leaves. They crossed obstacles amidst the confusion of fallen branches that burning causes in the woods. Along the way, they saw requests for help written with pieces of charcoal on cardboard posters tied to tree trunks.

They took food, water, and donations to houses that were up to 1.2 miles apart from each other. On the way, they met a resident who had saved the house by throwing water around; however, she had lost her crops. In another house damaged by the flames, they removed debris, piled up scattered tiles and leveled the ground. At the neighbor's, they cut and transported long tree trunks to rebuild the structure of the roof of the kitchen and they left him shovels and a work cart.

A volunteer from *Desafío Levantemos Chile* noticed: *It was very touching to receive Fraternidade members. They arrived with incredible energy, which lifted us up and gave us the strength to move on. Their visit was essential and it encouraged more youths to participate in the rescue.*

The group also visited the Animal Campaign Hospital, in Constitución. They walked dogs, cleaned kennels, prayed in the stalls of those who had been burned. Those who suffered from intolerable pain were subjected to euthanasia. Watching a cat with burnt paws, a missionary began to reflect on what the natural kingdoms feel towards the violent impulses of humanity, for some cases of the fire had been caused by arsonists. For him, it made sense that Nature reacted to human madness with earthquakes, hurricanes, waterspouts.

Among black skeletons of trees, rust-colored dry foliage and whitish treetops bordering the road, they kept driving to the town of Santa Olga, which had become a graveyard of broken walls. The lots and the streets had no more debris, because the public administration had done the cleaning, as the region was under the eyes of international media.

In the morning of the tragedy, six thousand fearful residents were disturbed by the gray smoke wall that rose up the hills toward the city. Quickly sparks, followed by a flaming red flash, began to encircle the

Biggest forest fire in Chile, February 2017

Donations brought to residents in remote areas. Panganillo, Chile, 2017

surroundings. The population was evacuated in the early afternoon. At midnight they received the anguishing news that Santa Olga had become completely destroyed. Among the remains of a thousand houses, schools, churches, city hall and police station, the missionaries prayed. Ricardo said: *It's done, now we can finish our mission.* And they left.

The group felt particularly moved by one story. During the humanitarian pilgrimage in the hills, they saw a blue lake among entangled branches of the non-populated forest. In the valley, they arrived at the lands of a young wine producer. He had been a famous national actor, that had done shows in Brazil. His vehicles, tractors, machines, and beautiful century-old house had been mercilessly consumed.

Surrounded by flames, the young man, his sister and a dog escaped by keeping their bodies submerged for hours in the river. They watched the smoke darken the immaculate blue of the sky, flakes of ashes float in the wind, flames fly high. Their possessions crackled, snapped, moaned, until there was nothing left. Slowly, amid absolute silence, the three re-

A missionary nun contemplates a scene of destruction. Chile, 2017

turned. Not a bird's song, not a buzzing of bees, not a sign of life. His cat also had succumbed.

Shen says: *He was a professional circus clown, and inherited the farm from his parents. When we arrived, we found his clown friends, two girls, and a gentleman. All disheartened, in shock. Only the black structures of the house were left, the twisted unicycle of tomfoolery. On the ground, melted metals that once were cutlery and silverware. What purification! We rolled up our sleeves. Before rebuilding, we need to clean.*

It was February and one of the most scorching summers since the beginning of meteorological records in Chile. The two siblings had set up a tarp and improvised a kitchen. Shen goes on: *We cleared up debris, over and over. Suddenly someone found the remnants of a burned book. There was only one sheet left with the image of Christ and one sentence of His. Paper consumes quickly... Christ words seemed as an invitation for the wine producer to seek His help. When we showed him the burned page, he started crying and said: "My life has changed forever. I'll redo it another way".*

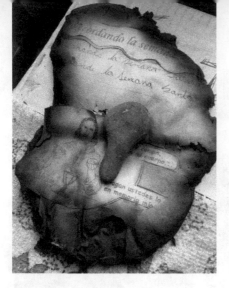

A book page with the image of Christ found during the cleaning of burned debris. Chile, 2017

For someone who has lived a luxurious life and lost everything, what is the meaning of watching fourteen strangers that came out of nowhere carefully clearing their rubble for three days? What motivates these solidary beings who offer a unity of conscience for these Chilean siblings to continue the journey?

The artist reflected. He felt the symbolic potential activated in him a more generous way of being. The test of detachment from the sense of possession demanded that he begin a path beyond material illusion.

Those who spread peace do not travel just to remove soot from homes or heal the third dimension. Material activity is the visible side of the iceberg. What about the two-thirds underwater?

The actions of the visitors strengthened those affected by the catastrophe. Magnetized by the archetype of Love, they encouraged the needy to react, to free themselves from numbness. Even without words, they conveyed a silent message: *Life goes on. Light the inner flame of hope and be reborn from the ashes!*

19th mission
VISTA ALEGRE, MINAS GERAIS
December 30, 2017 to January 8, 2018

20th mission
TARTAGAL, SALTA
February 12 to 26, 2018

ZONA DA MATA MISSION, BRAZIL
CONFRATERNITY MISSION, ARGENTINA

Flooded homes and hearts

Oh, falling waters, from where I come!
Oh, falling waters, I saw severe waters!
Oh falling waters! Baptized,
I'll cry.
Murilo Mendes

The water came to clean a lot of wrong things here, says a woman affected by the tragedy.

The morning was gray and in minutes the river overflowed rushing around the streets. It rose to the height of the roofs bringing raw fear. To escape the muddy stream, she and the people affected would cling to pieces of wood, a sofa, the edge of the balcony. People screamed in despair: *Come and get us, get us out of here!*

The relentless storm was swallowing animals, people's belongings, fences, bridges, part of a freeway: *The water entered the house, and we climbed onto the rooftop. Then, I took a ladder and with my girlfriend we climbed to the tall branches of a mango tree. We stayed there, wet, until nine at night. A neighbor improvised a small boat with a motorcycle engine and was helping two at a time. The engine kept shutting down,* a man says, hearing still the noise of the waters and the screams reverberating inside him.

Storms were raging all over the region for days. They devastated ten cities in Zona da Mata, in the southeastern part of the Brazilian state of Minas Gerais. The deluge left some people isolated and caused deaths. Water and thunderstorms chastised the residents once again, who lamented that the cleaning of the river had not been done before the rainy season.

Humanitarian aid started to come slowly. Three weeks later, ten volunteers from the Fraternidade went to Vista Alegre, one of the most seriously affected villages. The peace task was made up of secondary missionaries and members of the Light-Network—health professionals, a physician, a dentist, a psychologist, a nurse, a rescue worker, a naturopath—of whom six were participating in a mission for the first time.

They traveled for 300 miles carrying subtle and also allopathic medicines—serum, antibiotics, antihistamines, and dewormers. They left Figueira equipped with cleaning accessories—shovels, hoes, saws, high-pressure washers, squeegees, brooms, disinfectants, bleach as well as thermal blankets, boxes to capture snakes, food, and clothing for donation.

In Vista Alegre, the health team supported paramedics at the Health Center, who naturally opened their doors to them. The affected people saw the flood coming into their homes as well as into their hearts. The loving attention and the results obtained in the medical consultations, in the dental and psychological attendance and in the application of bandages also attracted victims from the neighboring communities.

The officials themselves started getting treatment, most of them exhausted and with bodily pain as a result of the incessant rescue services provided since the beginning of the catastrophe. *The health staff felt moved by our way of providing attention until the last patient of the queue was seen, regardless of the conditions and appearance in which they arrived,* says Vitório, the mission coordinator.

Two missionaries went to inspect houses to analyze what had happened. They found fifty-five residences destroyed and seventy-two damaged. *The residents live in great poverty, imprisoned in a way of life that is not worthy of a soul,* Vitório says. Some houses which has been submerged came down or became uninhabitable, with cracks in the walls. They said: *I lost everything, but, thank God, nobody in the community lost their life.* As a symbolic act of solidarity, the group decided to rebuild a residence.

Among those assisted at the health center, they met the oldest resident in the neighborhood, a seventy eight year old lady. *Dona Isabel burst into tears as she said how bad she felt inside. She lived alone, and the house was everything to this widowed woman,* says Wanderley. *We went with her to visit the cottage by the river. I was impressed! The only thing intact was an image of Our Lady Aparecida. We then learned that she coordinated an active prayer group in the neighborhood.*

For five days, they used shovels, brushes, nails, paintbrushes. They cleaned every corner of the house. They leveled the courtyard, refurbished the wooden structure and roof, washed furniture and utensils,

Surprised, Dona Isabel is grateful for the renovation of her house.
Vista Alegre, Minas Gerais, Brazil, 2018

bought a new bed and mattress. They painted the house yellow. It was gorgeous! So they went to fetch Dona Isabel. In the car, she remained quiet, observing the devastated neighborhood. Entering the room, she exclaimed to the image on the table: *Oh, Our Lady!* She joined her hands in prayer, and cried, deeply surprised and grateful. With brooms in their hands, the missionaries celebrated: *After the storm, new life comes!*

After making contact with the local authorities of Vista Alegre they were invited to attend a meeting to plan for post-disaster actions and to give a talk addressed to health officials. The Health Secretariat also organized group therapy to relieve people's anguish and traumas.

The activity was carried out by a member of the mission, Denise, a psychologist: *We gave them room for detailed testimonials. Accustomed to annual floods, the residents were surprised by the magnitude and speed of this flood. But, this event created strong union among them.*

Two neighbors, who regarded one another as enemies, were not dragged away because the short one, almost covered by the waters, embraced firmly the other, who is taller and stronger, and who, in her turn, grabbed a gate. With water up to her neck, the taller one was getting discouraged and exhausted: *We're going to die, I'm going to release my arms.* The short

Village affected by flood on the bank of Casca River, Brazil, 2018

one: *Don't do it!* Touched by the sacred laws of forgiveness and reconciliation, they later said: *We needed each other in the middle of the water.*

Denise realized to what extent the stories revealed faith and detachment from material things: *No-one complained, some said they were going to start all over, building more loving relationships among neighbors. We had great proof of affection and testimonies that they were receiving something unknown, far beyond what they could imagine.*

Vitório emphasized: *We feel that we have transmitted to people the impression that fraternal love exists and it is possible to experience it.* Doctor Stella reflected: *There was an exchange. They were very warm-hearted to us, love really did it all!*

Before saying goodbye, the missionaries raised their eyes to the surrounding hills. The cloudless blue sky was sending them a message: a rainbow, which crossed it from side to side, like an immense portal.

Indigenous people observe flooded street, Argentina, 2018

Confraternity Mission

Two months later, the Confraternity Mission in the province of Salta, in Northern Argentina, began. It had several points in common with the Zona da Mata Mission. It was also a response to the unprecedented overflowing of rivers that turned streets and roads into riverbeds.

Rain storms swept the lowlands of Chaco, affecting the lives of 17,000 residents of this area in southern Bolivia. Here are headwaters to the Pilcomayo and Bermejo Rivers—the first one at 1,800 feet altitude.

Confraternity Mission was made up of Argentineans from various regions and coordinated by Brazilians Cristiano, Helentiana, Rosi and Wanderley.

I accepted without hesitation. This kind of service first empties me of myself and then fills me with love, with compassion, with more joy, says Florencia, a volunteer from Bahia Blanca. Purity is also reflected in the innocent speech of Viviana, from Buenos Aires: *I merely offer my heart and my hands to help in whatever is necessary.*

The participants met in the capital of the Province of Salto, and traveled north together aiming to reach a certain rural area.

However, halfway there, after driving 220 miles, they found natives in the city of Tartagal who had not yet received aid. They were sure that they should remain there: *The mission gradually told us what to do. It was not possible to arrange the details before we left. We walked without knowing what would come up one meter ahead,* says Mabel, from North Argentina Light-Network.

When the rivers finally withdrew from the roads, the outcome was tonnes of mud, debris, pieces of pottery, plastics, metal, branches. It takes a long time for the sun to dry large puddles and, when it happens, the land cracks. In this muddy and filthy scenario, they had a warm welcome by indigenous communities of Fwolit, El Mistol, El Algarrobo, El Quebracho and San Benito.

With a thread of attention connected to their own essence, the missionaries divided efforts to give assistance to the first community. At the request of tribal leader Modesto Rojas, they built a wall to prevent future floods, especially around the sacred temple of the village. They collected debris scattered over public spaces. They did recreational activities with children, besides teaching them the practice of oral hygiene and distributing toothbrushes and toothpaste to the whole community.

Part of the team left to inspect the streets and the surrounding area, wondering what to do to prevent the invasion of waters. With an entrepreneur spirit, they turned to Tartagal local authorities, who soon sent a technician to study solutions with the missionaries and the natives, plus a backhoe and a grader to excavate deviations, clean and expand the watercourse channel which crosses several villages.

While the heavy machinery did the hard work, indigenous people, missionaries, and even the owner of the inn where they lodged, built a retaining wall with stacked bags filled with the sand dragged by the flood. *For the village Fwolit, that was a turning point. Cheerful children ran like the wind on the brand-new wall,* says Rosi, smiling.

The news spread. Missionaries made contact with residents. Local people finally started to undertake tasks. *Who are those coming from the most*

Wall of sandbags for the retention of floods; distribution of food in indigenous communities. Tartagal, Salta, Argentina, 2018

Rain is back again.
Tartagal, Salta, Argentina, 2018

diverse points of Argentina and Brazil, who make such efforts? Inhabitants and merchants became aware of the situation and opened the valves of generosity that the Creator deposits in each essence. Donations of clothing began to multiply, adding to diapers and milk sent by Argentina Light-Network. The missionaries classified, packaged, and distributed to families, according to the leader's indications. One shopkeeper sent out kilos of bread, which was shared to the community with chocolate milk.

The dogs themselves seemed to be asking for help from the missionaries who, seeing their affliction and the children being infected with scabies, photographed them and sent the images to an animal protection group. The group donated drugs and vaccines against parasites and scabies. For the first time in the history of that community, dogs and cats were given baths and vaccines.

In the meantime, several mothers began to call for help against lice, and that same afternoon missionaries started treating their long black hair and those of their children with vinegar and fine combs.

On Sunday the insistent rain returned. With it, anxiety. Part of the wall had been built. Even so, the missionaries kept filling up sacks to raise it.

Indigenous kids affected by flood observe the rain.
Tartagal, Salta, Argentina, 2018

It was Sunday, and it was raining, so only a few natives came to help. The preventive measures had protected almost all the houses, but the ones erected on uneven terrains were in trouble, and the servers rushed to help the residents.

During the wet morning, children and women took shelter in the temple. To dissipate afflictions, the servers talked to the ladies, played games with the kids and served them a snack with loaves of bread, cookies and hot chocolate.

A missionary stood by the window with the little ones. They contemplated the beauty of the curtain of water, which cleansed the air and purified the energy. When the rain was gone, the children rushed to jump into puddles. *Now I understand the reason for the name Confraternity Mission: the most important thing is to talk to them, listen to the small narratives of how they conceive life. I was surprised to realize their openness, as if we had known one another for a long time,* Mabel realized.

They said goodbye to the Fwolit community and headed to support others a few miles away. Received by chants of indigenous kids, they underwent similar tasks: sweeping and collecting debris from the streets, sharing bread and chocolate, developing activities with youths.

To meet families' needs, they distributed first-aid kits with natural medicines: propolis, espinheira-santa—*maytenus ilicifolia*, hepatobiliar for the liver and arnica, among others. In face of the vulnerable houses below ground level and the sacred temple devastated by the rainstorm, they taught those interested how to erect the water-retention wall.

In El Mistol, of the Wichi ethnic group, the tribal leader Roberio was sick, debilitated and regretted not being able to help the community as before. He was a communicator for the local indigenous radio station and was suffering because it had been defeated after the last elections.

Through the waves of the transmitter, the communities received useful news from one another, which enabled them to be less isolated and get help to win rights and improve social conditions. Wanderley, missionary who served on both missions, Zona da Mata and Confraternity, says: *We had a long conversation about the importance of the communities to maintain love and unity among the ethnic groups, respecting the differences between them. United, they would always be stronger. The leader thanked us for our presence and our words having brought them almost forgotten hope and renewal to them.*

Brazilian and Argentinian missionaries gave assistance and soothed wounds caused to the humblest among those affected. They were there to remind them of how important they are. They were resigned to the climatic phenomenon and were supportive of one another, although the trauma added to old pains.

Wherever they arrived, the lively and peaceful men and women dressed in gray, caused a positive response. Altruism generates altruism. Without delay, they created work fronts according to the particularities found in each village. Missionaries both allow themselves to be guided and guide, according to what life presents to them.

Under leadership, Brazilians from Vista Alegre and Argentinian residents of indigenous communities felt encouraged to cooperate. Their dynamism accelerates the energy of what it touches, elevating material life. The Fraternidade service cheered them up, generating a wave of life. The servers and those in need contributed to the general good. It awoke hidden potentialities and launched a silent inner appeal, which invites everyone: *It is time to wake up! The time for cooperation has come.*

PART IV
Brazil and Greece
Permanent Missions

Planetary Mission Network

Contemplate the passing spectacle of life
with a calm mind, for the ups and down
of existence are nothing but sea waves
in constant flux. Do not get involved
with them, but remain calm, cheerful
in your inner center.
Paramahansa Yogananda

Small altruistic groups, attuned with the new times, herald a future of peace for life on Earth. Even though they are not numerous, they are of immense value, for they take on evolutionary tasks. They apply love in every detail. They try to understand other people's needs in order to heal them. They silently paint veins of light over conflicts.

They go on short-term missions for a few days or weeks, or serve permanent humanitarian missions. The latter reach greater depth upon dealing, for example, with cultural roots of Argentinian, Brazilian, Paraguayan, and Venezuelan native people. Comprehensive knowledge is required to assist those people, in order to avoid religious traditionalism and other traditions.

In different degrees of awareness and surrender, FIHF members have worked in almost twenty countries. This entity brings together volunteers who conduct a wide range of actions free of charge. They work in its two pillars—Humanitarian Missions and Planetary Light-Network, as well as in its affiliates—Light-Communities, Light-Nucleus, Service Associations, Religious Associations, and Marian Centers.

Each step is accompanied by superiors. On February 16, 2016, they announced the foundation of the Planetary Network Mission and the union of FIHF's two pillars: In each region of the planet that has a Light-Network, there should also be missionaries in training, members of prayer groups and souls who will awaken through selfless service. The invitation was extended to hundreds of Planetary Light-Network groups: *The Missionary Network groups should gather for a Missionary Meeting twice a year at the Figueira Marian Center, where they will deepen their learning with the primary missionaries and will establish the semiannual service goals.*

One month after coming back from Turkey, the consecrated servers organized the first twice-a-year meeting including a basic course for rescue workers and advanced courses on rescue and nursing. Since then, they have fulfilled what was indicated in the petition: *Contribute to the Earth balance so this group consciousness can fulfill external and inner rescue needs.*

Two years before the Planetary Mission Network was established, the Carmo da Cachoeira Permanent Mission was created in Minas Gerais, Brazil. An unprecedented cycle began.

Between missions, the primary missionaries stayed at Figueira farms participating in the daily routine while waiting for the next trip. A growing urgency began to emerge in them to go on with the service of reaching out to the needy and oppressed with the same total surrender experienced in Nepal and Africa.

In response to this yearning, on January 25, 2014, two humanitarian aid houses, one for women and one for men, were inaugurated in the poor São José district: Casa de São José and Casa de Maria Rosa da Paz. The group started to assist various needs of the Human, Animal, Plant and Mineral Kingdoms, and soon began offering instruction to aspirant missionaries.

In the following year, at another part of the city, the missionaries set up a warehouse to distribute donations, the Galpão de Serviço São José, Service Shed of Saint Joseph. In 2016, in partnership with the municipal authorities, also opened the doors of the Casa do Acolhimento, House of Welcome, for homeless people.

Praying for guidance and help from the sublime world, the missionaries were gradually prepared during concrete actions. As they reached a certain degree of love for people and for the Kingdoms of Nature, two more permanent missions of humanitarian assistance were founded. In September 2016, the Missionary Base in Greece was founded, which for almost two years served Asian and African refugees and homeless Greeks.

A month later, the Roraima Permanent Mission was born in Boa Vista, Brazil, to assist Venezuelan refugees. For this task, all primary and secondary missionaries were instructed to travel to Roraima.

New dynamics always redesign the Planetary Mission Network. In the second half of 2018 began the Permanent Colombia Mission. The Permanent Missions Roraima and Carmo da Cachoeira continued their work, whereas the Missionary Base in Greece, sustained by volunteers from Europe Light-Network was temporarily closed.

Giving continuity to official missions, three others Recurrent Regional Missions were undertaken by the Light-Network. Since 2014, the Rede-Luz Norte and Northeast of Brazil has given immediate follow-up to the sixth mission, held in the Sertão de Alagoas. From then onwards, it has provided biannual services to communities around Palmeira dos Índios. The same happened after Chaco Mission, when the Argentinian Light-Network continued assisting indigenous ethnic groups. Six months later the Regional Paraguay Mission to help native people was started.

They are responding to the urgent needs of those affected by environmental tragedies, and they are providing support to groups dedicated to those living in poverty.

A missionary, aware that the divine essence dwells within each creature, says: *We take a drop of hope, of fraternity, of love to those who go through great adversities and need to heal the past.* Altruistic love longs to liberate the wounded humanity from suffering so it may learn how to be united, how to love, to be lighthearted and joyful.

PERMANENT MISSION IN CARMO DA CACHOEIRA, BRAZIL

Serving and ascending

Ceasing to seek personal gain and giving
in abundance is what is proposed to the
human being at this stage of the Earth.
Trigueirinho

Clara was born with a thirsty soul. As a child, imagining what she would do as a grown-up, she saw herself distributing soup to the needy. Life gave her different lessons, and her premonition fell asleep. However, this early image persisted in her unconscious, as a backdrop. When she got to know the work done in Figueira, the old burning thirst to help people came to the fore with redoubled vigor, and soon Clara became a missionary.

Whenever she and the group returned from the intense service in Africa, they felt a growing need to continue with the same tone and humanitarian pace of fraternal spirit. Between one mission and another a yearning was born. Clara thought: *These beautiful community mattresses, these clean sheets, all this is wonderful. But I need to be with the poor.*

Her dream world announced the right time for the transition: *I dreamed that we, the missionaries, were moving in a big car, and the driver told us he was taking us where we should live. We went into a slum until we stopped in front of a house.* This dream was soon reported to the community instructor Trigueirinho, and from then on everything happened quickly.

During a lecture, he explained to the audience the importance for the missionaries to give continuity to active service in their own home in Carmo da Cachoeira. At the end of the speech, someone donated a residence to them. It was still under construction, in the São José district.

The instructor went to visit the house right away, gave the endorsement and indicated it to be the men's house. *Would the women's house be far away? Where?* the group wondered. Ten days later, another landlady, not knowing about the initial offer, lent them a house for two years. It was in the São José district. There was only one little house between the two others. How impressive are life's responses! Such synchronicity causes enchantment and has been repeating itself since the group has chosen to live in poverty.

Three missionaries fully agreed to join in with what was proposed. After repairs and maintenance of the two properties have been done, Imer came to coordinate the men's house and Clara, the women's house. The former is known as the House of the Immaculate Heart of Mary. The latter, which later was transferred to another place, became known as the House of San Jose. Over time, other people and new consciousnesses attracted by simplicity arrived for an internship.

The pioneers brought beds plus kitchen and laundry utensils. For almost a year they had no stove or a refrigerator. They had very little, and nothing was missing. They had lunch about half a mile away, in the general cafeteria of Figueira's House 3, which provides free daily food to anyone who arrives: city residents, community, wanderers.

Both houses focused their activities on the building of vegetable gardens and on the weekly distribution of food. The Law of Manifestation constantly streams forth abundantly, both for themselves and for those who ask for help.

Clara collected stories: *It was about nine o'clock on a freezing morning. We had given away everything, and a woman with her daughter knocked on the door. They were shaking with cold and wore thin blouses and dresses. Three of us lived there. We asked them to wait and went in to talk. We had the same idea and gave them all of our blankets. At one o'clock in the afternoon, someone rang the bell saying they were bringing us a donation of goods in the trunk of their car. We went to fetch it. There were twelve blankets! We came inside, looked at one another and began to cry.*

The servers feel deeply protected as they realize how carefully every detail is looked after by beings of the inner world. How? How does the positive magnetic web work, manifesting itself so accurately? Do angels whisper in donors' ears? These are mysteries to be unraveled.

Donations come to them in a balanced way and are living examples of those who know how to read the book of life. Clara's dialogue with the invisible is very practical, intimate, constant. For example, someone asks

Weekly donation of clothing.
Missionary House, Carmo da Cachoeira, Minas Gerais, Brazil, 2014

for a bed and tells her a story. Clara can easily tell if the story is true or false. The missionary explains they do not have a bed. Then asks what is their religion and tells them to pray at home. If they are evangelical, she guides them to read a biblical excerpt. If they are Catholic, to talk to Our Lady, Christ or St. Joseph. If they are atheist, to remain hopeful. She tells them that her group will also call upon the Highest. If the person's request is true, the bed will appear in the same afternoon.

If a person asks them for a door, this symbolic request usually indicates they seek a way out of some negative situation. They schedule a visit to the home and usually face hostilities between mother and son or husband and wife. Clara tells us: *They invite us to go inside. We sit without asking anything. Then they start to vent. When we are about to leave, the host thanks us: "You did not bring the door, but you solved another problem". There are material services and non-material ones, such as reconciliations.*

In each missionary house, it is said: *When the bell rings, Christ is calling. He said, "I was sick, and you came to visit me, I was cold, and you clothed me".* However, to cooperate with a person's development, sometimes it is necessary to say *no*, which is a way to correct them with love. And they explain this no: *Today we are not going to give it to you because you*

Christmas meeting for residents.
Carmo da Cachoeira, Minas Gerais, Brazil, 2014

already came yesterday and came last week. Please come back in a month. The one asking understands. In the case a junkie knocks on the door, he is always given something, whether it is just a few words, or cleaner clothing, so that he may feel like a better human being.

They deal with stressful situations, but as missionaries see reality in a light and faithful way, based on philosophy, they spread healing balms on souls in a simple way. They ponder intimate aspects that reveal something beyond the concrete. As the group practices the art of wholeheartedly giving of themselves to every little action, so, their energy is transfigured into a living flame.

What must be done is crystal-clear before their eyes. Imer says: *When we consecrate ourselves to a life of service, we get to know people deeply. They ask us to intercede in family conflicts, such as when a grandmother complains about her daughter who would keep arguing with her and would beat her granddaughter. We went to visit them. We talked with the three, remaining attentive, in no hurry, and without discrediting anyone, realizing each one had their reasons. The stress naturally mitigated.*

They restlessly deal with a multitude of situations, which includes putting out a fire at a farm and taking a drunk who has fallen down in the street to the hospital. They may offer handicraft workshops, participate in building a house, repair plumbing or electrical problems. They may distribute food, help people finding jobs, assist homeless people who have had to live in the street because the couple has separated and one of the two has nowhere to go, or because an unemployed person can no longer pay for the rent. Since love heals, even a person who is having a psychotic fit, comes asking for help.

They work not only for life but also for those who are about to die. Once they were called in the middle of the night to be with a dying horse: the owner had beaten the animal and used it to exhaustion. They begged for forgiveness by caressing his suffering hindquarters, prayed and accompanied him until he died. On another occasion, they tied a shell on a long bamboo to rescue two kittens from a tall pipe. One of them was dead, but they saved the other kitten and watched it grow up healthily after they found him a good home.

Under the first rays of one morning, two missionaries drove many of miles to take a mother about to have an emotional breakdown, to see her imprisoned son. They waited for her all day to bring her back at night, filled with relief and gratitude.

As part of the humanitarian aid, they visit homes, institutions, and hospitals, as well as forgotten or sick people from urban and rural areas. In Carmo da Cachoeira, they work at the Association of Parents and Friends of Disabled People, APAE. In the vicinity, they have helped Colônia Santa Fé, with leprosy patients, clinics for the rehabilitation of people with addictions, prisons. They have collaborated with the House of Light on the Hill, by assisting cancer patients in the organization Vida Viva, in Boa Esperança, Minas Gerais. They have worked with prisoners in a semi-open regime and with children in risky situations of the Association for Protection and Assistance to Convicted People, APAC, which follows the motto: *Every man is greater than the mistake he made.*

Young missionaries give mattresses; dance in the home for the elderly and donate some of the harvests of the Light-Community of Figueira. Carmo da Cachoeira, Minas Gerais, Brazil, between 2014 and 2016

In the home for the elderly in Carmo of Cachoeira, the missionaries give joyful and loving attention both to the tireless employees and to the residents: fraternal listening, hair-cutting, nail-trimming, cleaning of rooms and the facilities, distributing clothes and food, praying.

Once, two servers lived a transformation process. They set up a group of residents to teach them to communicate beyond words, to speak through colors and paintings. They explained to the elderly who had never held a paintbrush, who had never been asked what their favorite color was: *Painting black ink on paper may mean that we are sad.*

Good-humored, kindly, and patiently, they went on week after week, inspiring hope in the residents who gradually came to understand. Each student assimilated what was taught in their own pace, either in the blink of an eye, in one day, in a week or in months.

Later, they would bring melodies for the elderly to listen with closed eyes. As bonds of affection were built, they began to open up, to tell ideas, sensations. By realizing they were being listened to, they exposed their bitterness, sorrows, and fears.

The primary missionary Luiz notes: *This kind of approach was wonderful. They first reported their feelings through images, next they listened to music, then began to speak at the end of each session, even if no one was asked to do so. We gradually got to know each one and were impressed by their means of expression. The process was extremely rich and profound. We not only offered something, but we were interested in each one of them.*

One year later, they placed the elderly in front of a large white screen for them to paint together while a CD played songs of Saint Francis Assisi prayers. One by one, each student would pick up the brush, choose a color and go to the panel to express themselves. Luiz goes on: *There was a disabled lady, one who was not able to do anything. When we invited her, an elderly man commented that she would not be able to paint. The others became silent. The man's remark had no repercussion. Then she took the brush, chose her favorite color and painted the canvas. She was there, fully present. A narrow window had opened within her, and there was light. With a shy gesture, the lady expressed herself through imagery.*

When it comes from one's heart, service may resurrect the people being served. Little by little, the residents were strengthened and transformed.

When the missionaries departed for the Africa Mission, Ricardo left someone to take care of the houses and chores. Alexandrina, recently arrived from Recife, took care of the houses, plants, and dogs. She received the donations and kept track of them, distributing them on Saturdays with the help of collaborators. At three a.m. on Mondays, she rang the great Bell on the Hill of Apparitions of the Marian Center connected to Figueira.

Punctually at 3 p.m., she recited the Rosary of Divine Mercy, in union with the Fourteen in Africa. One afternoon, Alexandrina penetrated another layer of life and had a vision: *On an immense mountain were carved the face, the hair and the bust of Christ. Two straight and parallel roads guided people to the stone wall. One was pink, and the other was blue, both colors transparent like the rays of the painting of the Merciful Christ. Along the routes, thousands of beings marched, one after the other, and went into the stone, which had no door or tunnel. She was absolutely certain these were souls being rescued from the suffering continent, in which 14 thousand children die of thirst every day.*

In September 2017, the partnership between Fraternidade and the UNHCR was established. All missionaries drew the sword of peace and departed for Roraima, a state that borders the Brazilian state of Amazonas and two countries, Venezuela and the Cooperative Republic of Guyana.

To continue with the Carmo da Cachoeira Permanent Mission, members of the Light-Network in Minas Gerais and São Paulo were summoned, and began to work along with two missionaries and collaborators from the town. Together they maintain the House of St. Joseph, the House of the Immaculate Heart of Mary, and the Shed of St. Joseph.

In the urban area, they continue with the home visits and with activities in the Nursing Home and APAE. In the neighboring town of Lavras, they serve in the kennel Francis of Assisi Park, which assists more than four hundred dogs.

In a helpful spirit of love, the two pillars of the Fraternidade—Humanitarian Missions and Planetary Light-Network—shed pure water of life.

Shed of Saint Joseph

My friend's fate is to suffer
the luck of her fellow being,
although this is blissful suffering.
Let me explain. Each person's
suffering worries her, and ignites
in her the torch of action,
which makes her happy.
Speak, Almond Tree,
by Carlos Drummond de Andrade

In a predawn hour, those determined to be the first in the queue walk through dark streets. They go towards the Shed of Saint Joseph, where the green gates are opened every Saturday at 9 a.m. They sit in arrival order on the sidewalk curb, their body warmed by blankets. The dew dampens children's coats and hoods. The sun rises, but they still wait for hours.

Since anything in there can be taken for free, the early risers believe they will choose the most appropriate if they are first in line. Indeed, they yearn for something else in the joyful solidarity morning which, in simplicity, offers them subtle surprises.

In the weekly meetings, missionaries and the people being served look face to face. Throughout the contact, the volunteers seek to know the history of each one. They exercise one secret of humanitarian work, that is, learning to put yourself in the other's shoes to understand one's situation, trying to feel it from the inside to help him dispel worries.

Inside the shed, there is abundance and diversity. As soon as people arrive to distribute donations—among them four former homeless people who used to live in the House of Welcome—they open six large wardrobes for women's, men's and children's clothes, sorted by size and gender. They remove sheets protecting shelves with shoes, handbags, and objects. They discover floor racks with hanging coats, sweaters, and dresses.

With everything in sight, the environment seems like a rustic store, filled with clothes, books, furniture, stoves, water reservoirs, building materials, hair stylist supplies. If something is still missing for someone's request, they take note in a notebook with name, address, and telephone number, and the group tries to supply their need during the week.

A former artisanal brick factory, the Shed of Saint Joseph was passed to Figueira by the City Hall in the early 2000s. A community resident had coordinated the production of clay bricks for years, which were donated to the people along with vegetables from the vegetable garden, planted along the steep terrain. Finally, once that cycle ended, the place started to be revitalized by consecrated missionaries.

As their first activity, the group distributed the stored bricks. In the large lot—lawn in the front, and in the background two balconies and a stock room—a warehouse was set up for donations, which arrive non-stop. On Thursdays, the material received is sorted out, and kits are organized to meet the constant requests, such as baby layettes for pregnant women.

The shed stimulates creativity. Workshops to restore furniture are held there since only ready-to-use articles are made available for distribution. Sewing classes were also created to repair and make clothes. These are run in between the harvest period in which people work for months on nearby coffee crops.

Someone had the Truck of Mercy idea. The vehicle ran through community farms collecting unused objects, as well as belongings left by guests who, during their stay, find certain things are no longer necessary.

Everything pulsates, moves, shakes. Soon after the missionaries were summoned to the Roraima Mission, there was a dynamic transition. Ninety-three Light-Network collaborators came from different parts of the country to participate in a group service. They plunged into a joyful creative wave. They changed windows, painted doors, rebuilt the sidewalk and even built a new distribution wing, raising walls and covering the cement floor. Each one gave their best and all returned home vivified by the breath of Love that rules that little corner of the world.

Before the green gate is opened, the volunteers gather in a circle. They make the Sign of the Cross, recite the missionary prayer and listen to instructions given by coordinator Mariandja: *We are instruments to radiate codes, values of harmony. Let us not pay attention to the material condition of those we assist, but rather to the beauty of souls searching for ways to stay alive, and confident. Let us be very attentive because, often-times, behind a material request, there is a greater need. Let us not miss the opportunity to serve what lies behind.*

The service is a bridge to direct the needy towards other veins of the same work. The one who has a health problem goes to the House of Light on the Hill. The one with educational issues, to the Art Education Unit. If there are animals, in need, appointments are made for neutering, and the care given to diseases and accidents at the House of Hope.

Mariandja continues to guide: *Talk to each one, ask them if that is real-ly what they need. Pay attention to the number of pieces donated, some want to take almost twenty pieces to each member of the family, and this encourages greed. Pay attention to the time. Be careful not to spend the whole morning with a single person who wants this and that. Just warn them, "Others are waiting." Sometimes the opposite happens: a shy person chooses a single piece and we realize they need something else.*

Then the tasks are distributed. Some will hand out numbered tickets, some others will welcome each requester, and some others will be in charge of the children's activity. Mariandja wishes: *Have a good day, ev-eryone.* With passwords in hand, the assisted people enter the green gate and sit on the long bench leaning against the wall shaded by branches. They are called one by one: *What do you need?* According to the answer, server and requester will together look for the article which, if chosen, is placed in a bag. If rejected, it is immediately placed back on shelves or wall or floor racks.

Some attendants give everything the requester wants. Others instruct: Let's think about the others. Missionary Claudia says: *Our little Saturday mission is intense. A lot of people come. We are always learning and being put to test. They may want to take what they do not need, which has no function. To deal with their craving, their material illusion, we must first contain the anxiety in ourselves. We reflect what we are. The job is not just donating objects, but trying to understand the other. This is an exercise of the one who serves. Some find this task too hard and cannot handle it.*

Weekly distribution of things and
painting session with children.
Carmo da Cachoeira, Minas Gerais, Brazil, 2018

A missionary apprentice had a lesson to discover on neutrality. There are those who come just about every Saturday and leave with full bags, perhaps to sell these clothes. The apprentice was too bothered with one of them who picked only the best items. His reaction showed a feeling of prejudice which had to be transcended. The group learned from the Missionaries of Charity in Greece that, if someone takes something to sell it later, that is a way for them to earn extra money. But the apprentice would not accept it, and kept talking about it until the evening, when a missionary disarmed him: *Detach yourself, go pray to clear it off your mind, go bathe with coarse salt.*

The care with each article helps with transmuting the energy of the one who wore it, perhaps someone depressed, a sick person. Claudia clarifies: The one who arrives receives harmony codes. We found a lot of clutter and met hoarders in the houses we visited. Here they may learn how to organize their own dwellings, simplifying them.

Over time, the distribution work became more consistent. The coordinator gathered the people being assisted to draw their attention to hoarding, as whole families come to the shed every Saturday. To get out of the situation of just asking and to learn to give, they made a proposal to start an exchange bank from the following week on. What is useless or is excessive to one may turn out to be valuable for those who cannot afford it. They were told to pay close attention to their homes and to bring back anything unnecessary, whether it was an earring, a broom, a garment. Besides, she invited them: *Join us to welcome the ones who arrive here.*

Over the years, the assisted ones reflect the generosity received and develop empathy. A mother came and said: *Here are my baby clothes. He has grown. I want to pass them on.*

A lady supports her unemployed daughter and two grandchildren with 600 reais a month, just over 150 American dollars. The children's father had left them. She says that, if the shed didn't exist, she would not know what to do. But the people assisted get something besides full handbags. They appreciate being cared for and respected: *God bless you and pay you back twice as much!*

Educational materials are delivered in the city's schools or used in the shed itself, in a parallel activity for children accompanying relatives. They sit on a tarp on the grass in front of a small pink tent. The coordinator instructs: *We will share all we have, as today we have only a few pencils and very little paper.*

She sits down among the children, around a sheet of cardboard, and says: *Our heart always warns us about something. Have you ever felt that? It beats fast if we're in danger.* Children: *That's true!* So, she asks: *What lives in our hearts?* A little girl answers: *Jesus Christ.* Another: *Mary.* Together they draw a big flowery heart. The coordinator manages to gather them all inside the large colorful heart embellished with flowers.

In the meantime, a young woman picked up bed linens for a layette. Marlene was getting married. She had arrived at four a.m. and was second in the queue. In front of her, there was just a mother with her disabled son. She entered the shed at 9 a.m., and it was almost 11 a.m. now. She had chosen what she needed, but liked standing there smiling, embraced by peace.

A few weeks before, Marlene came after her wedding dress. There was only one, gorgeous, all embroidered with pearls: *What a beautiful dress!* But it was too small for her. Then a volunteer from São Paulo settled the issue. She took note of the bride's measurements to alter the dress in São Paulo. She also committed herself to make the veil, the tulle garland and the bouquet. *I'll take a photo and send you an invitation,* says the bride, delighted. She picks up her cell phone and shows the picture on the screen with her husband-to-be.

At a given moment, with unique elegance, a gentle attendant asked a lady touched by the sweetness of Marlene's story: *Do you need anything?* They looked at each other for a long moment, and the lady answered: *Yes, I need a hug.* Both of them open their arms and... what a squeezing hug, a medicine given without a prescription! How many secrets fraternal hearts exchange?

A hug is a symbol of the shed, which opens it's arms to anyone's need. Those who have been assisted sit at the curb from 4 a.m. and only leave when the gates are closed. When they leave, their souls are relieved, their disillusions are comforted.

House of Welcome

Pay attention to the wanderers.
Something moves them and makes
them restless. More easily than others,
they realize the frailty of ownership.
They are not afraid of distances.
They are learning a lot. Among
them there might be messengers.
Brotherhood, by Helena Roerich

A men's house with open doors, the House of Welcome receives street-dwellers. Whoever rings the bell comes in. If they want to eat, they do. If they want to take a shower, they do. If they want to live in, they do. The house energy shifts its tone according to those passing by or coordinating it. The colors of charity are wonderful and they are created step by step. No one can set rules for charitable acts, establish what can or cannot be done. Missionaries must adjust to each person's peculiarities, people they refer to as brothers.

When walking by the district streets or when paying home visits, the missionaries listened to stories from alcoholic and smelly occupants. Some of them asked for help, guidance: *I want to stop drinking.* At first, they were taken to sleep at the House of Saint Joseph, before being referred to recovery clinics. To address this issue, they met Trigueirinho, who managed to get the commitment from the city hall of Carmo da Cachoeira to pay the rent for a simple corner house with a large yard and overlooking wooded hills. The Fraternidade established this connection between local authorities, civil society, and social assistance.

Since its opening, people who arrive at the House of Welcome, whether addicted or not, share meals with everyone. Assisted with respect and a tender smile, the rejected ones gradually get involved by the aura of the missionary work.

The first coordinator observed people coming and going. *Something was lacking: We were distributing food, clothing, but I was restless. We needed to have a broader, more compassionate look. We talked to Ricardo and I*

*was sent to the Community of the Trinity, "Comunidade da Trindade",
in Salvador, capital of Bahia for inspiration. For eleven years, a Catholic monk pilgrimaged with walkers between São Paulo and Salvador. He
shared his home with street-dwellers until he found a ruined Catholic
church. The diocese accepted that the temple would become a dwelling for
the homeless. There they sleep on cardboard or blankets. As time went by,
the work has expanded, and a community has emerged around it.*

Returning from the trip, it dawned on the coordinator that, more than
just offering meals and clothes, they should set up a small community for
four homeless who wanted to follow a new path, to try out a new standard of conduct. Aiming at this goal, he lived and worked in the House
of Welcome for eight months until this all came true.

Given that street-dwellers are usually very creative to make handicrafts,
they set up a carpentry workshop in the house, where pieces in bamboo
and wood are made. They have also built orderly seedbeds in the large
yard, where a vegetable garden produced in abundance.

In a dynamic coming and going of people, the house keeps a rhythm, a
daily and weekly schedule. For example, on Tuesdays, the people assisted
with making bread and devote themselves to the vegetable garden. On
Thursdays, they receive all sorts of health care at House of Light on the
Hill, which they can see from the porch of the backyard of the House of
Welcome. Sometimes they attend lessons taught in the Art and Education
Unit. Every Friday, they visit the local Nursing Home and, on Saturdays,
they help to distribute donations in the Shed of Saint Joseph. Sometimes
they join prayers in the Marian Center associated with Figueira.

In the first year, fifteen residents stayed in the house. With a firm but
warm voice, the first coordinator comments: *It was an intense experience, and hard work. Often, I could only fall asleep at 3 a.m. because the
inner world of street-dwellers is quite tumultuous.*

Since he left for new duties, other missionaries took turns, and the task
was later handed over to Light-Network members. The transference from
one to another has always worked because all of them are united around
a single purpose: to serve those that few want to serve.

Besides offering comfort, they can arrange bus tickets for those who prefer to leave or want to attend a recovery center to quit drugs.

The assisted people themselves learned to take on the daily house chores. The meals are fixed by them, and they share the maintenance and cleaning of the house common areas. They themselves receive trekkers who wander the roads, who arrive, take a bath, wash their clothes or get new ones, eat, rest for one night or more and then leave.

The choice of living at the House of Welcome implies obeying certain rules. And most walkers and street-dwellers don't want to have any order. If the person being assisted accepts the proposed lifestyle, he is evaluated and may stay. Once, a young man happened to arrive having walked all the way from São Paulo. During a fight, he killed a person in self-defense, was sentenced to a year in jail and had already served the sentence. But he could not cope with his terrible guilt. As it happens with others, someone at the bus station advised him: *Listen, there's a house around the corner, by the church, where you can get everything for free.* Then he came and decided to stay.

The missionary Luiz says: *We have no expectation. A person may do very well at their arrival, and the next day, go away. The house also welcomes those who sleep by the church square here in front. They spend some time here, even months, but then prefer to go back there. They keep coming back to eat and bring others along. Although they can't stand living here anymore, the place has become a good reference point. As we always talk to them in the street, a network of friendliness has been born.*

One December, street-dweller brothers and friends of the house celebrated its first get-together. When the time comes to serve the food, the bell rings. An exhausted old hungry man asks if he could eat something. *His name was José. It was Christmas! Wow, what a man's name! We immediately regarded him as a mystical visitor. He ate like a king, took a bath, slept. The next day he said he had to leave, thanked us and we never saw him again. What matters is the experience in itself, not rebuilding someone's life, like: "Now they will have jobs and this kind of thing." This house is beautiful,* said the coordinator who welcomed José.

Missionary Practices: I'm going!

Participate in the next Missionary Practice
and serve the most needy. The place for
this practice will be in Carmo da Cachoeira,
Minas Gerais, Brazil

A single army of servers expands throughout the four corners of the world. Even without knowing it, educators, scientists, financiers, men and women of any area and age compose this brave group. With intelligence and international vision, they work for the good of humanity and for the understanding among peoples and nations. The servers break down social barriers and prejudices and quietly build the foundation of future universal peace. They are linked to a subtle high potency network surrounding the Earth, protecting it and, little by little, healing it.

Some humans dare to plunge into the dizzying wave of transformation that summons everyone. They advance along diverse paths. The missionaries of Fraternidade have chosen to follow one of the paths, the one of unconditional service.

A month and a half after the primary group moved into two houses in Carmo da Cachoeira, the *Missionary Practices,* called *Vivências Missionárias,* was opened to introduce apprentices to the missionary life.

The consecrated missionary Imer, coordinator of numerous meetings, says: *I am happy to participate in the awakening of self-summoned people. They begin to realize the urgency in relieving the pain burning in themselves and in the world. They wake up to the truth awaiting us beyond the chaos and the horrors that spread through this dying civilization. I am willing to do anything. Whatever happens, I am open to being an instrument of the Divine.*

For one week, the apprentices who enrolled face a succession of challenges. If well understood and assimilated, this experience can lead them to a new vision of the world. The exercises are alive, loving and happen close to nature. They bring about unification among the participants, changing spaces in the inner world of each one.

For the first events, about 10,000 invitations were sent by e-mail in Portuguese, Spanish and English—a number that gradually diminished. The person reads the invitation, and their soul may say: *Yes, I want to experience missionary life!* And they enroll. Others find out about the missions through the website Fraternidade and make contact, wishing to participate.

People are awakening. The idea of enjoyment during one's vacation still permeates the collective consciousness seduced by temporal things. However, there are those who use it to do something positive and they summon themselves. They put a backpack on their shoulders including personal belongings, bed and bath linen, and toiletries. They leave fantasy and start their practical exercise.

In five years, six thousand people have been through the Missionary Practices. Although this model gives some experience to the participants, they rarely embrace a life dedicated to the Missions. Therefore, in mid-2018, the Missionary Academy was planned as a preparation path for primary missionaries through specialized modules.

At the first meeting, apprentices get together in a circle to introduce themselves and be listened to: *My name is etc., I am here for such and such reason.* They come from the most diverse places. The stories told by each one echoes in others: *What you said touched me, I was surprised, it confirms what I had already realized.* Many have read Trigueirinho books and regard his teaching as a guide. Their outdated individualistic concepts are plunged into a group life. The doors of fraternal coexistence gradually open as they share small collective men's or women's bedrooms.

The primary missionary presents the activities and explains the week logistics, where the daily group services will take place: in institutions, in the missionaries houses or some area of the community, where they will

Songs of service opening in nearby town, planting of trees and training in tree climbing. Carmo da Cachoeira, Minas Gerais, Brazil, between 2014 and 2017

be able to stay overnight on farms. They become a role model, accompaning and acting together with the group. Only by doing can one learn.

One Missionary Practice is never similar to another. Here, the participants go through completely different experiences from those of their daily life. They walk in a line in streets or on farms. They make contact with the beauty of the greenery, with broad horizons and with lakes, tall trees, animals. They may attend a meeting of Alcoholics Anonymous, play with disabled children, visit prisons, go to a home for recovery of addicts, take clothes to the needy.

There are unforeseen and striking situations. In two circumstances, city residents that the missionaries had assisted passed away. The coordinator participated in the funerals taking young apprentices who had never experienced anything like this.

Imer says: *At first, of course, resistance, discomfort begins to emerge among the apprentices. But soon, they feel renewed by the intense daily rhythm, which leaves no time for anyone to be discouraged or to complain. As soon as we wake up, we gather for group prayers. Then, always together, we clean the house, prepare and take the meals.*

In general, people are used to walking alone, doing whatever they please at their own pace. During the practice, none of this happens. Some say that, at the beginning, integrating into group life was difficult and eventually became wonderful. Once, a young woman went out on her own to buy a ticket at the bus station. On her way back, she felt terribly lonely and burst into tears. When she left the group, she could feel the loneliness that is caused by our old individualism.

The time each apprentice needs for reconstruction depends on themselves. Most human beings are rebellious, as the kind who say: *You are not my boss!* Clashes can occur for insignificant things, such as refusing to wear a shirt as directed by the coordinator.

The apprentice passes through several external and inner tests until they understand that, without obedience, one cannot develop well. Ricardo, Manager of Emergencies and Humanitarian Aid, keeps repeating: *A missionary must have seven attributes. The first is obedience. The second, obedience; the third, fourth, fifth, sixth, and seventh are obedience. If we learn how to obey, other attributes develop naturally.*

As they forget about themselves, some begin to understand what love for their neighbor is. One participant says in awe: *Hey, for twenty-four hours I have not thought of myself. I cannot believe it!* By giving priority to the other, he discovered the spirit of cooperation, what the soul came to do in this life, that is, serving others with dedication. The other can be any human being, any animal, plant, water, mineral.

The magic is that each apprentice goes through what they most need to feel free. There are cases of people who find out that a specific human relationship is blocking their evolution. In the nursing home, you can find a person who is similar to your mother and solve a particular conflict. This type of synchronicity is often reported. Alternatively, in a prison, a person meets a young man that looks like their brother or ex-fiancé. They are blessed by the certainty of the help received from their inner Guides, always around, and feel immense serenity with these invisible companions.

It's a joy to be in a group! There is always something to learn, to contribute, to share. Training instigates a healthy mental and emotional restructuring and, above all, brings about the maturing of faith. Every night there are meetings and an exchange of things learned so that each member may be aware of what is happening in the heart of their fellow being.

Here are testimonies of participants in the 34th Missionary Practice, coordinated by Mariandja:

By Rosi: *How did I feel when I paid attention to the trees and the thicket? In the ample labyrinth space of the F2 farm of Figueira, there were leaves and branches fallen off towering eucalyptus trees planted in circumference around the labyrinth. During our task, I felt an inner movement as if we were removing what does not belong to us for life to flow gently. The trees inspired us to go higher in search of beauty and light, just like them. Walking along the stone path of the round labyrinth represents our trajectory to the encounter of our true self. Sometimes we almost reach the goal. Sometimes we get involved with distractions, and we distance ourselves from the purpose. But we keep walking because we want to return to our Source, symbolized by the center of the labyrinth toward which the path converges.*

By Anderson, who was being prepared to participate in the Roraima Mission: *How did I feel in the Francis of Assisi Park, a refuge for dogs?*

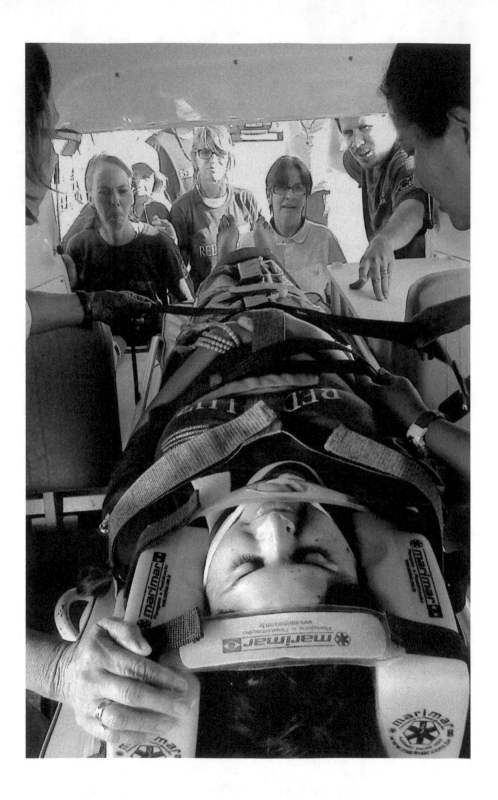

A missionary feels no boundaries. I listened to the barking of the dogs as if they were a symphony of someone calling for help. During a few hours of hard work, we were able to do a minimum for the sake of four hundred dogs. There was an exchange: they helped us to persevere on our path of the giving of ourselves.

Then they listened to Sueli Poeta: *How did I feel in the collective work in the Shed of Saint Joseph? It was a party today. We gave away more than five hundred pieces of clothing, donated mattresses, the children played peacefully, no rowdiness. I felt so much love in the people receiving the donations! I'm going to alter a dress for a bride to beautifully enter the church. We were exhausted, but it was great!*

Everyone laughed, agreeing. Yes, physically exhausted, but they were shining and full of vitality to apply the lesson to life from now on.

Many things can change in those few days. In the closing of the event, there is a meeting in which each apprentice expresses themselves and some share mature examples. Imer says: *Sometimes thirty people sum up their small story. They give impressive testimonies and there is so much crying! They feel super-touched by what was lived, by old concepts broken, by their effort to transform, reduce egocentrism, to lift their spirit.*

The apprentices are invited to expand this experience staying for three months in the missionary houses, to be able to cope with complicated emergencies. Roraima Mission also needs help and, now, they can participate. Those who are receptive accept the invitation.

Living in a mission within the whole apparatus of a Light-Community is one facet of service. Taking a plane to help refugees is another facet which unveils viewpoints of the Planetary Service Network.

To conclude, a coordinator raises her eyes to the sky: *In the Missionary Practices, we build a bridge between Heaven and Earth. Look at the sign, at first the sky was silent. Now the deva of the winds is giving us a shower of leaves as a gift. Our gratitude, Nature, for all you give us!*

One of the many first-aid training meetings.
Carmo da Cachoeira, Minas Gerais, Brazil, 2014

PERMANENT GREECE MISSION

To ignite consciousnesses

Do not wait until a crisis arises to
find out what is essential in your life.
Plato, Greek philosopher

Greece has a fascination for universal imagination. The small country attracts tens of millions of tourists who believe in a good life. Officially called the Hellenic Republic, it is home to eleven million inhabitants, lovely people who maintain their traditions. However, beyond the emerald sea, the paradisaic islands, the mythical Mount Olympus, and ancient monuments, statues, philosophy and culture, are multiple hidden facets of people in need.

The Fraternidade established itself for twenty-one months at the Greece Missionary Base, in the Palaia Fokea mountain range. Then started to collaborate with organized groups: the Missionaries of Charity, Caritas Hellas, the Orthodox Church of St. Theodore and the Young Volunteers in Action.

At first glance, Athens looks like the postcard of a healthy city, but you just need to walk a little beyond the illusory appearance to come across its brutal side. Street dwellers and miserable makeshift tents are an image illustrating the other side of the capital.

Over the last ten years, the hilly peninsula has been profoundly affected by the severe economic crisis of 2008, followed by the greatest humanitarian crisis since World War II, the refugee crisis.

The country's unemployment is rising. One-third of the population lives in poverty. More than one million workers have no source of income, and more than 500,000 Greeks have left the country since 2008.

Mortality increases. Pessimism is spreading and suicide rates have doubled. Greeks of the ascending middle class lose their homes and cars for which they were still paying, and cease to have social status. In a few months, the homeless begin to sleep outdoors, near the luxury shops where they used to go shopping in the tourist district and the Parliament. Former wage-earners and merchants owning three, four-store houses in excellent areas, like so many countrymen, cannot afford to pay electricity, water or telephone bills, food or clothing. As they do not want to get exposed, they refuse to follow queues to receive food and donations. They are being called "the new poor".

The missionaries found a dog on the street with a note stuck on his collar: *My name is Kriko, I am cheerful, I am vaccinated, but my owner is in trouble, she cannot take care of me any longer. Please, take me to your home.*

For the newly poor to survive, a social assistance program registers them. On nightly excursions, volunteers who keep the names of the needy in secrecy go door to door knocking, delivering food and clothing kits. The missionaries never had direct contact with the new poor. However, they brought donations for the program.

Sometimes a family breaks down. There are lonely men in the ranks of the Missionaries of Charity or those of Caritas Hellas, the Greek Caritas. Ricardo says: *I talked to an educated and intelligent gentleman who spoke four languages, but was ruined. Life made him stumble and fall. Skinny, with disheveled hair. He was taken off his alignment somehow, disoriented. Losing the basics shakes one's consciousness. He had had a good financial position as a ship captain, having come to Brazil a few times, but when his wife died, he went through a crisis and lost his job. Today he is assisted by the Missionaries of Charity.*

The missionaries never visited the Acropolis or other famous sites, only the Temple of Poseidon, which Anastasia made a point of their visiting it. She founded and has been coordinating the Young Volunteers in Action group for 40 years. They are located 8 miles from the Missionary Base of Fraternidade, which temporarily closed the doors in June 2018.

Since the day Anastasia asked the Fraternidade to tidy up a warehouse that held an enormous amount of donations, the joy in helping fellow beings united both groups. Anastasia deeply loves the country that welcomed her ancestors. Enthusiastically she led the missionaries to the temple on Cape Sounio, at the southernmost tip of Greece. There, in front of the Aegean Sea, they marveled at the dance of the shimmering waters that hide stories and the essence of the golden age of the ancient civilization.

Today, this sea is the preferred escape route for Asian refugees who head to Greek islands. Clandestine inflatable boats can be seen every day on the horizon. In orange life jackets and salted skin, they step on the ground, pray and kiss the sand, grateful to be safe from insane wars, religious radicalism, and the hazardous journey in which thousands drown. Since this sea route has been heavily policed, Syrians and Turks seek an even more dangerous alternative, to cross the Evros River, the also heavily patrolled Greece and Turkey border. Exhausted, frozen and lost, many died in brutal ways.

Being a strategic spot between Europe, Asia, the Middle East, and Africa, Greece welcomes immigrants of over one hundred nationalities, who delude themselves by dreaming of a better future. Few of them manage to settle down in a dignified way, either there, or in neighboring countries. Mostly in 2015 Greece was the destination of hordes of Syrian, Iraqi, Tunisian, Iranian and Pakistani refugees, among other nationalities. More than one million of them have crossed the Greek mainland towards central and northern Europe, but with the closure of the Balkan route, 70,000 remain stuck in the country.

The Greeks try to cope with the challenges and abysses of these times, which are far from over. They wait for help from the European Community. What an extraordinary opportunity for leaders to embrace peace!

It was about midnight on a Friday at the Greek Missionary Base. In Minas Gerais, Brazil, the time of *Angelus* was approaching. Just at that time I had a meeting via Skype with two primary missionaries, who were coming back from a meeting. They began to outline their weekly routine during the last year of intense service to others.

The first idea of a Fraternidade headquarters in Greece was to reinvigorate those returning from Middle-East missions. As these missions were suspended, the instructor Trigueirinho recommended the missionaries should interact with the Missionaries of Charity of Mother Teresa of Calcutta, who have two houses in Athens. The interaction of the two groups

Middle East and African refugees wait at the door of Caritas.
Athens, Greece, 2016

had begun in Nepal and in five African countries.

In dealing with these beings of kindness, the missionaries practiced obedience and acceptance. Although they are strict on Catholic religion subjects, over the months both groups wove a joyful soul relationship. The Missionaries began to help the Sisters in the house where they host mothers with children until they are referred to another place. In the second house, the missionaries prepared and provided breakfast for about fifty immigrants, refugees and people in need who hang around the place waiting for lunchtime. They would wash dishes, clean the kitchen and the house, organize and distribute the abundant donations the Sisters receive.

If requested by the Missionaries of Charity, they doubled their daily working hours. After lunch, the Sisters retreated and occasionally invited them to worship Christ together. They resumed activities at 3 p.m.

Since they have a pickup truck, but do not drive, the missionaries became their drivers and porters. Every week, on certain afternoons, they drove in Athens busy streets and avenues where sirens won't stop blaring. Now, they took them to buy food or to collect fruit and vegetables discarded in good condition in the market, with which they prepared food kits. The Sisters also took them to visit prisons, where they took food and clothing to support prisoners.

Ricardo recalls: *One day, the Sisters rented a bus to take the street-dwellers, who have lunch at their house daily, to a nearby beach, where there was a church. At the picnic, we helped them serve the meal and then we were asked to clean the area.*

The Sisters asked them to do challenging repair work; a clogged pipe, a broken faucet. They hardly knew where to start, but in the end everything got fixed. There were sudden requests, such as to clean and paint, with a few exiled people, a house in precarious condition lent by the Greek government to a Moroccan immigrant with her four children.

Missionaries took a subway and a bus going back home at the end of the day. A Spanish lady and an Argentinian man would walk along offering products given away by the Sisters to street-dwellers, such as noodles, milk, fruit and industrialized foods. In the icy winter, they also gave away gloves, scarves, coats. Then one day they noticed: neither of the two spoke the local language, they would just pray and radiate love, as Christ had told the Apostles to do 2000 years ago.

About five hundred people moved daily around Caritas Hellas, a Catholic service segment where work volunteers from various nations gathered and also studied in local colleges. Two of these people were from China, who fled their country due to religious persecution. The missionaries helped the organization. Now cleaning the entrance of the building, now organizing German donations, boxes with clothes, accessories, footwear, blankets, milk for children. Ricardo describes: *Early in the morning, two days a week, we would travel 37 miles to the center of Athens. Caritas remunerates volunteers with the purpose of developing efficient solidary social actions. As for us, we always served free of charge.*

Regularly they also sorted out and distributed the incoming clothes for more than eighty people a day. They put away on different shelves women, men and children's clothes. Ricardo goes on: *Imagine the patient work, the persistence: a person picks up a piece of cloth, looks, dislikes, throws it in a corner. We pick it up, fold it, and return it to the shelf.*

Missionaries distribute donations in the streets, organize a warehouse in Lagonise and serve lunch to 50 to 80 homeless people, mostly men, in Athens. Greece, 2016 and 2017

One piece more and another, and still another, and each time we take it, fold it, put it back on the shelf.

On Saturdays, they would help in the Orthodox Church of St. Theodore, in the town of Anavyssos. This religion has two hierarchical lines, that of monks, who do not marry and live in monasteries such as Mount Athos, and that of local priests, who are in charge of the church, the community and can have a wife and children. In the beginning, the missionaries only took part in the preparation of the lunches, distributed clothes, and assembled bags and food kits for Greeks in an increasingly difficult situation. Soon the relationship unfolded into friendly ties with the traditionally dressed in black priest, *patéra or πατέρα*, and his wife.

Active in the service, the priest rescued 150 children from the Bosnian war. Families in his community cared for them until the end of the war, when they were taken back home. While bombs exploded on his journey through the neighboring country, the *patéra* distributed food stocked in the trunk of his car.

Little by little, missionaries began sharing church life, from watching folk dance and music presentations to helping to cook and serve during seminars and gatherings. Imer recalls: *There a man usually doesn't help with cleaning and cooking. They were surprised in seeing a male volunteer and with a profession—a dentist!—cleaning, cooking, doing everything as willingly and as skillfully as any woman.*

Every three months, the group rotated. Once, the newly-arrived decided to introduce themselves by reading a message in Greek to the Orthodox. The *patéras* invited Imer to the stage. Having learned the reading in the unknown language, he greeted them: *Kalimera or Καλημέρα*, good morning in Greek. He went on: *We came from Argentina and Brazil to help the church, and we are very happy to be here.* No reaction from the audience. Did they understand? He also introduced the rest of the group, who went on stage. Other closing words and... and there came a cheerful applause.

From that moment on, they became part of the great and playful Orthodox family. The *mama*, the grandmother, who cooked for street-dwellers, adopted Imer. They felt immense love for each other. The mama shared news about her granddaughter's marriage or other issues with her son and had fun with Imer's accent when he repeated Greek words.

Making contact with a street-dweller.
Athens, Greece, May 2017

They had been introduced to the Orthodox priest and his wife by the couple who owned the Missionary Base, the house on a hill 1.2 mile from the sea. The devout merchant shipowner had built it for the son who, at the time, chose to take part in a mission in India to living in the sophisticated and modern mansion with white marble staircases.

The invisible hands of destiny had the merchant meet two representatives of the Fraternidade and the Brazilian woman who would pay for the rent of a building. The three were looking for a place in South Athens to implement their headquarters. The shipowner himself showed them around the residence, and soon after invited them for a snack with him and his wife in the gardens of their beautiful townhouse in the vicinity.

They were drinking natural juices when the man asked them how much they had for the rent. *Well, something less than the market value...* He did not hesitate, but accepted immediately: *That's it, it's a deal.* They should go to his office to sign the contract. And the merchant ordered his lawyer to remove several items from the mutual agreement.

For the cost of a stripped-down property, they rented the mansion in a wealthy district. The opulent residence is entirely out of their standard of simplicity. Life set the curious juncture for them to break prejudices and live a test of the vow of detachment to wealth. Sobriety guided them to furnish the house. They bought Franciscan beds, a refrigerator, a small table for the kitchen, and put yoga mats in the prayer room, the main room of the house. There, they asked for divine blessings to be poured out on the planet, and they followed broadcasts of events for peace and lectures by Light-Communities instructors.

The shipowner and his wife became good friends. He himself introduced them to the Orthodox Church, a Christian faith followed by almost all Greeks. They were overjoyed by the missionaries' carefulness with the mansion and the gardens surrounded by trees, a perfect place to recover from constant service in the harsh metropolis where citizens protest and await solutions to their lives.

Having settled down, their next step would be to register the FIHF in the country. The organization's lawyer in Portugal recommended a Greek colleague, with whom he had studied in England.

As the Greek lawyer would need to know the Brazilian statute, the missionaries spent three days translating it into English. Soon after that, the lawyer gave them a call: *I read the statute. That changed my life. The way you look at life is wonderful. Your work is wonderful!*

When they met for the signing of the statute in Greek, the lawyer warned them: *I wrote a note saying that, as you don't know the local language, I am reading the document aloud, in English, so that you may be made aware.* Ricardo said: *I believe in you, doctor.* The lawyer says: *Now we need to register it, but it's hard, we know a group that has been trying for two years.*

As time passed, and he couldn't get the official register, they decided to confront the bureaucracy as a threesome, the lawyer and two missionaries. He was quite assertive in talking with the clerk, in Greek, as if they were arguing. Then the three were sent to a boss, who put a stamp on the sheet. They went back to the clerk, and the lawyer said: *She doesn't want to approve it. I don't think it's going to work.*

The unintelligible set in. The missionary women sat down in a little corner, picked up the rosary, and, in silence, passed the beads. The clerk was asking for the service code of a specific book. *My God*, said the lawyer, *where do I find this?* He called his accountant, got the number, handed the papers to the clerk.

They never figured out how the document left her hands and ended up in front of a colleague, a gentleman in the booth next to her. He flipped the pages of the document, talked to the lawyer, went through them again, took the stamp and started stamping each one of the pages. The lawyer was speechless. It seemed like a miracle. He looked at the coordinator, at the missionary passing the rosary beads through her fingers. *Keep praying*, he whispered.

The male clerk got the papers together, and handed them over. They left. *I can't believe it*, repeated the lawyer. His faith grew. Since then, he asked them for prayers for hearings in court, such as that of a mother who might lose her son: *Please pray for me*. And it helped them in other situations.

After the entity was officially included in the list of humanitarian organizations operating in Greece, the missionaries went to a meeting to present it to the Brazilian Ambassador and to the Citizenship Council, which represents the local Brazilian community of 4,000 people.

Service unites, and whoever is on duty sees no barriers. The Fraternidade became a neutral bridge between religions and local entities in a mutual transfer of donations. Because of the lack of previous exchanges between the service groups, the missionaries began a previously non-existent activity: transferring the surplus from one to the other. They moved clothing of the Young Volunteers in Action to Caritas Hellas. The Sisters would give them leftover items to be passed on to the new poor or the street-dwellers. The Orthodox said: *Take it to the little sisters.*

Everyone knows everyone and that the members of the Fraternidade make up an ecumenical group that travels between religions and gets along with different rituals. They might get invited to attend a Mass in English at the Catholic chapel of St. Joseph on Friday or to commemorate the Assumption of Mary in Greek with the Orthodox on Sunday.

They celebrated Easter at the *patéras'* house. By tradition, they should roast a goat, but the missionaries are vegetarian. Family friends would come and go. They thought they themselves would leave soon, but no. Ricardo recalls: *We stayed with the family. Four prepared vegetarian food dishes that were placed on a long table: Greek salad, grape-leaf rolls stuffed with rice and herbs. We then spent the afternoon looking at photos, and listening to their stories. It was beautiful! They thanked us, not only our work but also for calming them down when they were about to lose peace.* They gave the group the typical Orthodox cross, and a book with old photos of the region where they were born: stone houses, sheep, fields covered with olive trees.

In September 2017, the unexpected news came to them. Another cycle of work would start. In two weeks, all primary missionaries, obeying the sacred vow of obedience, should be at the Roraima Permanent Mission in Brazil. The missionary Shen says: *It was a surprise, but that's normal. We are always ready for a new beginning. In this activity, we know that life can be something today, and entirely different tomorrow.*

The European Light-Network, affiliated to the Light-Community Flower of Lys, a branch of the FIHF located in Frazoeira, near the village of Dornes, Portugal, took up the focus in Greece. For a week, the last missionaries and three volunteers were together to go over the tasks that builds a fraternal love to overcome suffering.

The primary missionary coordinating the headquarters in the transition ponders: *As missionaries, we have chosen to live according to a format of service of constant surrender, readiness, obedience, sacrifice, dynamism. When an emergency arises, we don't hesitate but, in the case of Greece, the mission takes place day-to-day. The main thing is to touch hearts, being a bridge so that the Divine can reactivate codes of hope in those who receive help. The main thing is that the other person is able to believe again in the existence of good people.*

Food is meant for celebration and communion. The Holy Supper is an example to bid farewell, they offered a Brazilian lunch for Anastasia and European brothers and sisters: rice with beans, soy protein with potatoes and olives, and a large salad mixed with olive oil extracted from the long lived and generous olive trees mentioned in the Bible, trees that, century after century, have offered fruits for restless human generations. As a dessert, Anastasia served a Greek semolina lemon and chocolate pie.

For months, the European Light-Network have radiated peace. Their members loved and were grateful for every action and to everyone they met. With discreet joy, they glorified Life, did their best and delivered the result to the universal glory.

PART V

Roraima Permanent Mission
Brazil

You were not forgotten

Divine and powerful Mount Roraima,
sacred cosmic wonder, you guard the
archetype of the future race on Earth.
Mount Roraima,
song by Vera Lúcia Noronha,
from Boa Vista Light-Network

Waves of life run through the cosmos. In changes to the evolutionary cycles, they move from one universe to another, from a kingdom to another, from a planet to another. Across the Earth, smaller waves move between continents and countries. Migratory currents that set off to meet the unknown leave a trail of pain and human tragedy. Nearly seventy million people, half of them under the age of eighteen, are forced to escape their homeland due to conflicts.

In South America, an estimated 3 million women, men and children have left Venezuela since 2014. The exodus grew in the last three years. Most of them go to Colombia and from there spread out into fifteen countries of the three Americas and some of Europe. Tens of thousands have come to Brazil, counting on international protection and solidarity. A mass of Venezuelans enter neighboring countries daily, where they settle down or move to more distant places.

They escape the hunger, unemployment, food shortage, hyperinflation, violence and political instability installed in the Bolivarian Republic of Venezuela. Hoping for a better life, they feel the pain of leaving their homeland. Some leave behind their homes, their belongings, leave behind children, parents, friends, professions.

They come from ugly and dirty cities with broken traffic lights and, everywhere, burned tires marks, called *guarimbas*, made during the constant protests meant to draw the world's attention. While streets are filled with demonstrators, the market shelves are empty. Some emigrate so as not to be arrested for having spoken out against the government.

Schools, where children faint from hunger, are closed. The health system is in collapse. Patients die on the floor of overcrowded hospitals, families lose sick members due to lack of medication in pharmacies and medical care. Physicians, teachers, engineers leave the country. Refugees and migrants have no way of buying tickets nor places to go. They leave Caracas on foot. On the way, they run out of money, children die or are run over by cars. Indigenous people travel nearly 600 miles by canoe or bus, hitchhiking.

As the human crisis deepens, greed for money and power seems endless. The nation itself and other nations lust for Venezuela's ores: diamond, gold, oil, and coltan, used in most portable electronic devices.

A journalist from Venezuela visiting Pacaraima reports: *Every day, the border is packed with people. I have a small car, and I do not even know how many I brought from there to here. I offer a ride to those who walk, and I leave them just before the barricade. They cry when they say goodbye to Venezuela. In Brazil, they improvise tents on the sidewalks of the street that goes from the border to the bus station. Still, we sustain the joy of living, until the tares are separated from the wheat.*

White cement landmarks carved with the name Brazil, on one side, Venezuela, on the other, indicate the 1,250 mile international border. Countless newcomer's cross irregular routes through mountains or the savanna. Twenty-two indigenous communities live close to this border and, to prevent entrance of drugs and weapons, the border is continuously monitored by helicopters from the Jungle Battalion.

A daily flow of hundreds of Venezuelans appears on the asphalt road linking the two countries. After being received at the border checkpoint of Pacaraima, municipality of Roraima, the state at the northern tip of Brazil, they go through a reception center. At the Sanitary Screening Station, each participant is vaccinated by the National Sanitary Surveillance Agency, ANVISA, because many bring diseases eradicated here in Brazil.

The UNHCR is an organization created by the United Nations in 1950 and charged with providing assistance, peace, justice and protection of persons displaced by a government as the result of war, persecution or other reason. At a Reception and Identification Office, it registers and guides the Venezuelans on Brazilian entry rules, indicating the best route into the country, providing them with a permanency permit.

Roraima, Brazil's least populous state, started facing a crisis because it lacks human and material resources to meet the multifaceted demands, which multiplies at an accelerated pace and magnitude. Refugees and migrants yearn for jobs and better services offered by larger urban centers. Therefore, from Roraima, thousands are taken by plane to Brazilian capitals with wider employment opportunities, and some pilgrimage into other countries.

Inhabited by natives before the colonial period, Roraima was in the route of migratory currents. The first Portuguese settlers crossed the lands by sailing Branco River. Through these waters, the English and the Dutch sought Indians to enslave. Spaniards invaded the region. Three hundred years ago, Carmelite missionaries began the conversion of native people to Catholicism. In the last decades, especially in the 1990s, migrants arrived from the Northeast, North, and South of Brazil, attracted by the illusory possibility of getting rich easily with gold mining. Also, by governmental promotion of facilities, such as free food and urban land in the periphery of the capital.

Since 2015, once the border is crossed, the Venezuelans move towards Boa Vista by car, bus, taxi, bicycle. Those without money to purchase tickets do their journey on foot. Families with children, pregnant women, elderly people walk down the Pacaraima Mountain Range along the road lined with native forest, picking nuts and banana clusters, most of them green. Hungry and thirsty, they sustain themselves on water with sugar in plastic bottles.

Coming from 3,300 feet of altitude, they reach 330 feet above sea level, a slightly undulating savanna covered with grass. They traverse endless stretches of straight one-way road on the hot asphalt pavement without shoulders, among indigenous reserves of the desolate landscape bathed by intense light. They get past small isolated lagoons, clumps of scattered trees or *buritizeiros*, majestic palms regarded as sacred by the Venezuelan Warao people. The walkers get some relief when they cross the bridge over the Branco River, where they can bathe. Finally, they reach Boa Vista, the only Brazilian capital above the Equator. The planned, hot, flat green city seems to have no horizon. The sky, so close, calls the contemplative to infinity. Its streets have taken on new facets after the immigrants arrived dreaming of starting a new life where they can bring their wife and children.

In June 2018, there was an estimated population of twenty-five thousand Venezuelans in Boa Vista, a city with 330,000 inhabitants. In 2019, over six thousand Venezuelans housed in 13 shelters of Boa Vista and Pacaraima. Others camp in the streets or rent houses in group, where they sleep on the floor of the rooms, in the corridors or on the porch.

What to do for them

The non-governmental organization Fraternidade went to give comfort to indigenous Venezuelan families sheltered around Passarão Fair market. On the first day of November 2016, thirty volunteers left, most of them from the Southeast region of Brazil, to be part of the first group of the Roraima Permanent Mission—ten missionaries, six nuns of Grace Mercy Order, and fourteen Light-Network collaborators from the Northeast of Brazil and those from the host city.

They found a chaotic place. At their first approach, hungry native indigenous people pulled at their clothes asking for food. At once, the thirty split into service groups. One group knocked on doors of food shops for donations, when a shopkeeper offered them the use of his kitchen. They bought pots, spoons, and a gas cylinder, and while some were preparing the collected food, others went to the streets to inform them: *We'll have a meal later on, we'll have dinner.*

From that night onwards the missionaries served a daily dinner at Passarão Fair, where refugees spent the night, and also in other parts of the city. They also provided cardboard for those who slept on the cement. The missionary's loyal and affectionate presence brought them hope and was the best remedy to encourage them.

Focused on humanitarian assistance in the Passarão Fair, besides the dinner meals, they donated clothing and did activities with the children: playing, drawing, playing the guitar, singing. Starting medical consultations, they took an indigenous minor to the hospital with severe malnutrition. The media started making reports, and news about the first humanitarian assistance coming from elsewhere spread throughout the city.

At a traffic light, a Venezuelan asks people for a job;
a meeting with indigenous people at Passarão Fair;
food distribution. Boa Vista, Roraima, Brazil, 2017 and 2018

First dinner meals offered to Venezuelan indigenous refugees.
Passarão Fair, Boa Vista, Roraima, Brazil, 2016

Meanwhile, another group set up a newly rented house. The Sacred Light-Nucleus Tepui of Roraima was the first reference place for missionaries to stay and have meals. Beyond this, the production of a nutrient-rich flour called multi-mixture began to be distributed among the needy.

Known for their hospitality and friendship, many Brazilians were reluctant to cooperate. They rejected foreign neighbors asking for help without having, at first sight, anything to offer in return. There was tension among shopkeepers, who began to demand actions from the Civil Defense or the police to settle the issue. They said that in 2015 there were a few refugees, but the situation had now become chaotic. They pointed out the native people were peaceful and there were no episodes of robbery, but customers had left. They kept saying: *This is a Venezuela's problem, we already have ours, we have no jobs, we don't have this, or that.* The missionaries tried to open their heart: *They are not here because they want to be. Today it's them, and tomorrow it may be us. No one is immune to a crisis.*

To see volunteers coming from far away to do charity was impressive, it gave the local population an impulse to be more tolerant.

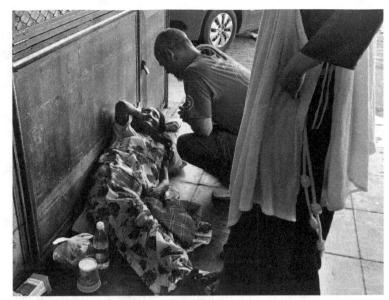

Giving assistance to a Warao indigenous person.
Boa Vista, Roraima, Brazil, 2016

Solidarity network of Boa Vista

In the scope of assistance service there are always pastors, churches, representatives of the diocese or the local parish. To get to know the solidarity network active in the city and introduce to them the work of independent humanitarian assistance of Fraternidade, the group visited political, religious and civilian organizations. They expressed their willingness to engage in joint actions on behalf of Venezuelans.

The missionaries then offered to help in the Institute of Migration and Human Rights, a Catholic Church organization, in the census of indigenous people settled at the Passarão Fair. During the registration, the migrants told them stories. Some cried for their parents who were left behind as they could not walk. They mentioned they eat every three days in Venezuela, and one of them had lost eighteen relatives to hunger and disease. The minimum wage in Venezuela—1,3 million bolivars—is barely enough to buy six loaves of bread or a chicken. An undernourished adult indigenous woman weighed 68 pounds and was hospitalized. They saw people's fingers with no nails and foot blisters for having walked for days inside their own country and another eight days from Pacaraima.

The missionaries also made contact with a shelter created by the Evangelical Church for sixty displaced persons, without distinction of religion. They also met generous citizens who accommodated up to thirty Venezuelans.

To identify the needs of different ethnicities, they visited the Casa do Índio Hospital of Roraima, an institution of the National Secretariat of the Indigenous People. Most of them did not intend to formalize their refugee status, claiming to have crossed the border only to get money, clothing, food and then return bringing all of it to their families.

The missionaries' relationship with the Civil Defense Agency of Roraima was special. It was a joy to collaborate with those who unite efforts along with other public and private entities on behalf of civil society. From the following week on, this agency would pass on to them food items and medicines. And also, they would make available a mobile health unit for the healing team of Fraternidade to expand their basic services.

Rosi describes a warning given in a visit to introduce Fraternidade to the City Council of Health of Boa Vista: *Six of us went to talk with the Secretary of Health to discuss the possibility of finding a place to assist refugees. We brought photos to alert the local authorities. The indigenous drank any kind of water and defecated and urinated outdoors, beside avenues, on trees. Showing him the pictures, I said, "These brothers and sisters need at least an environment with bathrooms. They have a culture and hygienic principles different from ours, and have serious skin problems. They can infect the people of the city, and this can become an epidemic".* He was startled, as he was not aware of the severe risk.

The group also traveled in three cars to Pacaraima finding a setting of poverty and abandonment. Dozens of people from the Warao ethnic group scattered in the streets, slept on the ground or in hammocks under decks. They begged for food and clothing, which the missionaries tried to provide.

In the last hours of their 15-day stay, the group participated in a meeting of the Integrated Cabinet of Migration Management. There were state representatives, the Civil Defense, and the Catholic Church, through the Commission on Migration and Human Rights. Throughout the conversation, Imer, the mission's coordinator, requested the opening of what he called the Care Center. The space would provide assistance to the displaced people, both in health and educational matters, but also guiding them to get official documents and other kinds of aid. The Fraternidade warned in a prognostic way: *We have little time for what will come. We must prepare ourselves because the Venezuelans will arrive in countless numbers and continuously.* However, nobody imagined the magnitude of what was about to happen.

On the same night, the missionaries passed the baton to a second group, who would be in charge of the contacted institutions list: the Diocese of Roraima—which had passed them a good stock of rice and beans, the Union of Pharmacies—which donated various toiletries and also the registration at the Ministry of Agriculture to receive seized goods. A flow of donations had been established, as well as the vow of trust from some shopkeepers at the Producers' Fair, who gave them fruits and vegetables.

Overjoyed, fifty volunteers from the first and second missions met at the airport. Thirty of them were going back home. Those arriving were greeted in a warm and kind house, ready for the labor that expands the consciousness.

Opening of the first Immigrant Reference Center

In late November the servers' aspiration materialized itself after the second Roraima Mission returned to Figueira.

The Civil Defense established the first Immigrant Reference Center, CRI. In an area lent by the Civil Construction Union, it set up chemical toilets, two tents, a truck with a mobile health unit—three offices for medical appointments, stretchers, bathrooms.

The logistics of food, health care and distribution of belongings concentrated in that place. From November 28th onwards, the missionaries would offer lunch and assist refugees seven days a week.

At the inauguration, dozens of migrants camping at the Passarão Fair and near the bus station were transported in cars and buses to the CRI. The music—guitar sounds, singing—flowed through the area. Monastics played with children, and missionaries distributed clothing, others practiced fraternal listening. Two physicians and three dentists from FIHM assisted them, and responded to two severe cases for hospitalization that afternoon.

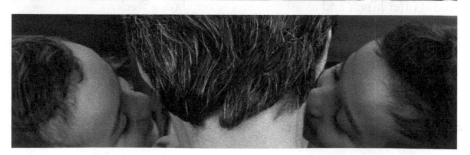

A big celebration was taking place, with the presence of government organizations and media coverage. Adding to the glory of the celebration, the meal was served. *The most important thing is that the Venezuelans trusted us, that is the crowning of the task. Some officials said this confidence made it possible to open the Immigrant Center in such a quick and harmonious way*, said Clara, the coordinator of the second group.

Closed wounds

The third Roraima Mission departed from Minas Gerais aiming at opening another service front. It included a doctor, a psychologist, a nurse, and two dentists to help indigenous people. In the Mobile Unit, the team dealt with the local chaotic health situation. Besides medical consultations, putting on bandages, and hospitalizations, it gave intense help to children with tooth aches or about to lose permanent teeth at an early age. It was assisting feverish babies and children with diarrhea, who were taken along by their mothers to beg or sell handicrafts at traffic lights, spending hours without water and exposed to the tropical sun.

An indigenous mother or aunt moved around the streets, and took the kids to have lunch at the CRI. The missionaries paid attention to the little ones, careful to prevent the hot soup from spilling on any of them.

A psychologist noticed a little indigenous girl. She was having a hard time putting the spoon to her mouth. She says: *She showed a painful shyness, and her sunburn face was spotted, looking like measles or chickenpox.* She started taking her to the office daily, to clean her skin and to talk tenderly. The case seemed severe, and the resources were few; only a non-allopathic ointment was available. The psychologist Mariandja thought: *We have this ointment and I count on the angels for treatment.* She opened the healing channel and invoked them: *Time for action!* The girl surrendered, never cried. She was about six years old. Natives guess their people's ages: they do not remember: *In nine days, when we said goodbye, her face was fully healed, quite smooth, perfect!*

A non-indigenous boy with a volunteer attitude always showed up at the consultation office to ask: *What can I do?* In the case of the little indigenous

Distribution of food and affection.
Boa Vista, Roraima, Brazil, 2016 and 2017

237

Playing with indigenous refugees. Boa Vista, Roraima, Brazil, 2016

girl, Mariandja asked him to fetch a pair of slippers, a *chola*, as they call it. The kid went to the warehouse, brought in a pair of the exact size and put them on her dirty little feet.

The psychologist explained to him that the girl was in pain, and that he could help by calling on the angels. He repeated in Spanish: *Divine Hierarchy, we open the door for Your light to come in. On behalf of Humanity, we now evoke Your Cosmic intercession.* Purity was there: *A child healed the other with his presence, his dedication, his self-sufficiency.* Silence became sacred, and the three hearts calmed down. The little indigenous girl smiled with her eyes: *I am in your hands.*

Sometime later, an indigenous grandmother came to her crying: *Please take care of my grandson.* She had come to sell handicrafts and left her daughter, her son-in-law, and this grandson in Venezuela. She did some shopping with what she had managed to earn and was taking it back to her family. When she reached the border, her little grandson was there crying to her: *Take me with you, take me with you.* He was alone, his father and mother were dead. He had come walking, hoping to find his grandmother, the only relative that remained. Mariandja recalls: *She showed the boy's sore feet, his toes in open wounds. It was painfully*

Pintolândia, the first shelter for indigenous people. Boa Vista, Roraima, Brazil, 2017

difficult for him to walk. The pain felt in those little feet is the pain of their path, the pain of the story they are living. We have never done so many foot dressings as we did in those weeks! Immigrants walk barefoot for days in the hot and rough soil. They take long detours to escape police barriers within their own country because they say the police take their money away as well as part of their belongings.

One afternoon, the health team left the clinics for a joyful moment, to watch missionaries paint children's faces with butterflies, Superman. The psychologist saw the border boy running on a scooter, his little foot learning to be a child again! Her life was profoundly touched by those little feet.

The Fraternidade has also been healing internal and external wounds in this people with various diseases: malaria, worms, tuberculosis, HIV, measles, whooping cough. Nurses treat health cases and register illnesses to notify the Army physicians offering consultations to those in shelters.

Opening of the second Immigrant Reference Center

The following groups kept up with the pace already dictated—donations of food and belongings, medical care, activities with children with sun burn. With the goal of supporting the Venezuelans, they met with representatives of local society, state and federal agencies, and gave interviews to the press.

Most aid received from entities started after the opening of the first CRI—Immigrant Reference Center. Volunteers from Boa Vista and Venezuela gradually joined the service. The registration of the assisted, with the statistics of the number of children and adults, helped more groups to collaborate.

In the meantime, the opening of a new CRI was being pondered, a place where refugees could sleep, live. On Christmas Eve, the Civil Defense took Fraternidade to the Pintolândia district, the west zone of the city. Assistance to immigrants would be transferred to a sports gym which was away from downtown, surrounded with a large area surrounded by walls. The shelter came to be popularly known as Abrigo Pintolândia.

The missionaries invited the indigenous leaders to visit the area with them. In the Warao language, the tribal leader responsible for family groups is called *aidamo*. They gave suggestions. In order to organize the space, a group cleaning with indigenous participation was scheduled. To better support the ethnicity and maintain the harmony of the shelter, they always met with the *aidamos* to discuss the standards of coexistence. The idea of a communal garden was also brought up on the first visit. During the 2018 rains, the vegetable garden produced watermelon, melon, banana, lettuce, pumpkin, chives and pigeon peas which were nourishing the earth.

Then, on December 28, 2016, indigenous people and creoles—descendants of Spanish born in the American continent—were gradually transported with their belongings to the Immigrant Reference Center. Indigenous taken off the streets, from the Passarão Fair or abandoned houses never resisted. There, they started to receive more assistance, although they still sleep on the floor of the sports plaza. The place and its services were slowly organized, as well as the lodging, the meals, the cleaning, the sanitary condition. At the same time, for over a year, missionaries kept delivering food to those who still remained sitting next to the bus station or gathered at traffic lights.

Sixty days before the Pintolândia Shelter was inaugurated, the pioneer group had served their first dinner at the Passarão Fair. At the time, there were no effective actions to protect the hundreds of displaced people in Boa Vista, nor clear plans to deal with them in the future. The missionaries took immediate action. This attracted more and more partners. And the reliability of national and international bodies and institutions that, since then, have relied on the Fraternidade as a support base to Venezuelan refugees and migrants.

One of the primary roles of Fraternidade was to give society time to think and take action. After a few months, the logistics to deal with the migratory emergency were organized. The UN, observing the missionary action, invited FIHF to be their partner through the UNHCR. On August 31, 2017, the two entities working for planetary peace signed the first agreement.

As the Brazilian President visited Roraima six months later, an inter-ministerial committee run by the Ministry of Defense and the Civil House became responsible for actions on the migratory crisis through the Brazilian Army Welcome Operation. To provide emergency support to vulnerable Venezuelans, on March 14, 2018, a scale-up of humanitarian assistance joined federal, state and city forces to international agencies and non-governmental organizations.

Twelve shelters were opened by November 2018. In them, the Brazilian Army is in charge of primary health care and provides food, security, building renovation and improvement of infrastructure. The UNHCR, supported by partners, such as Fraternidade, takes care of the management and registration of participants.

In May 2018, the missionaries offered daily voluntary support to five shelters. In Boa Vista—Abrigo Pintolândia, Abrigo Tancredo Neves, Abrigo Nova Canaã, House of Welcome, and also one indigenous refugee shelter in Pacaraima, called Janokoida Shelter.

Fraternal love for Venezuelans

*Roraima Mission comes to bring hope to our
hearts. Hope that our tired brothers, the indigenous
people, so mistreated and outraged by the world,
may take their place again in society and
may someday recover the archetypal codes
originated in the sacred Indigenous Consciousness.*
Testimony of an indigenous person

In Roraima, there are two shelters for indigenous people. The one in Boa Vista housed a little more than one hundred people when it was inaugurated. A year and a half later it had about seven hundred residents. Janokoida, in Pacaraima, was opened ten months later. As more Venezuelans escaped their country, many with just the clothes they were wearing, non-indigenous shelters were also settled in Boa Vista.

The Fraternidade groups are rotated and travel 3,000 miles to do so. They are determined to rescue the indigenous and prevent non-indigenous people, called *criollos*, from being shipwrecked in a sea of hopelessness.

Immigrants arriving speak no Portuguese, they are undernourished, sick, wounded by what they leave behind, just as the young woman who watched her husband being murdered by the police during the looting of a truck laden with food, a common scene in this hunger ridden country.

In the beginning, the indigenous were suspicious of receiving missionary help. In their country, they say, all aid is exchanged by votes. And indigenous people have no idea what political voting means. They feared the Brazilian government as they thought they would be expelled, arrested, violated.

They freed themselves from fear, as they saw promises being fulfilled and gradually established trusting relationships as they saw missionaries always cooking together, playing with the children, talking and listening to them: *Such and such a thing happened to my child today.*

Service to natives is a noble task, however none of those called to serve in the Roraima Humanitarian Mission had experience of how to treat them. Discovering the ancestral universe of native people is the biggest challenge, to be unveiled by looking them in the eye. Missionaries act with their heart: *Serving with the heart is to inwardly contact the one who is right there in front of you, knowing that an invisible bridge connects us with higher worlds.*

Most indigenous groups got far away from their archetype. Since the Europeans' arrival, they have been killed, thrown off their lands, and had their beliefs destroyed. There remained a rejected, sick, fearful people.

The Waraos of the shelters did not come from the original dwelling on stilts on the banks of the Orinoco River, in contact with nature and sacred life as they had lived for thousands of years. They were interacting with the worst of white civilization, surviving without rules or limits in streets and urban peripheries.

Throughout the process of rebuilding their behavior, the Fraternidade supports and directs this people hiding a treasure of purity in their inner tabernacle. It offers them respect, compassion, healing impulses. It radiates codes of harmony and of group life acquired in Light-Communities. It hopes hidden seeds of indigenous consciousness, apparently lost within each native, may be rescued. On the other hand, it embraces the collective life rooted in them. During their exchanges, the two groups build unity.

First week at the Immigrant Reference Center

It was December 31. It had been two days since those brought from the street were taken to the CRI shelter that came to be known by the name of the district, Pintolândia. The missionaries said goodbye to them on New Year's eve to return the next morning.

On the first day of the year, they arrived cheerfully. They came across cans and bottles scattered all over the place and a regrettable scene. Three-quarters of those in the shelter had drunk alcoholic drinks. By decision of the Civil Defense command, the missionaries withdrew, leaving them enough food for the day.

They left discouraged but the next morning came back in silence to begin the general cleaning. Two *aidamos* approached looking really sorry, asking for another opportunity.

Refugees arriving at the Pintolândia Shelter.
Boa Vista, Roraima, Brazil, December 28th, 2016

We had to develop our patience and non-judgment and serve adults shaken by alcohol excess, says Clara, coordinator of this shelter for more than one year. After another day, everyone was invited to a general meeting about pacification and coexistence.

The Public Ministry had the objective of safeguarding only indigenous people in exclusive shelters, however, 130 *criollos* were staying there. The opportunity came up when the Tancredo Neves Shelter was opened. About a hundred indigenous people had been taken there. An exchange was being planned between them and Pintolândia's *criollos*.

It seemed like a great idea, but when the *criollos* learned about the relocation plan, they panicked and fell into collective crying. They had learned about the kind of people who had been transferred to Tancredo Neves Shelter, and about stories of robbery, violence, and child abuse.

It was also difficult for the Fraternidade, which had accompanied them for ten months building bonds of trust. But what was officially determined would have to be done. The next day, a bus full of indigenous people arrived.

Pintolândia Shelter

The shelter went through three phases: at first, ten months of free entry through damaged gates that were always open, here the missionaries faced hardships. *Criollos* that did not live there came around to eat meals, sell drugs, and there were robberies, and people were stabbed.

After the agreement with the UNHCR, the gates were repaired, and there was some control, which significantly diminished the number of problems. An *aidamo* and a missionary, with a change of shifts every two hours, kept watching the gate, which closed between 8 p.m. and opened 6 a.m. in the morning. In a third phase, the army arrived, and as they were on duty 24 hours a day, the coming and going of people, as well as the atmosphere calmed down.

In the first phase, the non-indigenous lived under the bleachers on one side of the sports gym court. On the other side were six indigenous groups. The two groups settled down among mattresses, furniture, and several bags stuffed with items donated by churches, schools, or found on the streets. An incredible disorder.

By an irony of fate, they cohabited face to face, despite carrying a historic rivalry. At night, they spread mattresses across the green floor and slept side by side. This coexistence has always generated confrontations. They were having the opportunity, on behalf of their people, to break prejudices and resistances, liberating themselves from human pettiness. Some of them may have learned how to forgive, and found peace.

Around the gym, two other Waraos groupings built a big slum. They huddled blue or black canvas huts attached to the walls of the gym and old peeled walls. They did not like it when the missionaries got closer: *What do you want, sister?* It was clear that they hid something.

Soon after the Fraternidade became a partner of the UNHCR, a renovation took place, for the first-time order was put in the chaos. While the Civil Defense lined up thirty-two light beige stalls on the red earth for these two groups to live, a task force was formed to break up the slum and remove deep stakes that sustained nets. That was when the hen-house appeared: they raised chickens in there.

Since then, according to a rule by the UNHCR, animals are not allowed in shelters due to hygiene and health issues. Yet, a hungry dog once got

An indigenous person and her belongings. Boa Vista, Roraima, Brazil, 2018

inside unnoticed and grabbed a piece of chicken. Someone shouted to the family, who were cooking with their backs to the fire. The youngest woman ran after the dog, and from the hungry mouth, the piece of meat fell on the ground.

The sports court was also renovated. As natives prefer to sleep in hammocks, a series of hammock structures for dozens of them were built on cement posts. Even during the day, in a busy environment, they take a nap on the nets or lie back in them, watching time go by. At the time of the renovation, the indigenous groups were consulted and decided, in consensus, that they would remain where everyone was already, both in and out of the gym.

When the army arrived, people of three ethnicities were living there. The Waraos originating from the Orinoco River delta, who came mainly from the city of Tucupita were more than five hundred lived. There were about seventy residents of the western mountains, of the E'ñepá or Panare ethnicities, and a single Pemon representative, who had come from Southeastern Venezuela in search of medical treatment.

In addition to taking control of security, food, and health care affairs, the military began a new renovation. They set up more metal shipping

Refugees watch television. Boa Vista, Roraima, Brazil, 2017

containers in addition to those already used by the Fraternidade—offices, kindergarten, warehouses, bathrooms. After earthmoving, building a new hammock hanging structure, fire a area for indigenous cooking and clothesline area, the tents will be installed in both sides of the gym. The commander promises: *The shelter will become a park.*

At first sight

In any of these phases, at first glance the shelter disturbs. A lady from Minas Gerais went up onto the porch to go into the gym. She came across a few natives sitting or walking around. She stopped to take a closer look at the handicraft produced with fiber from the *buriti* palm, sold by one Warao. She took a few more steps. At the main entrance, she was paralyzed by the racket produced by that human anthill.

In a majestic dusk, a childish frenzy vibrated, shrieks mixed to the sound of fans softening the scorching heat. Naked boys ran, pulling plastic carts. On each side, crowded bleachers, stoves, refrigerators, bicycles, luggage, bags, suitcases, men standing without shirts, lying down, sleeping, watching a small TV. After a while, a beautiful little native girl rushed towards her and hugged her legs: What a surprise! She was barefoot. Natives are given sandals, but they leave them behind. Most have quite open toes, and prefer to walk barefoot.

With a smile on her lips and bright little eyes, the little indigenous girl offered her hand to lead her across the court. The buzz of voices in Spanish, Portuguese and especially Warao was intersected by the echo of vigorous serves of volleyballs by girls with an extraordinary potential for this sport.

Having no place to store personal things, missionaries worked in gray uniforms and carried a small backpack, solving issues and tensions. They had been active there for five months. A child cried. Without delay, a missionary approached her: *Oh, what happened?* In the back of the gymnasium, on the right, a group of men were fixing lunch, moving large pots. To the left, artisans wove costume jewelry with beads on a long table, some of them breast feeding their children.

The small guide crossed paths with the lady at the side gate heading towards the burning light outside. The women did the dishes and the laundry in the shade of a small tree and hung them to dry on a clothesline. A few feet away, in outdoor showers, men lathered themselves, laughing. Two boys played with a water hose in a puddle of mud filled with plastic bottles and trinkets.

A bit farther, a young missionary nun took off lice with thin combs from the long black hair of girls who do not like to have it cut, just like their mothers. Children would indulge in nail-trimming and hair-washing in that morning dedicated to beauty and hygiene. Another nun gently collected, piece by piece, the garbage scattered over the land.

All of a sudden, the childlike innocence held in that lady's unconscious re-emerged. With the fire of purity lit, she found herself united to that noisy life. She held the little girl by both hands and whirled, and whirled. She relearned to walk between right and wrong, between thorns and stones.

The Fraternidade

The shelter—the expression "refugee camp" is avoided for the stigma associated with it—became a great hospital for the treatment of degenerated ancestral human conditions. *It's lovely to be with so many people,* says

Missionaries give outdoor showers to an indigenous and a non-indigenous girl.
Pintolândia Shelter, Boa Vista, Roraima, Brazil, 2017

Clara. *Our instructor gave us a key as he told us not to have the illusion that we will change the world. He told us, "You will demonstrate the new world". To demonstrate the new world it is necessary to be new, not just seem like it.* She explains: *Sometimes I realize that we are in hell, here. That's when I need to feel hell as a cool breeze, plunge into myself and bring solutions from there.*

Having worked in other shelters since October 2017, in daily life, missionaries have similar commitments in each of them, despite some particularities, such as housing children or not.

The Fraternidade serves the meals—breakfast from 8 a.m. to 8:30 a.m., lunch from 12 p.m. to 1 p.m. and dinner from 6 p.m. to 7 p.m. Right before the meal, they count the lunch kits brought by the soldiers. If there are any kits left over, other shelters are informed. If any of them lack something, they send it to them. Networking works!

The Fraternidade organizes and guides teams that do the daily cleaning of bathrooms, floors, external areas. They follow the shelter people's entering and leaving. They record the departure of those who leave for more than three days. They greet each newcomer, register them on a spreadsheet passed on by the UNHCR and accompany them to the place assigned to them, informing them of the basic rules of behavior: no fighting, and no drugs. They provide advice on obtaining documents—such as refuge protocol, work permit, CPF—Register of Individual Taxpayer Registry—which allows the immigrants to receive the refugee's official status.

The Fraternidade also follows up on health issues and the nurse's team prescriptions, they also do the financial-administrative work and, if the army requests any quantitative data, it passes to them what is requested; for example, the listing of sheltered people by age.

Field coordinators need to be present in every step of the way and attentive to every need. If there is any problem, they will be asked to address it. In case of a health emergency, they call the ambulance.

The author follows the work of a coordinator. She goes through the external area, enters the sports court, passes by the hammock sector, goes to the kindergarten school taking photos for the Fraternidade website, crosses the kitchen renovated by the Mormons and checks some data, goes to the vegetable garden, passing by women washing clothes and kids playing, walks among tents, goes around the gym and returns to the container.

With a notebook in hand, she talks to one, to another. She takes notes of requests, any fights that may happen, visits of authorized entities, delivery of donations, anything that may need repairing, to inform the army official who provides repairs and what is appropriate. She makes the transportation schedule for the van of Fraternidade.

This vehicle meets demands from all shelters taking indigenous people to prescheduled consultations or hearings at the Children and Youth Court; transports children to schools and the malnourished ones to the nutritional monitoring program Ser Nutre.

Meal time

When Pintolândia still gave shelter to both indigenous and non-indigenous people, the group daily went through shops to gather food to prepare meals for up to 400 residents. Once they were nourished, everything else worked with greater harmony. The emergencies were exhausting.

Daily search of food items at markets and green shops for
Venezuelan refugees. Boa Vista, Roraima, Brazil, 2016 and 2017

The first task of a newly arrived missionary in the city was to help two other servers in obtaining ingredients to make lunch. Venezuelans eat meat every day, rice and meat, instead of beans, as in Brazil. And the missionaries are vegetarians. She recalls: *Then I asked. I didn't know the market or anyone, and I came to the butcher's area. I looked at the butcher and closed my eyes thinking... "My God, I thought that I would never have to ask something, and I'm here asking. Not for me. What? Beef!". I swallowed. Well... is this my mission? So, here we go! "Who is responsible here?" I explained to them that it was for Venezuelans who are suffering, and they had nothing to eat... "Can you help?" In the third butcher, we got bones, many bones! We took them with all our heart. They were cooked with the little meat that was left to add some flavor, and they found it delicious.*

She also asked for fruit and vegetables: *"You can pick them up there." I was glad. Wow! I looked at them. They were almost rotten leftovers. I lowered myself to select the good ones, and the shopkeeper told me: "You can take them all." No, I could not take garbage to the shelter. It had enough trash already.*

Sometimes they thought they would not get a lot of stuff, and suddenly the trucks were full. Shopkeepers began to take food from the stall to give them, and as the months passed, more people, trade, and institutions came to donate. One day there was a banana party. Another day, the watermelon party. Even today, faithful food donors give them fruits and vegetables.

Three from the shelter and a missionary were preparing lunch. The *criollos* were more willing to help, but for the native people that was harder. In the kitchen, everything was precarious, even hygiene. They had no knives, and when the Fraternidade bought them, they disappeared two days later. The tropical heat attracted flies in abundance, and they used vinegar on the tables to keep them away.

The cooks were generally male, and in spite of the small stove and little water, miraculously there was food for hundreds of people. The young missionary Gabriel, aged nineteen, ran the kitchen routine for a period: *It took a firm hand to decide who would help to peel, chop, and cook each day. We had to be alert, and keep an eye on everything: someone forgot to put salt on the food, someone else let the food burn. We took water from a little bottle outside in the middle of the mud. There was an old table to chop everything on. Convincing them to eat vegetables and flour was difficult. All they wanted was meat. But when donations of manioc, beet arrived, we made a soup and they ate it all!*

The kitchen is a reflection of the troubled situation in which they live. Human behavior is very similar everywhere, be it in shelters in Greece or elsewhere. There are those who don't stand in the queue because some of their friends cook and give them food separately. The privileged. It was up to the missionary to teach them that food is for everyone and should not be reserved for family members or for one's own group.

Time to eat: at the beginning, they would charge like a herd of bulls. Educating them was an arduous process: *For them to stand in line, we had to be firm, but they obeyed and respected us. Now I was very strict, now I would talk and play with them.* Gabriel shared tasks. Some served; one washed children's hands in two buckets, one had soapy water, another only water. They organized five rows some distance from the table—one for children, one for the elderly, one for pregnant women, one for women and the other one for men. Then they were called in groups of five.

An *aidamo* first released the children. An attentive missionary said: *Go put on your clothes, boy! You can't come to the lunch line naked.* He went running, all happy. The Waraos are a water people. When fearful torrential rains fall, the kids go play with balls outdoors, ride a bike and jump, jump in the puddle. And at lunchtime, they are covered in mud.

The Mormons were the ones who donated the most. For months, they provided the shelter with chocolate milk and biscuits for breakfast, baked chicken for lunch, cleaning supplies, did the inside painting, renovated the kitchen and bathrooms. They made other contributions to; supplies to disinfect the gymnasium; school and handicraft material; a rustic and robust wooden table; computers and desktops for missionaries.

In September 2017, the cycle of ordering food ended when funds destined for food and gas were allocated by the Federal Government—Ministry of Social Development, through the SETRABES—Secretariat of Labor and Social Welfare of Roraima. The funds were expected to feed two hundred people, but there were already four hundred by the time this money was available. Sometime later, the UNHCR donated foodstuffs to them. The SETRABES also hired multidisciplinary teams for each indigenous shelter of the state: a coordinator, an anthropologist, two socio-instructional agents, a psychologist, and a social worker.

Everything really changed with the presence of the army. They began to supply the lunch kits, which had good acceptance in the shelters for *criollos*.

As the indigenous people wasted food because they did not like meat or beans, it was decided to distribute them foodstuffs, which ten of the *aidamo*, distributed for each family to prepare their own meal. Every now and then complaints arose that the *aidamo* was not being fair: *We are five, he gave food to three people.* To respond to the complaint, twice a week the military supported by the Fraternidade began to deliver themselves non-perishable foodstuffs to families and chicken daily. The only meal in common for all was breakfast, prepared in the kitchen by the natives themselves: a pan of milk with chocolate milk, bread, and fruit.

Brasílio, born in Brazil

The new Warao baby would undoubtedly have died if he did not live in the shelter. His mother, an adolescent, was malnourished with nine months of pregnancy when she arrived. Brasílio was jaundiced at birth and stayed for days in the incubator. The native says that in Venezuela they would not have put him in the incubator, which is for whites only.

The coordinator, touched by the baby's crying in the lethargic mother's lap, her gaze lost somewhere on the floor, tried to understand her deep sadness: *What was going on in her heart, needing to surface a maternal aspect of herself to be able to breastfeed?*

The Coordinator, embraced the mother, saying her son was beautiful; but the native girl turned away, scared. Tenderness seemed to be a strange feeling for her. When she was asked who the child's father was, her expression was vague and she remained in silence. Clara comforted the baby on her lap: *I was delighted to hold the little being and always went back to the tent to see how they were.*

Jella Perez had arrived with her parents, Brasílio's grandparents. Her cousin, Ramon, gave a name to the baby, saying that Brasílio is the one who is born in Brazil. Clara decided to look for him. A particular leader, educated and cultivated, who had gone to college in Venezuela, he was

Jella Perez and Brasílio. Pintolândia Shelter, Boa Vista, Roraima, Brazil, August 2017

in charge of the school of the shelter. He was with the students when she asked if they could talk a little.

She said that in her view Brasílio's mother was a little sad: some women go into depression after babies are born. Ramon smiled and said no, that in the Warao lifestyle this is common, the mother is isolated in a hammock from forty days to two months. The only people that can touch her and the baby are her mother, and in this case, the grandfather, because he is a shaman. No other Warao can touch the baby, for the navel is for them the house of many eyes, and when the home of many eyes is open, evil things may get inside. Clara talked about having held the baby on her lap, if there was a problem in doing so. He calmed her: *No, not you, sister. You don't have to worry.*

Clara insisted: *I notice a different sadness in Jella.* Ramón added: *It is because she is a marimacho, a person of a special sexuality, partly man, partly woman. Among the Waraos, there are men and women like that. She is what you call homosexual.* Clara wondered if the ethnic group despise the *marimacho*, and he said no. She wanted to know how they can identify them. In a meeting of *marimachos*, they themselves recognize one another by their attitudes. It may happen that a woman marries a woman and lives with her for life or marries a man and a woman simultaneously. The same happens with men.

Clara asked him whether Jella might reject Brasílio. Ramón said that the Waraos do not reject their children. She indeed would take care of him.

The next day, she went to Jella's grandfather to learn more about his granddaughter's story, and to ask him for permission to approach her again. She remained sitting in the hammock with Brasílio crying on her lap, but now with a less sad look.

At last, she opened herself and showed Clara her bruised breasts. There was a doctor at the shelter, so Clara invited her to go and see her, who prescribed an ointment to ease her pain and recommended a silicone breast shield. Clara took her back to the hammock and went to the nearest pharmacy, to buy the shield and the ointment, including for Brasílio's rash, as well as disposable diapers.

Jella greeted her with a smile, and together they took things out of the pack. More relieved, she was able to breastfeed. She was pale, and Clara still asked her if she would accept special enriched milk. She went to get one of the cans and directed her to have it in the morning and at night. Jella thanked her.

Brasílio and his mother satiated their hunger, and simultaneously the mother-child relationship was eased. The grandfather was close to them. Grateful for the attention given to his family, he said that his wife had fifteen children. Ten died of diseases when they were children, and one was murdered at the age of twenty. Jella is a survivor. Every Warao has similar stories of many deaths in their families.

Missionaries support every person's life. From time to time, Clara repeats to Jella how important it is, for Fraternidade, for Brasílio to grow strong, healthy, to go to school. This future for the son is strengthened within the young native mother.

Coexistence rules

The group is immersed in a constant flow of learning, either during the interaction between the missionaries in the lodging houses or in inter-relationships in the shelter. They develop the art of distinguishing the

Playing with an indigenous boy.
Pintolândia Shelter, Boa Vista, Roraima, Brazil, 2018

good and bad side of every human being, giving special emphasis to the positive. Thus, it propagates peace and grows in awareness as it offers to those assisted basic instruction about values, which expands their love.

Clara wondered: *How can I deal with the indigenous culture, so diverse in values? What can I do when a husband beats his wife with a piece of wood? I can't simply stand before this man and judge him as everyone would. At that moment, she is the victim. But I don't know their whole story. What can I do? I will not be at peace with my conscience if I don't something for this woman. We have had several meetings with the natives on this recurring subject. The women let off steam, they say men beat them up for whatever reason, and that's cultural. I told them about the Maria da Penha law, implemented in 2006 to help prevent, punish and eradicate domestic and family violence against women. Women do want to live violence-free.*

In order to curb domestic and family violence, the missionary talks to the aggressor, trying to make him understand her. She explains his attitude violates Brazilian laws and the shelter rules. After three warnings, he will be expelled. In that case, the couple will be taken to the police station to file a report, and the wife will be submitted to a corpus delicti, as the victim of a crime, and will receive the protective measure provided

Pintolândia Shelter, Boa Vista, Roraima, Brazil, 2018

by law. If the husband enters the shelter, he'll be arrested. Clara continues: *There have been cases in which a dialogue settled everything. We have had miracles in here. We allow the aggressor to be arrested, knowing he will surely learn something and that this will serve as an example to others. We won't say he's just a poor little guy. He is a soul and needs to be transformed.*

The Waraos of the shelter have lived on Venezuelan streets since 1966. They do not come from *The Beautiful Land*, as they called the Orinoco delta when they lived on stilt houses by the riverside. They take on street habits, drinking, and distancing themselves from the right path.

Several Venezuelans had to be sent away. Others begin to make moral and ethical decisions, a sign the mission has positive effects. When they arrive, the rules of the shelter are presented to them: If an adult uses drugs, beats his wife or fights, he will have to leave. Clara says: *I'm not afraid, if anything has to happen to me, it's in the laws of God. In the first public fight, I thought "if I don't do something now, it's over." I separated the fight between two men. "What's the matter with you two? You'll will have to hit me first before you hit one another. Get on with your lives!" One was drugged, with red eyes. I called the police, who at that time was in a patrol car inside the shelter. We went to the police station to file a report. They never came back.*

Since the Army arrived, the Fraternidade went on dealing directly with indigenous people. The officers feel a bit lost in cases of drunkenness and conflicts, which arise as soon as the missionaries withdraw after dinner. They find it complicated to deal with the natives. A lieutenant said: When you turn your back to them, everything happens. The military say they are used to giving orders and being obeyed, but this is not the right way to treat indigenous people: We need to practice more humanitarian contact. *We're learning*, he explains.

Educating the body, emotions, mind, consciousness

Adults and children have been going through several educational experiences. The group keeps an eye on collective and individual education. It aims at the transformation of the little hearts. Each individual change reflects in everyone's behavior. Children who have no education, begging and cohabiting with bad characters, easily get involved with deviants' situations.

Shortly after the opening of the shelter, a young sergeant created the first school. She surrounded a corner of the gym with siding, made a list of students, arranged the morning and afternoon classes by age. She herself was the teacher. Even though she was evangelical, she asked for a neutral space, in which children would just search for knowledge. A volunteer teacher ran a campaign and was given crayons, slippers, A-4 paper.

For most students, that was the first time they wrote and saw their own name written. Eager to learn, the kids had to get ready before going to school: taking a shower, combing their hair, organizing their material. Some discipline emerged. They could not be rolling on the floor and then rush into the classroom. A non-indigenous sheltered teacher gave her first class and the next day the missionaries found the *aidamos* deeply moved. They had a xenophobic attitude, they would not allow the children to return to the school because a *criolla* was their teacher, and only indigenous can teach indigenous.

They and a few indigenous women were summoned for a meeting. The coordinator highlighted the benefits of the school, the fact that literate people cannot be fooled. She said: *Shelter children should grow learning. Now, if the parents did not open up to accept the others, who are different, how did they want to be accepted by society?*

She asked them: *Did the teacher mistreat any student, did she do anything to justify complaints?* They all said: *No, sister, no.* So, Clara emphasized: *The "criolla" woman is a teacher and definitely will go on teaching. She is here to help!* Little by little, the natives start healing themselves.

Shelter children get attention from official agencies that, at a given moment, considered incorporating them into the school system. They then realized that, due to cultural differences, indigenous children might suffer prejudice and never want to return. They lack hygiene and behavior habits. They just squat and relieve themselves in any corner.

After an analysis of which children were able to attend public schools, eight of them were accepted. This initiative was taken when a teacher invited the girls' volleyball team for a competition with his school's students. They were trained and the natives won ten out of eleven matches.

Gradually, this work attracted more volunteers and institutions, encouraging the turning of the educational wheel. The school was set up inside a container donated by the Embassy of Canada, with an equipped classroom—blackboard, tables, benches, chairs, cabinets, bathrooms.

On May 2018, the shelter had an average of 170 school-age children between four and seventeen. Their schedule was loose, dedicated to playing, until the Escola Janela do Amor e da Amizade Entre Dois Povos —School of Window of Love and Friendship Between Two People—was created, a bilingual intercultural education Project of Extension of the Federal University of Roraima. The program is carried out by the NGO Casa de Los Niños, a branch of the NGO Pirilampos.

Children in four groups aged six to 12 study from 9 to 11 a.m. and from 2 to 5 p.m. Eleven voluntary Brazilian teachers give literacy, art, physical education and math lessons, and teach them values and new customs.

They are taught basic norms of interaction: living in a collective area, using the bathroom, obeying the teacher and regarding him or her, instead of their friends, as a role model. Eleven indigenous people—three E'ñepás and eight Waraos—transmit their knowledge to the children, strengthening their cultural bonds, dances, craftsmanship, their stories and language in bilingual Spanish-Warao or Spanish-E'ñepá classes.

Aiming at having the children learn through play, on Saturdays the Pirilampos offer them fun activities. Kids Games, which is part of the

Mother and children of the Warao ethnicity.
Pintolândia Shelter, Boa Vista, Roraima, Brazil, 2018

Brazilian Sports Coalition, *Coalizão Brasileira de Esportes* group, works with physical exercises, such as *capoeira* classes. The shelter also has a partnership with the Methodist Church, which, three times a week, take forty children to external activities—recreation, Portuguese class, sports.

Anderson, a young missionary, coordinates the educational area of Fraternidade and the school. He teaches and follows up indigenous teachers: some of them used to teach in Venezuela. He explains: *Reality is our starting point. We connect education to everything, not only with the classroom. We follow up with parents and have an educational program for teachers, with the aim of retrieving Indigenous Consciousness, clear the dust that buries its richness, beauty, and importance. Tomorrow we will have an inter-cultural education seminar, as part of our partnership with UFRR, Roraima Federal University.*

The UNICEF—United Nations Children's Fund—invited Fraternidade to form a partnership with them. The organism operates in 190 countries promoting the improvement of children's life. They train agents who work on the front in friendly environments, offering them educational and psycho-social assistance. It also prevents abuse against children and adolescents, and distributes snacks for nutritional reinforcement.

Indigenous teachers have made together a drawing that has become the school's symbol. *Morich* palm fruits represent the Waraos; an arrow is a symbol for the E'ñepá ethnicity, and the Venezuelan flag is pictured with a heron, the Roraima Mount and a gold miner. The missionary adds: *People who lived in the streets can become mediators of their life, and be cheered up: "Today I have to teach, there's something in the world that depends on my actions". This activates what was stagnant within them.*

Visits to the shelter

The shelter moves national and international powers and receives all kinds of visitors, including ministers and presidents of organisms who come from the federal capital, to handle issues concerning immigrations and indigenous communities, among others. Some authorities make appointments before coming. Some of them keep a low profile. Some arrive with an entourage.

One visitor got off a jet plane at the airport and asked for military protection. The missionaries were called urgently, as they always accompany visitors to give them the necessary information.

When they arrived, the visitor had already gone. They met indigenous people very frightened by the arrival of those men holding heavy guns: *Sister, we thought they would kill us!*

However, another authority gave them attention, and invited them to write what they expect to get from Brazil. To everyone's surprise, they wrote a letter in excellent Portuguese, with just a few words in Spanish. It had certainly been written by them. The main message in the letter was: *We would like to have our own land.*

Immigrant stories

A young kind-looking man approaches a missionary and asks her for a pair of shoes. He shows her the only ones he has, a pair of white plastic sandals. He needs another pair to look for a job. He hopes to manage to bring his children and wife, who are still in Venezuela.

Missionaries at service.
Pintolândia Shelter, Boa Vista, Roraima, Brazil, 2016 e 2017

Venezuelan refugees leave the shelter seeking work.
Pintolândia Shelter, Boa Vista, Roraima, Brazil, 2017

Since they have daily contact with immigrants, the missionaries were able to tell official organisms why Venezuelans did not have official documents. By having a legal status in the country, they could be inserted into programs and then get a job: *Listen, they have no money to pay for the photos or the application forms.* For this reason, the tax for issuing documents and the one-hundred-dollar tax were suspended—that is, almost one year of minimum wage in Venezuela—so that they could get a two-year temporary residence permit.

Venezuelans are often regarded as good workers. Specialized companies refer them to menial jobs, such as bricklayer, or to do small maintenance services. They write down the employers' data, because often their labor force is exploited. They get paid half the salaries that Brazilians earn, or do not get paid at all. Sometimes they are abandoned in farms, from where they have to leave and walk back home.

This reality of the labor world is not rosy. Employees take advantage of the need of those people. The owner of a company was arrested for keeping seven Venezuelans in slavery working conditions. As most indigenous people have no professional qualification, they are called to weed. There have been cases of workers spending one month on a farm preparing the cultivation of the soil and, in the end, they received 15 dollars, with the employer's justification: *I gave them food.*

One of the first *criollos* families to be housed in the shelter known for their politeness and tidiness. Her grandmother tells her story: *I want to be in eternity with my mother, who was so good to me. I suffered a lot after she left. I went to live in the streets. I would hide in corners and couldn't sleep properly, to be always alert and not be touched by men who threatened me with knives. I couldn't take a shower, I couldn't clean myself, but some friends sometimes took me to take a shower and eat. I lived in the streets with my daughter and granddaughters, but later my son-in-law rented us a house. One day, he told me that in Brazil I would be able to eat well and recover my health. He and my daughter leave to go to work every day and I stay here in the shelter with my granddaughters. I like to work. I used to sell hot chocolate, and worked as a housekeeper at a hotel.*

The grandmother shows her abilities making sophisticated folds in the patterned quilt over the double bed. There the family set up a sort of impeccable studio apartment without walls. She says that her family has three races mixed, the mother is indigenous, granddaughters are blonde and black. She is Catholic: *God above all. If you don't believe in God, you can't believe in anything else. When I go to bed and when I wake up, I always talk with Him in my silence. It is because of God that we are alive, but most people don't know that.*

She intends to remain in Brazil: *This is a different world, where there is food, tranquility, peace. The president left our country in ruins and wants to bribe people, but money is not everything. We have disagreement between parties there, and its dangerous to speak against the government. Here, thanks to the support from Fraternidade, we can find jobs, get food, and send part of what we earn to the family members who stayed behind. We have to bring benefits to Brazil and never do evil.*

With affectionate and firm simplicity, Clara instructs the assisted. She gives examples of coexistence: *In the shelter, we walk here and there dealing with people's issues. All of a sudden, a Venezuelan man leaning on the bleachers shouts: "Sister, come here. I want to talk with you". Or, when we are assisting someone, one of them interrupts: "Just a little question". She explains to them, over and over: Brother, you have just arrived and you want a job. To survive here, you have to change your behavior. If I need* to ask someone a favor, I get closer to him and wait for him to receive me. We speak in a soft-tone voice, using the magical words: please, thank you.

Without hurting their dignity, the dialogue becomes instructive and gives lessons on good manners and professional guidance. Some will accept it, the prouder get annoyed and leave. She explains: *Their way of using the imperative in an arrogant tone gives people a bad impression. They need to be more humble.*

Clara analyses herself: *When I get home, I am exhausted. I take a good shower and start reflecting. Obviously, the reason for such tiredness has to do with myself, it's my mistake. Some characteristics of this people just put me to test. When I open the doors of impatience, my energy is drained. I need to find Buddha's path.*

A touching love for the homeland

Immense is the inner pain of the people taken away from their own environment. Although few immigrants get a job, most of them remain in Roraima to be near their home country. They keep sweet memories and yearn to return, when life goes back to normal. Before the crisis, they say: *Our nation was a little golden cup of natural beauty, music, art.* Their words, which express some bitterness and sadness, are not predominant among these extrovert people.

Olga Lorenzo, a Venezuelan volunteer, says: *Venezuela is gorgeous, with a wonderful climate, mountains, snow, beaches, deserts, prairies, thickets, the great Savannah where the Roraima tepui is. Geologically, it is one of the most beautiful places in the world.*

I am a half-breed, my grandfather was Italian, my grandmother was indigenous. There's so much history, love, pain, faith and hope impregnated in these lands of immigrants. I love my country, but I left it in 2015 and never went back. At that time, unemployment, malnutrition, and hatred had set in.

The crisis has been worsening. I was told that sometime in 2017, in the streets of Caracas they were collecting dead people from starvation. Here, immigrants are being rejected because they are confused. Some, confused and hungry, make mistakes and break the laws. Others that did nothing, are accused. The righteous pay for the sinners.

A true government, which improves lives, has to be peaceful. There, they manipulate, brainwash the people with aggressive and violent speeches. The real situation of Venezuela is spiritual, disguised of political, social, economic problems. We are excessively bound to material things and forgot the most important thing, which is praying and serving our neighbor.

The country was devout and I hope a miracle happens one day. We have gone through a karmic test, but we are responsible for it. All this is for us to learn about the many consequences we suffer when we make wrong decisions. Bad decisions have consequences not only in me or my family, but in my nation, in the continent, on the planet. I am grateful for the help I'm getting in Brazil, each cell of mine is thankful. Any nation that helps another in such a situation balances its own karma.

The end of the mission cannot be forecast, but life in the shelter goes on, effervescent.

With population above the suggested, indigenous people improvised again plastic huts between tents. The UNHCR and the Army have determined that no one else will be accepted in the shelter, since there is not enough room or food for more people.

Those in the shelter remain hopeful in their tents or swinging in hammocks hanging side by side. They are being protected, fed, treated, their conflicts and pains are being relieved. They have the opportunity to transform themselves, while walking on the bridge suspended between the past and the unknown future.

The Fraternidade office

To be like a river that flows,
Silent, into the night.
Not to fear the darkness of the night.
If there are stars in the skies, reflect them.
Belo Belo, poem by Manuel Bandeira

The Venezuelan exodus intensifies. Without access to the basics in their homeland, refugees cross the Northern Brazilian border to begin a journey into that country. The Fraternidade, a non-profit organization, was the first entity to arrive in Boa Vista to welcome them. Its members, of different ages and origins, most of them Brazilians, are guided by the hope of constructing a better future for the immigrants willing to ease their pain and plant seeds of peace in indigenous and non-indigenous people. At the same time, the volunteers take care of their own inner evolution.

Being the first shelter of Roraima, the Immigrant Reference Center was inaugurated by Civil Defense supported by Fraternidade. This organism started to implement a basic order among those assisted, increasingly immersed in afflictions. Besides, the shelter was a magnet to attract responses from organizations, which, united, started to foster a great humanitarian program. The constant worsening of the crisis awakened national and international solidarity.

Almost one year after its arrival, the Fraternidade was invited to sign an agreement with the UNHCR, the United Nations High Commissioner for Refugees. The partnership began on September 2017, when the missionaries helped the programme to inaugurate a shelter called the House of Passage, in Pacaraima.

What draws one's attention of this partnership is the absolute voluntary giving of those who persevere from Monday to Monday, simply out of love. Love, no greater power can move creatures with this level of giving of self. The missionary presence installs a more harmonious vibratory field among the people that are being assisted. The action of a soul that responds to an inner call has an unknown penetration for humans.

In previous missions in Asia, Africa, Europe and in Central and South America, the Fraternidade supported other altruistic organizations. Summoned by their superiors to the Roraima Mission, the members of the group started a new, more organized and professional stage.

At the Fraternidade office, we talked about unexpected humanitarian tasks with the primary missionaries, Ricardo, Manager of Emergencies and Humanitarian Help, and Shen, Manager of Institutional Relations.

Ricardo: *We were serving in the Greece Mission when we were informed that all primary missionaries should travel to Boa Vista, soon after the signing of our first agreement with the UNHCR. At first, we got surprised. But we are very accustomed to changes. Actually, we like challenges.*

At the first meeting with UNHCR, they explained: reports, deadlines, voucher missionaries... Wow! I thought, I am back to my professional days... and I like so much to take care of trees, water...

From then on, most missionaries continued to deal directly with the daily toil in the shelters, but a few took up the office work in our newly rented office. The UNHCR began to study our ability to respond. We shifted from an informal working style to being accountable for everything. At the beginning the group had some resistance to following a missionary program developed with logics, coherence.

We worked from 7 a.m. to 11 p.m. Sometimes we stayed in the office until 3 a.m. We wrote a manual of internal procedures and translated it into English. We had to learn about the administrative-financial rigor to respond to audits, for example. The first auditor was sent by a company from London to analyze details of each purchase, even to check every piece of furniture on our list. We are a bona-fide depositary, and have to be accountable for the resources that are sent to us and for the goods—containers, equipment.

On the other hand, we need to develop new projects with different methodologies applied to each sponsor, for example, to respond to an embassy donation proposal: "We want to support you financially. What do you need?" In addition to all that, we plan our personnel routine—which missionary goes to what shelter, in what transportation, what each one will do.

We take care of air tickets purchase, also of the fuel and renting of vehicles and real estate.

Today we have five houses with an infrastructure in Boa Vista to support the work: the office, the Nucleus Flower of the Sacred Tepui, the lodgings for men and women, and two houses of the Grace Mercy Order. In Pacaraima, we rented a house for lodging men and women.

Shen: *When we signed the agreement with the UNHCR, we were not sure what this would mean in practical terms. We found out about it as the project was gradually implemented, and periodically renewed. There was a significant change in our administrative structure. We set up the office and intellectually prepared ourselves to take care of the tasks.*

As we get financial support for several areas of the shelter—education, health, craftsmanship, food, hygiene, tents, containers—our administrative function is to deal with quarterly financial reports, institutional and accounting documents, the accountability of resources received both from the UNHCR and from groups involved in the provision of services.

Some parts of the office facilities are reserved for stocks of clothes, shoes, accessories, hygiene and cleaning products, foods, educational material, craftsmanship, medicines. They are separated and identified in shelves according to the organization donating them: the UNHCR, the Canadian Embassy, Mormons, Doctors without Borders. As we are a point of reference in the state, we receive donations to distribute.

Besides these steady contributors, a loving network has grown among Brazilian people. Having read in the papers about what is going on in Roraima, some ladies from Umuarama, Paraná, bought fabric and made more than one thousand pieces of children's clothing. The office made contact with a Light-Network group near Umuarama to take the boxes with more than 220 pounds of clothes to be loaded in a cargo airplane of FAB—Brazilian Air Force—to bring them to us. A television channel began a report about the dressmaker's generosity, filming the donation arrival and distribution at the shelters.

Another story: a collaborator of Figueira called. He had invited a group of entrepreneurs, clients and suppliers for a campaign. They rented a truck to be filled with twenty-three tons of any products that the Venezuelans might need, which would be dispatched from the state of Santa Catarina.

To get resources from UNHCR, our purchasing sector was acquiesced to formal procedures. We follow a complex and rigorous process with justified budgets for each purchase—eight documents presented in a certain sequence, signed, stamped. The methods differ for each amount: up to US$25, from US$25 to US$75, and so on. When the budget is over a certain amount, for large services or the purchasing of expensive items, a competitive bidding process is needed. At the moment, we are renovating the House of Welcome, before we can host vulnerable Venezuelans, we received three bids for the job, helped with the reformation work and made the employees payments.

Given the increasing requirements, the Fraternidade had to change its profile a little, hiring professionals by means of the UNHCR project. This is a challenge for a nonprofit organization. The Regency Council, which guides the work, studied it deeply for three months until we were authorized to hire specialists for areas we cannot support otherwise. We hired nurses and an indigenous person who is an expert in health management. Some arrived through someone's recommendation. Two nurses had worked in shelters as volunteers before they were hired because we felt we are energetically subtly connected. All the specialists are instructed, we show them videos about our values and principles, so they might reflect the energy of the institution they represent. Thus, the missionaries added, to their task, the welcoming of these new brothers and sisters.

Before signing an agreement with the UNHCR, we did a project financed by Canadian Embassy funds by means of the Pan American Development Foundation—PADF. Then we bought two containers with furniture, material and equipment for the Pintolândia Shelter. One is used as a medical office, another as a children's school. The ambassador was at the ceremony and cut the inauguration ribbon. The Embassy also donated food kits to the Tancredo Neves Shelter, which was chaotic at the time. This opened doors for other embassies to collaborate.

Different United Nations agencies are offering specific help. The UNICEF invited us for a partnership due to our financial-administrative capacity and a cultural education project we were implementing in Pintolândia Shelter. The International Migration Organization, closely connected to the UNHCR, is active in the relocation of Venezuelans from Roraima to other parts of Brazil. One of their most urgent needs is to have employment opportunities. So, we also help indigenous people to have a source of income with craftsmanship. As for the United Nations Population Fund—UNFPA—it focuses on the protection of the most vulnerable Venezuelans, such as unaccompanied children, pregnant women or the ones on their own. Without a job, many end up prostituting themselves.

Bimonthly, the UNHCR holds a meeting to articulate actions with partners working in Roraima. The idea is not to have more than one organism dedicated to the same service, which happens when there is a communication gap. In 2017, a small room was enough for everyone. In our last meeting, in the Army Brigade, the room was packed! The number of groups with an apparently genuine intention of serving is impressive. Certainly, there are hidden intentions, which I ignore. What each one says is: "We are here to collaborate".

As an implementing partner, together with the UNHCR we receive an increasing number of visitors. We answer questions about the shelters to international representatives, such as delegations from the European Union, USA, Israel, Japan, Italy, besides international organizations willing to collaborate. They do field surveys to identify the needs each one can supply: Red Cross, Doctors Without Borders, Pan American Health Organization—PAHO, International Organization of Human Rights—IOHR.

We have had meetings with the Brazilian Ministries of Social and Agrarian Development, the Health Ministry and the Ministry of Foreign Affairs. We also met with the Minister of Justice, the Minister-Chief of Staff, the Federal Attorney, the president of FUNAI—Brazilian government organizations dealing with issues related to indigenous communities and their lands. Besides, we have given interviews to local, American, Japanese and European newspapers. We only focus on our humanitarian role, and never talk about political matters.

The army arrived on March 2018, after the Brazilian President released millions of the official Brazilian currency, the real, for Roraima's emergency humanitarian assistance. The assistance quickly improved the situation. At the beginning, there was some concern about the army's powerful presence, since they are known for their aggressive approach. However, so far, we have only known their friendly side. Their cooperation surprised us. They have become great partners. Its members, who are many, quickly tidied up the shelters, took care of the cleaning, of discipline, brought in a certain peace. The people assisted automatically change attitudes when they are given food. The Fraternidade can now develop its work of human-itarian expansion of human consciousness with greater serenity, and learn about logistics with the army.

Months ago, the light at the end of the tunnel was not visible. Recently, with the opening of new shelters, we believe the main problem is nearly solved: to take crowds of people off the streets giving them the basics that human beings need to survive with some dignity—a place to sleep, to take a shower, to feed and to receive basic medical care. It is as if a fire had been extinguished. If we hadn't received the help from so many people, and the army had not come, none of this would have been possible. The army and the UNHCR are the main organizations protecting and assisting Venezu-elans in Roraima.

I can only fulfill my activity as a missionary if I constantly aspire to the spiritual mission for which I offered myself. In my view, the Fraternidade answers a call sent from the Divine to accomplish a spiritual mission. Their members try to overcome physical, emotional, and mental barriers, in order to be connected with the light of distant stars. What unites our group in a special way is the inner mission of each member seeking to manifest this fraternal work.

Tancredo Neves Shelter

Lord, I have a missionary soul,
take me to the land that is thirsty for God.
Take me where hope is missing,
where joy is missing simply because
they do not know about You.
Missionary Soul
song by Enrique García Vélez

Roraima has two seasons, the stormy one and a fierce humid tropical summer. On flat streets flooded by incessant rain, our car wheels create waves in the high-water. The driver drops us by the Tancredo Neves Shelter. Jumping over puddles, we crossed the half-open gate and went past the police officers. We did not show documents to enter, as we were identified by t-shirts with equal-armed cross, which represents the four Kingdoms of Nature—the Mineral, the Plant, the Animal and Human. In the former sports gymnasium are sheltered about 330 Venezuelan bachelors and couples without children.

I look around. Under a big high canvas cover, there is a lounge area. To the right and to the left there are colored metal shipping containers used by the Army and the Fraternidade as space, for medical offices, storerooms and bathrooms for members of staff. Some of them are air conditioned, such as the one in which the missionaries carry out administrative procedures, and receive the new arrivals to the shelter, passing on instructions and the rules for group-life to them.

I follow the steps of the missionary who is coordinating the shelter that day. An Argentinian teacher, Angelica has dreamed for years of participating in Doctors without Borders. Watching a Misericórdia Maria TV program, she came across their invitation for a mission on the Venezuelan border, and her fire of aspiration was re-kindled: *I prayed a lot and, on the following day, I wrote offering my help to Fraternidade. In two days, I received the reply and joined their second group to help indigenous people living around the Passarão Fair.*

She introduces me to the lieutenant responsible for the shift. The three of us went out walking beside the lounge area, where about fifty men watched an action film on TV, played dominos or were busy with their cell phones. We followed through the corridor between the wall around the lot, the clothesline and the gym's high wall. At the back of the terrain, the Civil Defense assembled twenty-three pearly tents. In each one lived ten bachelors or more than one couple. The place also has containers being used as men's and women's bathrooms, and laundry.

The lieutenant offers an adulation into one of the tents : *Long live Venezuela!* Male voices answer with ardor: *Long live Brazil, the UNHCR, Fraternidade, long may they live!* It was Friday, 3 p.m. Older men leaning on mattresses look at us. The military invites them to come out of the tent and talk. He tries to exchange information about both countries' history with one of them, who gets cheered up: *Brotherly people, our Latin-American origin is beautiful. Blood has been shed, more than half the people died... but we managed to get freedom, independence.* And he sings one verse of the Venezuelan national anthem.

Venezuelan vendors of brooms in the exclusive shelter for singles and couples without children. Tancredo Neves Shelter, Boa Vista, Roraima, Brazil, 2018

A man with dark glasses felt the need to express his sadness: *Unfortunately, our country is going through a critical situation. I arrived today and obtained permission to stay here. My mother has just died. I could not bury her as I had no money. My brother is physically torn apart, sheer bones.* Another man wails: *We were weak when we got here, with our bones visible.* He raises his shirt and shows his belly: *The government is letting many people starve. Here I have put on six and a half pounds.* The seven men quieted their dialogue, weeping silently.

At last, the first man tried to cheer the group up: *God's time is perfect until the end of times! Jesus said that. Each day I get more in love with the words of God. I was given a Bible and read holy words. I have found love in the shelter, people who are more than friendly, they are fraternal. I am grateful. At first, I was suspicious: "What do they want in return?" But they only give to us, without asking anything in return.* I took photos of that moment and we went ahead.

There was more to feel, more to see. I was astonished to enter the gym, the sports court covered with perfectly aligned individual tents. There was quietness and melancholy on the rainy afternoon. The orderly precinct can strengthen the homeless. Angelica says: *This is the atmosphere in the mid mornings and afternoons at the beginning of the day and in the evenings, the lodging area gets hectic.*

Two men enter the former gymnasium carrying a bunch of colorful brooms which they sell in the streets. To store them, Angelica unlocks the storage locker where the people being assisted put away their items not in use. I photograph the scene. Looking at himself on the photo, one broom salesman pointed out: *I've put on weight.*

Further ahead there is a refugee woman. One of her legs is missing, a chair was put outside her tent so she can lean on it when standing up. First, she and her husband lived on the streets. Then, in another shelter, until they were transferred to a collective tent with other couples. They had just moved out to two igloo tents, where they received some privacy. Independent and active, she weaves, crochets clothes, which she sells in public places.

Having finished the tour, we heard a truck unloading gravel outside the entrance wall. The rain had paused. The sky was dark gray. To repair the sidewalk, an enthusiastic group comes along and goes shoveling wheel-

Sheltered people repair the sidewalk.
Tancredo Neves Shelter, Boa Vista, Roraima, Brazil, 2018

barrow loads of gravel to cover up rain-filled puddles. Lieutenant J. Lima remarks: *Maintenance is essential, but the Army cannot cope with it on their own. We contribute with logistics and material through NGOs, but labor is done by the Venezuelans. We try to instruct them about the need to clean and keep the structure in good conditions. Everything is for them.* He rejoices: *I see what is to be done and call them to work. Of course, we encourage those who do not like to work. As they see one rolling up their sleeves, others are attracted by osmosis. They are rewarded for their hard work being the first on dinner queues and, if any dinner is leftover, they may have a second helping. This attracts more colleagues next time. It is fun out there. They play and we distribute juice and sweets.*

The Fraternidade humanitarian "post-graduate course" took place a few months after the opening of the Tancredo Neves Shelter, also called Tancredão.

The situation around the city bus station was intolerable. Packed in improvised tents under trees, *criollos*, Waraos and É'ñepás lived in unhealthy conditions and, at night, slept inside the bus station. A few organizations helped them until three hundred refugees were transferred

A dweller of a tent for couples only.
Tancredo Neves Shelter, Boa Vista, Roraima, Brazil, 2018

to the sports court which, by its fourth month, was sheltering nearly one-thousand *criollos* in terrible conditions. About one hundred indigenous people taken to the Tancredão were soon transferred by the Civil Defense from the Tancredo Neves to the Pintolândia Shelter.

One gymnasium is not built to hold a large population, as the sanitary facilities are precarious. Then the electric power had an overload, the sewage system, a breakdown. On the litter-covered floor, there were great mud puddles under filthy shacks and open sewage, a very smelly place! With a gate that was always open, anyone came and left at any time. The shelter became a place for prostitution and for illegal activities. But there were also frightened and intimidated good people living there.

Since the Saturday when the Venezuelans were transferred, on November 28, 2017, several organizations started to help. The Fraternidade was invited to support the UNHCR in specific actions, distributing hygiene and food kits, registering children for school, accompanying health cases on the public health system, among others.

The Fraternidade made the commitment with the UNHCR to set up there on a permanent basis, from March 2018, forward. Clara, the first coordinator, says: *There was violation of all rights. We received charges regarding sexual violence, drug trafficking and use, murder, all kinds of aggression. Groups that work with refugees, such as the Pastoral and the Jesuits, warned us: "Don't go there! An Evangelical pastor went to help, took on the kitchen, and received a death threat when she tried to organize the queues".*

Yet, four missionaries arrived to pacify the dirty overcrowded space. At the very moment they entered the gym, the police were removing some people involved in a big fight. The police force was there, but one week later the army replaced it to protect the displaced persons day and night. The four missionaries began the work by distributing food kits and cleaning material donated by the Canadian Embassy.

Soon afterwards, the 850 people living in the worst conditions were registered by the UNHCR and by the members of Fraternidade, including those of the office. Each person being helped was given their own card. One Sunday was a landmark day. They all left for the street, had a stroll around the block and reentered showing the identity card. From then on, the soldiers would only allow the entrance of people with ID cards. New efforts were soon made to educate the residents.

These movements built an alliance with the families that felt terrified. Having nowhere to go, they made serious complaints. Clara says: *Because of my way of being, spread the rumor I was an insider of the army. That was positive, in the sense that the people being helped started regarding the Fraternidade in a more respectful way.*

The missionary action was decisive. as the army cannot issue orders, it can only execute them. Clara explains: *I told the responsible military that all those from a certain tent should be sent away because they were caught using marijuana. He fulfilled the operational part. We made daily police reports, took drugs out of tents, sent offenders away. Others, having deviated from the path of love, spontaneously chose to leave. On leaving, they would look at us with expressions of hate.*

Who are those who now hug, then reprehend or send people away? The link was perfect: Fraternidade, with a profound maternal energy, and the army, with a paternal approach. Both had the same purpose, to gradually implement healthy collective norms.

Clara goes on: *We protected the residents. Delinquents who wanted to stay made fake charges against families. We investigated the cases with neighbors and asked, "Captain, we have a mission for you. Someone in that tent is being accused of doing such, and such. Please, investigate to-night if that is false or true.*

Just about everything happened in the first month. One week before the Fraternidade started its daily task, a much beloved young man was clubbed on his neck. He fell. Placed on a bicycle, he was taken to hospital. The missionaries learned about the incident while they were distributing food baskets to the families. The aggressor was still around.

How to deal with this kind of situation in a fraternal manner? Clara called the culprit to the police container: *We were told there has been a problem.* He defended himself. She: *We don't want to know who is right or wrong. There was an aggression, and the boy is in the hospital. Let us hope he recovers, but you will have to leave. If he recovers and says you have reconciled, you will be allowed to return.* She knew very well that this would not happen, but she was being diplomatic.

During the night, the aggressor came back through the gate that re-mained open and threatened to kill those he thought had exposed him, but they were not the ones who did it. As the situation was serious, Clara asked the police to intervene. A report was made and the guy left hand-cuffed. He never returned nor was imprisoned, as no eye-witness of the aggression was willing to testify, even being able to count on the witness protection program and having the possibility of an anonymous charge. No one.

In the meantime, the young beaten man's mother and sister arrived from Venezuela. The Fraternidade helped them with a food kit and some mon-ey. They came daily to give news. But the young man died one month later. The mother cried with pain. The missionaries kept her compa-ny in this painful period, doing whatever was possible for her, from lemon-grass tea to the step by step process of removing his body from the hospital, the biopsy process, burying on Sunday. The cemetery would close at 5 p.m., but the undertaker sympathized with the mother, who wanted to be with her son for at least 15 minutes, and all of them stayed there until 5:30 p.m. The lady wanted justice, made charges in Brazil and also in Venezuela. If the aggressor crosses the border, he will be arrested there, but he remains at large. The missionaries provided the best for the one who desencarnated to make a good crossing. If the Fraternidade were not there, he would have been buried as a pauper.

All that happened during the effort to uplift the energy of the Tancredo Neves, while the army determined an operation of cleaning and renovation of the building was needed. The strategy was to empty it completely, to reform the construction and bring the same residents back. The movement was done at the same time as the first relocation flight of 100 Venezuelans to other parts of Brazil.

For days, each resident was registered and instructed to take their belongings along to a soccer stadium one block away. Everyone would wait three days and two nights having food and a place for lodging until they would be brought back. What was left behind would be taken and burned. What remained was a horrible cardboard and plastic slum, from which twenty-three trucks of trash were taken away. The transfer period caused great tension and fear of not being able to return. However, the anxiety gradually subsided as the promises were true. In the interval they would have food and a place to stay.

A great dark force was occupying the shelter. The rains became partners to erase old footprints and purify the etheric plane. On the eve of the operation, the sky was clear. Suddenly, during the final arrangements meeting, thunders were heard and a violent downpour fell. If the rain had continued, the operation would have to be postponed. The organizers soon smiled to the sun painting the drops of gold. Everything went according to plan. An army meteorologist said that the rain was an out of season phenomenon and that it had been ages since it rained that much as in that same afternoon of the year.

Next morning, once the gymnasium was emptied, the army came in to solve the chaos. With impressive speed they installed a new form of life in a sub-human environment. The military disinfected, washed everything three times, transformed the bathrooms into storage rooms, eliminated the kitchen, painted the building, suspended the external area floor with sand and gravel to avoid puddles, stretched wires, installed plugs to charge cell phones, renovated the water system, built bathrooms and the laundry area created lounge areas, among other actions.

At the same time, the missionaries went through intense hard work. They would leave home at 5:30 a.m. and return at mid-night or later, sometimes not having lunch. They were exhausted, but could see the result: *We worked a lot, but it was worthwhile, it was wonderful to help dissolve their suffering!* As the work finished, the Venezuelans began to return at the first rays of a dawn. Each bag, package and suitcase was carefully inspected so that they would not enter with alcohol, drugs. Fire arms, big knives, swords were confiscated. The homeless had left a horrible place and returned to an unimaginable order. They looked stunned, with shining eyes. Angelica says: *They had expressions of awe, and couldn't believe their eyes: perfectly aligned clean tents.* Clara adds: *How thrilling to give dignity to these people!*

With the basic rhythm established, the environment was now peaceful. Now the souls could rest. Today, the residents live in a clean place, are well-nourished, and collaborate in the maintenance of their big home. Many couples live in two igloo camping tents, with doors turned to face each other. They are allowed to place their possessions in one tent and be together in the other one, as they please. One couple was extremely happy. The husband was living in the refuge area for three months, but since his wife immigrated after him, she had been on a waiting list until the day before. They connected their individual igloo tents with a carpet, a symbol of union and coziness of the temporary home.

Determined to get a job to help his family, a seventy three year old man from El Tigre rode his bicycle for nineteen days. Wherever he stopped, he asked for water, and also was given food. He hasn't gotten a job, but he feels grateful for not being hungry anymore. He likes to repeat his own story: *My son lives in another shelter for the last month. He will be thirty-two, and Fraternidade has gotten me sweets to give him as a birthday gift.*

Some organizations and citizens angrily state that the Venezuelans are all alike and do not deserve support. Xenophobic prejudice is difficult to transcend. Some even believe that the Fraternidade helps them because the UN pays them large amounts of money. Few manage to understand the missionaries work as volunteers, without any payment.

On the other hand, balancing the love-hate scale, there are compassionate people from Roraima. A paramedic was hired after working for two months as a volunteer for Fraternidade. She told me how shy, fragile or hesitant the people being helped feel about consulting the health team: *To*

Tancredo Neves Shelter,
Boa Vista, Roraima, Brazil, 2018

attract patients, we make an active search in the shelters, giving them fra-
ternal support, attention. Some arrive in the container saying they have a
headache. After a good chat, they feel nothing more. Others are depressed
for having studied and not being able to find jobs to express their talent.

Nurses select patients for psychological or clinical assistance according
to the degree of their need and transfer the cases to medical teams of
the Armed Forces or of SESAI—Special Secretariat of Indigenous People. They accompany hospitalization and help the control of diabetes,
hypertension, pregnant women and of vaccines for the "internalization"
program—German measles, mumps, measles, control of hepatitis B, give
a complex vitamin to reinforce their immunity.

When the Brazilian nurse studied in Venezuela, she had to cross by boat
to and from Margarita Island. During her trips she became acquainted
with a young woman who worked on the ferry boat. As soon as she returned home due to the Venezuelan crisis, she offered herself as a volunteer for Fraternidade. One day, she went with some missionaries to a
square to distribute donated things and recognized the woman from the
ferry with her two small thin children. Her eyes were filled with tears
as she recalls: *It was shocking, they used to live well, they ate freely. My*
mother and my grandmother accepted to have the three living in our home.
Both enrolled the children at school and helped the young woman to have
her documents issued.

Thousands of Venezuelans feel the living, real, brotherhood. Something
invisible and profound impacted hundreds of those who witnessed the
shelter reconstruction. The energy vortex rose, a new visual aspect and
ceremonial were implemented, and the place became a role model.

Clara wraps it up: *We have rendered a service even for the soul of Tancre-*
do Neves, a Brazilian president who died before taking office. Imagine the
soul of someone who dies whose name is connected with such wrong things.
He must have found relief with the new reality.

The examples of givers-of-oneself imprints altruism in those who are
served. An occult chemistry takes place through everyday activities leading people to overcome nationalism and separateness.

Nova Canaã Shelter

How to be at peace now? Reconciling
with the present moment. This moment
is the field in which the game of life happens...
We do not live our lives: it is life that lives us.
Life is the dancer, and we are the dance.
A New Earth—Awakening to your Life's Purpose
by Eckhart Tolle

In Roraima, all is intense, says a missionary: *The work is intense, love is intense, growth is intense, the pain is intense, all in the same degree.* Above the Equator, the sun burns hotter. However, a shadow darkened the Caribbean people. Full of vigor, they were placed in a gray moment by the well-known law of karma. What did they do in the past to have to go through this? What do they need to learn?

In order for the intuition of the immigrants to gain light and color, national and international organizations join into a network to meet the need. Each contributes to the neighbors to overcome material and psychic obstacles. Even though the Fraternidade attentively takes care of practical issues seven days a week, its focus is the souls. The missionaries are in this place for the sake of refugee and migrant souls.

The turbulent characteristics of the Venezuelan people surfaced during their stressful period of losses and uncertainties. One missionary notices: *The tropical climate influences one's temper. Although they bring with them the fear of a fugitive and the anguish of the hopeless, they carry a vibrant energy. They stay on fire, but must find a basic balance to overcome negative traits. I believe the main thing is to keep their souls shining. In Greece, we saw that dim eyes looking downwards reflect fading souls.*

Through the Humanitarian Logistic Task-Force, precise steps were taken to set up another shelter, the Reception Center, also known as Nova Canaã, name of the district where it is located.

Within three days, the Brazilian Army prepared the infrastructure and the landscaping. Then installed containers with bathrooms and showers, and set up UNHCR tents sent from Denmark, made of a light material with mosquito nets. In front of the stalls, rooms of two L-shaped corridors have been remodeled.

In two corridors are the office, kitchen, laundry area, storage room for food, hygiene and cleaning items. Nurses from the Fraternidade and doctors from the army meet in a consulting room. The building has rooms for art and craftsmanship, Portuguese and Spanish classes and one for seamstresses. In another room, people make baby food and prepare bottles for babies up to two years of age, as there is no food for them except the packed lunches brought in by the army.

After painting the walls white and the doors and windows green, the Army launched a humanitarian action with the UNHCR. They had the support of the Saint Francis Social Assistance Reference Center, the Military Police, the Traffic Department, the City Guard, the City Secretariat of Social Management and the Fraternidade.

On a Tuesday morning, something unexpected happened. Six hundred Venezuelans from the Capitão Clovis Square, one of the oldest squares in Boa Vista, and some others from Simão Bolivar square were removed. Without knowing their destination, the refugees and migrants had breakfast donated by the army, before being transferred by bus to the Selection Center of Latif Salomão Palace, downtown, where they spent the night.

There they were immunized and registered. Then, it was defined what shelter they would live in, and got access cards to it. Since there were many families with children living on the square, it was determined that the Nova Canaã would host sixty-five families, amounting to 350 people. The number of young pregnant women arriving in Brazil is staggering.

As soon as they crossed the shelter entrance gate under the surveillance of the military, the Fraternidade received them. In the area surrounded by white walls, they came across sixty-eight perfectly aligned white tents. With two rooms each, families that had never met one another before would live side by side. Even so, they began to have a better life.

A migrant receives an offer to voluntarily
move to other states of Brazil.
Nova Canaã Shelter, Boa Vista, Roraima, Brazil, May 2018

Venezuelans arrive emotionally and physically wounded by insecurities of the arduous journey between their homeland and the city squares, where tropical rainstorms were flooding their possessions. The newly sheltered experienced three moves in their first 24 hours. They were still recovering from exhaustion when, in the early hours of the night, a downpour soaked their belongings and documents. The water level came up to their knees.

The next day, while the army brought tractors to raise the ground level, Venezuelans dug ditches to avoid new floods and pushed construction carts filled with gravel. They were told that a large canvas would arrive to overlay all the tents protecting them from the rain and the sun-rays helping to reduce the heat inside them.

A few days later, five other families arrived. As always, the missionaries led them to the tents, gave them mattresses and kits for personal hygiene and cleaning. Hours later, one family—husband, wife and two young children—threw all the items they were given over the wall and left. The parents had lost their sense of responsibility. Everything in the shelter needs to be put away, locked.

The coordinator says: *These are the human beings that we have to love unconditionally. At the same time, we must be fair, convey codes of behavior to them, and never overlook wrong attitude, because non-action is a contrary action. At the same time, we must be correct and just. We must pass on to them the proper way to behave. If we see a wrong attitude, do not remain silent because to say nothing is to condone their wrong action. There is a need to set limits. This is a function of the coordinators and also, it depends on each personality, of each missionary. Sometimes this is difficult and we enter into an existential crisis.*

Just as that family fled, life sent another—father, mother, five children, the youngest with serious malnutrition. They were filthy from head to toe. The surprise of the mother as she received the kits was touching. Looking at the soap bars, she kept repeating: Is it one for each of us? Taken to a tent with seven mattresses, she was perplexed and grateful: *Are we going to stay here on our own?*

As soon as missionaries arrive at Nova Canaã, at 8 a.m., each one takes up their task. Two distribute breakfast with the soldiers, chocolate milk,

Young man observes the rain.
Nova Canaã Shelter, Boa Vista, Roraima, Brazil, May 2018

sweets, bread, fruit. Later on, they serve lunch and dinner. The coordinator has barely arrived at the office, when she receives the news from that night: drugs, robbery.

In order to prevent people from arguing in the queues, saying things such as: *I arrived first. No, I was first!* To solve this problem it was arranged that only one member of each family would receive a booklet to pick up food for the others. First, one missionary checks his own list with the number of the family document. Then the person is free to pick up their allowed portions.

After one week, the people being assisted deceived the missionaries. They went to the office, saying they had lost their papers. Out of trust, they were given a new booklet written "duplicate". The fraud was discovered when packed lunches were missing. They took two lunches instead of one, ate the meat throwing the rest away. In a surprise meeting all the booklets were collected and put on a table. Several of them were duplicated. After that, the method of control was changed to laminated cards.

Before breakfast, the coordinator takes the microphone to speak to the group waiting behind a rope: *Has anyone ever heard about UNICEF? No one? It is the United Nations organization that looks after children. They will be here on Saturday. We will inaugurate the Child Friendly Lounge. Indigenous children from the Pintolândia Shelter school will also come. So, all the kids will be able to interact. Our idea is that we, Venezuelans and*

Brazilians, should not have borders. A child is a child, it doesn't matter if they are indigenous or "criollos". Let us play and learn to co-exist. Clara added: *Those who want to work with the children, come and talk to me after lunch.* People, especially women, rejoice. Some of them raise their hand and accept the invitation.

Clara welcomes cheerfully those with an incredulous look. They sit in a circle of chairs. She makes jokes. After sometime they all start to feel at ease, laugh.

In order to set up the shelter's board of teachers for the children's school, she makes an introduction before each candidate presents themselves: *We want each one of you to put your talents and capacities into practice. We hope you may turn this shelter into a home. Of course, there are problems, just like in any family. One brother argues with another, but they let it go. In general, we need to be united! Let us show the children that this is their home.* Tears roll down a woman's face.

Relaxation gradually sweeps the circle. People start to speak up. They have taught science, math, language, drawing, and physical education. A university teacher says: *We are here to help one another.* A feeling of kinship is born. Some are eager to speak, be heard and valued by the thirty people around. Clara explains: *The UNICEF will train volunteer helpers with a course at UFRR. We will give the adults a general training so that they can be attentive, so their children don't get hurt.*

She goes on: *The hairdresser is invited to set up a beauty salon, cut people's hair and create beautiful hairstyles. No one can charge for their work, but all can work as volunteers. The lady that brought a sewing machine will stay in the dressmakers' room. The woman who is a specialist in birthday parties will plan monthly celebrations for the children's birthday. Please, bring us the list of the decorations for the hall.*

At last, Clara adds: *We will help the children not to lose what they've previously learned. The schools of Boa Vista are overcrowded, so we must teach them here. The army has placed a TV set in the hall, and the teachers can request movies to watch with the students. Some of these have positive messages, they are excellent for family viewing. We have to decide the program together, so there is no risk the children fight among themselves, imitating what they watched on television. We need to be very alert, analyzing what we show to our children. You can also suggest programs for the*

Breakfast at the Nova Canaã Shelter, Boa Vista, Roraima, Brazil, May 2018

adults to watch. Not Brazilian soap operas, please! These teach us the very opposite of what should be done. We will not prohibit them, you will decide what to watch, but pay attention to what principles are behind the scenes! People's hope reappears: *For adults who want to continue studies, there is a path. It is not easy, but it is possible to validate your university diploma.*

Once the meeting is over, they are all cheered up. Clara tells them to go to the office to get an A4 sheet of paper and a pen to write down their projects. Having arrived from a country that has excluded them, they feel devastated. The power to build something new, to collaborate, rekindles their spark. They start trusting themselves as citizens and strengthening their positive aspects. *No one can be happy only with food and a mattress, a minimal condition to be on the planet,* she concludes.

The law of the eternal return acting upon these people gives them the opportunity to mature. A karma can be either for a family, a group of people, can be national or planetary. Venezuelan souls have chosen extreme tension to recover qualities and grow as a group. Actually, they ask for help to learn how to follow the path of love. They are called to take steps to reverse rooted negative tendencies. Life places Venezuelans in

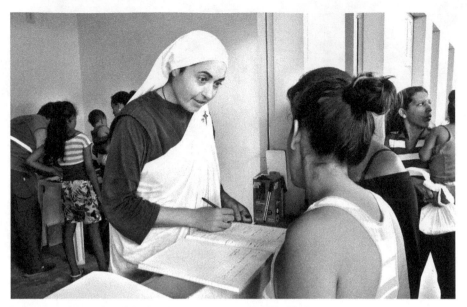

Registering. Nova Canaã Shelter, Boa Vista, Roraima, May 2018

contact with humanitarian organisms in which they can find new references about altruistic values. They can learn to be generous and to serve their neighbors. Encouraged to express their best qualities, they must respect group rules to find collective peace. They receive basic education about behavior, order, cleanliness, and community life.

Since some personal decisions are not allowed, some sheltered people feel they are losing their free will, which upsets them terribly. Dissatisfied, they rebel against the coordinators who make them feel they are not so unique. Their egos cannot even accept what does them good, because it was not chosen by them. Some of them keep complaining, saying they are being mistreated. They feel profoundly empty, and nothing fills them.

They think only about themselves and, not seeing the whole, try to impose themselves on others. Sarcastic comments trigger conflicts in the environment, which makes the missionary work harder. For example, some Venezuelans get angry when milk and diapers are distributed demanding a certain brand of these items. Even being at the bottom of the pit, their arrogance is still there. Many have lost ethics, and are emotionally sick, even in the moral sense: they lie and deceive people.

Missionaries and children from the shelter.
Nova Canaã Shelter, Boa Vista, Roraima, May 2018

Another common issue is their impulsiveness. While missionaries are attending to someone, an anxious refugee interrupts: I *have just one little question.* The servers repeatedly explain to them one by one: *In Brazil, the one who comes later waits for the one in front to finish talking. Is someone dying in your tent? Did anyone get hurt? Is a baby being born? No? So, just wait!*

It is normal for mothers to leave their child alone in bathrooms. The kid relieves himself wherever he pleases, his mother comes, picks him up, does not clean the floor, and goes leaving dirty diapers behind.

Many people that are being assisted live in promiscuity. They had just sent a man away who had left his wife to be with another woman. Furious, the newly married woman wounded him superficially with a knife and she was not sent away only because she had a baby.

In the Tancredo Neves Shelter, married women would take a shower and walk fifty yards wrapped in small towels among dozens of men, nearly all of them bachelors. The missionaries had to meet with them to explain they must not do that. In the breakfast queue, they would go wearing a transparent gown. Clara asked them: *"Hermana", is this your underwear? They laughed. You can't come for breakfast wearing that, you must change your clothes. Don't give food to her.* Slowly, after three of them were told the same thing, they understood.

During the daily tests, in less than half an hour there are two blatant scenes. Clara repeats to a frustrated man: *You have to share. You are all Venezuelans.* In a little while, she gives some explanation to a young woman who, without telling the coordinator, went to live by herself in a tent after arguing with her parents: *We are getting many requests from people in the streets with young babies, under this rain, and you are occupying the space of one family.* Unconcerned, the young woman gets annoyed, her face deformed by anger, saying she will leave the shelter. Rude reactions happen often. Most take their words back, and stay. The coordinator soon sends them all a new message over the microphone: *Please, return the trash cans that you have taken away from the bathrooms, otherwise all tents will be searched.*

Some wonder how would Brazilians and people from other countries react to these situations. A missionary-nun says: *In the humanitarian service in Roraima, we feel we are growing spiritually. By realizing the other person's difficulties, we grow in consciousness, as this leads us to revise our own attitudes. We end up finding out that we make the same mistakes, only to a lesser degree.*

Later in the morning, the coordinator receives a phone call and heads to give another general notice over the microphone: *Couples with children who are interested in being taken to other Brazilian capitals can come and see me now in front of the office.* She is immediately surrounded by tense faces, eyes questioning about a possible future. It is a relief when they accept relocation to other parts of Brazil. Roraima gets less crowded.

The missionaries serve lunch and then get in the car to go eat in the Light-Nucleus of the Sacred Tepui of Roraima. They laugh recalling a dear firefighter whom they met in another shelter. At Nova Canaã, they met a military man with similar compassion. He started talking in a harsh tone with a Venezuelan who had committed an offense, but gradually attenuated the tone: *Well, we can reconsider...* Later, he called the coordinator to one side: *I wonder if it's better not to send him away...*

Nova Canaã Shelter, Boa Vista, Roraima, Brazil, February 2019

Service brings people closer

When we are face to face with people,
we had better avoid the curiosity vibration,
opposed to charity, from molding our
discernment, leading us to judgment,
comments, and condemnation.
Silence, Beloved Silence, by Friar Luciano

In painful times, humanitarian groups join efforts to build peace amidst humanity. When they achieve harmonious mutual cooperation, they sow love, order.

Boa Vista was the setting of a humanitarian action involving 877 refugees from Venezuela and more than 400 servers united by fraternal service.

With overcrowded local shelters and Venezuelans maltreated by a harsh journey, they were living for months in the Simon Bolivar square—name of the leader that led their country to independence. Clustered under old trees, they set up camping tents or improvised ones made of blue and black plastic, or slept outdoors in hammocks or even on beds of cardboard. When rain storms blew in, they ran towards a marquee. Some had fever, others asthma.

Accustomed to living in homes and having their jobs, they untiringly look for employment. Life in the plazas is restless. It undermines and shakes people's consciousnesses and can trigger deviations. Being in the street, they cooked on wood burners, selling meals and other products, gave people haircuts, repaired shoes.

At any given moment, the square was enclosed within walls of siding panels, which made it difficult to receive the already scarce food donations. Then they saw drones flying over them. They did not know these were being monitored by the army, which were counting the number of residents to be transferred soon—from eight hundred to one thousand.

On a Sunday, at 3 a.m., they were taken by surprise. Soldiers isolated and divided the round square in quadrants. It would be empty within hours.

The action was jointly coordinated and achieved by the masterful Brazilian Army and the UNHCR.

The military team, supported by the City Civil Guard, installed forty chemical toilets, while three ambulances for emergencies were parked in waiting and three buses for the transfer of the refugees. Bread and butter, chocolate milk, apple and cookies were served to each immigrant. Having eaten, they started to be removed by stages in order by quadrant one, two, three and four. First, the families, then the women and the children, then finally the men.

The military searched each piece of luggage, item by item. Part of it was sent to trash, such as blank weapons, toys that imitated guns, old and dirty mattresses. People's belongings were packed and identified in the presence of their owners, to be returned to them later. Before the Venezuelans embarked, the humanization team of the City Secretariat of Social Management put a little identification bracelet on each person's wrist.

The precise choreography, directed by admirable logistics, continued as Venezuelans entered the temporary shelter Latif Salomão. The human flow walked around a welcoming circuit, going through tables arrayed under a tent structure.

City Hall attendants received them, checked their vaccine cards and papers, and filled in a form about how each person planned their own future. If someone's vaccines were not up to date, they were attended by the immunization team. From there, people moved on to the UNHCR agents, who took a photo of each person and immediately printed and laminated their card with basic data and the shelter name where they would stay.

The place was very orderly with chemical bathrooms, filtered water, seats in a row. The army, which supplies all shelters with three meals daily, distributed snacks to those who had arrived and lunch for the nearly 500 immigrants who were settling down in the Latif Salomão.

After they received the card, the Fraternidade directed them one by one to their new accommodations. Friar Luciano, general manager of the missionaries, who was there at the time, says: *Our focus is on supporting the needy, not on a religion.* Wearing long white and beige habits, the monastics rolled up their sleeves and made as much effort as the missionaries in following the guidelines given by the UNHCR coordinators, a lay organization.

Throughout the work, an occult chemistry took place, and no one discriminated or excluded the monastics because of their garments.

The Fraternidade followed up with every Venezuelan. Some of them to the waiting room, those who would catch the bus or vans to their respective destinations. Families were sent to the Nova Canaã or Jardim Floresta Shelters, and bachelors to Santa Teresa Shelter, which was opening on that day. Their luggage went with them. At their destination, they were met by other teams of Fraternidade. A peaceful flow was the main note of the humanitarianism.

To those who stayed in Latif Salomão, the missionaries handed out hygiene kits, and took them to the tents or bunk beds, showing them the bathrooms, the laundry area, the TV room. Their talks highlighted something positive.

During that brief and respectful direct contact, the Venezuelans' tone of complaints and criticisms dissolved. A clash of values occurred: *They started to realize that there are other things in life, equality, giving of one's self without expecting anything in return. The attitude of expecting nothing from them, not even that they be from our group, that they pray, makes them wonder: After all, who are those who help without asking anything, who welcome us even if they get offended? What voluntary work is this?! This is the work up front, without mysteries, which occurs in an impersonal and kind way,* adds Friar Luciano.

Those individuals cross the border in despair, where love is lacking and healing is needed. They bring feelings of despair, fear and uncertainties in their auras and also in the inner world. Most of them feel hatred, resentment. Besides their personal conflicts, they take along feelings crystallized in their country of origin.

On that Sunday, the Venezuelans walked along a compassionate line of humanitarian servers. At first, they showed the usual mistrust that dwells in humans, which was disarmed during the constant care they were given: food, vaccine to prevent diseases and epidemics, being looked in the eyes, short dialogs and smiles, a hand touch, a kit, and a roof for shelter.

Everything has pros and cons. On the square, if it rains, it floods, but they eat whatever they want, sleep wherever they want. In the shelters, food is provided by the army, there are regulations and order, and the gates open and close at fixed hours.

At the end of the operation, the servers clapped their hands, celebrating: *The square is empty! The square is empty!*

After dismantling the reception court, the military immediately swept the place, which was now clean and tidy, as if nothing had happened there. *Spectacular!* exclaims missionary Shen.

At the beginning of the day, they thought they would spend the whole night emptying the square however, at 5 p.m., all Venezuelans had been transferred.

On the way back to their homes, strolling on Sunday avenues and streets, the missionaries became aware of the unraveling of the work. They felt happy for being Brazilians and unanimously declared: *Congratulations to Brazil.* They were very grateful.

The goal of fraternal practice is profound, and aims at expanding the love of the one who serves and also of whom is being served. With greater or less feeling of kinship, 1,300 human beings were busy in the process, each one with a role and a lesson to be learned. The result shows that the planet is on a pilgrimage toward a new cycle, gestated in the unity among people and hearts for the benefit of the needy.

For decades it has been prophesied that Brazil will be the granary of a new humanity, peaceful, and uplifted. The experience has enabled comprehension to flourish among nations.

Mediators and peace-makers

The chilly mountain breeze, you sing golden legends,
diamonds shining under the sun, glorious Pacaraima,
my home, my future, my ground. Angels fly in the skies
revealing Universal secrets. You are a star in the darkesh night,
illuminating the border. My beautiful Venezuela, dear sister:
nations united by a single song, bond in a single heart.
Song of the Little Canaries Ambassadors of Peace
Lyrics by Míriam Blos

Thirty volunteers from the Brazilian Southeast, Northeast and North, following the motto, "Only love can heal the pain," landed in Boa Vista. From that morning on, they did their best to relieve the hunger of indigenous people and *criollos* camping in a public market and established a routine of offering food and basic services.

Four days after arriving in Boa Vista, they went to the town of Pacaraima to understand the circumstances of the main entrance of the Venezuelan exodus and to introduce themselves to the local authorities.

The missionaries greeted the street-dwellers, the Waraos. They were taking love, charity, clothes, fruit and other foods. Since the first contact, they had the inspiration to have a base of the Fraternidade in Pacaraima. During that visit, they were invited to participate in a meeting in the parish hall with governmental and religious entities, focusing on how to collaborate in the face of the growing number of people entering Brazil.

Missionary groups came and went to strengthen bonds with indigenous people. Each time, they saw a larger number of silent travelers of all ages and social classes carrying suitcases. Among boxes, bags and handbags, they waited for their future under marquees or sitting on the floor of the crowded bus station.

Being lost, with no jobs, and not knowing if they will ever return to their homeland, the despair runs with those steps trying to escape darkness. On a dirt road parallel to the street that is the borderline between both countries, some Venezuelans cooked on a camp fire next to an abandoned bus.

There were calls for other meetings, in one of them the mayor questioned the missionaries in front of the official commission of the federal government arriving from Brasilia: *When will the Fraternidade get here? We need a group like yours.* Someone who is willing to love the native people as brothers and sisters is needed. The answer stayed hanging there in the air. It only materialized when the FIHM signed the agreement of cooperation with the UN. Funds were available, and so was the blueprint of an exclusive shelter for 200 indigenous people. Soon, the structure, an old glazing shop, would meet the minimal standards required by the UNHCR in an emergency.

Humanitarian work provides people with shelter, food, and health. It is different from humanitarian service. A missionary explains: *We may give them food, satisfy their hunger, relieve their pain, but how does love enter into all that? You learn love through daily living. The most beautiful part of a mission is to get to know the people. Some situations require our presence because of these bonds. We are peace-makers, mediators, facilitators between the refugees and different organizations.*

The Pacaraima Mountain Ranges have one of the highest peaks in Brazil, Mount Roraima, a pre-Cambrian formation that gave its name to the state. The word derives from indigenous language, Pemon, and means green-blue mountain—roro-imã. Pacaraima town is among its tree covered ridges. It is considered a relaxing resort for vacations and weekends. Tourists also used to come to shop in Venezuela.

Twelve thousand Pacaraimans lived peacefully in the simple border town. People joking say that the town is Roraima's North Pole due to its rainy, cold climate in a tropical state. From 2015 onwards, ten to forty neighbors a day began to take refuge in town, causing health, sanitation, security, and education issues.

Three years later, the local authority decreed a state of emergency. Hundreds of displaced people lodge in an abandoned condominium or on an open-air platform for parties. The refugees protected some parts of it with black plastic, which was swinging in the wind. Some distance further along is an endless line of poles painted white that delineate the boundary between the countries. From there, the border-control building can be seen. Disappearing into the mists on the horizon is the sacred

Newly-arrived Venezuelans wait under a marquee.
Pacaraima, Roraima, Brazil, 2018

Roraima table-top mountain. A police car arrives distributing food. To get it, dozens of people, among them young mothers and children, begin to come out from behind black plastic sheets that are used as doors.

In October 2017, two missionaries walked around the streets to be closer to the indigenous people. They were waiting for the renovation of the exclusive natives' shelter. On the first days, they lodged at the home of the Spanish priest named Jesus, who, since the beginning of the immigration, has been offering daily breakfast in the parish at 5 a.m. There, the missionaries helped to serve 400 refugees, a number that doubled in six months. Father Jesus gives religious assistance to Waraos, who are evangelized and supported by Catholic missions in the state Delta Amacuro, the area from which they come.

Days later, another two Fraternidade missionaries arrived. The four stayed at a hotel near a Warao sidewalk settlement until they managed to rent a house. They started to evaluate health issues and photographed people's skin diseases derived from the unsanitary conditions of where they slept and cooked, which brought embarrassment to passers-by. They took the photos to be analyzed by the Health Secretariat, which would begin vaccination and primary emergency attention.

Life in town had changed quickly. Hundreds of Venezuelans wandered in and criminal cases of thefts, including one murder, began to increase. Resentful, the Pacaraimans were against humanitarian help. *They spoke to us in the streets, in shops, thinking that we were there to make money and did not meet the needs of Brazilians*, says Imer, the first coordinator of the group. They complained that refugees left trash in public areas and consumed alcoholic drinks. The missionaries listened to them and tried to calm them down: The situation is really critical—children begging in the streets, prostitution on the increase, there are health issues, but... During their dialogue, the residents gradually sympathized with the harsh reality of their neighbors. As they got to know the missionary's actions, they started to accept it: *We've come to help with the human aspect, we don't deal with political issues. We've come to seek solutions to dignify the immigrants' life.*

Obtaining documents is the first step in the process of reconstructing refugee lives in the new environment. To do so, a group was created for their registration according to the UNHCR's standards. The Migrant Pastoral, some representatives of the Migration and Human Rights Institute, and six Fraternidade Missionarieswho also participated. In five days, they registered 800 people, with photos and finger prints. The census also showed how many indigenous people and *criollos* chose to stay in Pacaraima.

On the third night of registering, a young missionary, newly-arrived from São Paulo, had a dream after praying for the indigenous consciousness: *I dreamed I was inside a hut in an indigenous community. They gave me their artisan articles—baskets, hats, straw rugs— desperately asking me to hide them. I hugged the objects. They were so beautiful!* The young woman had never had any contact with indigenous people. One week later, she was in charge of the Pintolândia Shelter artisan sector. For the first time, she got to know what they weave, similar to what she had dreamed about. She says: *Then I knew people were entering their homes in Venezuela to steal what they had made. And that even happens in Boa Vista. They began to fear selling at the traffic lights, because drivers stop their cars to steal their handcrafted articles. In a minute, they lose what took them months to make.*

To learn more about Pacaraima's life, the missionaries participated in some local altruistic groups. One started giving them organic greens. Between the groups there was a warm spirit which opened their contact with sectors of the community. They also established a partnership with City Hall, which yielded them a former round indigenous house for the storage of donations made by the UNHCR—a small but well provided stock of cleaning, educational, craftsmanship and sewing material with needles, threads, spangles, beads, fabrics.

They would attend rehearsals of the refugee children's choir, the Humanitarian Channel of the Little Canaries of the Amazon, Canal Humanitário dos Canarinhos da Amazônia, which brings back joy to children and adults. Among them was a Venezuelan musician couple. The wife, a young flute player, was psychologically afflicted and sad when the couple arrived in Brazil. She had lost hope. Having been welcomed, she started to play, sing, and smile again. She and her husband, himself a conductor, now teaches music to Venezuelan children, some of which live in the streets. She regained the beauty of a mother, wife, teacher by means of this work.

Míriam Blos, the Brazilian who created and coordinates the choir, said: *In this place of music we try to make the life of Venezuelan children less painful. They will continue the journey of their people. We have chosen music to convey to them the message of the evolution of consciousness. We are aware that several spiritual colonies exist in the etheric plane of the tepuis that are schools for children. They emanate energies and feelings to us that we express in our musical meetings. Incredible transformations have taken place in the lives of these children and mothers, the most vulnerable among those coming to Brazil. They arrive emotionally unstable, without perspectives, and we teach them to "re-enchant" their gaze and their heart. We use music, this wonderful tool, to bring them back to radiating love, which generates the miracle of self-giving.*

Fifteen days after Fraternidade arrived in Pacaraima, the City Hall agreed to move the natives to the shelter, even before the bathrooms and the hammock areas—iron structures to hang hammocks—were finished.

Imer says: *The city is at the end of the line, where the country ends. Building material, trucks, logistics, everything takes ages to happen. We started to transfer some 200 indigenous people and their objects and food they gather to take back to families left behind. After being taken from a downtown area near the bus station, a truck of the fire brigade cleaned the sidewalks where they had been living.*

Young girls newly-arrived from Venezuela, in the bus station near the Brazil-Venezuela border. Pacaraima, Roraima, Brazil, May 2017

Thus, was born the Janokoida Shelter, "big house," in Warao. It began to be visited by delegations and by the national and international press, always welcomed by the guardian missionaries. Different from the shelter of Boa Vista, which was installed in a sports court without any structure, in Pacaraima there was preorganization and a larger group experience.

Groups working in humanitarian emergencies move around as much as the indigenous people. The small missionary team changes whenever the general coordinator asks them to go to another shelter or start a rest period to revive themselves in Figueira. Missionaries replacing one another give continuity to the projects and their deeper/inner purpose.

When I visited Pacaraima, there were four missionaries—a thirty five year old woman and a fifty six year old, and two men aged twenty one and forty seven. They worked in the shelter from 8 a.m. to 6 p.m., in two shifts, pausing at lunchtime to eat and pray. The ones needing to rest or to work at the computer—on registrations, administrative documents—stays at home. For spiritual nourishment, they also pray early in the morning and before going to bed, at night.

Sincerity and dialogue make the difference in our group. This way, we gather positive energies to cope with the external world. Our strength lies in union. If anyone gets rude, I ask them if they want to stay home, resting, says Debora, the coordinator.

In this simple house on the top of a hill surrounded by woods, the water shortage happens daily and is not stabilized even in rainy season. The light is repeatedly out, the Internet is constantly off and the border town often runs out of gas. Once Pacaraima had no gasoline for over a month. The missionaries had to climb up and down the hills on foot. The nearest and only gas station of the region is in Venezuela, but since Fraternidade needs a Brazilian bill of sale to justify the purchase of supplies, they could not fill up the tank. Only after the Fire Brigade brought them a gallon of gas from Boa Vista, they went out to buy mineral water.

At breakfast, while they made fresh juice and tapioca, the good-humored missionaries told stories. Young Gabriel laughs: *Having no drinking water was an interesting experience. Life goes on and we are happy anyway. One and a half blocks from here, there is a fountain of non-drinkable water, where indigenous people wash clothes. We would fetch water and do our laundry and had a lot of fun with them. Life is beautiful regardless of the situation. We have to persevere. Since the day we ran out of gas, all I want is to walk to and from the shelter on foot, it is good exercise.* But no one is indifferent to the lack of water. When it comes back they celebrate: *Dear Pacaraima, my delightful town, in the daytime there is no water , at nighttime, you have no light.*

Alexandrina exclaims: *Everything is hard work. We have a thousand problems. But when I see the faces of the most beautiful, sweet and pure kids of the shelter, wow, my heart melts! The ladies do gorgeous handicraft work, dance for the visitors. We encourage men, "Come on, let's do it!" And they help us in this or that.* She has the ability of visualizing an innocent poem written on each indigenous face, noticing sweetness in every gaze. She smiles and leads little kids in a line among the tents: *Here comes the train, chugga, chugga, chuugga, choo choooo!*

Pacaraima is the gateway from the Caribbean region into Brazil. In the town, refugees and those who work with them directly have established a united family. When there is a concert given by the Canarinhos Choir, everyone attends. The same happens with the Mass. Clerks of Social Assistance, of the Health Secretariat and the Mayor himself transfer their excess donations. A missionary says: *We take on difficulties together.* Someone reports: *"Three children were found in such-n-such a place." We leave together to help them. Walking downtown it's a joy whenever we meet indigenous people at work carrying packages or looking for casual*

Venezuelan refugees, a hundred yards from the border.
Pacaraima, Roraima, Brazil, May 2018

jobs. The way the local residents look at the missionaries has changed. At the arrival of those four tall, white bearded men wearing similar gray clothes, rumors spread that they were foreign spies, but over time the missionaries' service managed to soothe all anxieties.

Having dinner on the balcony of the missionaries' house is a soothing experience. Night crickets and birds singing are lullabies to them. Sacred energies emanate from Mount Roraima, one of humanity's heritage and a mysterious dwelling of warrior nuns. Before the sun rises behind vegetation-covered mountains, a ruby light blazes the clouds and paints in gold the frames of the illusory boundaries created by humans.

Hidden currents of solar energy project an invisible light of armor on the borders. Day by day, they protect people's consciousnesses battling for peace, and for violated Venezuelan lives. The powerful union of local, interstate and international groups guide the steps of the refugees towards a less troubled life. In partnership and with the same goal, servers are precious pieces in the building of planetary healing.

Fraternal groups form constellations of sister stars that sparkle with fire, but their feet are firmly grounded. Since they love life in spite of difficulties, they radiate renewing energies, healing, love among lost souls in conflicts and mayhem. A few people's arms are enough when the consciousness strives in the quest of the imperceptible goal and knows that the Sun shines from the bottommost of each human essence.

Janokoida, Big House

The influence of the Sun over different levels of consciousness
is expanding, and the spiritual impulse from this star is
very important for the current phase of the Earth, a phase
that will place it in harmony with subtler vibrations.
The Healing of Humanity, by Trigueirinho

Human beings are extremely heterogeneous. The missionaries have no intention of changing any of them according to their personal views, but to help them solve adverse situations and bring peace to those who ask for help. Believing the human beings are greater than their own mistakes, they seek to love each essence of life, without getting influenced by external factors—color, nationality, social or cultural status.

In eighteen months, the members of the Fraternidade made contact with about 3,000 Warao indigenous people. Mutual respect has largely expanded between both groups which have become teachers of each other. *Indigenous people have a pure heart, they are more emotional and not so intellectual as we are,* says Debora, a coordinator. *I feel that our role is to bring them a little peace, to calm them, because almost all of them are sick, either because of a decayed tooth or a wound. Their relatives are dying in Venezuela and they want to take them medicine and food. We try to keep them busy, to organize the school life of the children, to provide craftsmanship for women, work for men. This is our task until a blessed soul or institution donates land with water and buriti palm trees where they can give continuity to what they do as an ethnic group.*

When the Brazilian government and international organizations assumed responsibility for fulfilling Venezuelans basic needs—hygiene, food and health—the Fraternidade remained in their task of uplifting the indigenous consciousness while sharing in their daily routine. Inner and outer transformations take place in a simple and natural way.

Indoor and outdoor areas in the Janokoida Shelter.
Pacaraima, Roraima, Brazil, May 2018

Several activities help to solve the refugees' main problem, which is their idle daily routine in a confined place, which causes multiple conflicts. People need to focus their energy and thoughts in intelligent activities.

Indigenous life is hectic. Sometimes a group of twenty or thirty arrive or leave at dawn. They go back and forth around Pacaraima, Venezuela, Boa Vista, Manaus. However, as the crisis in their homeland is aggravated, they are becoming more stable.

The army remains in the Janokoida Shelter around the clock, working in shifts. They watch the gate and the shelter and provide security to the missionaries. After 9 p.m. no one enters, unless the soldiers were previously informed. The army brought food, order, cleanliness. They installed water reservoirs and six containers: one for themselves, two dorms for soldiers, one for SETRABES and Fraternidade, one ambulatory and bathrooms for men and women. Two large tents were set up in the yard; one for meetings, talks and playing, another for the distribution of donations.

The military and missionaries solve several daily issues together, such as talking with families about their disagreements. Firm, yet flexible, they spread harmony. Coordinating the Janokoida shelter is an easier job than the Boa Vista shelters, since it is smaller, has fewer people, and the mild climate is a relief.

The army also brought leisure games to the shelter, which pacify the environment: table tennis, volleyball, soccer for children, dodge-ball, dominoes, cards. Captains often take part in games with the children, playing dominoes, ping-pong.

Since the beginning, workers of SETRABES began their psychological and pedagogical support to the indigenous people, especially to children and adolescents. They encourage their education. Students first had classes and playful activities at the Caminho de Luz School of the shelter. Then, they were invited by the priest to attend classes with other Venezuelans in the Children Pastoral, which, just like the Fraternidade, has an ecumenical side. It assists people of all beliefs and ethnicities. In the mornings, ten Waraos teachers of the shelter organize into queues 160 students between four and eighteen years old, by age, size and gender. The smallest one holds the hand of the teacher who leads them. Clean

Indigenous people gather wood to cook lunch in the shelter.
Pacaraima, Roraima, Brazil, May 2018

and tidy, they walk smiling in the streets towards the parish, where they are given classes of Warao, Spanish and Portuguese.

On rainy days, the kids walk to class in small groups carrying a canvas over their heads. Back from school to their Janokoida home, their cheerful screaming lightens up missionaries and soldiers, who rush to play with them, in joy.

In the afternoon, the kids watch educational movies, engage in games or in a new project between the Fraternidade and the UNHCR, to continue the morning classes. The ten Waraos and another three hired teachers: a musician, an educator and a physical educator participate.

Aiming to rescue the native cultural roots, SETRABES promoted a cultural festival for youths, who learned with the elderly a typical Warao dance. According to a Fraternidade coordinator: *It was the most serene moment of the current dense experience. We remain faithful that there is a deeper hidden meaning for the painful situations happening.*

Soon after the opening of the shelter, a food supply agreement was about to be signed. It took a while before the army started to deliver the items for a balanced menu, according to the nutritional standard of the World

Each family cooks their own meal at the back of the shelter.
Pacaraima, Roraima, Brazil, May 2018

Nutrition Fund, which sends them through the UN. However, five months later, the shelter was overcrowded—it lodges today 500 indigenous people, about 120 families—and the food amount had to be doubled.

The proposal is to respect the indigenous culture, and the feeding method being used works very well. Instead of having meals prepared in gigantic pans of a communitarian kitchen, which never satisfies them, the missionaries, in the presence of *aidamos* and soldiers, daily distribute fruits, vegetables, fish, chicken, eggs, manioc flour, oil, salt, sugar, pasta, rice, corn flakes, milk powder. Families are called one by one according to a registration list, that a missionary updates daily the number of dwellers.

Before the distribution, the missionaries talk, give messages, recommend people never to throw away fruit and plastic leftovers on the floor, a deeply rooted habit among them. They also warn parents that children are escaping over the fence or about an odor of urine in a corner. All are warned to be watchful, and, if any problem arrives, to let the missionaries know. The natives listen and respect them, but suddenly ignore the queue and help themselves to the food. If one does it, they all do it.

Many natives leave at 4 a.m. to have coffee with milk and bread in the parish of Father Jesus, a ritual they had developed when they lived on

At the yard of the shelter, indigenous people wait for the distribution of flour.
Pacaraima, Roraima, Brazil, May 2018

the streets. Just as in their lands of origin, early in the morning they start to gather wood in the forests. Pacaraima's mountains are covered by wonderful trees, from which they pick up dry branches respecting and acknowledging Nature, never harming it.

Followed by a relative, they come back to the shelter with enormous bunches on their shoulders. Then, the women prepare the meals side by side according to their feeding custom. Each cook at their small fire, and then they sit as a family to eat. They knead *domplina*, a typical Venezuelan bread. In front of the shelter's main entrance gate, the bread is sold daily by Venezuelans bringing people from the border city Santa Helena to buy it.

As time passed, the health problems decreased. Three volunteers, one doctor and two nurses, come from Venezuela once a week to give medical assistance, out of sheer love and without material reward. In addition, small health services are made by missionaries in the shelter, such as putting on bandages, referring patients to the health centers with malnutrition, diarrhea, parasitic intestinal disease, night fever, cold, chickenpox, headache, dental infections. However, respiratory problems, measles outbreaks, serious infections such as HIV, are referred to the Pacaraima hospital. Patients with serious dehydration and precarious nutritional conditions are transferred to a hospital in Boa Vista. There was a time when the Pacaraima Health System collapsed, due to the demand of medicines and anesthetics. Nevertheless, it granted assistance to the needy.

The arrival of the army on April 2018 brought peace to the shelter. In previous months difficult situations had already taken place. The first coordinator of the missionaries was an Argentinian, which made the Spanish communication easier, although many indigenous people only speak Warao.

Imer says: *The consciousness of community life is well ingrained in natives. There are similarities in their behavior, way of acting, thinking, and habits, but they have another view of life, different from ours. For example, about time. They live in the eternal present. They make us realize how hurried we are. We call this preparedness, but they do not believe that being fast brings benefits. If every action perpetuates itself, as it must be done again and again, why rush? They start to do something but, if anything else draws their attention, they leave it behind. Why finish it? Life is eternal. It flows like the water of a river... this simplicity is a challenge for us, who were taught to live in another way.*

Natives in the shelter must learn how to live with 500 others in the same space, without privacy. What is done or said is watched and heard by the others. They need to adjust themselves to the rules of a new community style. For example, they do not turn off faucets. For thousands of years, they have lived at river banks and have the concept that water flows and never ends. Why should they turn off the taps if water comes from some place and runs to another? How to make them understand that we need to turn them off? Water from the water tanks will eventually be gone.

Missionaries insist on them keeping the environment clean, and preservation and maintenance of the building. Since they believe Nature recycles everything, they throw packaging on the floor, and children relieve themselves on the cement, just as it used to happen in the woods. Besides, they produce extra trash because they gather aluminum cans, metal pieces, and copper to sell to recyclers. Objects scattered on the ground has been a wounding place for the children running all over the shelter, without precaution. Imer says: *We don't know who is right, who is wrong. We? They?*

An everyday scene in the shelter for indigenous people.
Pacaraima, Roraima, Brazil, May 2018

Stories circulate about the cruelty, the mistakes, and self-destruction happening in the neighboring country. And its government denies them, masking reality saying other countries want to undermine their image. For instance, indigenous people report that they grow crops of large potatoes in the delta of the Orinoco. Along with fish, it is the basis of their diet. Taking these kind of yams to be traded, they may be stopped by police officers who say they have to pay taxes and that they are trafficking.

The natives wonder: *What can we do if this is our only way of doing exchanges?* On their way back home from Brazil, they are stopped by three police posts, where officers take their food and money.

Primary and secondary missionaries experience a model of harmonious creative life in the Light-Communities where they live. They find similarities of it in the peaceful manner of some indigenous families coming from the Venezuelan countryside, such as the E´ñepás group. They are quiet people who never complain, never cause a problem. Children always stay quietly by their mother, while their father goes to look for a job.

In the past, the Waraos used to live in different communities away from one another, finding identity through ethnicity and their language. On the river bank, when they disagree, they move to a new stilt house a few

yards away. In the shelters, proximity causes small outbreaks, and they become confused. Everyone participates and gives opinions about other people's problems. The *aidamos* take a position in cases of vandalism, quarrels between women, separation of couples, a man beating his pregnant wife, a woman beating a man.

Open to changing their minds, they call the missionaries to give an opinion about their family conflicts. They all sit on hammocks or on the floor. The missionaries try to help them make conscious, non-impulsive decisions. If a relative complains: *This mother left, and grandma does not want to look after her kid, an uncle decided to look after the kid...* Together, they try to find ways to protect the child with the help of neighbors.

There are difficult Warao families led by vicious behaviors, alcohol, drugs, fights. They battle in their own homes. Careful not to get involved in aggressions, missionaries try to solve these issues with discernment. They warn them that natives must not break Brazilian laws and, if they persist in doing so, their destructive acts will have bad consequences.

Before the army arrived at the shelter, after the missionaries went home, the place might become chaotic with drunk indigenous people. On the following day, they were calm, as if nothing had happened, and did not even talk about it because they forgive easily, do not hold grudges, rancor. However, recurrent scandalous cases brought collective tension and danger—fights, lesions with knife, women being beaten, robbery. In some cases, calling the police was really necessary.

A conflict involving theft took place soon after the shelter's inauguration. After families and *aidamos* turned against one another, Imer called a general meeting.

The sun had set. In the starry sky, Orion was visible and its open belt poured strong energies to the region. One hundred people made a reconciliation circle in the yard. A dialogue might repair open wounds, clear up misunderstandings, and bring order back.

Imer based the conversation on a symbol. He asked the eldest man for a cigar. Paulino picks and dries *açaí* palm tree bark to roll tobacco on it. As an analogy of unity, Imer determined that only the person holding the

Pacaraima, Roraima, Brazil, May 2018

cigar in their hands would speak. The missionary was the first. Putting himself in their shoes, he said he realized they were in a difficult coexistence situation, that food was not guaranteed, but they must work on themselves to carry coexistence forward.

He reminded them that, when they slept in the street, they used to look at the gymnasium on top of the hill and called it *jonokoida: janoku* means house and *ida*, great. That was their home. It was made for them: *I told them that the cigar would be available for those who wanted to speak, but no one should interrupt. Usually, when one speaks, moods get excited, everyone moves their arms giving opinions at the same time, chaos reigned. Gradually, women and men took turns to speak. Others, emotionally touched, were not able to speak.*

Their auras interpenetrated during the fraternal talk. The young son of an *aidamo* reflected on what it is to be an *aidamo*. He pondered that it means being the one who, interested in the community peace, seeks solutions. But no one was behaving this way, not even his father.

In the end, they all remained silent. And turned their eyes to Imer, waiting for the verdict. The cigar was handed back to him. Calmly, he said: *We respected and listened to one another. This is important in community life. But in case we have to have another meeting, each one should speak of their own mistakes, without pointing to those of the others. We must understand our differences and try to help one another.* Everyone cheered enthusiastically. And the conflict dissolved. At the same time, an occult reconciliation happened, some pain was eliminated from the broad indigenous consciousness.

Peace-makers act for the benefit of group unity. The missionaries' presence, their attention and their activities, manage to transmute conflictive situations into peace. Working with souls while one's own soul develops is the greatest opportunity for the one who serves and the one being served.

PART VI
Recurrent Regional Missions

The Light-Network seeks to quench the thirst
for love, forgiveness and peace among people.
To do so, it serves indigenous, Portuguese and African
descendants in Alagoas, a Northeastern state of Brazil.
In the Argentine Chaco, they work with the indigenous
Qom ethnic group. In Paraguay, it embraces
Avá-Guarani, Yvú Porä Rendá and Mbya-Guarani.

Support for the backcountry people

*True fellowship among men must be
based upon a concern that is universal.*
I Ching

On a weekend just before Christmas, five ladies and a man spent hours on a plane and a car trip to bring hope to solitary communities of the backcountry dryness. They let go of the reins of their own lives and surrendered themselves to destiny. After distributing food kits, snacks, clothes, toys and cakes for Christmas celebrations, people began to invite them to baptisms and Eucharistic celebrations. At one point, children and young people, rehearsing for a small concert with choreography asked the missionaries to enact the Three Wise Men story. Just like the biblical characters, they went great distances to be there. After three days, they returned home on a Sunday to resume work on Monday.

Members of Brazil North and Northeast Light-Network continued the Backcountry Mission of humanitarian help, carried out by consecrated missionaries one month before. From then on, they return twice a year to the surroundings of Palmeira dos Índios, in Alagoas, each time taking along an increasing number of collaborators from six Brazilian states. They spread love in the arid life of Baixa Fria, Bem-Te-Vi, Quilombola da Tabacaria, in indigenous villages such as Fazenda Jarra and Cafurna de Baixo, and in a community where prostitution had flourished.

Since 2014, the bond between the residents and the region has deepened. The missionaries are greeted with joy by religious representatives and the local people, grateful for the effort to improve their daily life and general health. The word gets spread. New communities request their presence. They scatter seeds of knowledge and inspire the residents, who feel encouraged to look after the Planet.

Dozens of inhabitants gather in schools, parishes and outbuildings to be with the regional missionaries. Lessons emphatically given at each meeting are being taken seriously and put into practice. The countryside people gradually change consciousness. The coordinator Celina says: *We support Caritas locality, and their representatives continue with humanitarian actions we have started, such as vegetable gardens, and medicinal herbs beds. There are now communities dehydrating fruits and vegetables, and residents eating more greens to improve their physical health. They also have improved the attention given to domestic animals.*

The servers experienced the difficulties of rural areas. In 2017, news programs announced the most severe Northeast drought in the last one hundred years, they saw empty dams, dying animals, some of the thirsty and hungry 300,000 people. The water distributed by water tankers is not enough to supply them.

In rainy seasons, the missionaries had to reschedule visits due to muddy and rough roads. To help the countryside people, they have formed a group in Palmeiras dos Índios who prepares and distributes seedlings of *Moringa oleifera*, whose leaves, green berries and flowers have rich nutritional value and whose seeds purify contaminated water, making it clear and potable.

Each mission lasts three days. In larger communities the work goes from morning until late afternoon. In smaller ones only half a day. Before their first daily activity, the missionaries pause briefly to align their energies. They have worked constantly to meet the needs of children, adults, the Kingdoms of Nature—about 4000 people in the last four years.

Always working in pairs, to render mutual aid, they pay home visits to the elderly and to sick bedridden people. An engineer advises them on a better distribution of water from a spring. They hold workshops on the preparation of enriched flour as a nutritional supplement—multigrain mixtures, dehydration of fruits and vegetables, and on building a low-cost solar stove. They donate agricultural tools, in addition to garments, personal hygiene items, bed and bathroom linen, layettes for babies, home utensils. They assist and deworm domestic animals and leave medications for them, tutoring about animal care. They share vegetarian lunches and snacks. Aware that the missionaries are vegetarian, the people they help bring them fruits and greens.

Regional missionaries tread firmly, but lightly. They smile and look into the eyes willing to fulfill people's needs. Caritas and communities' representatives send them request: to give instructions on the creation of a vegetable garden in one village, teaching the building of dry toilets in another, a comfort few residents know.

On each mission, health professionals—doctors, pharmacists, nurses and medical students—offer hundreds of free medical treatments. The Light-Network produces and distributes herbal remedies and a booklet, *Living Pharmacy*, about the use of officially recognized local plants used by the Brazilian Health System. It gives back to the people what originally came from them. And families are planting and using those plants, and also practice simple external treatments and procedures, such as water suction for headache, high blood pressure and emotional tension.

The missionaries can be recognized by the sparkle in their eyes. They are meek, simple. They follow the teaching: *Your heart must be pure as a child's, but wise as that of an elder.* While they learn to overcome restrictions that separate human beings, they heal deep wounds in themselves and in those being assisted.

Living on a school-planet, we are both masters and pupils of one another. The group received a fraternal lesson from an unforgettable countryside housewife. As food was given to her, she asked for it to be taken to her next-door neighbor, who needed it more than her family.

The people call them missionaries of peace. They remember each one with tenderness and ask: *When will they be back?*

Strengthened by service that unites humans, the group says goodbye. They carry with them the impulse found in the exercise of solidarity, as well as another challenge: finding solutions for the salty water of the African descendants' community, whose high level of salt causes cases of hypertension, even in children.

They arrive at the airport. Instead of visiting little shops while waiting for their flights, the missionaries retreat in the ecumenical lounge. And inwardly they confirm their commitment to give themselves to the infinite.

Visits to the Qom people

Altruistic service is the way by which
the divine Soul contacts the human soul
and manifests itself as group consciousness.
Albertina de Castro Fernandes

On each new mission, they gather for the official photograph. Standing or crouching, volunteers stretch their arms and hug one another. One carries a little dog. They look at the camera with sincere smiles. They are the ones who, out of kindness, do not hesitate and leave their own homes without looking back. As a single heart, they move forward side by side with Qom people, during the long journey of returning to their planets of origin.

The Qom ethnicity—with sixty thousand individuals according to censuses—populates the Northeastern Argentine Chaco. Its communities are among the poorest of South America. The first service provided by five of them during the Chaco Mission, softened the material and emotional needs of these people. Even before the mission ended, it became apparent how important it would be to continue the assistance given to Costa Iné rural community, 28 miles away from Resistencia; to the Mapic district in Resistencia, to Cacique Pelayo district in Fontana, and two other communities in Puerto Tirol and Margarita Belen. This is how the Chaco Recurrent Missions began, under the responsibility of the North Argentina Light-Network, coordinated by Mabel.

Since 2016, every couple of months, thirty to sixty people enroll to join these missions. Some travel almost 24 hours, not for tours in museums and restaurants, but to take themselves along with their own talents to be with the Qom.

There might be one or two who come from Brazil or Paraguay, but most come from Northern, Central, Southern Argentina—Bahia Blanca, Buenos Aires, Capilla del Monte, Cordoba, Corrientes, Eldorado, Formosa,

Garuhape, General Roca, Mendoza, Necochea, Neuquen, Paso de los Libres, Posadas, Resistencia, Rio Cuarto, Salta, San Luis, San Rafael, Santa Fé, Tucuman, Villa Giardino. Not all of them are members of the FIHF. Their diversity draws the attention of a volunteer from Cordoba, who participated for the first time. She had met the group a few hours before, and said: *These are people from diverse cultures and places, but they understand one another because they speak the language of love for the sake of our indigenous brothers and sisters.*

During the past two years, Mabel has seen changes resulting from the persistent presence of the Light-Network: *As the missions take place— there have been ten of them—the indigenous people open themselves and become more self-confident and accessible. At first, they were distrustful, always evaluating and observing us. Then they became convinced we had no hidden agenda nor the intention of preaching or imposing anything. We are quite tactful in respecting their customs, ancestral beliefs and thoughts. We are here with the heart, interconnected with the One to live brotherhood. This is what brings us life and nourishes us.*

At the end of a mission, the dates for the next three-day meeting are scheduled, and its preparations begin. They stay in the city of Resistencia or Puerto Tirol, where they are strict on punctuality: a scheduled time to begin the tasks, to start each meal, to pray, and also a scheduled time to end the tasks with reflections and a final attunement on the day of departure. However, in the communities, they cannot always follow the program printed on paper learning more about flexibility and surrender. *We never know how things will flow. We learn how to have faith and adapt to the reality in the moment,* says Mabel.

While still in the place of their lodging, after they finish their first prayers, the servers sort through the donations and the material to be used by each team. They split the tasks into groups: sing songs, tell stories about Kingdoms of Nature, play games and do handicraft work with children, sew bed sheets with mothers, serve as hairdressers, deworm animals, make lunches, visit native people, plant, deliver donations.

During the Vest Campaign, the ones all over the country who cannot be there dedicate themselves to help as they can. In groups or individually, they knit socks and coats to warm up babies and children. Feelings of charity, beauty and caring get intertwined in colorful balls of wool.

Even in 122° F heat in the shade in summer or under very cold temperatures in winter, the messengers of peace return to the five communities. The reunions rekindle the joy of living in the visitors and in those visited. They look at one another with the softness of flowers, take their hands and hug with blazing hearts of meeting with the dearest close relatives. The indigenous women know how to welcome the missionaries. Just like the mothers, Qom children greet in good Spanish and offer to collaborate. Perfect hosts, they take lunch to those who work. They are quite different from Paraguayan natives, who just look shyly from afar in silence.

The power of the group begins to manifest itself when, with the tenderness of grandmothers, servers prepare soft towels, a warm atmosphere, without any movement of the air, and gently put babies into the lukewarm water. They make use of the therapeutic baths and examine the little body's needs. Small drops of water run down the thin skin of the native children and splash attentive mothers. The little one's sleep in warm arms, they are breastfed, close their eyes and dream with maternal wings.

Another group makes donations of clothing, food, soap, toothbrushes, personal hygiene items, first-aid kits and medicines coming from several Argentinian provinces. Qom men and ladies humbly accept the gestures of love. During the ritual, whisperings can be heard. The quasi-silence mirrors the beauty of the moment. From it, ascend truths not registered by sounds.

Visiting and serving the Qom is like attending a school of an altruistic love, which heals egocentrism, intolerance, rejection. Mutual respect matures during tiny actions that build peace.

Outdoors, as the powerful sun is behind heavy clouds, calm children and adolescents have their dark hair cut and washed, and lice removed. They sit on chairs beside a group of trees on a lawn. Around them, white-haired gentlemen and ladies are bent over using scissors and combs. The purity of the bond between the youths and the hairdressers is endearing.

Chaco Recurrent Missions, of the Light-Network Argentina, serve indigenous communities around Resistencia, from 2016 to 2018

A volunteer plays with children.
Resistencia, Chaco, Argentina, December 2016

Their colorful auras get mixed with vegetable emanations. The misty scene hidden to the eyes is real and not a poetical image.

From a house beside them, come the giggles of children. There, imagination mixes itself with origamis and ball games. Children and volunteers in a circle play at the sound of a bamboo flute and guitar strings. They sing repertoires of old lullabies and swirl, swirl around. Others paint the sky, the earth and girls' faces. Holding puppets, they dramatize animals, teaching about cooperation and kinship.

A wave of energy cools off the sultry air. The wind blows at lunch time, during the meal prepared right there. A Qom woman places pies she made on the table. A native embraces the guitar and sings in Qom L'aqtqa. The silenced voices of the deep America expand in the ethers, seeking to caress the hungry for justice. *The leader Dom Hilario blessed the table of food, and we shared the food as a big family. Bonds with the Qom are strengthening as the years go by. The five communities have become more united since the Light-Network began their visits,* said Patricia Sanchez, one the coordinator of the Chaco Recurrent Missions.

From community to community, professionals of oral health make dental prostheses for adults. There are workshops for brushing teeth, nail-trimming and child hand washing. They feed and deworm, internally and externally, hundreds of ill-nourished dogs and cats, with scabies, ticks, borers and infected wounds in their bodies.

The coordinator of the Paraguayan Light-Network trims the nails of an indigenous grandmother. Resistencia, Chaco, Argentina, 2017

The Qom appreciate being visited. They invite missionaries to enter their shaky homes, to share their intimacy. Warmly welcomed, the missionaries listen to them, trying to understand frailties. They seek to decipher their meekness, in spite of the cruel history of insecurity and exclusion. From certain lips can spring stories full of pain and resentment about massacres suffered at the hands of white men, who decimated their ancestors. However, an elderly woman recalls childhood memories without rancor.

Two coordinators, one Argentine and another Paraguayan, had striven to reach the community. The former traveled ten hours by bus. The latter drove six hours.

Together they went to visit a grandmother: *In spite of the bitter icy wind, she was sitting on the porch next to a fire that had almost gone out. She needed to talk. In clear Spanish, she said that she was the daughter of a tribal leader. When she was a baby, her father became involved with another woman and her mother fled with her. She searched for a new horizon until they were warmly welcomed at this village, 500 miles from the one where she was born. The mother married again to a native man who always treated them both well.*

When the visitor asked for permission to trim her nails, the Qom grandmother was thrilled: her swollen knees ached, she barely walked. The Paraguayan took an anti-inflammatory ointment from her purse, which the Argentine used to rub the woman's inflamed knees. The grand-mother was stunned. As a farewell, after blessing both servers in Qom, the grandma said: *I loved sharing with you. We are sisters, and God is our only Father.*

Native people hold treasures. They have stories, joy and pains similar to those of any family anywhere in the world, since our human nature is the same. They yearn to be listened to and contribute with their knowledge of the world and of Nature.

At the Qom Council, the elders educate youths orally, and parents transmit behavior and values to children. Wounded by being despised and exploited, they hope to gain community lands to help keep their culture, to receive bilingual education and to participate in national life.

Before the Spaniards arrived, about thirty-five dialects were spoken in the Argentinine territory. There are now fourteen: Avá-guarani, Chorote, Guarani, Mapuche, Mbya, Mocovi, Nivaclé, Pilagá, Qom—with many speakers—, Quéchua, Tapiete, Vichí and Tehuelche—with only one speaker. Recent surveys revealed the Vilela, nearly extinct since the 1960s, and the Chaná, an enigma for almost two hundred years.

A few decades ago, a child who spoke an indigenous language in public schools had to wash out their mouth or was chastised. Each native cries out for respect and for a future in which no one will speak nor act with violence and hatred.

Ethnically, the Qom are hunters and fishermen with a nomadic spirit. Their agriculture is precarious, but sometimes they plant native seeds—pumpkin, corn, manioc. Under the same sun, visitors and the Qom hold hoes, pull weed and cultivate the earth for sowing. Yes, under the same sun, visitors and the Qom communicate and evolve in mutual understanding.

The visitors relieve the hardships of the Qoms' lives sowing peace and hope amidst them. But they also harvest seeds of fraternal mysteries from those who someday will recover the gift of communicating with the natural sacred world.

Aguyje peeme cheirukuera: thanks, companions

...my language, my soul flies like birds.
Clouds draw flowers,
taking my breath to the edge of the woods.
My language and my singing accompany it,
and depart like birds towards my ancestral people.
Alba Eiragi Duarte

We must be pure again, be fraternal again. We must be attentive to the rain and migratory birds, to the movement of trees and waters. We must walk towards the Sun.

To find wisdom, nearly thirty volunteers leave their homes every three months and head to seven villages of native people, all of whom are trash recyclers. They forget about their cities and belongings, to take action in the surroundings of Ciudad del Este and Presidente Franco, in eastern Paraguay. They travel hundreds of miles by car, bus, plane, coming from several places of the host country, from Argentina, Brazil and sometimes Uruguay. The multinational service has defined goals: enabling peace to thrive among humans and heal historic wounds open in the consciousness of these nations.

Members of the Light-Network gather to quench the thirst for love that dwells in them and in native people. They had never worked together, but a spiritual kinship unites them. *Since our first meeting, there's been so much joy among us! It seemed that we'd known one another forever. This is so beautiful,* says Faustina, the coordinator of Paraguay Light-Network. Their bodies may be fatigued, but their fiery energy keeps growing.

The Paraguayan territory, occupied at least for 1,500 years, perpetuates images of suffering. Diverse indigenous ethnicities were at war when, in the sixteenth century, the Spaniards began their settlement. Two centuries later, Jesuit missions arrived aiming to convert them to Catholicism. Up until they were ousted out, they converted more than 100,000 natives in over 150 years.

The history of the nation became even bloodier when wars with neighboring Brazil and Argentina resulted in the death of two thirds of their male population, mostly indigenous.

The natives keep struggling to preserve their own culture and values. They understand life in community, as they have always valued the family life associated with the villages.

There are now 115,000 natives in Paraguay, in different degrees of helplessness and poverty, split in nineteen groups with beautiful names: Ache, Angaite, Avá-Guarani, Ayoreo, Ayoreo Totobiegosode, Enlhet North, Enxet South, Guarani Ñandeva, Western Guarani, Manjui, Maka, Maskoy, Mbya Guarani, Nivacle, Paitavytera, Qom Lyk, Sanapana, Tomaraho, Yshir Ybytoso.

To decide what villages to support, a team of FIHM visited some, talked with their leaders, with natives who begged in the streets, with those who worked as masons or cultivated manioc and corn in well-structured communities. At last, the seven communities whose survival depends on trash recycling were chosen.

During the fourteen days of the 15th Paraguay Mission, Awakening Seeds, the Fraternidade Missionaries got in touch with an overwhelming reality. In very poor houses, the natives starve and are cold. They are sick, sad, discouraged.

From then on, the Recurrent Regional Paraguay Mission was formed, with the commitment of supporting Avá-Guaranis who live in extreme poverty. The servers run campaigns to collect tons of non-perishable food: rice, pasta, oil, coarse salt, beans. They donate big pans and ladles, mattresses, first-aid kits, toothbrushes, working tools and garments, including rain boots and leather gloves to protect the native people during the collection of trash.

The group brings crayons, paper, and beads to play with the children. Since craftsmanship with seeds and fibers extracted from Nature is part of the Guarani culture, they watch children and mothers delve in the multicolored strings and beads, intertwining wrist-bands and necklaces.

They offered their services and resources to build two prayer houses, called *opys*. For one of them, they also left money for the purchase of musical wind and percussion instruments used in ceremonies. As one leader

Volunteers from the Light-Network cross the community of Yvú Porã Rendá, Ciudad del Este, Paraguay, October 2017

requested, the missionaries helped the drilling of a well in a school yard. They always offer haircuts for men, washing and combing for women and children. Once, an Argentine coordinated veterinarian care for dogs and cats in poor condition.

But what most pleases the natives is receiving long visits. Their copper-toned faces open in smiles. First-time missionaries are surprised at native people's hospitality rules. From village to village, the Light-Network takes their time to deal with each of them, for one or two whole days. At the farewell, they always ask when the visitors will return. They say most arrive quickly, give them some objects, turn their backs and go away.

The leaders express themselves mixing up Guarani and a word of Spanish languages, but most natives speak only their mother tongue. There are places where they do not even understand a word Spanish. To make contact easier, they have compiled a mini-dictionary with basic Guarani words: Good morning—*Mbae'ichapa nde koe'*, How are you?—*Mbae'ichapa*, Thank you—*Aguyje*.

The energy emerging from these movements attracts loyal collaborators who do not belong to the Light-Network, but offer help. Paraguayan doctors and dentists surrender wholeheartedly, using their own money and time and, with professional excellence, offer clinical consultations and oral health services to indigenous people who are losing their teeth.

A couple from Ciudad del Este stores the material used on the missions and even buys what the group needs. The driver who brings the volunteers from the capital, 220 miles away, charges them very reasonable fares and, in addition to that, works hard helping the Light-Network distribute food to the seven communities.

They pay a minimum sum to the owner of the hotel where they stay, who lends them his kitchen when it rains. So they have a place to cook the food to be served in the communities, when its streets are muddy and their wet firewood is unlikely to burn.

In one of the visits, they felt sorry for the Avá-Guaranis scattered in the streets, dislodged from the land they rented beside one of the trash dumps. Men and women, elderly and children ceased to have protection from the inclement weather. They are suffering a lot. So, these natives were included in the network of protection of the group, who felt immediate empathy for their pain. They seek to help them, interact with mothers and children, leave food to improve their frugal diet.

Some time ago, even the current servers themselves used to turn their back to the natives. They eventually understood how blind and deluded they were by old-fashioned prejudice, and they finally entered another evolutionary stage, ruled by love, not by egocentrism.

Transformation is a process of awakening to a harmonious collective work. *We used to feel an almost total indifference towards the indigenous people. Now we hug children, learn their names, look in their eyes, smile, sing, talk with adults, cook lunch to eat together. For sure, we have perfected and polished our egos,* says Faustina.

Paraguay Recurrent Regional Missions serve indigenous communities, Ciudad del Este, between 2016 and 2018

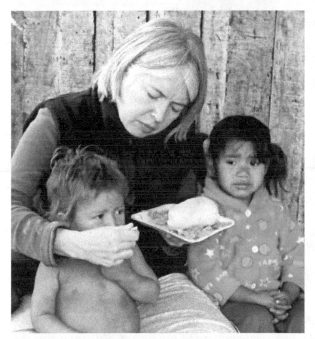

Volunteers from Paraguay, Argentina and Brazil with indigenous people. Puerto Barreto, Presidente Franco, Paraguay, July 2017

The constant and diligent selfless service is both a symbol of reconciliation between the representatives of the three countries, and also between whites and native people. It creates a prototype of good that radiates and expands the planetary consciousness: *May the white man learn how to share, in order to bring hope to the natives,* says a Paraguayan collaborator. The paths of interaction open as we lovingly watch for one another. They become a field of challenges, of personal tests and of group learning.

During six meetings, volunteers' comments were recorded. They weave a vivid panorama of memories. Here is a selection:

Ederlene, from Brazil: *Everything was done in an extraordinary way. What impressed me the most was the synchronicity between the smallest events and gestures, including the weather. It rained cats and dogs one day before the visits began. They forecasted continuous rain. But then the sky began to clear, and when we arrived in the village, on Saturday, a radiant sun was drying the red mud. Each volunteer seemed to know exactly what to do, and felt an unusual joy. People we had never seen before, participating on a mission for the first time, seeming like old friends. All of us felt integrated, everything worked perfectly. As soon as we finished the last task and meal, the sky became overcast again. We only had time to collect everything and get on the bus. The rain fell and wouldn't stop.*

Volunteers from the Light-Network cross the community
of Yvú Porã Rendá, Ciudad del Este, Paraguay, October 2017

Nilda, from Argentina: *First I was afraid that things would be too precarious, but there was such love, companionship and dedication, that my questions dissolved, one by one.*

Míriam, from Brazil: *There was so much purity in the natives and in the servers, a silence, sweetness. This charmed me. The missionaries transmit a wonderful divine energy.*

Alicia, from Argentina: *I have been a nurse for thirty-four years and had a fantastic experience while working with the doctor. I had never seen a doctor working with so much love, dedication, reaching the level of each child.*

Adriana, from Paraguay: *Connecting with the indigenous consciousness is a gift from the universe. I feel unity among brothers, among souls, above and beyond any difference. Sharing with them brings me a sense of completeness. On each mission, we make up for a little of the mistreatment that we have done to them, for our discrimination against those people.*

Azucena, from Paraguay: *With their loving presence and generosity, Argentines and Brazilians help us carry out the tasks. The simplicity, humbleness and union of the natives of Puerto Bertoni are also role models for us to grow spiritually.*

Leandro, from Argentina: *In that place blessed by Nature, we found a community filled with virtues, which thanks us lovingly for the little we did for them.*

Mara, from Brazil: *When we were together in the jungle, it was very moving to observe an elderly couple. They had nothing at all, but they opened the doors of their little house to welcome us. They expected nothing from us, and when someone gave them food, they didn't eat, even though they were hungry. They held the food in their hands, just looking at us with so much sweetness. As for the kids, they wanted to be caressed, touched. When we washed their hair, massaging, they closed their eyes, loving it.*

Elsi, from Argentina: *The exchange between us, who came from far away, and the natives, enriched everyone. There were meetings of souls. We were called to learn what was simple, realizing the abundance that life gives us, even in poverty. Above all, we were invited to deepen our connection with what is invisible, with the whole.*

Teresita, from Argentina: *What struck me most was the beauty of the fire lit by the tribal leader, his perfect technique.*

Faustina, from Paraguay: *Actually, the missionary work makes it easier for us to discover ourselves. At the end of each mission we feel more fraternal and reinvigorated to keep participating with others.*

Marcia, from Brazil: *The most moving scene was when we said prayers asking for forgiveness on behalf of the white people, which decimated native populations in the four corners of the world.*

Throughout the precarious settlements of the Avá-Guaranis, the Yvú Porã Rendás and the Mbya-Guaranis, the group creates a refreshing breeze and leaves a glow in natives' eyes. In a farewell, an eight year old boy cried intensely, wanting to leave with them. The missionaries were moved and left with broken hearts.

The servers weave part of the mantle of peace that someday will be extended over all people of all continents. They become antennas for the Divine to dissolve pains. Understanding and sharing are means of opening doors to invisible planes to rescue the Indigenous consciousness, which safeguards original purity and protects the Kingdoms of Nature.

PART VII
Behind the scenes

Coordinating missions for Fraternidade

Our imperfection is a sign of
a transitional state, a still
unfinished growth, an effort
that is seeking its path.
Sri Aurobindo

Ricardo, you've been the Fraternidade coordinator since the first mission, in 2011, in Nepal. Tell us about your responsibility in this voluntary group service, which is quickly expanding to broader horizons.

First, I am one who needs to see the big picture. Coordinating is interesting, but it's not easy. When I volunteered to be a missionary, I never thought I'd be the coordinator. I was caught by surprise when asked to do this task and from then on, I've dedicated myself for its materialization.

In the beginning the work was grounded in simplicity, divestment, discipline, and a certain austerity. We were instructed to prepare the group to overcome difficulties in crucial emergency moments, such as during food and water shortages. If they had to walk 30 miles, a missionary would not think twice, they would just start walking. They also wouldn't hesitate to start more dangerous activities, being careful, of course.

Until then, my life had been the very opposite this, but I quickly adjusted to this idea of readiness and of doing things, whatever it takes. But this takes people out of their comfort zone. Some missionaries stuck to the rules. Some others stepped away.

Many forces are set in motion in each mission. We have learned how to work well in missions that take from 30 to 60 days in several countries, with different groups and people's demands. We have developed the ability to be in tune to meet the needs of each moment.

On the other hand, the Roraima Permanent Mission, which has run long-term and is not expected to end soon, demands us to go deeper.

Coordinating is a difficult task because we have to look at everything, for everyone, and in detail. We must not make small mistakes so as not to make big ones. First of all, we need to be punctual. If we have to leave at 8 a.m., it can't be 8:03 a.m., for the boarding gate closes and we'll miss the plane. We need to stop being negligent with small things. Even here at the office, when we run out of paper for the printer or of toilet paper, they're not replaced. Someone leaves the light or the air conditioner on, the chair out of its place. In a more important context, distractions can be fatal. The daily effort of the coordinator is to keep repeating, insisting for everyone to be attentive. This can be a little tiring.

We have the image of the Fraternidade to protect, an image of order, beauty and harmony cultivated during forty years of instructions given by Trigueirinho. For this reason, we need to unite efforts and undertake a number of initiatives, from walking in a single line, wearing appropriate clothing, using clean and well-identified cars, to refilling fuel tanks when they become half empty.

A mission has distinct stages: the periods before, during and after it. Planning delights me. The pre-mission period involves a myriad of predictions. Who will be taking part? Does that person fit in the mission, will they keep up with the pace, does she get along with the others?

It also involves issuing plane tickets, getting visas at embassies, taking photo-copies of passports, telephone and contact lists, and organizing the budget, food, lodging, transportation in Brazil and where we will go. What to take: warm clothes, cool clothes, size of the uniforms, safety material. Weighing backpacks and suitcases—calling Mr. So and So to remove their excessive weight, locking the suitcases and labeling them.

Right before we leave, we have a double-check: "Did you get your passport and your badge? Let me see." Once someone had no passport when we arrived at the airport for our flight. Then we get in the van, phew! We can relax for a while. We arrive at the airport. "You and you, pick up the suitcases, please." We have people specialized in taking care of the luggage. "You, please, pick up the carts."

When we arrive at the destination, only one particular person picks up the suitcases at the baggage claim area and checks everything. The daily routine of the mission begins: making contacts, taking care of each other throughout it. Someone feels ill. "Do we have the right medicine? Shall we send them back?" So far, we haven't needed to send anyone back, but we have faced all kinds of setbacks.

Coordinating involves being there accomplishing and at the same time being attentive so that no one gets hurt. For example, in Kathmandu we were asked to go barefoot and wash a ward for children with cancer. There were needles on the floor.

"Either we wash it wearing boots, or we don't wash it," I answered. They accepted it, but asked us to wash our boots well before getting inside.

On our way back to Figueira, we wrap up the process collecting all the materials, rendering accounts, storing things, making reports, organizing the photographs. Summing it all up: "It's over!" This is what usually happens one month before, and one month after. And then a new mission starts and we resume our path.

We put our theoretical and academic knowledge into practice in totally different circumstances. We plan so that we are not caught off guard: this is why we have few problems with unforeseen circumstances, because we always have a plan B.

I have always valued group work ever since I was a boy scout. However, I have a handicap. I am a person of action. I accomplish tasks, but I'm not a people promoter. Just tell me what needs to be done, and I'll do it. But it takes me a while to realize that someone is not feeling well or dislikes doing something. It's hard for me to see their needs.

Patience, that's what I need! I still do not have much... it is a learning process. I am learning to work with more patience, more humbleness, less arrogance. Except for the difficulties, constructive situations gradually transform aspects of our old consciousness and inspire us to be better human beings.

Conversations about Ethiopia, DR Congo, Rwanda, and Uganda

*A drop of action is worth more
than oceans of theoretical resolutions.*
Mirra Alfassa, the Mother

Five missionaries reflect, with thoughtful expressions and occasional smiles, about their fourth Mission in Central Africa. They recall sensations, learnings, intuitions, personal and group experiences in Ethiopia, Rwanda, Uganda and the Democratic Republic of the Congo or DR Congo.

Twenty years before you were invited to join the fourth Africa Mission, you had worked with the Missionaries of Charity and needy communities in the interior of São Paulo state, right?

Rosi: *I started getting closer to missionary activity in 1990, when the instructor Trigueirinho explained that service was a keynote on the spiritual path, that no one gets anywhere if they don't renounce themselves and seek to find and serve God through the other. He gave us the example of the missionary activity of Mother Teresa of Calcutta, which I ignored. Wishing to live according to that teaching, I found a base of the Missionaries of Charity near the city where I live, and volunteered to help sick people in difficult situations, which is their routine. And I was shocked when I saw a sacred painting of Christ in a bathroom! Instead of the mirror, there was the image of the Merciful Christ. At once, I went to ask them, feeling embarrassed, about my doubts... They laughed and answered, "Don't you get it? We have to mirror ourselves in Him. This is why His image is spread in every corner." I calmed down: this answer confirmed the instruction that Trigueirinho was planting in my heart.*

Was the service in Africa similar to the one done in Brazil?

Rosi: *Yes. On my first trip, super intense, with the Missionaries of Fraternidade, I often found the same kind of people I had seen in Brazil. People* born in poverty, in extreme poverty, which never had enough resources, food and assistance, but are grateful for every little thing we do for them. On the Turkey Mission it was not so. The refugees used to have everything, and had lost it all. I realized Africans were more grateful.

Bento adds: *We found many Congolese in Turkey. They were impressed by our choice of going to their country. I remember the children in the Congo. When we approached, they were scared and screamed. We were like white bearded ETs. You can picture the scene, all missionaries had beards. Eventually they got closer to us, hugged us and were extremely loving.*

And what caught your attention most, Shen?
Shen: *In general, it was the increasing number of perplexities. After the episode of genocide, Rwanda received rebuilding funds from the UN and other countries. Kigali is beautiful, orderly, it has well cared-for squares. There is silence. It was the best of the five countries we visited in Africa. From the capital, we drove four hours inland, on a dusty dirt road, getting past trees, and simple houses, but everything was clean, tidy. They cut trees with huge machetes: they don't use modern tools. At the hotel of Kigali we found role models of order and politeness, and the Fathers' house where we stayed in Kibeho was a sort of seminary, too. It was gorgeous, with plants all around it, and new buildings. We commented that we were being prepared for what was about to come. And that was really so.*

You were shocked, Elamed, by the difference between Rwanda and the DR Congo.
Elamed: *Rwanda is a silent place. Many people walked down the streets, but it was quiet, there wasn't this incessant noise as was in the Congo, which is too noisy. Everything is remarkably hectic there.*

What about your impressions about Uganda and the Congo? Another day a missionary said, *Congo is hellish*, and she left without explaining.
Shen: *Uganda's capital, is messy, a little dirty, but there are "reasonable" areas, asphalted avenues. A crowd circulates around the trade area with a world of stands selling an infinity of trinkets and food on the sidewalks, but there were also businesses in shops. As in Brazil, there are better and worse districts, but they're clean and not overcrowded. We didn't see open sewage as in the Congo, which is like hell because... What do I imagine a hell is like? A state of consciousness, which may be mental, emotional and even physical. But there are islands of relative peace in Kinshasa.*

Kinshasa, Democratic Republic of the Congo, April 2015

We lodged in an oasis. In the Congo, everything happens in the street. Even the bakery is someone carrying bread baskets on their head. Wherever we went beauty, order, harmony, silence were missing. We saw chaos, ugliness... Human degradation is extreme, misery is extreme. All sorts of vile and wrong things are visible in the streets, are common place! Sewers give off a bad odor. Commerce: a world of street vendors selling an infinity of trinkets. Citizens throw all kind of trash on the dirt roads. People live in a garbage dump, lost, and what's worse, regard it as a normal thing.

Are there many street-dwellers?

Shen: *Too many. Under the viaduct, with no hygiene at all. We've been to horrible places. People have entirely lost the awareness of inner balance. To enter the Congo, we had obtained our entry visa from the Congo Embassy, in Brasilia but, even so, you ran the risk of having it refused when you land. The decision about being accepted or not in the country is made only at the airport. Our entry was made easier by the help of a super influential lady.*

On the missions, you met realities that you've never come across before.

Shen: *No missionary had gone through the extreme deprivation as those we had to face during that mission. There, lack of food is common, medical assistance is rare. People are alone with God, at least in the range of the ones we dealt with. You cannot tell whether the scrawny street-dwellers are twenty or forty years old. They have suffered need since birth. That's the only reality they known. He who is able to have a meal a day is in a good situation. If he can have two, that's excellent. There's no hygiene. As it's hard to find water in faucets, they carry water in buckets in certain localities. Even in some Missionaries of Charity houses, water was not drinkable , and people drank it all the same.*

In Uganda, we understood better the two sides of the missions...
Luiz: *We found out what we went to do in Africa. Not only rolling up our sleeves; but also to discover the other side of the coin. Material service plus prayer are a perfect marriage! We would get home from the morning task, have lunch and start our group prayer. We'd sometimes pray eight hours straight. To be able do this, lodging in the house of retreat was essential.*

You do a visible and also an invisible work: a material and an immaterial.
Shen: *Before traveling for the fourth mission, we were instructed to balance service and prayer. When we left Brazil, we didn't know how to put this into practice. As we arrived in Kigali, the very routine established by the Missionaries of Charity showed us how. We had to leave their house at noon, since they close it to retreat in prayer. Since it took us more than half an hour by van to go and come back, we decided to remain in the hotel in the afternoons, to pray. At the beginning, we'd pray for three, four hours. At the Kibeho shrine, we participated in many prayers and Masses. When we went to Uganda, we had established a very intense daily prayer schedule, always singing and using a guitar. And it was that way until the end.*

Did you play the guitar as a child?
Shen: *No. I learned in Africa. We prayed and sang so often that I ended up learning.*

After having been in contact with the inner purity of Kibeho's faithful and devout people, the missionaries say Rwanda is the heart of Africa.
Elamed: *Rwandans today live a courageous reconciliation path. They are summoned for monthly community work such as cleaning parks and building highways or homes for the needy. The aim is to give people the opportunity to repent, to increase their ability to forgive, and also to uplift everyone. In Kigali, we made a quick stop at the Genocide Memorial, where the history of Rwanda is portrayed. Made up of tribes before the colonial period, these people were very united and strong and lived in peace. The two main ethnicities were the Tutsis—the ruling class, with kings, princesses—and the Hutus, predominantly field workers. When the European invaders learned how strong and organized these people were, they*

realized that the only way to gain power over them was to divide them. They began to classify them according to very superficial data—the Hutu is smaller and has a flatter nose, the nose of a Tutsi is thin and they are taller. In order to encourage rivalry between the two ethnicities, the settlers also started to make their ethnicity explicit on their I.D's, sowing discord, "Are you a Hutu? Why do you let yourself be dominated by a Tutsi?" By using the media, they managed to generate separation, until hatred was finally unleashed in the genocide of 1994. Within one hundred days, radical Hutus, enticed by the government and the media, massacred almost one million Tutsis, moderate Hutus and Tvás, another ethnic group. Today, Rwanda is united under a single flag. Families herald a time of peace. One of the most important lessons this country gives to the world is the ability to forgive what we regard as unforgivable. Learning about Rwanda's recent renaissance history enabled us to understand the importance of group unity and the value of forgiveness to achieve peace. In this land there are those who seek the path of reconciliation within themselves, with fellow beings, with their own essence, with the Divine.

Convincing the black man that the color of his skin determined inferiority was a perverted strategy in the process of domination. This prejudice still brings us serious consequences.

Bento: *Even so, the Rwandan peasants greeted us with great joy. The European influence had not altered their courtesy. Simplicity, politeness and humbleness are superior attributes. How many evils have we caused them, how much lack of affection? Yet, I was able to notice love on those farmers' faces which held no grudges or rancor. To me, the synthesis of the mission was to understand how divine qualities live within the most simple and humble people.*

In Rwanda, you experienced a moment of revelation.

Bento: *We went to Kibeho crossing the beautiful Rwanda, the land of a thousand hills. On the undulating road, I'd observe women with their children on their back carrying hoes in their hand. People do not use modern tools to plant potatoes and vegetables around the heavily-cultivated fields in the valleys. As the women heard the engine, they stopped and turned to follow the van taking the white people away. They opened broad smiles and greeted us until they lost sight of us. How charming! For a moment, I felt a synthesis of knowledge, a very lively comprehension when I fixed my gaze on one woman among all if them. I penetrated a mystery. I saw the*

Missionaries organize the firewood storage. Nairobi, Kenya, May 2013

Black Virgin Mary inside her. I was face to face with the same maternal virginal purity, despite her painful woman's history. White people have a heavy debt to be paid off to the blacks... but those women had forgiven us.

You had an insight while working with the firewood.

Luiz: *I will never forget the firewood. In the house of the Missionaries of Charity in Nairobi, there was a great yard filled with logs, wood to be chopped, pallets piled up in a disorganized way. As soon as the coordinator proposed to tidy up the area, they split the chores: part of them chopped it, the others piled up the logs. Then, something began to happen. There were many black people around, surprised by the fact we were doing a job not done by white people, who regard it as inferior. I looked up, and there were smiles on their faces. At that moment, there was a paradigm shift. If we did the work they do for the Sisters, we were serving them. There was a reason for their joy: they were being freed from old chains of prejudice! And I had a "déjà vu," suddenly remembering a Debret artist drawing, which illustrates Brazilian History books. In it, a group of black people are working, being watched by well-dressed men. Here, it was the very opposite. It was a shock. "In a past life, might we have been the white men only observing?" In another occasion, black people also stopped to stare at the white group painting and gardening in front of the Sisters house. We even took a photo with one of them.*

You've always wanted to be a missionary in Africa
Luiz: *Since I was young, I've identified myself with African culture. When I studied with Jesuits and Franciscans, a friar would tell us stories from the time he'd been a missionary in Africa, and that touched me. One year before I went, I read the book by Immaculée Ilibagiza, I Survived to Tell, and I cried a lot. Then I read it again, but never thought I was about to come to Rwanda, where she had lived an impressive history. When we entered the rural area towards Kibeho, I felt I was entering a different space and time. I traveled backwards centuries, I seemed to be visiting ancient times in history... the purity, everything touched me deeply. In Kibeho, they turned off the electric power at 8 p.m. Contemplating the starry vastness, listening to whispers of distant talks, I entered a time within time.*

The group had an extraordinary experience.
Clara: *It was impressive. We went to Ethiopia three times. On the first mission, we kept a certain memory of the hospital of the Missionaries of Charity. A huge house with 1,500 patients, and an enormous mortality rate. In the third mission, they seemed to have fewer people and we thought they have painted the rooms. The Sisters said the number of patients remained the same, and they had not painted it. The impression of the group was so real: the place was brighter, cleaner, the walls whiter, there were fewer people. After returning, we asked Trigueirinho what was happening to us. He explained we had worked the astral plane of the place, and a lot had been liberated. If that happened there, a similar thing may happen anywhere. We can change the astral level of any place. This is invisible work, and it's not done by us. "What did we do?" We put on bandages, we did the laundry, we swept the floor. Apparently, that was it. But on other levels... mystery is operating.*

Conversations about Greece and Turkey

Today, this is the condition of the planet:
darkness still reigns in the world of appearances
while, at the same time, the man who is about
to come is blossoming. This future human,
in incubation, already lives with us, he lives
within us and is destined to remain here definitively.
Juan Mihovilovich

Let us not close our eyes to what happens in the four corners of the world. Missionaries tell us about the consequences of global crisis and chaos in lives of people they meet, which illustrate brutal human selfishness.

A missionary recalls her memories: *How brave these people are of so many nationalities and foreign languages! They only know their mother tongue and when they enter another country, they leave everything behind. The prisons of Athens are packed with these people. They did nothing wrong and are waiting for documents or to be deported. Not knowing their languages, we looked at them and placed our hands on our heart. Respectfully, they answered doing the same gesture, slowly lowering their head and closing their eyes. Then we give them clothes, a meal, bread. But the way they look at us is worth more than any material thing. Little faces from different countries, each one looks like a child... many were young people, many. It is sad. You see they have faith because they make the Muslim salutation "As-Salamu Alaikum!"—Let Peace be with you!.*

Dangerous mafias beguile naive and usually poor foreigners, ill-informed and uneducated. In the Detention Center, the missionaries met a Haitian who spoke Spanish, Portuguese, French and English. When he recognized the Brazilian flag on their clothes, his eyes were wide-open: *I was around so many people for over a month, and I don't speak with anybody! Not even the police officers speak English.* He cried with happiness, from inside the bars, the missionary group being outside. He told them his story. He was not a criminal: *In São Paulo, I paid 2,000 euros, and they promised to get me a job earning 1,000 euros a month. When I arrived in Greece, I found out it was all a big lie. I ended up living from hand to mouth. Eventually I was arrested because I had no money to renew my documents in time.*

Another missionary reports on how to connect without speaking the same language. He use to distribute men's clothes with the group: *We didn't speak the language of those on the queue, but created bonds with our eyes, with gestures. It was a silent conversation. Our Latin blood made it possible to have warm exchanges. The men felt they were not alone, and no longer went only for clothes, but to be given a smile, a touch of joy. And if there were no donations at the moment, they would get affection but, above all, they would remain hopeful. Sometimes my heart ached: the hardship of a needy person was reflected in my own deprivation.*

Having seen so much poverty, madness and impurity in Greece, the missionaries realize: *Souls are fading out, growing cold.* The context of a country that has exhausted its forces and whose borders have been closed leads the foreign immigrants and Greeks under the same situation, to walk discouraged up and down streets, hurt by past calamities and afraid of future prospects. Their feeling of defeat strengthened the missionaries' impulse to spread love, to encourage them: *Move on, come on, brother, don't give up hope!* Even though only a speck of joy is put in the life of these beings, the servers make the effort. The aim of a missionary's activity is not to provide people with housing or a way of survival. Such tasks are in the hands of governments and large social organizations. The missionary's activity is about offering unconditional love.

Thoughtful, a missionary is silent for a split second, and lowers her voice: *We met people with sad, bitter, resentful looks. It is extraordinary, it seems that everyone has their lives messed up. Greece is tough. This is not something you realize straight away, but its psychic field is deeply contaminated, saturated with the energies of immorality, such as laziness, lust, gluttony. No one goes hungry. There is an abundant donation of food distributed by churches and other institutions. One of the miseries is the lack of control of moral energy: people get much too involved with that. There is a large number of sex-shops in Athens, lots of drugs and prostitution, all that mixed up with the beauty of the country. It is a dangerous place. You have to be careful not to neglect higher values and go astray with illusion.*

There is a striking contrast between the residents of this small country. There are those who live in sumptuous homes at resorts on the beach,

Boats in the marina of Bodrun, Turkey, February 2016

with no money or food, while neighbors throw food away—they are called "the new poor"—while, a few meters away, neighbors throw food in the trash. With the dissolution of the middle class, the one who has nothing today had a full table not long ago and was also wasting food.

Given the sudden social and economic fall, an altruistic network grows. For example, what a bakery produces one day, by law cannot be sold the next day, hence it was thrown in the trash. Today the owner agrees to give the leftovers to the missionaries to distribute to those who need it.

The discrepancy also occurs in the neighboring country, Turkey. Here is the description of another missionary: *We passed by gorgeous jewelry stores, fine restaurants in boulevards closed to traffic in Bodrum, a top-notch tourist resort on the Aegean Sea coast. In the marina filled with mega yachts, customers drank tea on decks by the seaside. It was winter. Arabian refugees, 200 yards away, boarded fragile inflatable boats trying to reach Kos, the Greek island 2.5 miles away. The City Hall gave orders for them to hide in the bush not to be seen, avoiding embarrassment for tourists. There, human blindness and indifference were visible. The heart of humanity is sick.*

Conversations about refugee children in Turkey, abandoned children in Africa

Don't make of yourself a dream to come true: Go.
Without a marked path.
You are the one of all paths. Just be a presence.
An invisible silent presence.
Canticle XXIII, by Cecília Meireles

As missionaries were learning to see beyond appearances, they communed with the profound suffering of Arabian and African boys and girls during activities at ASAM, a Turkish organization that supports refugees, and also in different houses of the Missionaries of Charity.

I asked the same question to some missionaries interviewed for this book: *What was the most touching interactions you have had during the missions?*

Bento: *In the Ankara office, an ASAM manager assigned us to be with the children in a room. We opened the door of a 40 foot cubicle packed with children dancing to a loud techno song, doof doof doof. "My God, what is going on? We come to do our work and end up in this madness." In a lapse of time, I saw myself as a child leaving my bed to sleep between my father and mother to feel them closer. Then, I understood those children's feelings. Close to each other in a cathartic movement, they were trying to forget their pain. Most were orphans and many had seen their parents beheaded. I looked at one of them, and she rushed to hug me. I hugged her for a long time and understood that the Divinity was there looking after those souls, even amidst that craziness, which repels us so badly. I understood Light working in many different forms, way beyond any format or rule.*

Alexandrina: *"What am I doing here? What is my mission?" I kept repeating these questions to myself. We have ancestral relationships with countries. Since I landed in Turkey, I felt misplaced, strange, until I had my first contact with a Syrian refugee girl about 5 years old. While we played with dolls for the children to feel at ease with us, she kept her hands in her coat pockets without doing anything, not interacting with the group. Something in her* drew me towards her. Slowly, I put both my hands outside her pockets, over hers. She looked at me, and I at her. She took her little hands and placed them on mine, tilted her beautiful head to my side and said in Portuguese: "Mãe!" What a gift to be called mother! I was deeply touched. I don't know... maybe she lost her mother. I don't know... so many children have lost their families. We hugged. I had found a daughter. She had found a mother. I felt the Divine Mother pulsing in my chest together with hers and I understood: "This is what you came here for, to give your heart. You don't need to speak their language, nothing. Just look, just feel." I placed her back on the floor, but we remained holding hands. Other children came... we started playing in a circle, and she joined other children's games. It has been two years now and I have never forgotten her. Every day I remember that sweet look, her dark hair. Deep inside, I baptized her as a spiritual goddaughter and pray for her, I pray for all the children in the world, especially for those who loose their parents and are in wars. It was the most unforgettable moment of so many missions. From then on everything flowed, and I stopped asking what I was doing there. We went to distribute codes of love.

Rosi: I can't even draw a house but I saw myself in the room of a Syrian plastic art teacher, who taught drawing to children from Aleppo. He spoke English and Arabic and I asked him: "Can you please ask this girl how I can help her?" The twelve year old Aisla answered: "Say a prayer!" I was surprised... What prayer? I began to write in English the invocation for the children in wars: "For the Angel of Peace, we implore to God, calm the suffering of the little ones. Angel of Healing, restore the wounds of the innocent." As I wrote, the teacher translated it reading out loud. A boy whispered something in his ear, grabbed the paper I had written on and left running. I wanted to know where he'd gone. "To the office, to print copies and distribute them to his friends." In the meantime, Aisla finished a drawing and showed it to me. From a heart pierced by an arrow flowed drops of blood and, inside it, she wrote: "I love Aleppo." Just below the drops, she drew a large burning candle. I asked the teacher to ask her the meaning of that. I thought she might have left a boyfriend in Syria. Aisla explained that it was her heart, broken by the war. The spear and the drops of blood were symbols for what she was suffering. "What about the burning candle?" The blood dripping on the candle without putting it out represented the hope that Allah would put an end to all that when He decided to. She was absolutely sure of that. I was speechless!

We think the war takes place on the other side of the world, in the East, that the hurricane is in the United States... We don't see these things are also here, as we all are one. If they suffer, a part of us suffers. If they are in pain, we are directly or indirectly causing it, we are co-participants.

The core of disorder in the consciousness of humanity is continuously fueled by small nuclei of discord within our own little families. Disagreements with a brother or a sister, with the father, with family members echo in waves around the world and result in wars.

If something negative vibrates in us, it generates consequences, conflicts, and differences. Each one of us is responsible for this lack of love because if each one fully lived love, there surely would not be space for chaos. May we recognize this and collaborate for peace, acting according to the teaching of the Missionaries of Charity: "Be the mirror of Christ in each movement, in each action."

Cristiane: *In Rwanda, in the House of the Missionaries of Charity, we were divided into groups. I went to work with children in a simple, very tidy room. As I entered, an acid strong smell permeated the air. The children had cerebral palsy in different degrees. Some were tied to chairs by pieces of cloth, others drooled and crawled on mattresses left on the floor, and, when we got closer, they grabbed onto us. For a moment, I felt an immense rejection, something I never imagined I might feel. At the same moment, a delicious flower scent permeated the air. I had no doubt, that was the poetical answer from the presence of Our Lady! Grateful, I closed my eyes in prayer and had a vision of our group supporting me in kinship. From that moment on something changed in me. I began to feel so much love for all of them, to notice the radiation of their eyes, to understand the children without needing to speak their languages, and vice-versa. Over time, my communication with children improved. In the Congo we went to a house for males where boys abandoned in tragic ways live. The first time they opened the gate greeting us with joy, we hugged them all and gathered to sing. They loved it. One boy, Nathan, held my hand all the time, began talking with me. At first, I didn't understand him, since he speaks Congolese and I, Portuguese. He went on and on. Suddenly, I began to understand him beyond words and mind. He also understood me. It was so natural. Every day, we were greeted with joy, and played, sang, talked. Our last meeting was special. When we got out of the car, Nathan ran towards me. We hugged warm-heartedly, child by child giving them all the loving energy pulsating in the group.*

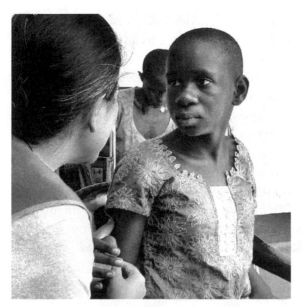

This girl never smiles. Kampala, Uganda, 2015
A Syrian refugee. Izmir, Turkey, 2016

A missionary: *The joy and the radiant smiles we see in films and photos of African children are not just effervescence. They come from a genuine purity and depth. The Sisters told us about their harsh reality, and I too lived some dramatic moments. A small boy told me, in a very straightforward way: "I have two brothers. You will take us to your home." He didn't ask, "May we come to your home?" Then, he ran away and called the two, just as if his dream would be coming true right then. I had to say: "No, you can't come to my home." The boy: "Why?" I told him: "Because your home is here." He had bet all on that. It was difficult, very difficult. Since children found our names funny, while we created songs together, some boys began to sing: "I want to come with you, but I know you can't take me." A feeling of adversity lives within them. They fear the future. They want to be saved from that place, from the eternal insecurity and anxiety. There is no perspective regarding jobs or money. Tension about politics is constant. They live in a paradox. People are cheerful and have energy, but carry the fear of hunger, of evil, of a world which is out of control and may get worse. In that place, it is easy to be pushed into an abyss.*

Shen: *African children are extremely musically inclined, they sing in tune, and learn songs quickly. In Uganda, every day they received us singing:*

"Peace, peace, peace on Earth." But I was particularly touched by a little girl from the Congo. Children have horrible stories, the worst of them, involving witchcraft and superstition. People believe that families are cursed when babies are born with malformations or even skin blemishes. Since malnutrition is widespread, many have diseases at birth. Parents loath them and quickly get rid of the children, abandoning them in streets or forests, or tying them to train tracks to be killed. Passers-by save some, taking them for the Sisters to take care of. Wounded children arrive with marks of beatings to cast out evil spirits. I was touched by one survivor. The little girl with motor difficulties due to a mental problem, was in a wheel-chair. In spite of her physical disabilities, she was quite lucid. One day, while she listened to us singing, she began to conduct. She conducted perfectly. She lived music. From then on, she always followed me. Wherever I played, she was around conducting with her little hands. I did a song for her. She smiled, her eyes shone, innocent, as if there was not a drama. There was music in that gaze. She was wonderful. We played, laughed with each other, sheer joy. Someone took a photo of us together. I also remember Maria, with the most awful story. She received love from each missionary, however, none of us has ever seen her smiling.

Rosi: During the missions, we found out how powerless we are to solve world miseries, illnesses, wars. Yet we managed, somehow, to plant seeds of peace. A power brings life to our souls, enhances our perception and gives us wisdom to silently sow seeds in the people we serve, in our families, in our friends, in our neighbors. Today, all we need to do is to pray and plant invisible seeds.

Conversation with Friar Luciano

A disciple of today drinks directly from his inner source.
A disciple of today walks firmly, even if he does not know
where he is going. A disciple of today transcends the concept
of frontiers: he recognizes in people of all nations, flowers
cared for by the same Gardener. A disciple of today knows
he will not cross the Doorway until he gives way to a brother
or sister who is nearby. A disciple of today keeps attentive
vigil, and prays in secret, permeating spaces with light.
Words to the Heart, by Friar Sivanum, aka Friar Luciano

The mission work is followed closely by Friar Luciano, a consecrated monk of Grace Mercy Order, an affiliated member of the Fraternidade—Humanitarian International Federation, the entity that promotes and supports the missions. He is one of the four members of the Council of Regency and Permanent Guidance which fosters the sectors connected with Fraternidade—International Humanitarian Federation—FIHF. In December 2017, he started to follow the missionary work intently. He regularly travels to Roraima and Brasilia to participate in meetings with partners and players in the humanitarian network woven to support Venezuelan refugees.

In May 2018, we met in Fraternidade's office in Boa Vista, and he explained topics related to group service.

The FIHF discovers new ways of expression as it expands it's missionary service.
Yes, FIHF works on many levels, including the spiritual one. Two of their affiliates are religious institutions: Association Mary and Grace Mercy Order, both are autonomous Christian organizations of interfaith relationship with groups connected with Catholicism, Islamism, Judaism, Buddhism, and other beliefs. Besides those two, FIHF has another facet, the missionary one, started in 2011. The missions of Fraternidade do have a spiritual root, but don't teach any dogmatic or religious belief. However, behind the walls of the lodging houses, the missionaries do a profoundly inner exercise and practice hours of prayer.

The values we represent are shared in daily life, without any mystery, and our work is gradually known through its selfless voluntary service. Our work is done more through the heart, through fraternal co-living, rather than through words.

The UNHCR and Fraternidade are partners and work hard to protect refugees from Venezuela. Since the UN is a secular organization, how do they relate with the monastics?

As everything in life, there's nothing like a transparent dialogue to clarify a situation. We made it very clear to the UNHCR as well as to the UNICEF— which recently invited us for a partnership in activities with young people and children of the shelters—that the presence of the monastics is similar to that of the other missionaries, the residents of the communities or of Light-Network collaborators. It is not religious. It's concerned with service, to do whatever is necessary. They know we are not theorizing, nor teaching any catechism, nor attracting devotees. The Council of Regency prohibits, in the shelters, any spiritual practice that we develop, or even making any reference to them.

However, our garments make people wonder. "Where do these men and women come from, these people wearing religious habits, cleaning the floor, feeding children and playing with them, carrying boxes and bags, without any trace of a religious activity? What is this, after all?" Male monastics are particularly rare nowadays. We always cause a surprise whenever we arrive; in airport queues, in shopping centers. Some situations are embarrassing, because people laugh, make comments and may show an irreverent attitude when we are around. Some become interested, and move closer to ask us questions.

A few days ago, we were received for a meeting with the Chief of Staff of the Presidency of the Republic and the Army Command for the Roraima Mission, plus thirty-five officers, as well as representatives of other entities. All of them respect us because, throughout our task, they have observed that we are as missionary as any other. Monastics of the Fraternidade have served in Boa Vista since the first mission, when indigenous people lived in the Passarão, an outdoor market in which there's sewage in the street, a real mess. The local authorities and the populace are accustomed to us and, when they meet us, make a point of talking to us and reinforcing their admiration for our availability for service.

Friar Luciano. Pintolândia Shelter, Boa Vista, Roraima, Brazil, August 2018

But there are those who show prejudice. The captain of a shelter told me that the habit itself implies a dogmatic aspect. I replied saying that the use of Army uniforms is associated to wars, conflicts, imposition. In the same way the Army is in shelters, fostering humanitarian actions, so are the monastics. As they've already noticed, we never talk about God, about Jesus, because this is not part of our activity in the shelters. He became a little embarrassed.

In Brazil, a country of interfaith exchanges, there are many spiritual nuances, from Umbanda to the Catholic Church. Today, religious intolerance may be the reason for someone to be put in prison. This is not an ethical issue only: it is a legal matter, a great takeover of the country. By law, people are free to have any religious expression. No one is compelled to join a religion, but they have to respect all of them. We may not be accepted, but we accept other religious expressions and want to be respected.

The purpose of the Fraternidade missions goes beyond the fulfillment of material basic necessities.
Missionaries fulfill various levels of needs, from the most unimportant and trivial—such as giving clothes, food, medicine, diapers, cradles, tents, bicycles—to the abstract needs, which are emotional, ethical, humanitarian.

We try to undertake a silent task to rescue human dignity and its consciousness, to rescue people's hope and joy of living in order to educate souls and help the planet and the Kingdoms of Nature. We seek to touch the core of the wounds caused by the loss of self-esteem in families with unhealthy children, without hygienic care or adequate food, for women without preventive assistance, for men without education.

Everything asks for help. Inequality is at the basis of all conflicts, and the consequence of so many mistakes may end up as a mission, where the assistance process begins. The most important thing is that the one being served, be he a Nepali, an African, a Syrian or an indigenous person, may rebuild the consciousness of their own value, respect their unique characteristics, their feelings, their own history.

Gradually, the refugees realize that Fraternidade is not there just to give them objects, make medical appointments. During the field work, the principles we try to develop in our own lives and in the inner world of each one of us are taken to them, along with the assistance activities. The people who are being helped notice that there's no competitiveness, no yearning for power and no need to be right. At the same time, we are disciplined and make our presence clear when something is not going well. Our examples and attitudes foster their reeducation and activate corresponding values within those helped.

What is the current situation of the Venezuelans in Boa Vista?
Besides those who rent houses for groups, there are more than 4,000 people sheltered by the joint work of the UNHCR, Fraternidade and the task force of the Welcome Operation of the Brazilian Army. These three organizations offer them a range of direct services, from bandages put on indigenous people to socialization and group activities, and even collaboration in the relocation of refugees and migrants to other states of Brazil.

The presence of the Defense Ministry, through the Army, has been positive. The military are taking people off the streets, although their focus is national security—settling issues connected to drug trafficking, human trafficking, prostitution, and measures to impose some order at the frontier. The Army provided the most consistent logistics of the last months, with a task force that allows those in the shelter to have a tent, food, shower and be vaccinated and registered. If it were not for them, it would be much slower. We have to make it clear that now the military provides us with the human and financial resources and the kind of help that we are not capable of offering. In addition, they give some protection to the missionaries in the shelters.

Without making any political position, it was through the Army's efforts and experience in humanitarian missions that thousands of Venezuelans now receive drinking water, food, documents, dental service, vaccines. They no longer live abandoned in squares, under heavy rains and threatened by the local police. Those who used to relieve themselves behind a post now have facilities made from modified containers where they can take a hot shower, do their laundry, and they are protected.

Attitudes of cordiality and amiability of the Brazilian Army have drawn the attention of the UNICEF and the UNHCR, who are in contact with international missions in several countries. They compared other nations degree of military arrogance in dealing with people with the way Brazilian Army officers walk among the assisted people, respecting them, working together, talking, playing and laughing with the refugees.

What are the orientations given to a missionary?
To do neutral, simple work. On the spiritual level, neutrality means going deeper in what we call impartiality. Missionaries should address situations with neutrality. If they get involved with any external issue, if they take sides or think there is anything wrong in Venezuela, the mission will not help to build new routes for these people's lives. We should know about each country's reality. But it's not up to us evaluate what happens in them and neither discuss this issue with their inhabitants. We welcome everyone without fueling their concerns: we try to listen to them but don't encourage criticism. When they ask us something, we answer, clarify, go deeper in the subject. When nothing is asked, we keep silent. We should handle each situation by itself: "Do you want to return to Venezuela? To look for a job? To go to other states of Brazil? To go to other countries in Latin America?"

In the shelters, our goal is to provide them with a better quality of life and educational process. The case of the indigenous people is a very different issue. Their background includes being abandoned in their homeland. There they used to beg and were no longer valued or had any interest in their own origin. They arrived in Brazil in a process of deterioration, with the intention of preserving their previous street life style. However, they came across the Fraternidade, whose purpose is to stimulate activities that may allow them to resume their culture and inner life based on their own beliefs.

What are the future perspectives of indigenous people in the shelters?
Regarding their settling, the Fraternidade hopes that the organizations responsible for these issues are sensible enough to provide some area for them to live in. There, they could be accompanied in their activities, so the indigenous consciousness can be appreciated through craftsmanship and cultivation of crops, so that they can eventually create a village legally established according to Brazilian laws. In Venezuela their lands are being seized by the government and they don't have anywhere to stay. This would be a path for the children from the Shelter to grow up near Nature, in better conditions.

It is the first time Brazil has had this kind of situation.
Brazilian legislation recognizes the refugees' right to work, education, health, mobility in the nation's territory. It allows them to rebuild their lives. The task of a humanitarian mission is not to be a substitute for governmental actions. It is an offer to fill non-structural gaps with preventive and specific activities in the cases of health, education, conflicts.

Recent statistics in Venezuela indicate that the situation is getting worse. More than three million citizens, in addition to the 1.5 million that have already migrated, intend to leave the country. However, the shelters are temporary, and the contract signed between the Fraternidade and the UNHCR, as well as the action of the Army, are being renewed according to the situation of the neighboring country and the way the Brazilian government decides to implement humanitarian actions.

Traditionally, Brazil is not a belligerent country, prone to creating animosities. Spiritually, this is a relief and represents protection to the soul of the nation. It is also a devout country, which recognizes Our Lady Aparecida as their patroness. This spiritual background grants some support to all missionary activity.

In conclusion, can you explain how the missions are defined?
The Council of Regency and Permanent Guidance follows the guidelines transmitted by the Divine Messengers, through the visionaries of Grace Mercy Order. For example, they have just indicated that a mission has to be set up in Egypt. Each movement of the Fraternidade is determined by the Celestial Hierarchy and a role of the Council is to materialize and support each one of the assigned missions.

A call to the youth

You know well that the most correct path
is the path of altruism. The heart holds
the testimony that it is precisely the good-
will that helps in hard times.
Morya

The Universe speaks, making us remember infinity. The eternal light flashes in the cosmos, inviting young people to abandon their material illusion to get to know the pain of the world, since their immense energy helps to heal this pain. It is magical to see a young person reflecting joy in the shelters. The spring spirit is contagious and transforms those who serve and the ones being served. At the end of the day, no one feels exhausted, on the contrary, they feel even better.

Youth brings a renewing impulse. If a young person is determined to do something, they change life around them for that to take place. Young people attentive to signs in the sky aim to practice fraternity, respond to the call and join this great adventure in Roraima. They take along universal values: serving common good and emanating love. They are the expression of a new era that is flourishing in the Earth-home, time for transcending cultural, ethnic, religious differences and resistances.

The missionary task is renewed every day. An environment of constant discoveries attracts the youth. When they wake up in the morning, they know they will be experiencing something unprecedented with different people, that they will be receiving new instructions, and participating in a unique movement. The creative energy of youth may be suffocated by the institutionalized system, and it awakens when they have the opportunity to work in a team, being respected in their feelings and knowledge. This gives them energy to transform this vitality into positive actions.

Although this phase of life is regarded as rebellious, the young persons know how important it is to obey the command of the coordinator, recognized as the one who is knowledgeable of the task as a whole. Besides, they become good partners for the adult who, with good humor and enthusiasm, works side by side with his apprentices.

We call them youth, but there are people here from twelve to seventy years old. Children may feel old and elderly may feel young, chronological age does not matter. An eighty one year old proactive lady took part in the first Missionary Practice with lively enthusiasm. Young minds are flexible, open to change. If one day they just have bread and bananas to eat, they do not complain, and even say: *Look, what a wonderful banana! Let's make some banana candy.* A young person is permanently flexible and welcomes change: *Today we'll have lunch at 3 p.m.* They even think that's good, it's a new adventure.

Changing schedules to deal with urgencies is one of the missionary rules. Once, a group went to a neighboring town. They had planned to spend the afternoon there and they were soon given a test through a phone call: *Something is happening here!* The missionary gave them a swift answer: *Ok, we are coming back now!* If someone starts complaining, moaning, suffering because of the altered programs... the missionary work is not for this person. The one who creates resistance becomes a rigid cell, an inflexible block inside the eternal flux of energy.

In Boa Vista we had straightforward talks with the young people, apprentices who had come from far-away areas of Brazil or from other countries. They spent hours in flights and stop-overs in order to share with Venezuelan refugees. We also talked to young volunteers from the city itself, who bring joy, beauty, enthusiasm and faith to those in the shelters once a week.

An apprentice says: *What I take home is more than what I bring. It is incorrect to say "I am helping." The help we get is certainly bigger than what we give! During the missions, I was healed of things I did not even know I suffered from. How invisible are our shortcomings and mistakes! There are issues we need to solve, but we get stuck, unconsciously blocked. I had heard that the problem is always in us, and that, from the moment we transform ourselves, our relationship with others is also transformed, but I had never understood such a thing. But this is true, everything is connected! If we let go of criticism, guilt or fear, this gives us freedom in our future steps.*

At first, she did not say *no* to refugees because she believed only a *yes* could ease their hard life. She did not say *yes* out of love, but because she compared her life to theirs. Actually, she said *yes* to mitigate her own guilt. Over time, this attitude became a burden. She was helping out of obligation, not out of love. One day, a group was praying, and someone accompanied with the guitar. This young woman clearly saw a pink ray penetrating her own heart. Tears appeared on her face. All became clear to her. Unconditional love for all beings, for her family burst within her. Since then, she has been learning to listen to others and she allows herself the possibility of changing her viewpoints. She understood that people learn from a yes and also from a no. She is now able to say a firm and friendly no, an instructional *no*, explaining to that person the reason for that. In short, she improved morally and intellectually. She adds: *How can I thank the refugees for all that I learned? Giving back to them!*

A physiotherapist who works with auriculotherapy says: *My heart asks me to serve. Whenever I watched documentaries about Doctors without Borders or about the Red Cross, my eyes used to mist over. I felt as if I had to be there. Then, I enrolled to participate in the Missionary Practices, and my attitudes and life changed. I began to see the world in a different way, to care for the other, to analyze the dynamics of the street-dwellers, to look in their eyes, to talk with them. I went to a Missionary Practices, then another, then two more. I participated in meetings of the Planetary Mission Network. That work gradually pulled me... and here I am, in Boa Vista. At first, I found it strange, the heat, the energy, the intensity of the everyday pace, to be giving of myself all the time to others. I felt exhausted, and heavy. Now, the service is flowing well.*

The third young woman recalls: *During a certain Missionary Practice, we went to the APAC, an association that gives assistance to inmates with good behavior. I'd never been inside a prison before. I thought: "I have nothing to say, but I will surrender, and ask Jesus to help me and, whatever I need to do, I'll do." I stood there, looking around. During a workshop, the inmates were asked to create a drawing to be sent to their families. One of them called me thinking I was a foreigner. We began to talk and I suggested that we color some mandalas. We talked about what we felt while coloring them. That was more than a therapy. I felt united to him. Other people were attracted by us and joined us. I am a little mistrustful, kind of buttoned-down, I like to plan everything: "I am going to do this, and say*

A young missionary puts on dressings.
Pintolândia Shelter, Boa Vista, Roraima, Brazil, September 2017

that." I set goals. I'm scared of letting myself go. At work this works well, but at the missionary service something extra always happens, and the situations get out of my control. Learning to trust is not easy, but I know I need to live here and now. I keep telling myself: "Let yourself go, just be available. At the right time you will know what you have to do, let yourself go like the water of a river. Let yourself be taken." I can't figure out what happened, but on that day, inside that prison, a subjective part of myself that was imprisoned was released.

Another apprentice, a volunteer from São Paulo's waste collection cooperative, tells us how she came to Figueira. She was looking for a vegan veterinarian for her animals, when a couple was suggested to her. She looked up to them because of their generosity: having a good income, the couple defined a budget for themselves, and donated the rest to humanitarian campaigns and projects. The veterinarian recommended the community of Figueira to her. And now the volunteer had just arrived in Boa Vista. Among other tasks, she was offering flower essences to indigenous and non-indigenous mothers and children.

A primary missionary gives guidance to the young first-timer instructing them to connect themselves exclusively to their task. Inexperienced, they report unnerving stories and news spread by the press and the social media channels. If they remain surfing on this dark wave, their minds and emotions are not able to contribute with the rest of the group. They must learn to be selective regarding the news.

Each missionary's attitude is observed by the coordinators. At their arrival, their willingness for serving is similar, but, a few days later, their emotional facets come to surface while they work and live together. If one turns out to have a "trouble-maker-consciousness" during a mission, they do not recommend their participation in another one until they mature.

In difficult situations, volunteers who are too susceptible and those who get sentimentally involved with those being helped or with the servers, can put the group at risk. Individualistic actions of reckless people are also unsettling for the whole group. There are those who are excessively shy, who remain in a reclusive attitude and not attentive to the needs of the team. They need to be pushed into action as they hold up the group. However, to everyone's joy, there are promising revelations taking place.

In the Pintolândia Shelter, a young woman surrounded by kids played the guitar and sang along with two sisters and a friend. They are about 20 years old and doing Environmental Management, Pharmacy and Senior High School courses respectively. Our chat took place in the lively environment, with hundreds of assisted people of all ages walking by, running, lying on mattresses, sitting on the bleachers.

About helping the others in whatever is needed, she said:
We have been volunteers for six months. People here need more than food and clothes, they need to talk, get hugged. I have just given a shower to a girl, if it were not me, who would approach her? Helping the other is the role of every human being, not only of missionaries. That's why the four of us come on Tuesdays and Thursdays. We interact with the children, teach them the alphabet, to form words. Sometimes we talk with preadolescents about prevention and about some wrong behavior we see here, behavior that young women need to be careful about. We help in anything. At first, in the kitchen. Then, assembling kits of clothing and hygiene material in the storage room of the Green House, the missionaries lodging. The missionary women teach us to identify the newly-arrived, to welcome them and give them the kits, since we have never had any formal training for voluntary

service or for interpersonal relationships. We learn how to look in the eyes of the sheltered and tell them that we are here to give them support, you see?

About how they got to the Shelter:
We were talking with friends at the Catholic Church and realized how much needed to be done to ease the humanitarian crisis. Some friars had told us about the shelter, and we decided to make a bazaar. We spread the news on the social media channels, collected clothes donated by the community, sorted them out, washed them. We thought we wouldn't sell anything, and everything was sold out in fifteen days! With the profit, we bought personal hygiene materials for the refugees that came to visit the place. We didn't know that Fraternidade looked after them and we decided to assist them. We were shocked to find out that we wouldn't be able to change the indigenous situation, we couldn't take them home, find them a job, send their children to a school. At first it was scary and we even felt some bad energy, but as we started being around the Venezuelans, this changed. The children came to hug us in such joy! Parents talk with us. Now it is very good.

On putting yourself in someone else's shoes:
Everything we don't want for ourselves, we do not want for our fellow being. We place ourselves in the refugees' shoes. We get upset and defend them if someone shows prejudice when talking about them. The work we used to do in the church was distributing monthly food kits and helping the needy. Feeling the other person's pain is difficult, it's difficult to figure out the feelings of someone who flees their own country where they once had a home, food, a job. They are sometimes alone, without the family. To be sheltered in a place like this, is a physical and psychological shock. We have to keep encouraging their hope, tell them it's going to be all right! If someone is going through a difficult situation, it doesn't mean they should be sad. They have to cheer up, and create solutions to be able to improve.

On the joy of doing good:
Being here makes us happy! People are so lively. At home there's always so much to do. Here we forget about everything. Being a volunteer here ennobles our souls. This week I've helped a child to write her own name. How rewarding! Some ask me, "What am I going to do here? I'm lost!" Those in the shelter want to learn and are open to change, especially because they need to discover something new.

On a voluntary heart:
It's the one that doesn't want anything in return, no recognition. If the Venezuelans trust us when we offer them help, that's enough. A smile and a tender look are enough. They have wonderful, shining eyes. We have never seen them with lifeless eyes.

On music:
Songs energize and have an important role here. I find it so beautiful when nuns sing along with children! The kids cheer up, sometimes shout, jump, and the adults accompany them. They've taught us some lyrics in Warao, I don't know if I sing them correctly or not, but we communicate with joy. Everyone gets united when there is music, this greater force. It is something beyond matter, you know... We're not here to give them consolation or something like that, but to be near people who trust us.

Adventure attracts young people, who immerse themselves in films and reading books and dream of being inside these stories. They do not like stagnation and feel incomplete in traditional classrooms. Just like the planet rotates, they prefer to rotate around the world. A mission motivates them, they yearn for getting to know the reality of those who suffer from discrimination, and also because this is an adventure for the spirit.

Anxious, the young people ask: *What course am I going to take in college? Where am I going to work?* During a missionary experience, they may see glimpses of hope arising from the depth of their soul. Some of them manage to express what they feel, grateful for being able to know realities of human deprivation. They feel fulfilled when they are not afraid of cooperating and surrendering to voluntary activity. A primary missionary says: *In this group work, no one needs to compete with anyone, but simply be led by the currents of life.*

Exclusive dedication to being a missionary may not be the young people's task. They can join the mission for a couple of months, or for years. The opportunity of giving something of themselves reverberates within their cells and nourishes them.

Charity is a powerful means to influence people's consciousness and lead them to embrace growing faith. By being charitable, young people strengthen their ardor and love more. And look around, hopeful in the glorious future approaching the Earth.

Sunday meetings

Everything has its time,
and there is a set time for
every goal under heaven.
Eclesiastes

September 3, 2017, Sunday, at noon. In Boa Vista, twelve missionaries intone protection mantras while waiting for a Skype call. *Hello! Can you hear me well?* The coordinator of Roraima answers: *Here the Garden of the Green House is in full blossom with servers.*

A surprised laugh joins the laugh which comes from the cell phone placed on the laundry sink, where twelve missionaries sit in orderly rows. Participating in the general meeting that takes place every Sunday, there are four missionaries in the Greek base and ten in the Fraternidade head-quarter. They make up a small army of gardeners that cultivate flowers of the spirit in themselves.

Ricardo gives them the best news: *The general coordinator will indicate new tasks in a week's time. It will be presented to 1,400 participants of the General Meeting of Figueira. Get ready! Our life is going to change. The coordinator of the missionaries guides people's consciousnesses: We have to stay committed, faithful and obedient to everything that is indicated. By doing so, we will always be in the right place.*

Attentive, the team listens to the preliminary communication: *The Fraternidade has changed. Trigueirinho has been preparing it with his instructions in the past forty years. Since 2011, we have been trying to re-spond to each mission proposed. Without talking about religions or ex-pecting anything in return, servers are moved by the heart. We carry out an ecumenical integration with secular and religious entities. Due to the expansion of our fronts of service, as well as the engagement with other in-stitutions, FIHM has reached a maturity that allows it to expand the task.*

So, as Ricardo asks about Boa Vista, Clara sums up the events of the last seven days: *Here we are in the blazing fire of ascension. Everything is dynamic, it's a continuous learning. For each day has it's task. This week, the agreement with the UNHCR was signed. We've made good progress with the terms of cooperation with the Civil Defense and the Federal University. Refugees are greeted every day in the shelter, yesterday there were nine; altogether, they're almost 600. We had a meeting with the mayor of Pacaraima on Friday night. He said non-indigenous Venezuelans will be sent to Boa Vista. For about two hundred Waraos living in the streets, they will open a shelter only for indigenous people. Next, we met a Warao group camping under a marquee: it was a celebration. Boa Vista is completely full with non-indigenous refugees. The situation is tense. That is good, because when the situation gets complicated, we receive help. The Doctors without Borders will send us more donations. Also Venezuelans who have lived for years in Rio de Janeiro will send a lot of things to their fellow citizens on a Brazilian Air Force plane. Today we cleaned the rented house which will become the office for logistics and the financial organization of the Fraternidade. It was a stroke of luck, a perfect place to receive the authorities. Part of the house will be used as a warehouse for storing donations.*

News comes from the Greek base. The everyday routine is running smoothly. About the Carmo da Cachoeira Permanent Mission, Imer, the

A meeting of missionaries via Skype.
Boa Vista, Roraima, Brazil, September 2017

coordinator, explains about the whole involvement of the missionaries with the community. In both missionary houses there is a continuous flow of people: they bring their problems and leave feeling better. Within an hour, he will drive a convoy of vans and cars with pilgrims to pray on the hill of the Marian Center of Figueira.

Who will volunteer for the closing prayer? asks Ricardo. As he himself is appointed to do so, he continues: *United to the missionary works of Greece, Carmo da Cachoeira and Boa Vista, we will say the Prayer of the Sacred Unity three times, to be, in fact, able to live inner and external unity: "Sacred Unity of God, unify our lives, unify our Being, unify us in profound fraternity. Amen." As a conclusion, the Missionary's Prayer: "In God we all are, to God we all respond, in the Hands of the Most High we rest, in the Heart of Christ we transform ourselves. Under the mantle of the Universal Mother, we are protected, on the Holy Spirit, we are fed for all Eternity. Amen." In a spirit of brotherhood and under the light of the three Sacred Hearts, in the name of the Father, the Son and the Holy Spirit. Amen.*

He concludes: *Let's be connected to the General Meeting news, which will change the direction of our work. Let's welcome everything with our hearts in peace. Well, we are ready for whatever comes our way! Next Sunday we'll have further information and details on how the changes will take place. Have a good, intense week. Be with God!*

In the late afternoon, tropical birds of metallic voices announce another meeting at the back of the yard. Eight missionaries sit in a circle. Immense wings fly over them. Their peaceful faces reflect the hot colors of the tropical dusk tinted with solar tones.

As a starting point, Clara says: *I'd like to hear a little from each missionary. How do you feel and see the task of the missions?* In a mix of Portuguese and Spanish, a genteel Argentinian smiles and runs his eyes around the circle: *Ladies first. We have to be polite, don't we?*

A lady, also from Argentina, describes the health situation in Pintolândia Shelter during that week: *We completed 207 forms with data from children and adults listed according to their illnesses. They have headache, discouragement, sore throat, diarrhea, skin problems, sight problems, etc. The doctor who will accompany the treatment of five cases of light syphilis has asked us to explain the treatment to those infected.*

Clara says: *Well, the question was about how you are feeling. Since you started talking about practical things, let's go on with this theme. In a few days, the FIHM, as an institution, a UN specialist coming from Geneva will give us a training course based on the reality of Boa Vista. Whatever the UNHCR tells us not to do, we will follow their instructions. They've given us signs that we are going beyond what was previously indicated, taking on issues that are the responsibility of governmental organizations.*

Next, the participants talk about actions to transform unhealthy hygiene habits. With the booming coming of residents in the shelter, two family groups built a kind of slum around the gymnasium. There are cases of illness in one of them. In the permanent heat and dust, they sleep in hammocks under plastic sheeting. The place is cluttered with objects, and needs cleaning. As a preventive action, the missionaries agree: *Let's get together tomorrow and ask for permission from the "aidamos" for our group to help them clean up the trash? If he allows us, this will begin to solve the health problems arising.*

Clara says: *We need deeper healing work in everyone. Mothers take their children to beg in streets, and they are burned by the sun, dehydrated and we don't even know what they eat. Then the mother comes to us, "Sister, they have a fever!" Next, we take them to the hospital, lecturing them for hours, just like yesterday. The fever goes away and, in the following morning, the mothers take their kids again to beg. We have had times when missionaries were at the hospitals daily, from 7 a.m. to 9 or 10 p.m.*

With the signing of the agreement, a team will be formed for outward accompaniments, especially in health cases, which are many. Since service also reaches people's soul, the missionaries feel the time has come to take a more mature step to tackle evils such as HIV and syphilis, which are serious spiritual diseases.

What do these diseases mean for the indigenous people? How to tackle such diseases with them, who have no idea of their significance and continue to contaminate themselves? What health issues are under the responsibility of the municipal or the Roraima authorities?

Someone reported a scene witnessed the day before: *A woman was making a fire to cook fish, another one by her side was pouring water on the flour. Then, a child got burned in the wood fire, and she threw water mixed with flour on the kid's hand.*

An eighteen year old, coming from a recent Missionary Practice, begins to confess about her suffering when she witnesses the indigenous people's condition: *Am I recognizing and feeling grateful for the simple but vital things I have? I used to think that everyone had food to eat, clothes to wear.* With tears in her eyes, she goes on: *One thing is to know that there are human beings who have nothing. Another thing is being with them daily. What can we do to take them away from the situation they are in?*

Clara answers: *In the face of so many negative situations, we must think: "This will change. This is what is going on now, but it will change!" There must be a great transformation in the shelter. It is hard to watch the able bodied men, who are used to working, just doing nothing. Their idleness attracts negative energies to them.*

Another young woman adds: *I believe education is a way out. What they are now is the result of what they didn't get in their education. It's wonderful and magic to see indigenous children expressing themselves in the shelter, having the opportunity to learn. In the classroom we have a deeper contact with them and understand them better.*

To sum up the meeting, Clara thanks everyone for sharing the house work, and in providing services to the Venezuelans. She's thankful for how much they enrich one another when they exchange reflections. They say a prayer and each one stacks up their own chair. Those human beings who plant flowers of light raise their eyes to the stars, exchange a quick thought with their bluish light and resume their domestic chores. The Argentinian sings with ardor, in Spanish: *"Cambia, todo cambia"*— *Changes, all things change.*

Perfecting the way we look at the Waraos

How does love blossom in humanitarian help?
When the hearts of the one who serves and
that of the person being served connect in fraternity.
Testimony of a missionary

The Waraos, that is, the people of the canoes or of the waters, believe that, in their genesis, they came from the Sun, where the great leader of their race possessed a bow and an arrow that opened a doorway wherever it was hurled. Although it was forbidden, he shot it at a sacred bird in flight. As he could never hit him, the arrow hit the Earth. This was his first disobedience. When the archer learned about the place where the portal had been opened, he communed with Nature and the waters, feeling that the people of fire should have an experience here. Therefore, he asked permission from his superior and received it under the condition of never bringing in a pregnant woman. Waraos came and went freely between the two spheres until the doorway was closed when a pregnant woman entered. They got stuck inside here and now wait for this planetary cycle to end to return to their homeland, the Sun.

Spiritual disobedience such as the one of the Warao leader caused historical errors and generated cosmic karma. Much of it is being balanced during the stay of our humanity on the blue planet.

In 2016, a star brought the Warao and the Fraternidade closer so that they could create a new destiny together. They met one another among grains, seeds, flours and tapioca gum of an open market. Families that improvised camping there, along with others who lived around the bus station, in vacant lots or who hang their hammocks in abandoned houses came together in the Pintolândia Shelter. Having come from different Venezuelan communities, some already knew one another, others had met on the way to Brazil or in the shelter. At first, the assisted people were just above a hundred. One and a half years later, there were 750.

Preparing lunch. Pintolândia Shelter, Boa Vista, Roraima, Brazil, February 2019

In a permanent humanitarian mission, such as the one in Roraima, servers and refugees strengthen their bonds while they open their hearts to each other. In the vibrant environment of the shelter, filled with an endless range of events, they mature. Even so, it is challenging to run the routine of the shelter and render service to indigenous people.

Members of Fraternidade seek anthropological knowledge about the Waraos in order to better deal with them. Two missionary monks study their culture, their habits, their history, their *modus vivendi*. Sister Maria Auxiliadora, who has been daily with them since 2017, clarifies: *The Warao people is heterogeneous in their way of being. Despite the differences between their communities, they keep the linguistic unit. They have values and customs that are very diversified from the white people, as they call us. They live in another mental and emotional universe. I have realized that I had to be extremely careful not to make the same historical mistakes, regarding them from my educational background and expecting them to adapt to it. I was extremely restless. We took up the role of maintaining harmony inside the shelter, and we certainly should correct them, give them guidance about hygiene, send away those people who insist on having behaviors that affect the group, yet, we have to know who we are dealing with.*

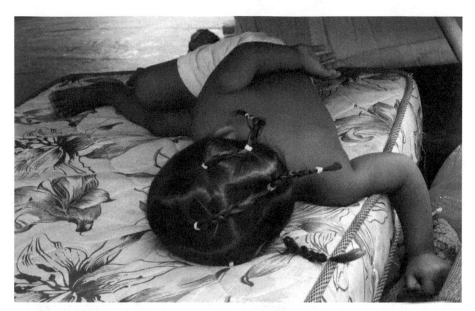

A Warao child in the tent.
Pintolândia Shelter, Boa Vista, Roraima, Brazil, February 2019

Today there are 49,000 Waraos. This is the second largest ethnicity in Venezuela, after the Wayúu, who live in the west of the country. They are deeply connected with the waters, which makes these people friendly and peaceful. Nomads, they navigate up and down the river moving long distances through navigable canals, having formed hundreds of little communities in the Guianas and in three Caribbean states of the delta of the blessed Orinoco River, which opens into the Atlantic Ocean.

For thousands of years, the Waraos have lived on stilt houses. They communed with the exuberant flora and fauna of the *buriti* forests, swamps, mangroves, a prehistoric cave with petroglyphs. Nature offered them fruits, palm heart, honey, crabs, fish, wood for making canoes. In their traditional way of life of hunters-fishermen-gatherers, they occasionally cultivated bananas and roots, such as manioc.

They make the most out of the *buriti* palm tree, known as *moriche*. They accompany the collection of its raw material with ceremonies in gratitude to the sacred tree. They use its leaves to make roofs. The ripe sprout generates the fiber to weave baskets and nets. Out of its trunk they make harpoons for fishing. Out of the cluster of the female plant they harvest over 650 pounds of fruits, which the male tree does not yield.

They obtain flour from within the trunk and out of the *moriche* they make medicine for throat problems, cold, fever and against lice.

A Warao tells a story: *My grandfather, now in another world, told me about the "buriti." Our people were hungry for bread. Men left to hunt at night and came back home empty-handed. The woman cried from hunger. Then the world darkened, the day no longer existed. A shaman intermediated with the great spirit praying, singing, praying, singing, asking for the dawn to come. When light was back again, everything was different. Some thirty Waraos had vanished. One boy went fishing in the river, saw the "buritis" and knew that the men and women who had disappeared had been transformed into palm trees, and they would no longer lack their daily bread. They all celebrated, sang, and laughed.*

Excelling at canoe building, they had sophisticated knowledge about shipping. It is said that Christopher Columbus was amazed at seeing canoes taking up to one hundred people in the delta of the Orinoco River. In 1499, the first European explorer gave the name Venezuela to that extension of green areas and waters, because the indigenous stilt houses on the banks of the river reminded him of the Italian city of Venice.

Due to the natural difficulty of access to the region, these people of the water kept their way of life for centuries after the arrival of the Spanish settlers. This lasted until the wave of monocultures took over its territory between 1920 and 1940, when the *buritis* trees began to be deforested. The government decided to transform the place into an immense farm, where cows and buffaloes were taken. In 1966, it built a water dam, and the new undertaking made the people lose their autonomy, basic for their survival. In the same year, most indigenous people abandoned their homes exchanging them for urban, riverside, coastal and rural places. Later, in the 1990s, companies of the oil sector settled there. Today, few Waraos still live in the area.

Nature has responded to the greed. Ecologically irresponsible actions caused the acidification of the soil and salinity of the river, killing fish. The water level rose. Strange diseases arose. The Waraos have a cosmological explanation to all that, based on the feminine creative power. If a tree is chopped in a wrong way, the Mother of the trees remove its healing properties. If anyone fishes for more than they need, the Mother of waters and of the fish diminishes the number of shoals.

Lady of Warao ethnicity. Pintolândia Shelter, Boa Vista, Roraima, Brazil, September 2017

This ethnic group experienced the pain of contact with the "white man". It was forced to become dependent on a technological society. The nun says: *They settle in the worst places in the cities without being able to be who they are or adapting themselves to what we are. For generations they have mixed and assimilated the worst of our culture.* Similarly to most Venezuelan ethnicities, they survive in poverty, social helplessness, malnutrition, and suffer from diseases that they had never had contact with. Epidemics, such as cholera in the 90s, caused the death of hundreds of them.

Despised and marginalized, since 2014 they have increased entry into Brazil, searching for resources and access to better health. Coming from the Northeast of Venezuela, they move about 600 miles by canoe, bus, hitchhiking or taxi up to Brazil. Always in family groups, they rarely bring their elderly relatives. Many of them cross the border on foot. However, they maintain a strong bond with their homeland, to where they dream of returning, taking money, food and clothes to their relatives.

Led by an *aidamo*, who is responsible for their unity, men and women have specific roles. On the riverside, men are charged with fishing, hunting, and taking raw material out of the *buriti*. The woman collect honey, fruits, produces handicraft work, makes flour, cooks for the family. She

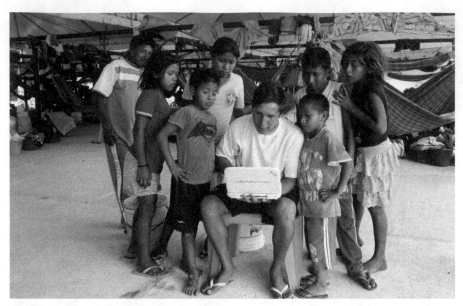

Waraos. Pintolândia Shelter, Boa Vista, Roraima, Brazil, September 2017

is the axis of the social organization. If a father sees a son fighting with someone, he does not interfere. He calls his wife to settle the argument.

Away from natural life, men try to perform small jobs: shining shoes, selling ice cream, working in plantations and cattle farms, working as a housekeeper, jobs that are extremely difficult for them. In the shelters, they work whenever they want, if asked and encouraged.

Trying to leave their prejudices behind, a view that regards older men as lazy people who spend the day lying in hammocks while the woman go to beg for handouts, the missionaries started studying Waraos culture. Grandfather used to tell very ancient stories in family circles at night in order to give instruction, heal and embellish family life. Spiritual practices transmitted to him beliefs, values, and all that shaped his generation.

As for the woman, she changed the activity of harvester of fruits and honey in forests for the collector of handouts in Tucupita, the Venezuelan city with the greatest concentration of Waraos. They do not regard begging as a demeaning activity, but as a solution and a job as any other, which makes them feel valued for being able to provide for the family. They administer what they earn, and the husbands come to them to ask for money. Being aware of these women's attitude regarding begging changed the

A missionary and indigenous people get ready to present a typical Warao dance at the Federal University. Boa Vista, Roraima, Brazil, 2017

missionaries' perspectives. It made them more sensitive when dialogging with these women about the issue.

While in the shelter, they often left to beg for handouts or to sell handicrafts taking their children along, even if they had a fever, diarrhea, skin diseases due to the scorching sun of the streets. Touched by the consequences of begging on the health of the little ones, the servers insisted they change these habits. When it became possible to supply what was necessary for those assisted to live well, the missionaries explained to the parents that Brazilian child protection laws forbids taking children to beg. They gradually abandoned this practice, which was no longer attractive when the population stopped giving them handouts. This happened as they learned about the exclusive shelter for indigenous people, and that the *criollos* were in more serious privation.

The indigenous logic is to live in the here and now: *I need food to eat today. Tomorrow is another day: I will solve it then.* They have another perception of time, act from their heart and do not plan for the future. A woman, after earning 400 Brazilian reais, 100 USD, from selling a *buriti* hammock that took her three months to weave, went back to Venezuela on the following day to take the money to her family members.

After the breastfeeding period, mothers leave their children free, running back and forth. Teachers say that they lack rules, limits, and parental references. The missionary sister does not agree: *I don't know the big picture of the process these people are going through, but they certainly have well defined rules and limits, based, however, on values that are different from ours. There is something important to bear in mind. Children are confined within the chaos of the shelter. Besides, there's their energy, typical of their age and their great suffering for having left their homeland and witnessing the conditions their family is living in. They are very aware. They feel the pain for those who stayed behind, the pain of witnessing the father beating the mother, which is a very common scene in the Pintolândia shelter and is virtually nonexistent in the shelter of Pacaraima. What can we expect from these children? What's more, they are indigenous, and are not used to a traditional classroom. This is a long-term adaptation.*

The nun continues: *Since the children imitate the adults, they might get violent while playing with one another. Whenever I decided to teach them that this is not correct, I used a severe tone. From the moment I changed my strategy and began to speak to them with tenderness, looking within their hearts, they began to obey me, to do what I was asking of them. I learned to love them: I really did.* Speaking in a soft voice and reflexive eyes, Sister Maria Auxiliadora ponders: *We do what we can to give them our best, but I always wonder: "What do they need besides material things?"*

Throughout the year, the kids and the missionaries play, laugh freely, to the surprise of those who observe them from a distance. When some enter the shelter, children run to hug them. Three, four kids surround the person's waist with their little arms. This exchange of love is touching.

The missionaries have shared daily routines since 2016 and always insist for the Waraos to sweep the place, to keep it tidy. Having come from natural areas, they were used to dealing with only biodegradable materials easily recycled without causing pollution. In their language there are no such words as trash or car. They use the Spanish words *bassura, coche*. They keep throwing packages on the floor, plastic, bottles, clothes, and children relieve themselves in front of the tents.

Roraima is a Brazilian state created in 1988. It has 450,000 inhabitants, of whom 56,000 are natives, the greatest indigenous population in the country. Many of them have access to education, they understand their

A notebook with listing of words in Warao.
Pintolândia Shelter, Boa Vista, Roraima, August 2017

own process within society, they know how to dialogue and to represent themselves. The leaders come together through the Roraima Indigenous Council. They have formalized entities such as the Roraima Indigenous Women Organization—OMIR, whose struggle is for rights to be recognized by society and also for issues to be transformed within their own cultures, such as taking actions against alcoholism in the villages, women's health, domestic violence, indigenous education, land demarcation.

The Waraos are deprived of education and the ability to establish a dialogue. They may improve their self-esteem if they accept interacting with Roraima's indigenous people. There are appropriate places to do so, such as the Insikiran Institute of Indigenous Higher Instruction of the Federal University, in Boa Vista, which is the first in a Brazilian university to offer courses of professional training oriented to the indigenous reality.

In 2018, in partnership with the Fraternidade, the Institute organized the 1st International Fair of Culture, a meeting of the native people of Roraima with the Venezuelan Waraos and the Eñepás. They danced and exhibited crafts. Each one of them was able to tell a little of their history and share their knowledge. Missionaries accompanied and helped them get along with Brazilian indigenous people. In addition, a closer relationship with the National Foundation of the Indigenous People, FUNAI, was initiated, which has allowed them to collect the raw *buriti* leaves in the Ianomami territory. Doors started being opened.

I made an informal appointment to talk with the *aidamo* Ramon. The sun was growing dim as I bent over to get inside a long blue canvas tent leaning on the wall of the Pintolândia gymnasium, where he lived with relatives. He showed me a hammock. I sat down in it, he, on a chair. By our side, an aunt on a mattress over plastic seemed oblivious to my presence. Further away, an adolescent cousin swung on a hammock among piles of bags.

I gave him the recorder. He spoke freely in Portuguese including a few Spanish words, pronouncing each sentence clearly and calmly, taking time to think of the words he needed, giving emphasis to some, repeating others with effort.

Good morning. My name is Ramon Gomes. I am an indigenous Warao from Venezuela. I am thirty-two and have two daughters. I arrived in Brazil on December 14, 2016, and I live with the Fraternidade.

The Warao people used to live in the "morichales", the "buriti" forests, which is our source of life. Out of the "buriti" we get food and various types of crafts. Our travel was done by the rivers. We are fishermen and artisans. It was like that until the Warao had contact with the white people, who changed us little by little, and finally changed our way of living.

In the sixties, politicians contacted us, and the people began to be more aware about politics, but our consciousness was gradually dominated by money, by salaries, by alcohol. Unfortunately, Waraos don't think as they used to. Now they think in an individual, selfish way. They originally were united and communitarian, they left together to fish. This has been interrupted by the white people. Now, the Waraos live in the city and try to survive.

I also want to talk about what made Venezuela sink. In order to follow the model of the party, politicians had to close private organizations. As indigenous people, we didn't readily notice that since the year 2000 our food, health, education, and work had been getting worse and worse. And the price of food was rising. I work with teaching and education, and my salary was not enough to sustain my family anymore. Now, indigenous people are faced with political partisan threats. The police also threaten us. We used to bring money and food from Brazil to our families, but now they take everything from us and point weapons at us to kill us. And they do kill. They are very violent nowadays.

Waraos have always traveled to sell handicraft articles and honey in the countryside, but they earned little. Then we started coming to Brazil taking our family along. Speaking and understanding Portuguese is difficult, the currency is different, but we feel better here, it's easier to get food. Here is a new, very different world. At first, we lived at the Passarão Fair: it was dangerous, and I worried about how to protect my family. We've continued the struggle, and arrived at the shelter. Now we are learning from this experience, which makes us stronger.

I thank from all my heart for having found the Fraternidade. The missionaries gave great support to the creation of this shelter, with transportation, with food, with medical treatments. They say we are all the same like a family, as brothers and sisters.

I've found that Brazilians are very affectionate, they like to share and work as volunteers. They bring us games and songs, and new orientations. I like to work as a voluntary immigrant of Fraternidade in the education of the shelter school, to strengthen the children. I expand on what I know by giving to them and to their future. I teach Warao as a mother tongue, Spanish and Portuguese, three languages for them to have a new experience. I am preparing a dictionary of the Warao language. It's important not to let the mother tongue die but also to speak the second language, Spanish, to communicate with the white man. And Portuguese as well, to express what we are. To God we are all alike, but here in the shelter it's interesting to have exchanges in these languages. Thank you.

Ramon himself suddenly stopped the talk.

The Waraos are fragile and susceptible to influence. On the other hand, their strength cries out to find lost roots and, by doing so, value their own history, their knowledge, what they are and believe. May they regain their knowledge and transmit it from generation to generation. Above all, let them lift up the offended soul and unite with the latent essence within them, remain in fraternity with family, with their own ethnicity, with other ethnic groups and all living creatures.

The respectful bond between the Fraternidade and the indigenous people contributes to paying off the immense debt that the "white man" has with the indigenous people. From the contact between both groups echoes a mystery, whose secret meaning will be unveiled someday.

Be in chaos without being a part of it

The fetters break not by force,
but by surrender to the Supreme.
Trigueirinho

Sometimes missionaries are in the middle of cross fire and may have the impression that they will not survive from the inner or external pains. After an intense effort to expel tiredness and discouragement, they re-kindle the service impulse.

They may wake up in a bad way, feeling consumed by inertia, by a physical ailment or by thoughts of complaint brought from battles fought during sleep. The physical body tries to become a hindrance. A negative wave of feelings throws up from the subconscious trying to subjugate them to the chaos that is afflicting the world.

Missionaries have bodies that have been stripped of their skin, they say. To be protected, they put into practice the instruction: *Be in chaos without becoming part of it.* They do not try to run away from pain but, giving priority to the sacred duty, they get stronger after each inner crisis is reversed.

Servers on the way to a shelter witness a valuable primary missionary's fight against her own lethargy. Holding the steering wheel of the van with firmness, in the first curve Clara gave herself a brave command: *Go away, laziness, go away apathy that leaned on me today! What is that, no way! I am here to serve God! I can't indulge in being tired. You have to give everything, and after giving everything, discover that you gave nothing!*

She gives herself this command and appeals to the vigor of a song to expel her weaknesses. And she mobilized the rest of the group to turn their voice loose and to decree with a powerful impetus: *Holy Fire, come and blaze. From my clay make a new creation.* She starts the next song:

Sacred Mother, establish Your door of Peace in Roraima. From song to song, people's voices cheer up: *Now let us ask Saint Joseph to bring peace to this planet. "With Your power, awaken the missionaries of love. Peace for this Planet, peace. Peace for Roraima, Peace."* Come on, folks! Now let us sing to the King of the Universe: "Sacred and glorified Heart of Jesus, have mercy, mercy for the children, for the sick, mercy!" Now let us sing in honor to the Indigenous Consciousness. "Sacred Sun, Sacred Moon, Sacred Unity, be present in our bodies and dissolve forever the illusion that in them dwells."*

Her extraordinary enthusiasm grows, the van vibrates. Suddenly, the dark barrier of prostration is overcome. Her story changes completely. Once the doldrums are overcome, the disturbed soul is realigned.

The splendorous and painful life jumps when, at a traffic light, she sees a dog crossing in front of the vehicles: *What a skinny dog! Look at his ribs, the poor thing. Many of them have been abandoned.* She no longer looks at herself, she does not struggle anymore. She gets appeased when her eyes turn from herself to the other. In mutual cooperation, the group helped her win the battle.

My eyes have become older

You talk about service. But you
will only be able to serve God
after you stop serving the ego.
Paul Brunton

Clara had been called for a meeting.

While I drove her on a dirt road among alleys and portals of trees with intertwined treetops, I heard her courageous testimony. I was being transported by her sincere voice to inner landscapes that yearn to be transformed. She revealed to me the beginning of her awakening in Africa. She brought back to her homeland an urgent wish to overcome herself in order to light the way for those she meets.

After parking the car, I watched her attentively. Talking about her struggle to rebuild her own being, love and faith overflowed from each sentence. Sparks of her missionary vigor shone vividly and tenderly in each pore and in each word:

I understood better what it is to be a missionary when I plunged into Africa. There, I learned to give my life. I was so sure that I would die there... I even left a letter to my children telling them not to be sad because I had died doing what I liked best. As I returned to Brazil, I had to tear it up and throw it away.

I know a minimal part of the pain of the world. But I keep imagining the Divine Beings observing the Calvary through which the planet goes. So, I do my best to eliminate a little of Their hearts suffering. I think this is the mission of my life, to be a pencil to write something different on the track of the needy. It's not easy.

I know it's not I who loves, it's something much bigger who loves in me. Sometimes I catch myself reflecting about the Biblical passage in which the prophet Simeon foresees a sword of pain piercing the heart of the Mother of the Child Jesus. I love my children so deeply and, although I know that part of the learning of life involves letting them go through difficult moments, I would be unhappy if I knew in advance about future evils waiting for them. But She, a Divine Being, knew everything Her son would go through and, still, let Jesus express himself as a child, with joy. I ask for this wisdom when I am faced with the human anguish of one of Her children. During the missions, this is crucial for me.

Why does life want me to see so much evil? All I see is pain. I have been on many missions. I have watched so much agony that my eyes have become older. For sure, this is for my maturity, because I now realize the meaning of compassion more clearly. Of course, I feel one thousandth of the compassion taught by the Buddha. For example, I am in Roraima trying to understand the refugees more and more to help them with love and wisdom. I try to do the best I can for them, but without getting involved with the situations. This is part of my lesson.

Rwanda was a turning point. Symbolically, I died there. I surrendered my life. Not even the missionary group was able to understand my physical and inner problems. I got too sick, and a sick missionary disturbs the mission. I disturbed it in several moments, I had nausea, high blood pressure, etc.

I was thrown to the floor when I heard stories of the massacre in Rwanda. There, the most wonderful thing was to go to Kibeho, in the heart of Africa. A gift for this existence. I returned to Brazil as if I had been drained, as if nothing were left of me. I needed to slowly re-emerge as a new being.

There I discovered many of my subtle shortcomings and I have slowly been healing them. Because they return. For example, when I judge people in my thoughts. Then I say to myself: "I will improve, be patient."

We live in a constant giving, and when someone that came to serve became sick, my mind would judge. Not with words, but with thoughts. This shortcoming needed to be released within me, or put in a coma, or at least begin its death process. As planetary beings, I think we will never completely liberate ourselves from judging others. We always judge, either positively or negatively, but we judge them. Besides judging, I saw in myself the shortcoming of being imposing. I impose myself, or rather, I used to be imposing. I thought: "The task has to be done my way, and that's it!" Then So and So came and wanted to do it another way, better than what I'd thought. This was a great setback for group life, we are here to express unity.

I was unconscious, I found excuses, kept falling into mental traps. I be-gan to work on this from my experience in Africa. When I began to see my shortcomings, it was a great stage! Wow! I would do something and keep looking at myself as an observer: "You did something horrible." But I couldn't fall into the bottom of the pit. Life was giving me a great opportu-nity to change.

The word Fraternity is written on my shirt, on my coat, on my trousers. Being fraternal means what? I started looking at the printed cross on these clothes, to analyze its meaning. I have this word close to my body and am not fraternal?

First of all, a missionary assumes a mission as a truth, and goes into the world to express this truth. I have to embody in myself the best I receive and learn. I have to live the teaching sincerely.

We, as first missionaries, have created a kind of twisted idea about the task believing we have to be a mix of Superman with Wonder Woman. This also penetrated the group consciousness, to be a jack-of-all-trades who eats little, sleeps little. This is not real. We are humans, we get hun-gry, feel cold, get sick.

We have to be deeply sincere, true. What can I say to a woman whose child is hungry? I know her child will starve. Then, I cannot say something just for the sake of saying it.

What can I say to someone in front of me, who I know I will only be able to help him for 10 or 15 days? And when I leave? It's pointless to find excuses for that. I have to live this crude truth. I don't say a word. I talk with that mother only through my eyes. People's eyes are strong. I have had deep gaze exchanges. I have never looked at people as deeply as I did in Africa.

PART VIII
Pulsing chronicles

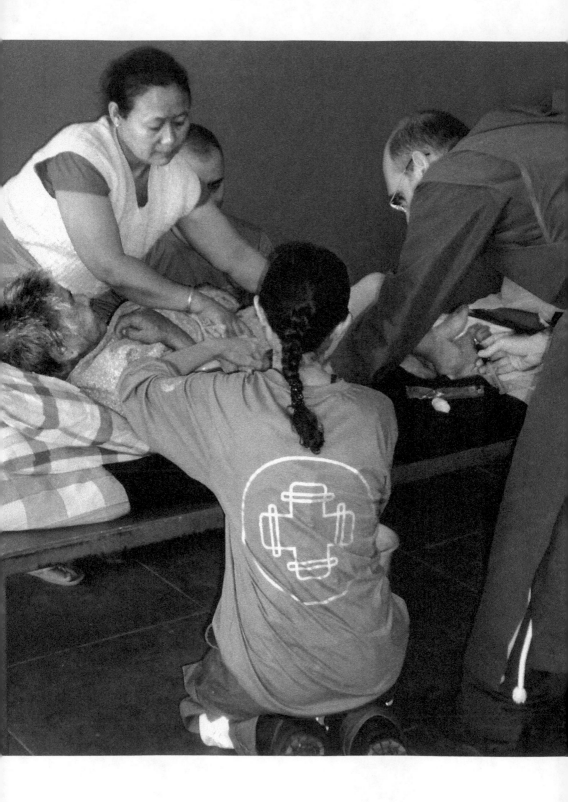

The therapist and the monk

The hand that gives will never be empty.
Helena Roerich

A therapist and a monk were about to witness the recovery, which was abnormal, to say the least, of a great wound. They already knew that the healing work is not limited to the physical restoration of the sufferers, but they were perplexed on testifying to the action of Divine Providence.

In Kathmandu, in Nepal, the Missionaries of Charity asked them to evaluate internees of the Home for the Elderly, which triggered a process of alternative therapies in dozens of elders. Among the cases, there was a lady with a putrefying lesion on her leg. It was wide and deep, the inner muscle was visible.

The therapist and the monk began treatments. Day after day they washed the wound with serum and spread a propolis ointment. During nine sessions they gave the patient chromotherapy treatments, a practice that acts from the physical to the most subtle levels. In the first sessions, they projected green light, then, the mysterious violet light. In the tenth, last session, on the eve of their departure, the pus and the bad odor had disappeared from the woman's wound, and half of the lesion had scarred.

They gently placed the Nepali woman on the stretcher, and exchanged looks and smiles with her. They decided to bathe her with violet light, which, as it hits the crown of the head, eases universal energy connections. The therapist on one side, the monk on the other side of her, whispered a prayer in deep reverence. They all closed their eyes.

At a given moment, the therapist looked at the wound. *This is an illusion, it can't be true!* he thought, quickly closing his eyes to recover from the shock. He opened them, slowly. The great lesion was scarring visibly.

He and the monk looked at each other, and with renewed vigor, repeated the prayer calling out to the Source.

A process that would take days was happening in twenty minutes. As if they were watching a slow-motion movie, the therapist and the monk saw the flesh regaining life, the skin healing. They were witnessing a miracle!

The limitations of matter were transcended because they serve the other without any personal interest. This was added to the unconditional surrender of the lady of pure mind and heart. And the miracle of healing reflected in the consciousness of the country, it helped to heal an ancestral wound that the people carry in themselves.

The therapist and the monk understood the meaning of true service. By means of the channel of compassion formed between both, the high voltage of the impressive manna of spiritual healing was flowing, more powerfully than any technique created by scientific minds. Having witnessed something inexplicable, the healers entered quietude and silence. Life taught them the lesson of Grace, ready to manifest itself whenever love overcomes darkness.

Helping the hungry, the great challenge

For I was hungry and you gave me food,
I was thirsty and you gave me drink,
I was a stranger and you welcomed me,
I was naked and you clothed me,
I was sick and you visited me,
I was in prison and you came to me.
Truly, I say to you, as you did it to one of the least
of these my brothers and sisters, you did it to Me.
Holy Bible, Mathew, 25:35-40

It happened in the Congo. One of the millions of forgotten people suffering around the world knocked on the door after closing time. All the food for that day had already been distributed to the patients and visitors. There was nothing to give. The man walked with a crutch and his swollen legs had open wounds, elephantiasis. He came as other beggars do, knocking daily on the Missionaries of Charity door.

Two Fraternidade missionaries looked at each other. One asked: *If Mother Teresa were here, what would she do?* The other replied: *She would answer the door.* So, they went to him: *He was very, very needy. I asked him how he'd gotten there, what had happened... He spoke English, and said he had walked three days looking for food, without eating. Mercy! That hurt my heart. There was nothing left in the kitchen...*

A bond of love formed immediately between the two women and the son of God before them: *And now what?*

In their backpack, they carry a survival kit, which included *tsampa*, an Eastern super-nutritional dumpling used by nomads and other travelers. It is made by the Light-Network of Brasilia with substantial ingredients such as dried leaves and fruits, roots, chickpea, peanuts and other seeds. One little ball nourishes a person's body for one whole day. Used as a nutritional supplement, it is, in general, consumed in bits with a sip of tea or of water.

Both took the little they had and made the man a package, and the Missionaries of Charity joined them seeking medicine for the man's legs infected by a tropical disease.

The man, leaning on the crutch, took off his hat, placed his hand like someone who is going to receive a Eucharist host, a consecrated food. He closed his eyes. He bowed receiving the food in his little hands, made the sign of the Cross, put the package in his pocket.

She insisted: *Eat it.* He said no, he would take it to his six children left at home. *That broke the rest of the heart I had. He thanked us, turned his back and left slowly back home taking raisins, "tsampa," dried banana and individual packages of snacks given in airplanes. He was taking so little, but expressed such a heartfelt thanks.*

The man was bathed by the balm of love without borders. However, even knowing that all beings are united in essence, the two felt deeply insufficient in face of the drama of hunger. They remained silent.

Months later, one of them whispered to me: *In the missions, the lack of resources to better help a fellow being inflicts a profound pain on us. Extreme helplessness is our greatest challenge.*

The universal sign language

The deeper the person has gone within,
the more authentic is their communion with others.
White Eagle

Spiritual instructions teach that fear is an enemy of love. *Will you take on the risks? You may not return, you may die.* The missionary group said: *Yes, we take it on.* And left for Ethiopia.

An immense number of very thin people survive in the streets of the capital Addis Ababa. On each corner, they sleep on sidewalks covered with plastic bags. Life expectancy in Ethiopia is thirty-five years, however, people appeared to be fifty when they are only twenty.

Lying on sixty beds beside each other, men wait in a dormitory of the Missionaries of Charity. Brought to die, a young one was sitting in bed trying to breathe. A terminal patient of tuberculosis he had a high temperature, and could not lie down.

The first time Clara met him, she offered to trim his fingernails—she always has a nail-trimmer in her backpack—and gently did it: *I asked him if I could do a massage on his feet. He said "yes". I took his socks off and noticed his nails were very long, I pointed to the trimmer, and he accepted it. We talked through sign language since he spoke his tribal language. I trimmed his nails and did a massage. Finally, I left the room and returned the next day. He was still there, and a Sister informed me he was at the end.*

The young man waved for her, and Clara came very close to him. He made signs, and a nurse, who spoke English, translated them. First, he snapped his fingers, and the nurse said he had known her for a long time. Then he pointed to his own heart, to hers, and to the sky. The nurse explained both would meet in the sky. Hours later, he passed away.

In the lodging area that night, when Clara retired, the young man came back intensely in her mind: *I had to cross the ocean, step on the African continent to meet that consciousness. Without being able to speak, almost with no breathing, with a few gestures, he said enough for a whole lifetime.*

In that country a leper-like disease is common: the skin peels, open wounds all over the body and head that reach deep tissues, and do not scar. Besides this illness, another man had mental problems, which made it difficult for the Sisters to deal with. His wounds had bandages, but they and the man emanated a bad odor as he refused to take a bath, becoming rebellious when the Sisters tried to carry him. So, their coordinator asked Imer to help, and stood by his side, watching.

At first, Imer made the invitation and tried to convince the patient. In vain. He insisted, tried to lift him, but he became angry. Imer is tall, strong. Suddenly, he lifted the man in a single impulse, as you do with a child. After the shock, the small thin man weighing approximately 90 pounds embraced him strongly. And gently let himself be carried.

The unexpected became evident. The Sister, who was also short, followed the two fixing her eyes on the expression of the face lying on Imer's shoulder: *He likes it, he's smiling!* Wounds discharging puss touched the missionary's face and neck. Feeling the secretion on his ear, Imer gave himself a daring command against his own disgust: *Come on, come on!* The three passed the corridor towards the bathroom.

The man was placed on a chair and smilingly looked at Imer, his gaze half lost by the mental blockage. Through the universal language of gestures, Imer said: *Stay here, I will give you a bath.* The man was peaceful. Imer lathered him, threw water on his body, dried him well and took him in his arms back to the newly made bed. The man was happy; the Sister and Imer were smiling.

Anastasia

In truth, for the one who is well-intentioned and
always understands from a spiritual point of view,
all sufferings and occurrences turn into blessings.
Meister Eckhart

A positive wave expands through the Earth. From East to West, from North to South, talisman-beings work for peace. Even in dark periods of grave conflicts, they develop qualities and become even more lucid. In Greece, the missionaries joined forces and energies to those of a lady, Anastasia, who almost forty years ago set up and still coordinates a voluntary group. She tells her family story: *With my grandparents and parents, I learned to love, respect, create. Nothing works without love. My family was and remains generous in offering love.*

Descendant of refugees, Anastasia grew up hearing reports about the pains and hardship faced by her maternal grandparents coming from Russia to Athens in 1922, to escape their homeland Civil War. As for her paternal grandparents, in the thirties they had escaped Turkey, which was undergoing violent changes, and moved to Greek territory. Both family branches were Orthodox Christians who suffered and worked a lot until they managed to settle in Greece.

During the forties, horror and drought devastated the country, spread by those taken by hatred, fanaticism and greed. First, it was occupied by the Nazis and, right after the end of World War II, it was devastated by a civil war.

A grandmother of Anastasia was a Red Cross nurse, and the other, a volunteer at a church. They say the family members were saved thanks to the help they offered and the help they received, as well as the respect that they always had for the workers. Given the goodness that they exchanged with the fellow citizens, they remained alive. Food was scarce in the cities and burnt or stolen in the fields. So, Anastasia's father, aged 8 at that time, walked for hours to Athens to get a meal served to children by Red Cross volunteers, by churches or by the North-American help. The boy took what he could to his parents and, thanks to the volunteers, the family survived. With tenacity and the consciousness expanded by the positive experiences lived during the wars, he was able to serve Greece as a consul inspired by a greater purpose, that of helping the other, an attribute he always taught his daughter.

Anastasia Ioannidis sent a letter to two missionaries: *I could write a book about how the cruelty of wars and of human ego destroy existence, but this is not the way I see life. I'd rather talk about the good things that make me what I am and make me do what I do.*

Educational consultant and coordinator of the Young Volunteers in Action, which operates in the town of Saronikos, explains: *The group is relatively small, but dynamic and is in an ongoing process of adaptation to the changes in the surrounding world. It acts in various fronts: distribution of clothes and food, registration of food donors, protection of dolphins and corals with divers, firefighting, cultural rescue of an old port city.*

Likewise, it supports social causes, such as the refugees, and provides psychological service. It offers practical classes on cleaning up the sea, the beaches, the hills. It also offers seminars and recitals, theaters, musical and dance presentations, video shows. It sets up painting and graffiti exhibits, and bazaars. It inspires teachers and librarians with story-telling and book-binding. It offers varied workshops and courses on how to make portfolios, and teaches elders to deal with technology as well as those of cooking, sewing, decoration, chess, gardening, first aid and how to protect oneself and others.

Having lived in several countries in Europe, North Africa, North America and Japan, Anastasia, who is a teacher, learned to appreciate the beauty of each one and it's people. She says: *While I was helping adult and children refugees, in and outside fields, with the Red Cross, with the International Schools, the UN, the International Social Service and many other organizations, I learned about the importance of goodness, feeding, security and education. These are rights that each human being deserves.*

Both her husband and her son, now a young leader of the group, believe and work for that. *The beauty of life is hidden in great and small things.*

Anastasia and her father.
Sofia, Bulgaria, 1938

Everything interconnects and is important for harmony in family, among citizens, with the environment and animals. This is what I try to teach those who join the activities of the group. We learn, act, teach and, by doing so, we improve.

Invited by this lady, Fraternidade took charge of tidying up a warehouse packed with clothes weekly. After sorting them out by type and gender, they assembled kits and distributed them at hospitals, homes for the elderly and wherever there was a need.

One day, three missionaries were called by Anastasia for a beneficent opera recital in homage to a famous Greek singer. The revenue would help her projects. As they rarely go to social events, which are not in tune with the missionary discipline, they hesitated. Determined to take them, she contacted the general coordinator, who was in Brazil, and he sent the three a message: *You do have to go to the opera!* A friend of Anastasia picked them up at home. On the way to and back from the theater, they philosophized about living.

Similar beings are attracted by inner magnetism. Like magnets, those who understand the world by means of the sacred fire of the heart have mutual attraction. As the missionaries serve others, they are impelled by an expression used by Anastasia at the end of her letter to the missionaries: *Let us do our best.*

We are all family

Ephemeral! What are we?
What are we not? Man is
The dream of a shadow.
But when the gods cast
Their light on him,
A bright splendor surrounds him
And then life is sweet.
Pindaro

Who is my family? Those with whom I am at the moment.

The mission and the practice of treating all as equal is challenging. The training to develop community occurs when a member of humanity no longer manages to distinguish what they feel for blood relatives—their own mother, son, brother—from what they feel for those with whom they come to intersperse with throughout life.

How can we attain the consciousness of fraternity? How can we regard everyone as brothers and sisters? As we share joy and difficulties during close and intense co-existence with each person we meet, those who arrive, those who stay around, those who go away.

European, African or Eastern women refugees either with children or alone, street-dwellers in a tough situation, are all invited to live in one of the houses of the Missionaries of Charity in Athens until they are transferred. A missionary of the Fraternidade served there, helping them in maintenance work. He was the only adult man and he felt like a brother to all the women and children.

At that moment, they were his family and fraternal love was his happiness. He remembers: *All the boys wanted to handle the screw-driver, the hammer, the drill. It was difficult to work with them running after me. For them, I was something different. We didn't know each other's languages, but we understood one another when doing things or exchanging a few English words.*

He shared the pain of a mother whose baby was hospitalized with pneumonia developed when they crossed the Aegean Sea by boat, and who

Imer feeds Abdul and Fatima. Athens, Greece, 2017

later died. He also established bonds with Abdul, 5, and his eighteen-month-old sister Fatima. They were with their grand-mother, who had a sad expression because of her daughter's addiction to heavy drugs. The mother of the children had chosen to live as an addict in a large park where consumption is permitted by the government. Sometimes she came to take a shower and change clothes in a little bathroom in the entrance hall.

One day, the young girl showed up, her body in declining health, without some of her front teeth. The missionary went to talk with her. Abdul and Fatima wanted to stay on his lap looking at her, just looking at their mother while she cried a lot, saying she couldn't get a job.

In the afternoon, Abdul asked if the missionary was his dad: *I didn't know what to answer. At first, I didn't reply. Then I said "no". He wanted to know: "Brother?"* Their mother spoke English, and Abdul, a little. Their father was an Algerian immigrant who had lived with their mother in the street using drugs. They had the children and never saw each other again.

Since his arrival, the missionary had adopted Fatima, who at first cried incessantly, but gradually improved. She climbed the stairs crawling after him. The love bond strengthened the little siblings, and the Mother Superior also gave them full attention. The task was shared between the feminine and masculine energy: *None of them would accept breakfast if they were not with me. I taught them English and pointed "fagithó", food in Greek. I asked Fatima to be quiet and when she cried because I was going away, I told her I would come back. I spoke no Greek, and she couldn't speak either, because she was only eighteen months old, but we understood each other.*

The three-month stay of the missionaries in Greece was coming to an end when he went to say good-bye finding Abdul and Fatima in a baby buggy walking with the grandmother. Imer says: *It was a very cheerful meeting, but my heart was broken when I returned home. The dependent mother, the depressed grandmother, the rebellious children... I went to the prayer room of the missionary base to talk with the Divine Mother and plunged into a state I had never known before. I made Her a passionate request and felt something inexplicable.*

The missionary returned to Brazil, but soon learned that the mother was arrested and sent to prison. They would deport her with the family back to Serbia, her homeland, from where she had escaped with her own mother during the Bosnia war. The grandmother was thrilled, and was sure the daughter would get rid of the drugs there. In a week's time, the four of them departed.

The missionary clearly feels that his prayer and request activated this movement, the best that could happen. He lost contact with the family, but keeps a strong bond of compassion for Abdul and Fatima, two little members of a great family called humanity.

An unexpected visit

Acts of love are acts of peace.
Mother Teresa of Calcutta

Originating in South America, the Missionaries of Fraternity have been working together with the Sisters of the Order of the Missionaries of Charity, the congregation founded by Mother Teresa of Calcutta since 2011. They have worked in Nepal, Nicaragua, Ethiopia, Rwanda, Uganda, the Democratic Republic of the Congo and, in 2018, Egypt.

During the Greece Mission, their work lasted for months in a row. Bonds of respect and increasingly deep mutual trust were gradually created throughout the period they worked together pouring charity over Athens.

One day, the Sisters said they wanted to visit them. What a nice surprise! At last they announced the day, on the anniversary of the congregation, a date in which they do a special trip.

Their dogmatic rigor is positive because it makes them firm in their discipline and, as a result, transmits immense power to those who approach them. The Sisters know that the missionaries are ecumenical. Something surely happened within them, as they rarely visit non-Catholic residences, making them realize that the service relation of both groups went beyond religious rules.

Months before they had been shocked to find out that the Fraternidade members are vegetarian, since one of the rules to be consecrated in their Order was to eat meat. India, where the congregation was born, is, by far, the country with the greatest number of vegetarians in the world. Since many Sisters are Indian, the founder determined they would have to eat meat because of the challenges they would have to face in the streets.

In the morning of the visit, everyone felt overjoyed. The sisters climbed the stairs looking up to the great sunny house. As they came into the kitchen, they celebrated: *Watermelon!* Besides Brazilian coffee, they tasted fresh fruit juice and bread donated by a bakery.

Around the table, the servers of Good celebrated the richness of their altruistic service union. Both groups surrendered to humanitarian assistance with the aim of softening and elevating the life of the unfinished human nature.

Soon after breakfast, they watched a screening of photos of missions of Fraternidade, where they were seen working with other Missionaries of Charity around the world. Sheer joy! At the end, the Sisters stayed quiet, as if they wanted more.

Seating in front of the banners of Christ Jesus, of the Mother of the Divine Conception of the Trinity and of Saint Joseph. The Missionaries of Fraternidade with the Missionaries of Charity—dressed in white saris with a blue edge of the same color of the rugs of the room—prayed the Rosary contemplating the Glorious Mysteries. They made the angelic salutation in English, *Hail Mary, full of grace*. Together, those hearts of pure diamond attracted a better future for Greece. And they sang, with their souls merged in the virtue of love.

In the splendorous morning, the warriors of Light reposed and were mutually strengthened during the hours of serene interactions. Reinvigorated, they would continue to assist the neighbor of the same nationality, the foreigner, the detainee, the street-dweller.

The world goes around

*Rich are those who know how
to live without possessions.*
Trigueirinho

Three homeless men met in curious circumstances. They had walked around streets and roads, went through cities and abysses until they met again years later in the House of Welcome, in Carmo da Cachoeira.

Determined to start walking on his spiritual path, one of the three arrived in the Toca de Assis, in São Paulo to help street-dwellers in the Catholic fraternity whose members follow the example of primitive Franciscan radical poverty. He dressed in mundane clothes, colorful tennis shoes. One of the homeless people was wearing ear plates, had tattoos on his hands, arms and neck. He got closer: *Listen, from now on you will be wearing flip-flops. You don't need this pair of tennis shoes anymore. Why don't you give them to me?* He agreed: *Ok.* The homeless man went on: *You can't wear the watch either. Can you give it to me?* That is how they met for the first time.

Years went by when the third man, Peterson, met the spiritual seeker in the house for homeless people in Campo Belo, in Minas Gerais, Brazil. The seeker was coordinating it. He was not a rigorous person, and accepted even those who did not have the documents demanded by social assistance, that is, most of them. But Peterson, the newly-arrived, presented to him all the documents in order.

After three days, feeling well-treated, Peterson told him: *That story that I had argued with my parents is not true. I coordinate the drug trafficking in the capital, have been sentenced to forty years. I'm here because we are having a fight between criminal gangs.* The coordinator put his hand on the head: *But you putting us amidst such confusion is a tragic comedy!*

Peterson said his real name. His documents and name were fake. A week later, he left.

The world goes around, and the spiritual seeker has become a missionary. He was coordinating the House of Welcome in Carmo da Cachoeira, when he traveled for a week with the primary group for a Course of Rescuing in Remote Areas. When he came back, he met the residents of the shelter sitting around the dinner table. He was surprised: *You are Peterson!* And he was corrected: *No, I'm not, that was my fake name! My name is Camilo.*

Human beings have multiple facets. Camilo had learned in a video how to create bamboo objects, such as lamps, chandeliers, and began to decorate the house until the missionary made a comment: *You are always confined within the workshop, shall we build something outside?*

So, in the yard, the project of the Prayer Room in bamboo began, next to a flower garden and green beds of the vegetables. For six months, all the people of the shelter, including the tattooed man with ear plates, who had come to live in the house some time before, helped to build it. The altar of the temple was set up by the three men, who met the coordinator again years later.

Each person leaves his contribution. On the floor at the center of the room, a six-pointed star was carved, a symbol of cosmic worlds that act according to the Plan of God. Camilo did not see the star when the carving was over. He could not tolerate the discipline of the house any longer. He was last seen selling pens in a square of a neighboring city.

What do we know? What radiation found in the aura of the spiritual work will Camilo bring to the streets? Magnetized as he gave himself to the building of the small bamboo temple and by the prayers done there, what positive energies does he radiate on his path?

The sun light pierces the crevices between the bamboo of the Prayer Room, making ethereal drawings in the place and on the people who pray. Through the openings, hills, clouds, the sunset can be seen. The semitransparent walls lead the prayerful person inside and outside, and allow the heart to follow intangible paths beyond the horizon.

Asylum—welcoming the other

If things are intangible... well.
That is not a reason for us not to want them...
How sad the paths would be, if it were not
for the distant presence of stars!
Of Utopias, by Mario Quintana

How might be the heart of Angela? She was taken to be a housemaid at the age of 12. For three generations, she worked from sunrise to sunset in the house of one family. She becomes ill and is immediately abandoned in a home for the elderly, because they no longer want her.

No one wants to hear what she has to tell about her history, about the rejection she feels. One day, two missionaries began to visit the home to interact with the patients. Angela vents her frustrations, the loss of being needed by the family she loves so. As she is listened to, she changes.

Meeting with an elderly in the home, Carmo da Cachoeira, Minas Gerais, Brazil, 2017

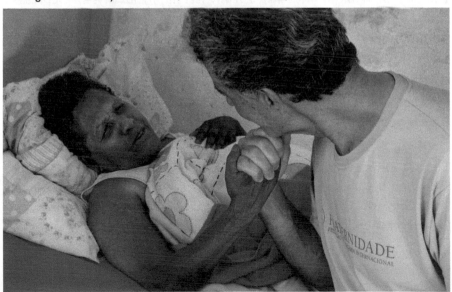

The two invited me to visit the home. They smile opening its gate, their faces lit by the 4 p.m. sun. Since most elderly people were already in their beds, we walked to the rooms stopping at the first door of the corridor. A woman dreaming was calling: *Come, Antonio, come, don't you hide from me.* We stayed attentive for a minute, imagining the dream-like scene before moving on to the next dormitory.

Angela and another lady were lying in beds next to green walls. They and the two tall men arriving were thrilled as they met. They laughed gently, so gently! Both were arriving from Greece, on their way to the North of Brazil. Each one of them sat on the mattress with one of the ladies.

I was introduced to Angela. She told one missionary: *I don't feel anymore these things I used to.* Then I asked her: *What did you use to feel?* She turns to him: *Tell her what I had!* He laughs again: *You used to be nuts!* Angela laughs her head off, and says: *I'm serious, I am so thrilled about your visit I won't be able to fall asleep tonight.*

The bliss of the reunion continues in the room lit by the sun setting behind the hills.

Angela and the missionary, hand in hand, recall: *We worked together for a year. We talked and prayed a lot. You were very sad, but learned to accept what you have. Today you are joyful, Angela!* She agrees: *That's right. Thank you! With all my heart, I really feel happy for myself.* Depressed because she had been rejected when she couldn't walk, she would hear from him: *Being happy has nothing to do with anyone nor with anything. It has to do with our own heart. You can be happy even if you can't walk.*

He contemplates her fraternally: *Remember what you told me when you were not well? You used to wake up at night and see someone by your bed.* Angela confirms: *It was you all right, in the middle of a large blue banner. Yes, I saw you more than once.*

The second missionary gets closer, asking Angela if she wants another pillow on her back. Both lift her to better accommodate her on the pillows: *One, two, three, you are as heavy as lead!* Before leaving, she says: *I feel sheer happiness. I swear before my saint I love both of you.*

Leaving the room to visit another elderly, I hear the missionary mutter to himself: What did you do to this woman, Lord? She used to be so depressed!

Support for the soul

Only the service that does not ask for
anything in return is pure and authentic.
Paul Brunton

Among pains and beauties that broaden the consciousness, missionary life is a school. It trains the process of overcoming of the self for the other's good. To do good work, a missionary should be whole, entirely given. At the same time, he should observe his own inner feelings.

In spite of his benevolence, he may be overcome by bitterness, sorrow, bad temper, impatience or tiredness since he continuously deals with the injustice done to those who do not have bread to satisfy their hunger, nor where to go, nor shoes, nor jobs.

If non-positive feelings begin to emerge within a missionary, they must interrupt their mission to regenerate themselves in order to turn their crisis into still greater compassion.

There are few missionaries and the amount of service is immense. They spend their time dealing with individual or group issues of hundreds of people responding to people's demands with kindness. To maintain the spirit of charity, they need to be daily supported by group unity, fraternity, by prayers and by unprecedented gestures of tenderness. Just like the episode of the little six year old indigenous child who captivated a missionary.

Every morning, right after he entered the shelter, Tamira appeared by his side and held his hand as a daughter. She had the shine of a cloudless sky in her eyes. *Always by my side, she became my secretary,* he recalls. *I'd get inside the shipping container to assist someone or put on dressings, and she followed me. She spoke very little, only looked at me with purity and devotion!* When he had time, he played with her.

413

One afternoon, they were visited by nine officers of the American Embassy. The missionary gave them attention, with Tamira on his arm, smiling and breaking the ice. This relic of love remained recorded in his heart: *After one and a half months, she left with her parents and never came back. Tamira's tenderness bathed my being. Remembering her is a support for my soul.*

During tough episodes a missionary often faces, they must learn to observe themselves in a loving constant way so as not to go beyond certain physical and emotional limits. They may occasionally start to react to the same circumstances not as clearly as before. If they wake up one morning and no longer feel the impulse to serve, if they feel heavy, tired, impatient and getting lost with inner conflicts, they need to find methods to dissolve these negative energies.

The missionary says: *As I went to bed after months of daily serving an indigenous shelter, I began to see images in my mind—faces, scenes of the day, talks, one after the other, unceasingly. When I realized I was totally involved by that, it was a shock. The time had come to stop for some time, to empty myself before moving on. This is part of the path. I never lose aspiration, but I need to step out to keep the light of service always lit.*

He soon traveled to the Light-Community for a spiritual retreat. On his own, he made a synthesis and reinvigorated from the pressure of months spent in a whirlwind.

Angels work together. He has Tamira's purity imprinted in his heart. In a subtle way, the little indigenous girl and the missionary continue on the same path. They scatter seeds of peace and love, which will germinate in the new Earth yielding flowers and fruits.

A Warao birth

Break your body in caves
So that within you
The free force of air may roar.
Expand yourself.
Be the great breath that circulates...
Canticle V, by Cecilia Meirelles

Life placed together two very diverse human groups—one rational and practical, another symbolic and magical—to walk together, given the aspiration that they learn from each other.

It took the missionaries a while to understand the indigenous resistance to prenatal exams. They follow other rites, values and methods concerning birth and preservation of a child's life. During pregnancy and birth, the pregnant woman retreats and has no sexual relations, while the husband remains in her surroundings. He cannot hunt far away, for the father protects the child in development against negative spirits.

They believe in the *rebo*, good or bad Nature spirits. When the child is born, the mother buries the placenta in a ritualistic way, because part of the baby's energy remains with it, otherwise a bad spirit might harm her child. A bird flies over the villages daily: sometimes it shows feathers of one or another color, one masculine, the other feminine. The bird sings to protect the newly-born, and the villagers sing back to it.

At the beginning, only the Fraternidade members worked in the Pintolândia Shelter. There was no health team they could depend on. Debora, a young coordinator, tells us about her intense experience:

I went through a dilemma. "Sister, sister," I was called. I rushed to see an indigenous woman about to give birth. I said, "Get your document." And I took her to our office at the container next to the gate. I called two ambulances. Busy, they would arrive within two hours. The woman was suffering. "Call my mother." I called the firefighter: they were putting out a fire at a gas station. Some liquid began to drip from her legs. I pushed the table,

415

got a big map banner of the shelter and unrolled it on the floor. Well, it is brand-new, it is clean. "Lie down here." Her pain was worse when she laid down. She sat up. Her mother arrived and began to direct the head of the child. I looked at one, then to the other, and then at the cell phone. Outside, a bunch of curious people, "Come on, move, move", I tell them and close the door. The mother made the woman stand, she was shaking, blood was dripping, have mercy! She won't make it... neither will I... She grabbed the table with her hand, I held her by the other hand so she wouldn't fall. The baby began to come out! I ran to the gate, and saw no one. I looked at the cell phone, and said: "Jesus, I will have to help with this birth and I don't know how!" I ran back. The baby's head had come out. The woman was about to fall and I help her to stand, the grandmother pulled, and the baby's shoulder came out, the baby slipped down, and there was blood, and water, O Lord. When the grandmother took the baby on her lap, umbilical cord stretched, and she asked me, "A knife". "Knife? Never!" They knocked on the door. The ambulance was there. The mother made undulant movements with the belly and plop the placenta fell, wow! The warrior woman expelled the placenta while standing up. The driver came alone! He brought instruments, "Can you help me?" "Yes." I picked up the child in my arms, that mushy, sticky thing. I didn't even know how to hold the baby, O Our Lady! The driver placed the oxygen mask on her. I stayed there. Neither the mother nor the grandmother could get up from the floor: the grandmother feeling a backache and the mother almost fainting. Then the doctor came inside and did the usual medical procedures. I helped him. The mother was put in the ambulance receiving IV fluids, the child on her breast to warm up. I also got in and we all went to the hospital. The mother brought the baby to her breast. O, she is feeding all right.

Knowing nothing, two missionaries went inside the office, saw the mess, and no one there: *There was a lot of blood on the table, on the floor, on the banner. It was the first day of work for a Venezuelan who came inside with me. He fell from Heaven like an angel with wings! A veterinarian technician, I did all he told me to do. Everything was cleaned up, immaculate.*

Debora sums it up: *Later, I gave her clothes, diapers. One day, the family came to visit me, the grandma, the papa, the baby on the mother's arms. I later learned that helping the birth of a soul creates a positive dharma, connects us to the universe through service to the other. Once the emergency is gone, it is gratifying. Thank you, Lord, for this baptism of fire!*

Artisans and missionaries

We carry the aura of what we are.
Let each garden be different and unusual.
Human beings must tend to unity, not to
uniformity, as each one has their own talent.
Dorothy Maclean

There are so many problems to be addressed in the shelters, but when artisan women touch colorful threads and beads, they attract peace. Remaining unruffled, they disconnect themselves from people's babbling and children's cries, and seem to be weaving a portal that leads to somewhere far-away. Having forgotten the practice, many retrieve the ancestral collective memory and keep their culture alive bringing three to twelve year old daughters to weave together.

Artistic skill perpetuates the sacred. The process of creating goods encompasses more than just generating an income. It is deeply related to the history of their ethnicity. The artisans intuit, they see internally what will be woven, related to life and Nature, before creating shapes on necklaces and collars worn as talismans to protect themselves and their family. Unaware, customers trivialize asking them to write names and weave flags.

Barely knowing symbolic meanings, one missionary gave an artisan a rattle she had received. She bent over to put it around her ankle, and was perplexed by the silence that urged to express itself. All the women had stopped weaving, saddened faces observing the scene. They explained to her that a rattle can call evil spirits and can only be used in sacred ceremonies for specific aims. The missionary apologized, and took off the rattle to bury it far away and deep in the earth.

Some missionaries are charged with overseeing the artisans. At first, the work was done on a long table where the mothers barely managed to breastfeed their little children. Things got better when the artisans were invited to sit on the floor, as they originally did.

417

Indigenous artisans prepare *buriti* leaves to weave baskets.
Pintolândia Shelter, Boa Vista, Roraima, Brazil, 2017

Mate sanuka, which means wait a little, were the first Warao words a young missionary in charge learned while anxious artisans stretched out their hands to get beads and threads. Discouraged or sad artisans become soothed while threading beads. While checking the quality control of the pieces for sale, she wanted to know: *What happened to this wristband?* The artisan, depressed: *Look, sister, I am troubled, my husband is gone, I am afraid he may be drinking.* They raise five children in the noisy shelter and still manage to keep their daily routine pace. At the beginning, the husband even came to ask them to cook.

The missionary in charge says: *You can take everything away from them, except for the crafts. That balances them, they recover self-esteem, and people's appreciation for the beauty they create touches their consciousness.*

Clara, coordinating the shelter at the time, says: *If we focus on the external world, which upsets us so much and overwhelms our thoughts, we'll never find a way out. But if we act with the purity of our heart, another energy emerges, and things change without our knowing how. In the physical realm, what we do seems too little. But our continuous presence and giving generates incredible results in other dimensions. It is not helpful feeling inadequate before visible issues of indigenous people, for there is the spirit life behind everything.*

Now and then, missionaries raise questions to the group of artisans to help them think. In a caring but sincere dialogue, they ask about their

Indigenous craftsmanship. Pintolândia Shelter,
Roraima, Brazil, 2019 and 2017

perspective for the future family sustenance: *What to do in the long run in a country that is not yours, in a shelter from where you may be taken away at any time? How would you live from then on? If you are not given beads to weave, will you put away part of what you earn to supply future material?*

The soul-to-soul contact grows between artisans and missionaries. In December 2017, they decided to celebrate that the natives had not been selling or begging in the streets for five months. Once they planned a picnic in Anauá State Park. They made *arepa* bread and left. *Leaving the noise behind to breathe Nature's harmony,* says a missionary nun, *was like putting a fish back into the water.*

Each artisan left the group walking alone to be fed by the peaceful atmosphere. Their feet on the earth reconnected them with life. Serene, they breathed aromas while looking at leaves, touching trunks. Or closed the eyes to feel the breeze.

Artisans and missionaries sat calmly side by side to contemplate the river in silence for a long-time. Reaching toward purification, the women threw in the waters the dryness of the streets, of the shelter, of banishment, and became what they are, floating flower petals, a part of Creation.

An endless dance

Daughter of the Light, seek light because
you are light. I speak from the Sun.
I touch you with my fingers. I touch myriads
of lives, and these also are part of us.
Dorothy Maclean

The moment pulses. Listen to its rhythm. The right time approaches. They rehearsed for days, over and over. The Warao women are about to step on stage to begin a dance in praise to the country that welcomed them. This is why their faces and foreheads are striped green and yellow to celebrate Brazil, blue and red in homage to Venezuela, from where they came. They had hand-sewn, stitch by stitch, the long green and yellow satin garments donated by the Fire Brigade commander.

They enter in a line, they softly raise their bare feet to step onto the gym floor. Then, they start running together to the center of the court, their shining fabrics floating. Side by side, they intertwine their arms in the waist of one another.

Now!

On cue, bare feet stamp strongly on the floor. Perfectly synchronized, they sound like percussions echoing in the gymnasium. The rhythm resounds on the walls and inside the missionary souls. The impact makes the eyes of the audience run to them. Indigenous, *criollos*, volunteers, members of government, society and religious groups gather to watch them.

United and orderly, the dancers come closer, and then recede. Their long silky black hair flying. They glow and swing like leaves of a palm tree.

They sing a hymn of love to Porê Child, the Orinoco River, imagining they are dancing on the fresh waters reflecting the blue sky. The dancer's memory runs on the flowing water. Gliding canoes furrow their moist eyes. They raise their voices: *I have lost the oar while I sailed on the Orinoco waters and, now, I travel towards the infinite.*

They twirl and twirl. They go through blazing minutes, fifteen, thirty. The afternoon Sun filters through the big shelter portals, and they persist, untiring. Clouds of rain drops cover the dancers. For another half hour they narrate their age-old existence.

Some people in haste in the audience got tired of their delay, because they could not enter their endless time. At each beat of a foot, the natives break the future and rebuild ancestral life. The repetition creates strength. Their flight is high. It follows the immensurable, the unending, the vastness outside of time.

A sincere cry and clear smile spring from those who watch and are touched by the moving spectacle of the women found on the streets with lice and wounds. Clara reveals: *I cried and laughed on that day, a proud mother applauding her exuberant daughters.*

The perpetual dance of little light feet still resounds, made eternal.

Making of garments and a typical feminine Warao dance.
Pintolândia Shelter, Roraima, Boa Vista, Brazil, 2017

Sacred names and human names

Work in such a way as to avoid idleness,
the enemy of the soul, without however
losing the spirit of the holy prayer, to which
temporal things must be made less important.
Santa Clara

The missionary was in the van, about to leave for a new mission when she got a phone call. She was asked if she would accept to be called Clara. The word hit her like a lighting bolt and, in bliss, she said a decisive yes.

New values had been springing up in her. Returning from the second Africa Mission, she realized it was time to change her personal name, as the baptismal one had closed a cycle. However, she feared receiving a complicated one, spelled with *hs* and *ks*, as of other residents of the community. So, she wrote to Trigueirinho about her concern: *I deal with the poor and I would like them to have no problems understanding my name.*

A name can reveal an inner truth, and also someones hidden spiritual task. Related to numbers and geometrical forms, when its sound reverberates in the ethers, a name draws energy structures, which may transform the surrounding environment.

Her new name Clara creates a thread of light to a high consciousness: *I was given my name after St. Clare of Assisi, for whom I have a deep devotion, and I hope I deserve to use it. She incarnated the Divine Poverty, and is the inner companion of Saint Francis of Assisi which, nowadays, is the Lord of the World. He represents the Sacred Will for the human race that lives on the planet's surface. This sublime consciousness responds for this world before the Brotherhood of Light. Such a desolate and slipshod world, so filled with inequalities, has a Lord like this, of infinite mercy. It seems a dichotomy, but Mercy can only descend into a field of pain like what is here. It does not need to descend into a sacred world, where humanity does the Will of the Father, where life is in accordance with Eternal Laws.*

The Earth is the best planet for the experience with Mercy. There is no error, everything is correct.

We have to be more humble to discover cosmic life, to remove the veil that humankind placed before itself that makes it feel so alone, so self-dependent, so lost.

Clara says: *Without cosmic life pulsing in us, we cannot bear the current of suffering that hits us during the missions. We face so much misery, so much injustice! We need to connect with the Greater Brothers and Sisters that have been on this planet since the beginning of times leading and protecting mankind. They live the Law of profound sacrifice, as they renounce their own cosmic evolution to walk among us, as Mother Teresa of Calcutta and Saint Pope John Paul II.*

In the cosmos, Great Lives do not have names, but here they use those that symbolize a part of the immensurable work they conduct. These Lives anchor their consciousnesses in Planetary Centers and Retreats of Love scattered on the Earth, but, just like Presence, they are omnipresent, they are all around us.

Four years after being renamed, Clara had a new view about people's names. During the Roraima Mission, she met Warao adults and children who had no names. Only to please the missionaries, they make up one but, if they are asked it again, they cannot remember it. Babies until one year of age are not named because their relatives say that, if they die, their pain becomes greater.

A couple was asked: *What is the name of your son?* Speechless, husband and wife just looked at each other. An indigenous woman was also asked about her husband's name, and she could not answer, as she only remembered the name of her former deceased husband. She asked the *aidamo*, and half an hour later came back with the answer.

The people in charge of the shelter constantly fill out forms and make resident lists. They register the entering and exiting of indigenous people, give them certificates and health system cards, besides making this data available for the bureaucratic system of society as well as for academic surveys about the ethnicities.

A young missionary in charge of a registration list was surprised at the organizational skills of an *aidamo*. They arranged to list all together the

List made by an *aidamo*, of indigenous people under his care-guard.
Pintolândia Shelter, Roraima, Brazil, August 2018

members of his group on the next day. Just as she arrived to the shelter the next morning, the *aidamo* brought her notebook sheets with the families, classified by names, I.Ds., number of children, of pregnant women, even though most of them do not even know when they were born.

Once, a refugee of the shelter asked the missionary, in halting Spanish: *My mother has been crying for two days because she has lost her health care card.* The lady was not crying about the card, but for her unceasing losses. The missionary calmed the daughter and wiping her mother's tears: *I'll get you a new card.* For reasons like this, the office keeps copies of the indigenous documents. It is normal to receive the documents one day and not find them the next day.

The volunteers may wonder why we give so much importance to our own names, to dates of birth and birthday celebrations. The loss of a card, the lack of a name for their children or the ignorance about the husband's name: are these signs of a disorder instilled in them? Or does it mean a different outlook on life? There are strange worlds on this planet and surely still more extraordinary ones in the cosmos.

PART IX
Inspiring lives

Be others

Be like the ocean, which receives all rivers
and creeks. The immense calm of the ocean
is not stirred. It receives them and does not
feel them.
H. P. Blavatsky

Something kindles our joy when we are with primary missionaries. These volunteers are determined to be hand in hand with the most vulnerable and unprotected human beings and also ready to help the Kingdoms of Nature. I talked with four of them at the headquarters of the Fraternidade, their base, their living quarters. Their home from which they travel, the refuge of peace for the warriors. For each one I hold vivid images and examples that rearrange atoms and touch souls.

Aiming at unveiling secrets of themselves and of everything, at a certain moment of their lives they heard an inner whisper that attracted them to the Community of Light of Figueira. As they plunged into revealing philosophic-spiritual instructions, added practical and prayerful training, their minds, feelings and physical bodies were refined, and becoming more compassionate.

Years passed before they entered the missionary activity. A common attribute among primary missionaries is their creativity to serve others. They advance side by side sharing smiles broader than the challenges overcome in the corners of the world. And they aim to be a single serving heart guided by the eternal Presence.

Here are biographic episodes of the senior missionaries, two women and two men. One comes from Argentina. The other three are Brazilians, from the states of São Paulo, Paraná and Minas Gerais. They unreservedly let me enter the chronicles of their lives, so they might be shared with the readers.

Changing was not painful

Being a source of help for the Rescue Plan.
Selfless Action, Attributes of the Monastery

A glow came from the depths of Ricardo's consciousness with the urgent certainty: *I want to go to the Nepal Mission.* He had never thought of this before, but at the first call, his missionary soul was activated. Without a doubt, the impulse already existed in him. The hidden seed emerged with the speed and splendor of thunder. In a month, the group should be in Asia, and he already saw himself disembarking among the debris of the recent earthquake.

At the time, he was the director of the Irdin publishing house. After the meeting with more than 1,000 people in which the mission was announced, he told the instructor, Mother Maria Shimani: *I want to go.*

As he was beyond the age limit, he left and thought: *My time is gone, let me leave this for my next incarnation.* To his surprised, a few days later he was told: *You will go on the Nepal Mission. And you will coordinate it.* He had his typical reaction: *Wow!*

We made appointments and canceled them until at last we could all get together. He laughed surprised: *Wow!* I asked him to tell stories of his own life from his childhood that had moved the flow of his education that later applied to the missionary practice.

In São Paulo in the 1950s, he lived in a farmhouse with his parents, grandparents, cats, dogs, ducks, chickens. As a boy he was often in the top of trees. He loved to be with his grandmother, a granddaughter of a native, with long white and black hair in a braid. She did everything: she cut wood, processed soap in a stove in the earth, baked bread in the

Ricardo, coordinator of the Missionaries of Fraternidade.
Carmo da Cachoeira, Minas Gerais, Brazil, 2014

wood stove, raised, killed and cooked chickens, took care of the huge vegetable garden. Her retired grandfather drank. His parents were very strict. If their only child misbehaved, his mother hit him with a branch from the shrubbery. He remembers, without grievance: *I was spanked often. I think I deserved it... I was a naughty child.*

There was a large bicycle he inherited from his uncle. With friends, he would ride on soapbox cars made by his carpenter father. He had family gatherings at the end of the year. He just did things without quite knowing the real reason behind the action.

Given his difficulties with school subjects and, even more, with math, he repeated one year. That was good, after all, because new friendships uncovered his enthusiasm for learning. He started working as an office clerk at age 15. From job to job, he was able to pay for his Management course, in Accounting, the major for his Master's Degree in Finances. He had become a close friend of numbers, and became the financial manager and partner of several companies.

He married early. Invited by a friend to go sailing, the hull breaking the vastness of sweet and salt waters captivated him. However, what attracted him the most was the nautical skills, handling knots, cables, ropes.

One day, walking down the street after leaving work, he saw a boy wearing a scout uniform; shorts, shirt, cap and handkerchief. He wished he had been a scout, but his father could not afford the price of the blue uniform. So, he asked the boy: *Where are the meetings held?* And was soon involved with his wife and three children in the volunteer organization: *I'll do what I didn't as a child!* The pedagogical scout training is based on respect for God, for our fellow beings, for animals and on dexterity trainings. Scouts camp, train outdoors, until their values and skills emerge: being alert to help the others, rescue techniques, dealing with emergencies.

Since parents must also participate in the group, with boundless enthusiasm Ricardo became the director of that unit. Soon, the chief of the region and later the state.

Amidst the daily bustle, other quests led the family to move from the metropolis to a calmer city, on the way to Minas Gerais. That is when the couple found out about Figueira, a community the wife started to visit regularly. Even having married in the Catholic Church, as the respective families were catholic, the couple was thinking about spiritually beyond this religion. So, they had been attracted to the Spiritist doctrine, where they assisted the poor. But now they opened up to a new spiritual path.

Material life grew quickly but, years later, the couple went through a financial crisis, and learned to count their pennies. They had already sold their car and were not even able to pay for bus fare, when surprising meetings and invitations begin to indicate new directions.

Taking inspiration from a scouting technique, Ricardo wrote a daring three-day project for outdoor training for executives, and a consultant to small companies offered to be his partner in it. At the same time, a friend asked him to take care of his stationary store for a while. Others invited him to teach in two different universities and to finish an innovative master's degree on costs applied to hospitals. So, he started to give lectures in Brazil and abroad.

With a partner, he opened another enterprise, through which he was invited to work as a consultant to the Health Ministry of Angola, where he began to relate with local ministers and leaders. He explains: *The postwar country was destroyed, a mess. It had no hospitals or doctors.*

In the seaside African capital, he and his partner set up an office with thirty clerks and were planning the opening of a similar office in Lisbon. They created courses for hospital specialization and management with interchange programs between Angolan and Brazilian hospitals. They started to oversee the reformation work in nearly all the public hospitals in the country, and also to train doctors.

Learning about the number of villagers dying due to lack of asepsis and health care, they began to invite the most capable health workers of each locality to take first-aid courses in Luanda, make small bandages, help mothers in labor, and provide basic assistance.

The whole project was working out well. Ricardo took international flights, went through urban avenues, hospital corridors, lots of figures. There was the construction of a beautiful house on a small farm with araucarias evergreen trees, on top of a mountain in Minas Gerais.

He had come back from a trip, when he found boxes piled up in a room: *What is this?* His wife's reply: *Books. In Figueira, they're asking you to give them out in Africa.* He resisted: *It is not easy to go through customs, they control everything.* At last, two trips later, he took half a dozen of them to a public library. On the next trip, he filled his suitcase, but was halted by custom authorities. The agents did not believe the books would be donated, Ricardo spent the rest of the day at the airport filling out forms, paying taxes to free his luggage.

At that time, he began to read books and watch lectures by Trigueirinho, drawing closer and closer to the Community of Figueira. Always good-humored, he explains: *The trigger for my involvement was the Immediate Action Team. We went to clean a creek, and the man who only wore suits and carried Montblanc pens in his pocket got all wet carrying logs, removing tree leaves! This is what I want to do!*

Then, he got involved with the building of a new area of Figueira: *I had one foot there, one foot in Africa, but was frustrated by Angola's corruption. For instance, if a project cost $100, the contractor would demand $30 for himself, as a commission.* Ricardo objected: *But the professor costs such and such, we could not bring him.* They replied: *Bring us a trainee.* Ricardo: *But this won't work...*

To clear up his doubts, he counseled with the community instructor, who warned him: *Leave that place before you become corrupted.* So, he decided to go on a spiritual retreat in a mobile home by a lake: *It was freezing! I drove back home thinking about what to do. I didn't fit in that old life anymore.*

Arriving at the office on a Thursday, his partner asked him: *How was it?* Ricardo: *The retreat was very good. But... look... I don't fit in here anymore. I will stop working. I don't want anything.* His partner did not understand: *You are ill.* Ricardo stated again: *I'm leaving. I'm going back to Angola to say good-bye to the team and to let go of the apartment.* In short, he left everything, and his past gradually dissolves in the twilight of his memory. He became a volunteer and was never paid again for any work.

Skiing vacations in the Argentine city Bariloche and other luxuries were now part of his past. He began to direct his vigorous energy to the Fraternidade. At first, he lived in a tent from Tuesday to Sunday, monitoring the construction of three modules and twelve igloos on one of the community farms. His wife and three children lived there for some time, and his daughter, with a broad smile like her father's, is still a resident.

Two years later, he became the director for the community publishing house, Irdin, using resources brought from the past, his executive know-how. He has worked with the Management sector of Figueira and with the Trees Group, where he applied his safe-climbing skills learned in scouting. With this new practice, the group started to be more daring, climbing to the tallest branches or moving to others without going down the tree trunks.

At that point, I ask him: *How do you explain the change to such a strange lifestyle to most people?* Ricardo reflects: *I don't know if it is so strange. Changing was not painful. I used to be in the wrong place and movement, losing time with this stuff of counseling, professional, and academic life. I believe there is a group of self-summoned people. At some moment of the remote past, I raised my hand and said: "I want to be ready to do what has to be done during the transition of the Planet into the new age. This moment has come. The hour is now." If I have to return to the old life, I'll die! I spoke so much nonsense, I taught so many wrong things.*

About the two different phases of his life, he says: *Sometimes, people end up choosing other paths because the ones they had been treading did not turn out well: they lost their job, had a great disillusion or faced difficulties that forced them to seek spiritual life. In my case it was the very opposite. I was at the peak of my professional career, doing very well financially, doing well in everything, everything. And then, that was over. It really happened in this way, indeed. It is different, because, really... leaving everything in this way.... To my children it was a big shock. In our annual vacations, we traveled to Europe or went skiing: always traveling... Then, the moment came when I told them: "It's over." "What do you mean, it's over." It made no sense to come to Figueira and than say in July: "Now I am going to Bariloche." I couldn't see myself as a tourist. Today I travel, but with a completely different view.*

Ricardo had the rare courage to accept another way of traveling around the world. I ask him to explain: *When we travel in normal life, we do what everyone else does: I will taste that food, go to that place, to the museum, even if only to say, I visited that place, ate at that restaurant, drank that wine. Now I travel with all simplicity. I used to travel only in executive class, and now, in "economy class," tight among four seats, but in full peace. I began to see the other side of life. The world of illusion sees everything beautiful, but it is an illusion. I began to see needs wherever I went, not just façades of hotels, tourist places. I began to see what is behind the appearances.*

At an airport, destiny wanted him to run across an old acquaintance. They shook hands, exchanged words. The man, analyzing him, somewhat perplexed, said slowly: *Your partner says you are ill... but you are sun tanned, joyful, look in perfect shape.* Ricardo heard him quietly and responded with a wide smile: *Well...*

Madness of missionary love

The love of God is everywhere, however, we see
destruction, misery and inequality all around us.
If we preserve the good things within us, we
will be able to supply the lack of beauty using
the supply of beauty we have within our heart.
The Sufi Message, by Hazrat Inayat Khan

Everything began under that one hundred feet tall *jatoba* tree, *Hymenaea courbaril*. The tree, sacred to the indigenous people, follows Clara's life cycles. The seed pulp was served before meditation rituals of the native people, for it facilitates mental balance, an effect recently verified by scientific researches. Fruits leap from high parts of the tree and roll on the pavement of the flowery garden in the yard of the missionary headquarters, where, sitting on a bench under the high branches, Clara evoked facts and reflections that framed her life:

Everything began as a missionary offering. I had known Figueira for years and stayed on that attitude: "I'll never live there, at most one week, though I admire those who live there".

Before the missionary call, I considered my life so well organized! I even thought I would go to heaven for having gone through hard moments as Vania de Fatima. Now I see they were not hard at all. I find my birth name beautiful. "Why this name?" I asked my mother. She said I was born around 3 p.m., when a radio was transmitting the novena of Fatima. Thus my connection with Our Lady of Fatima. Today, I am Clara. I have changed my name.

I had a poor childhood. I know well the face of poverty.

Therefore, I struggled very much, fearing to become poor again. By the way, as a child, I found everything excellent, I did not even know I was poor. Only later did my mind consider the difference of social classes. Different from my children, who always had a notion of what it is to have or not to have.

The primary missionary Clara. Adis Ababa, Ethiopia, 2013

I grew up in the countryside, surrounded by chickens, cattle. As my grand-father was manager of a coffee farm, we went to live in a house nearby. I am the second of eight children. The first four were girls, the fifth born was a boy. I have a male characteristic, this decision thing, probably because my parents wanted one so much! It comes from the desire of not having been born a boy to please them.

My father was always absent. He was ethereal, an artist, he wanted to play the viola, do shows. He got jobs, but they didn't last. My mother is earth, she worked for the children to study, "You can't have the life I had." Obviously, their relation did not succeed. I was fourteen when he left. I thought that was a cruelty. I interpreted it as rejection. I felt so bad that I was hospitalized, and took tranquilizers to sleep. We were seven children, my mother pregnant with the eighth and so involved in her own suffering. In this abandonment, I got to know aspects of human pain. I only saw my father after twenty years, and another twenty years passed until I saw him again.

I married a jealous man, although he had good principles. I worked at an office, was independent, but he asked me to leave the job and I stopped working for more than twelve years. I thought, I will make an effort for him to be present as a father and we will never separate. I discovered that we do not control these things.

I did not want to have as many children as my mother, to be with them more. The Mother of Love took care of this. I had a son, and then a girl was born. I made the time with them into sheer joy. I would play hide-and-seek, roll on the lawn, relived childhood, as I missed my mother.

Just when my daughter was fourteen, my husband and I separated. Even with so much care, he fell in love with another woman, and messed up his life. The betrayal was the greatest surprise ever. He was so jealous. I considered myself the most loved woman in the Confederate Universe, and suddenly...

It had to be that way, to hurt, because with me things have to be intense. I heard quarrels between my parents, many, I even covered my head with the pillow not to hear them. For my own family, I had prepared a beautiful story, the tidy house, two children, everything in its place. I cried for one year, asking my guardian angel not to let me go into depression nor do what happens to so many women, "He got another person, I will get one even better." I cried, and cried.

I woke up one day headed to work and I saw myself so ugly. Two years before the separation, I had gotten a job at the best private school in the city, an inexplicable fact at the time, a miracle of the Divine Mother. It was a shock to see me in the mirror. God gave me a quality: good humor. I said to myself, "You fool, you were not deceived, you were liberated. Now you can do what you always wanted to, help people. You are failing to help, in order to be navel-gazing," as I tapped my own face.

Five years before the separation, in 1996, I went with the family to Figueira. I did not even know who Trigueirinho was. We lived in São Paulo state and left in two cars to a place in Southern Minas Gerais, because we were told that vessels descended there and they knew how to invoke them. I was always fascinated by vessels, I saw several while I lived in Nature. I would wake up at night with the house surrounded by light. As an adult, I never saw them again, perhaps because I had lost the child purity.

First, we went through the secretary of the community to decide where we would lodge: different from today, when the guests are informed by e-mail. I wanted to go to a farm, and they said, "You will stay in the city." I tried to negotiate, "What do you mean? I travel kilometers to see vessels and will stay in town?" I said how many kilometers... I stayed here. Under the jatoba. Looking to the sky the whole night, but no vessels.

When we returned home, I told my husband, "I want to know Figueira more: to go after the spiritual quest. There are study groups there." He refused, "No way!" He had the normal fears, "If you enter this group, you will abandon home, children, etc." That night, I cried. I had to choose: either

Figueira or the family. I chose the family, the children, the two precious jewels that God gave me.

But I received the "Bulletins of Signs from Figueira". I was attentive to the time they arrived and saved all of them. One year after the separation, I began to make a life synthesis and I read them again in another way. After all these years, I called them and returned. It was 2003.

I lodged in the same house, here in the Fraternidade, but I did not recognize it. It was not like this before, the building was completely different... The first time I had such a headache that they made me an appointment in a circular room... Where is it? It was bright... I looked for it. It does not exist? I discovered that I was treated on a subtle level, not on the concrete level, a revelation!

Then they told me there was a study group in Jaú, where I lived. Its coordinator became my best instructor: when I cried because of a human drama, she gave me a CD recorded with the correct instruction from Trigueirinho, and I began to read his books, to understand Figueira. I coexisted for years with her, now Mother María del Salvador. Since the beginning until she became a nun, I accompanied her surrender. I thought, "She left her professional life, she was super-acclaimed, so well established, had everything and left it. I admire such people. I will never do this, never.

Then, she came to live in Figueira, and I took on the coordination of the study group in the city. Besides the meetings at my home, we continued the service programs started by her; visiting prisons and poor districts, bringing clothes. This was my basic training school.

I had recovered my joy of living while managing a pre-university school. I love working with youths. I happily left home at 6 a.m. and happily returned home sometimes at 10, 11 p.m. I had a good salary, made my schedule, was the owner of my life, the way I liked it.

Every semester I came to the General Meeting for updates in Figueira until, in 2011, I was surprised by the first public apparitions of Mary, Jesus' Mother, to a visionary of the community. That had an impact, because I had always had a strong love for the dear Mother. As the apparitions would continue for another seventeen days, I returned to my normal life, to be back on the weekend with my city's group. Several problems occurred on the road, but we arrived on time. It seemed it might rain, and the apparition was transferred into the great hall of F2. I was surprised, the mind playing games, how absurd, "How will the Most Holy Mary Hierarchy fit inside a hall?"

When we came in, people were praying. I was looking where to sit and my heart beat intensely. It seemed to leap, the skin on my chest trembled. It swirled in a clockwise direction, and I was asking myself what that was. I felt a fire, neither cold, nor hot. I cannot explain, no science can explain. I only know it was not of this world. A high-speed movement, as if fitting gears. I never felt that again.

I starred at the stage. So much aroma of roses, they must have put rose essences in the candles. Then the Virgin Mary asked if some members of the group would accept to go to Africa. She explained it was a request for help.

In a few days, I learned She had asked for the formation of a group of missionaries. I thought, "Missionaries, how heavy! A tall story. Wherever the missionaries went, people's culture was destroyed. They colonized, indoctrinated, catechized and all. In short, they really spoiled everything."

But her request and my swirling heart resounded in me. "Missionaries... I must go! I'll go to the Africa Mission", I could see me there. I was quite surprised to receive via e-mail the registration to be filled out by those who felt the appeal. I had imagined that only in dream worlds. We had a thirty-day deadline to answer. I took a photo, added health examinations, answered the questions. Every day I tried to send them and before the click, "No, let me think, there is still time."

I needed to find a mental way out, a plan as perfect as the one made for my married life: I will go to my training and return home, when the call to Africa comes, I will anticipate my vacations. It will be all right! I clicked, "Enter" and... Thy Will be done!

I did anticipate my blessed vacations indeed and found many people, some one-hundred twenty candidates on a community farm. They rented big tents to lodge us, and the process began. Talks with psychologists, health examinations. From the first selection, forty were chosen, from those fourteen were selected.

I learned the training would continue in the Light-Community of the New Earth sierras, called Crer-Sendo at the time. Wow! I hadn't planned that. I explained to the person leading the mission, "I will take the leap, but beforehand I need to inform my boss I will quit. I like to leave by the front door, not by the back door. I talked with my children, who were living with me. My son is a teacher. My daughter had become unemployed, but she gave me the impulse, otherwise I wouldn't have made it, "Mother, go, be at peace, I am well trained, I'll send resumes and soon will get a job." In fifteen days, I quit my job, quit the school, released the past.

After Crer-Sendo, the groups split in three. A part was trained in the House of Light on the Hill, part went to the Light-Community of Fraternidade, in Uruguay. I coordinated the third group to Granja Viana, Light-Nucleus of Figueira in Sao Paulo. We stayed there for three months. It was a wonderful missionary school, one to tame life. I underwent a hard test: I could only call my children once a week.

The reality of the missionary process gradually unraveled. It was a much greater step we had imagined. It was not the training for a mission: total surrender of ourselves was being asked of us. For this reason, the candidates gradually left. From the one-hundred twenty, only seven were left, the seven that went to Ethiopia. We still had another enormous test: Africa Mission took one year to occur. We were tried all over again!

After Sao Paulo, I spent one month with my children. They were beginning their careers. I had left the money of the work agreement with them and also my unemployment insurance. My daughter still had not gotten a job. I found her worried, "I have interviews, but nothing happens!" My heart of a mother was in my boots, but I returned to the Fraternidade obeying the date to present myself: obedience to the deadlines was a fundamental matter.

Here, they did not know quite what to do with a missionary arriving. I spent some two months in a little room taking care of this garden with a Japanese lady. I weeded, saw people come and go. But they didn't announce the date of the mission. They didn't even touch the subject. I thought: "I am going crazy if I stay here, my body needs movement."

Once I went early to check the bank balance left for my children. Zero! I returned, sat here under the jatoba tree, thinking. I felt like crying, and went to my room. It was a test of faith.

I sat on the bed, picked up an image of the Divine Mother and said, "Dear Mother, you know my offering, my story, my madness of love for You. You know my children's stories, I don't even need to say that the bank has no money. The school director keeps calling and making me incredible proposals for me to return. I can resume work at any moment and supply my children. To my despair, they are going through needs. You promised to take care of the families who has surrendered. I believed, Mother. That same afternoon, my daughter called. She had just gotten the work she wanted, the way she wanted, with a good salary. And, better then that, in the same company and city where her fiancé works. They were living far from each other and were losing their love story. Now they are married. The Mother hand-picked everything. We arranged to do one-hundred fifty Universal prayers to thank the Holy Mother at the same time, also we were hundreds of miles away from each other.

I can never again doubt anything. Everything was guided, I get emotional. Then my first mission came. I am still discovering what it is to be a missionary, I am still not one completely, because it is very mysterious.

During my madness of missionary love, sometimes I catch myself wondering if I am abandoning my children. I always took care for our relation to be close, but without attachment. I released them to the world. I go months without seeing them, but they are not hard on me.

Today I received a reply on the cell phone. I could hardly believe what I was hearing, "Mother, I am taking a course. One of the activities was to choose seven mentors who gave meaning to my life. We have to send an audio to each one. Here it is, "Mother, you are my first mentor, the most important person. I feel totally grateful for the way you brought me up. I am what I am because I am your daughter. Seeing your happiness today makes me happy. Thank you for teaching me the purest sense of the word love, for being present, for teaching me that love is everywhere."

On hearing the message, Clara and I cried in silence. She raised from the bench under the jatoba tree that follows her life cycles. She took some steps towards the white sculpture of Our Lady of Graces. She smiles as she bowed to kiss her hand.

After months, at the office of the New Canaan shelter for Venezuelan refugees, in Boa Vista, Clara made the reflection: *Whence came the yes that I gave to be a missionary? It did not come from my conscious level, no, it didn't. As a personality, as a person, I didn't have the slightest condition to give this yes. This yes came from a very distant world. To be part of this is an enormous mystery.*

Life for others

The heart is not a place. Look within.
The heart is not physical. It is the central
point from where all things emerge.
Ramana Maharshi

From the marine rock, the young man extended his eyes on the straight golden path of sparks over the sea to the horizon. The semi-hidden Sun was rising from masses of light blue water. The first rays broke the shells that suffocated his inner core, liberating old accumulated pains. He cried. The salty tears washed the non-coherence with the morning light. He wept until he felt embraced by an unknown state of peace coming from beyond the horizon. It took him a long time, but one day he understood that he had been enveloped by the radiant original purity of the Center of Lys.

Twenty years later, while Imer told about the episode that happened in that Mediterranean island, I whispered: *What is the Center of Liz?* He summed it up: *It is an energy center in the Iberian Peninsula. The energy of Lys has been guiding us from the beginning of our consciousness awakening until we consecrate ourselves to the Divine.*

To talk with him, I drove 30 miles on the interstate highway flooded by a white rising sun. In the curve leading to the city, still veiled by a soft winter mist, I saw him walking with long strides. Tall, with the gray uniform of humanitarian assistant, he was carrying a small yellow bouquet of newly-picked wild flowers for group tea that evening. Coming from the farm, he had been picking the medicinal flowers by the dirt road.

I parked my car. Imer came closer. I lowered the window, he bent over, holding the little wild chamomile flowers in his hand, his big green eyes, sparkling: *A synchronized meeting!* Yes, a sign that we were being driven by a silent command.

The daily toil was his master. Born to help, he has been involved in the service to others since the age of five. With the separation of his parents, his mother worked to support the family, entrusting him and his two brothers to make the bed, tidy the house, wash the dishes, do the shopping. He said: *There my attitude of collaborating and dealing with daily matters was being born. We lived in a peaceful seaside city, and early on I had contact with the street, gradually becoming independent.*

A descendant of Basque French, Spanish and Italian immigrants of Arabian influence, Gaston—Imer's name at the time—was born in Argentina and inherited the love of labor from his ancestors. Nothing came easy, nothing was solved for his family in which all had to seek sustenance. When he was thirteen, he would take the train with friends to sell raffle tickets in a neighboring town to earn money for his own expenses.

The situation became worse. His mother, who had been ill for many years at home, was now hospitalized. To receive better treatments, the family moved to the state capital. While adapting to the big city and his new school, Gaston and his brothers would take care of the home. As he turned 18, he found a job as a video-club clerk to help with the rent. To pay for the expensive university courses, he had two jobs, a regular one on weekdays and work as a waiter on weekends.

The time came when he compared his life with his friends. Why was his experience harder? Only in the future did he understand how instructive his beginning years had been for training his determination, courage, discipline, continuous work.

The young missionary spirit awakened while working in a university extension in a needy regions of the country. He would go to the field with colleagues to offer dental service and orientation about the health of children and preventive health through oral hygiene. He would rather help there than be under artificial light, dealing with patients pains at a dentist's office. He says: *My intention was to give an impulse to raise human conditions by means of Dentistry. In those places, we became a reference, a doctor, even if we hadn't finished our studies at the university.*

Later, he participated in the UN humanitarian help program of the White Helmets, on a mission with his colleagues on the dry border between Brazil and Argentina, covered by dense Araucaria moist forests and marked by Jesuit missions for the Guarani culture between the seventeenth and

Imer, a primary missionary. Addis Ababa, Ethiopia, 2012

nineteenth centuries. In vehicles with dental equipment, they assisted inhabitants of the region who spoke Portuguese and Spanish and moved easily through the jungle, regardless of officially established borders.

Once graduated, Gaston crossed the Atlantic Ocean to Spain, seeking professional success in a country that still did not have a Dentistry Faculty. He failed. In fact, he went to Europe to expand his consciousness, and his way of looking at the world. He learned from the cleanliness and order that existed there. Also, about the value of accepting human diversity without judging. Above all, he reconnected with the golden thread of life. On the Mediterranean island, he glimpsed the invisible supra-physical Existence. He had crossed vertiginous years until climbing that rock where he relived the sorrow for his parents' separation, his mother's illness, the effort to sustain the maternal home.

On one hand, adventurous life stimulated him. But with some suffering, the karma always returned. He says: *I have always been eager to experience things to gain my own knowledge.* He had launched himself deeply in material life, both at work and in sensations caused by addictions. He tried once, then another time, to learn: *Is that all? And what else is there?* The pleasures go away, and did not sustain themselves. Life needs higher fuel!

At last, the emptiness throbbed in him, a good point to start over. He asked and learned: *Everything is energy. Only Life will show you new paths.* He did not fit the normal path of the majority, neither the young, the adult nor the old age: to graduate, work, buy, raise a family, go on vacations, grow old, retire. He knew, his future would be different, a to-morrow that would be created step by step.

He went back to his home country to run the course of illusions in the whirlwind of his brother's clinic. For two years he was in practice, learned about the profession, earned money, took shifts on weekends attending dental emergencies called in by cell phone.

The time came when he faced the first self-rejection signs of his lifestyle. He recalls: *I became ill, had headaches, allergy. Working to make money did not satisfy me. I recalled what I had felt at dawn in Spain and won-dered if life was that trivial. A feeling of unease for the lack of answers was growing within me.*

He went to an allopathic doctor for the headaches, who immediately pre-scribed a computerized X-ray. He wanted to know: *Why? All I feel is a headache. Inside the tube taking digital photos, I noticed something was not right. At last, I got the results: nothing. The doctor just prescribed some pills for me.*

He also had allergies: *After waiting two hours for my appointment, I went into the doctor's office. He asked me what I was feeling and immediately prescribed a medication. In two minutes! The consultation took him two minutes. I left.*

Gaston thought it all over. He did the same with his emergency patients prescribing antibiotics, corticosteroids, painkillers, anti-inflammatory. He received what he was giving to the others: *I began to understand, to go through my consciousness awakening.*

To treat people's physical symptoms, he learned about alternative medi-cine. When the human being is ready, an angel appears to guide him to the next step, which, in his case, was a colleague who had advanced a little further on the path.

He says: *The first discovery is that we are being manipulated by the system. We saw that as something negative and wanted to escape. My colleague recommended an anthroposophical doctor to me. "Anthropos what?" I had no idea what that was, but I was afraid of allopathy, so I went to this doctor. He looked at the iris of my eyes and gave a diagnoses and explained what was happening to me! I thought it was wonderful! We talked for one and a half hours. I was introduced to a new diet and to sports.*

With new aspirations circulating in his veins, he found an elderly alchemist who gave courses: *With him, I began to uncover the world of medicinal plant preparation, the real Medicine, and not the one that comes in capsules. I took a course on distillation, to obtain active principles, and even set up a small laboratory at home. I was taking small steps. However, suggesting alternative treatments in the clinic would not be appreciated.*

His angel-colleague was enthusiastic when he came back from a visit to Figueira. He had found answers to the pressures from the system. Sometime later, they both accepted the invitation for a course on Dentistry and Inner Healing in three segments, at the Community.

Imer recalls: *There were sixty dentists; three Argentines, the others, Brazilians. We hardly talked about dentistry. We studied alternative medicines, Chinese Medicine, energies, the cosmos, the Sun. We learned that souls dissatisfied with everyday life are beginning to reveal themselves and get together.*

At that point, Gaston was experiencing a life more in tune with his inner yearnings. He worked fewer days a week, lived in a house across from the sea. Since his trip to Europe, he had been having a conjugal life with a professional colleague, and together they attuned with the vastness of the cosmos until they chose to eliminate sex from the relationship. Then, as companions, they went to take the third module of the course.

They had barely returned home, when they began to fight an inner battle: *Shall we live in Figueira, leave our home, work, family, car, everything, or not?* The decision came from the ocean, from the infinite. In the middle of their crisis, one day they sat looking at the sea. Two gigantic whales emerged. Again, and again! They were partying in the waters for three hours. It was a sign to them that they needed to leap the barriers that opposed their new goal.

Touched by subtle wings, the couple closed the commitments, put back-packs on their shoulders, stayed for a few days in the Healing Center of the Light-Community of Aurora and arrived in Figueira. He recalls: *Five days later, chaos exploded in Argentina. The government took all the money from the people, who went to the streets. We had just taken our money out of the country and could live for five years without a regular job. Everything was perfectly conducted by the Brotherhood, the Greater Hierarchies. It is a jubilation for the Universe when two souls decide to tread the Path!*

I asked him: *What is a Greater Hierarchy?* He smiled: *Hierarchy is the Brotherhood that guides us, the Elder Brothers that wait for us to work with Them. Since they have more experience and wisdom, we can have them as references to take our steps. They are invisible to human eyes, but we can feel Their love in our hearts.*

To renew the visas, the couple came and went between Brazil and Argentina, visiting sacred points in both countries. At last, they decided to set up, with other doctors and dentists, a consultation office near the Light-Community of the Brotherhood, in Northern Argentina. They were putting into practice what they had recently learned about Dentistry and Medicine. They also drove an old Jeep to forgotten towns around the mountains to offer healing services to the needy.

At that time, they started to participate in a spiritual work in the highlands of Bolivia, in the *Puerta del Sol* of Titicaca Lake. From there, the couple went to meet the Doctors without Borders, to help the Peruvian indigenous and non-indigenous people for one month. They left the plateau to arrive in the jungle.

They took along the book Miz Tli Tlan, by Trigueirinho. One night, deep in the forest, the dentists asked Gaston: *You talk about intraterrestial centers. What is this?*

He began to share some knowledge received in Figueira about the network of light that surrounds the planet, about the Centers of Love Miz Tli Tlan, ERKS, Mirna Jad, Aurora, Iberah, Liz Fatima, Anu Tea. *These are bases where extraterrestrial visitors stay, headquarters of the Cosmic Brotherhood living in other dimensions. From there, these evolved beings radiate instructions and light to our planet. They may contact us in a subtle, silent, sometimes extremely bright way. In many ways, they invite us to awaken. He spoke with enthusiasm: I found out that chance does not exist, for we are guided by Something Greater, or God, or the Universe, or the One and Only Life.*

In the background, a large river murmurs, the melodies of nocturnal animals and chirping sounds. At that moment, splendid gigantic domes of light appeared in the starry sky. They sparkled, disappeared, flashed here and there. Everyone saw them. They were being contacted by the energy of Miz Tli Tlan. Abstract information was made clear, resulting in a material revelation. That group of Doctors without Borders received that grace.

Once their trip was over, the conjugal life with his partner ended. In him, there was a question about sexual energy to be solved. In Light-Communities, the proposal of sexual chastity as a path to help soul's evolution is clear: *But as I couldn't transcend the sexual desire, which was getting in my way, I decided to experience marriage life and a child. It was wonderful. My new partner was from the town where I was born. Life's paths surprise us, I went back to where I was born!*

The couple decided to have their child at home, being the first ones in the city after a long time. Unable to find someone who would help with the labor, they made contact with a young mother in a neighboring town who had had three children at home. The third one was born at dawn, in the laundry area, on her own, without even waking up her husband.

As they made up their mind, the next day the midwife and the doctor who had previously refused to help them, decided to assist the birth. *A person's inner decision, when it is real, attracts collaboration,* Imer concludes. A boy was born peacefully, and his parents made a home video to help other couples do use the same method.

However, the marital bonds began to undo little by little. Fantasies started giving way to a growing stir. *I'm suffocating,* Gaston said, at last. His sexual desire was uprooted, his crisis with his wife dragged on, generating conflicts, sadness, mutual sorrows. The couple entered the same battle that is taking place in so many homes in the world and, just as it had happened with his parents, their relationship ended.

Now he was convinced. He had a different mission, than the dedication to family life: *Not that one path is better or worse than the other. I even tried to organize a place to take them. I went alone for three months to*

Sierra de la Ventana and, right on the block behind where I lodged, there was a Trigueirinho group, in which I did not participate.

His experiences with free-will were ending. His soul aspired to follow other footprints. During this transition, the philosophic ideal seated at his heart's altar was rekindled. He recalled mantras and sang them. However, he still had to work on humbleness. To survive, he had to work as a bricklayer assistant and to cook meat at a bar, although he is vegetarian. He says: *I was purifying from the period in which I lived by myself.*

He yearned so much to contact Trigueirinho's teachings again, that he attracted an unplanned encounter as he went by a street corner. He was given a book called Aurora about an intra-terrestrial center in Uruguay and learned that, in Paysandu, they were beginning to build a Light-Community. And soon a service group would leave to help them harvest oranges.

He decided to go. He even decided to live in Aurora and made the request via e-mail to the secretariat. No reply. The same old story happened again. When someone wants to take a spiritual step, everything gets stuck. He waited for forty days! No answer.

His aspiration grew, and as a pilgrim he decided to participate in the orange harvest anyway. He brought clothes for two days. And stayed there for two years. When he arrived, he learned that the e-mail message to his request for residence had gone astray: *The response is yes, stay with us.* In view of this, he joined the other pioneers to manifest this spiritual community.

He felt embraced by the love and the joy of the brothers and sisters on the path. The white Brotherhood that dwells on other planes of consciousness also celebrated. The prodigal son had returned home.

From that moment on, Imer has lived among the Light-Communities. In Córdoba, Argentina, he learned about the Africa Mission. His heart connected to the heart of that continent, but he kept silence. Soon he received the invitation to join the Ethiopia Mission team, and never stopped.

Imer says: *My spirit is missionary, adventurous, entrepreneur. I have always liked to help people: "Leave it to me." At the university, I founded and was the president of a Student Council, which to this day represent students' interests.*

He surrendered himself to his soul, to his spirit, to his personal mission. He moves inward, studies the mysterious side of the planet, gradually revealed to those who reach the right evolutionary degree: *I felt the Call and decided to surrender to God, to follow what He indicated to me. And to accept the consequences that the decision would bring to me and others. After three years of separation, I still tried to talk with my son's mother, who hung up the phone when she heard me. "I'm not supposed to insist,"* I thought. *There, inside the telephone booth while holding the telephone, I let go of that suffering, of that guilt. I felt in peace. "Christ, I deliver both to You." I understood the Sacred is in all, unify all, that pain is just of this material level, that souls have to live what they have to live, and that my surrender would help other beings, not only my son and his mother. Imer smiled widely. Now I serve children, the elderly, everything and anybody with the greatest joy.*

In the meantime, he noticed it was time he changed his birth name for a spiritual one. He acquired it. Imer was a young Essene priest and therapist, a faithful follower of Christ. He explains: *After Jesus died and ascended, the apostles had the task of spreading His words. Persecuted, they took refuge in Absalom tomb, near the wall of Jerusalem. There lived Imer, who, besides being in charge of the sepulcher, attended, healed and safeguarded those who gave their life to Christ.*

Baptized by the vibration of the new sound, Imer's transformation sped up. He tells us about his inner healing and the liberation of old standards of behavior, feelings, thoughts: *It is not easy to undo bonds we have created and begin a new way of life. Families resist changes. Determination is essential for us to liberate ourselves, to overcome life's trials. We go through difficult challenges. But the blessings we receive are immense.*

The three-dimensional world does not let us easily break new sparkling ground. But Imer advances, his feet guided to the golden light trail over the infinite ocean masses of water. He goes toward the Sun.

Offer one's life

Always keep in mind that God and human beings
need one another. Both are necessary for the full
and final eternal experience of realization.
The Book of Urantia

Shen's soul came to Earth with a goal: to build a joyous server. With a meek but determined personality, since adolescence she has experienced countless selfless services until she became a missionary. As she gives of herself to others, fiery rays emanating from the Soul of the World, train her so that she may attain increasingly deep spheres of consciousness. One day, filled with lessons learned in everyday life, Shen's soul will penetrate non-material spheres.

Being the only daughter of parents who doted on her, she holds luminous memories of her childhood, playing and studying year after year. No family problem ever reached her, and only later did she learn about conflicts between her parents.

However, preadolescence arrived: *I encountered the rebellious teenage years. I wanted to turn the world upside down, even being a good student. At the age of sixteen, my spirit said: "Enough with that!"* Crossing the street, she was run over by a girl learning how to drive. The car wheel had to be lifted off her leg. Unable to walk for a year, she stayed at home in retreat. She read, did lessons brought by classmates, and only left to do school tests.

After the first breakthrough in life, everything changed. She had other friends and became a different person. Then she scared her parents by telling them: *I want to be an airplane pilot.* Her loving and friendly mother was shaken at first. However, the adamant daughter got her pilot's license. Allowed to fly small airplanes, on a late afternoon she soared the air alone for a panoramic flight beyond the metropolis.

She flew over the jungles and the waves of hills tainted by the dusk, then she saw the sun reflecting on the waters of a golden lagoon. The young pilot plunged all of her being into that light. And, in the heights, the luminescent sparks opened her eyes. She merged with the sky, the valleys and peaks, the beauty, the Magnificent. She allied the sun-rays to become their bearer: *For the first time, I felt God burning in my heart. I began to question the meaning of existence. What did I come to this world for? I returned to the Aero-club, landed the airplane and said to myself: "I need to find some answers."*

Restless, she asked questions here and there, until she mustered enough courage to ask a friend: *Do you believe in reincarnation?* The friend replied: *Are you nuts?* But the torment of doubt needed to be relieved, which began to happen during a theater play, while the actors were acting on stage. She was with her group of Mechanical Engineering friends, a course she took only because it had to do with piloting and to calm down her mother, who insisted: *All right, be a pilot, but you need to complete your university undergraduate course.*

In urgent eagerness, she asked the teacher beside her: *Do you believe in reincarnation?* Then, a magnificent light dripped in the curve of time.

In an environmental catastrophe, the primary missionary Shen helps to rescue animals. Mariana, Minas Gerais, Brazil, 2015

The teacher gave her the saving indication: *Ah, I will introduce you to an author called Trigueirinho.* He lent her the book ERKS, which she could not put down.

She wanted more. She read all of his books even the last one published at that time, *Searching for a synthesis.* Trigueirinho's words resounded in her being and enlightened it intensely. She says: *I took the first step, I stopped eating meat, and a revolution began to take place at home. My parents are passionate Catholics, and grew up in this environment until I abandoned the religion in my years of rebelliousness. Now, all I wanted was to meet this author.*

The philosopher would give a public lecture in her town, she dreamed of that day, but it was canceled. Trigueirinho had closed the cycle of public lectures and, from then on, he would only give them in Figueira: *I have to go there immediately! I went. I entered a hall with perfectly aligned chairs. People's shoes were kept outside. Everyone stepped lightly to maintain the reverent atmosphere and a place of absolute silence. Sitting behind a small table, Trigueirinho began to uncover other universes in a slow tone of voice. That was it, my life changed!*

In 1990, her thirst for knowledge and answers started being quenched. She immediately began to dynamically participate in communitarian life, returning to Figueira every two weeks. During a strike at the Federal University, she stayed for a longer time on the farms, praying for the strike to go on forever. But eventually it ended.

Resuming classes, she faced her predicament with her parents. They thought she was going mad. Naive, unprepared, she had reported to them with great enthusiasm the new world that she had discovered: *I was very young. I had discovered the cosmos. I wanted them to do it also.*

To undo this painful disharmony, she was instructed by a wise resident of Figueira: *You can't do that to your parents. Always tell the truth, but don't go into details. For example, tell them you've come to participate in the reforestation of an area. You study Geology, they will understand that.* Since she hated the Engineering course, she had changed it for Geology. Because she was successful at the university her parents were relieved.

She intensified her participation also in an extended area of Figueira in Belo Horizonte, Blue Sky, today called Light-Nucleus of the Sacred Heaven. At this stage of life, she discovered service to others. Along with collaborators, she raised donations of food from restaurants, spent several hours before dawn processing the food to distribute nutritional soups in the early morning, along with clothes and other things needed in the communities. She eventually was in charge of one of them: *It was great! I met residents and paid home visits with two other young people. They used to call us if they felt ill. Even at night we went to assist them with herb compresses, foot-baths.*

In Figueira, she participated for years in the Immediate Action Team, now called Solar Group, coordinating its meetings in the Blue Sky: *There was practical training at the Red Cross and in the Fire Brigade. We attended classes, watched films and videos about rescues, so that we could provide urban and rural first-aid services. We exercised survival in extreme situations, such as very high temperatures and lack of water. We also learned what to do in natural accidents, floods, fires, landslide, earthquakes. The group went through a powerful inner work at the same time to prepare our consciousness to maintain balance when dealing with adverse situations.*

Then, a new rule from Figueira came to the Blue Sky: *A member of the Immediate Action Team should remain permanently there.* Being its coordinator, she decided to move out to the Nucleus, while finishing her last year at the university.

Having graduated, she chose to live in Figueira's farms for five years. Deepening her inner process, she expanded her knowledge and reverence for the kingdoms of Nature and for the Sacred Life. At the time, no one used cell phones and there were only telephones in the secretariat office, in town: *Non-materiality was almost palpable, as if we were entering another dimension.*

Her original name was Ana Maria. However, because of the purity of the task she was taking charge of—the spiritual retreats of the community—she got a letter from Trigueirinho suggesting she change her name to Shen, which means, in Chinese: the "spiritual strength is in the heart." When she accepted it, birds sang in glory to the Most Divine.

For two years, she never left Figueira. One day she went to the neighboring town to ask for a document. Immersed in a subtle vibration, she was surprised at the number of cars, and had to re-learn how to cross the street... she was living in another world.

However, at a certain moment, the wind of human dreams dragged Shen from community life to personal life in a mountainous region in the state of Rio de Janeiro. Needing to learn about the love of the world, she says: *It was wonderful to be married, with a home, a good job. I went to Figueira sometimes, and participated with my husband in the communitarian life of Crer-Sendo Service Nucleus, in Teresópolis. Everything was perfect.*

For sure, her essence knew, but the mind did not even sense the upcoming big new change. An internal tornado brought Shen to her real destiny.

In September 2011, she was in the Figueira General Meeting, and at the first public apparition of Mary, the Mother of Jesus, to visionaries of the ecumenic Grace Mercy Order. She thought all that was very weird, and climbed Crystal Hill with more than a thousand silent participants. A tender breeze mitigated the noon heat. Sitting on rocks and on the sandy ground, the multitude waited, eyes floating between clouds and the sea of ridges and woods, when the ceremony began.

Lulled by prayers and songs, at a certain moment Shen felt a balm of purity open in the atmosphere. Unexpectedly, she connected again with her childhood, perplexed: *I nearly knelt down when She manifested Herself to the visionary, who saw her on top of a tree five meters from me. What I noticed was indescribable... the same affectionate energy protecting me as a child was back, and so strong! I revisited scenes when I played at school breaks, feeling embraced by the same maternal presence.*

In another manifestation at that time, the Divine Mother requested: *I want a mission to Nepal.* Shen began to insistently ask: *How can I not go? How can I not go because I have other things to do?* She loved the life she was living, her job, but, despite this, the call to become a missionary could not be postponed: *What shall I do now?*

In the meantime, she was invited to work at the Missions secretariat of the Fraternidade, and her doubts were soon gone. She quickly sorted out each detail of her life and departed for Figueira, without looking back, without a husband, without an income, without fear.

When she surrendered to the mystery of the new stage in her life, Shen received knowledge of one task of her soul. The perpetual flame shone higher. In view of the quietude achieved, she could cross the narrow portal to serenity: devoting herself to the intense cycle of missions. Convinced and at peace, the warrior entered the battlefields.

Epilogue

The Fraternidade responds to the
growing humanitarian crises, which tend
to intensify in this era of contradictory
values that we are all experiencing.
Between June and December 2018,
the Egypt Mission took place, the
Roraima Permanent Mission expanded and
the Colombia Permanent Mission began.
Other doors to service are to be opened.

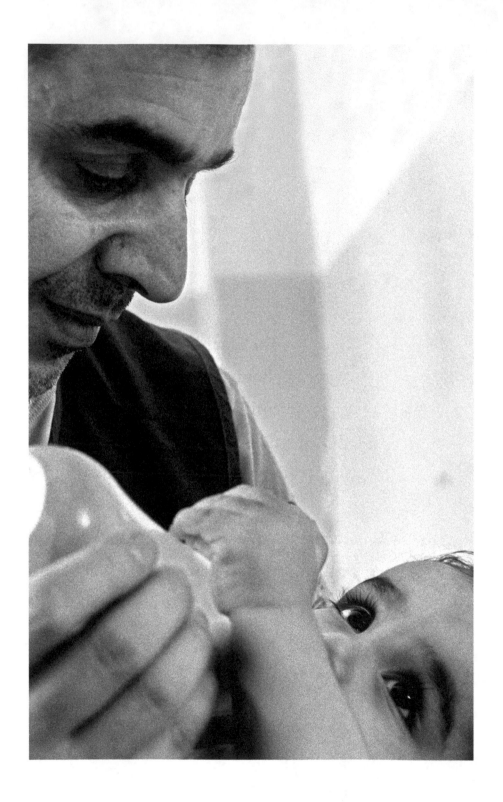

Egypt Mission

...for Egypt is the image of things of the heavens and...
a temple of the whole world. When Egypt confirms that,
then the Lord and Father, Supreme God, First in Power
and Governor of the World, will scrutinize the hearts
and acts of human beings and... will be able to bring
them back to their old magnificence, so that the world
may appear as the lovely work of His hands.
Secret Egypt, by Paul Brunton

Wonderful, exclaimed the missionary about the days five Brazilians and two Portuguese provided humanitarian assistance to the elderly taken off the streets of Cairo and to babies and children of trash collectors. It took me some time to understand the reason for so much enthusiasm.

She had just described the location of the home for the elderly and the nursery located in dark buildings of a huge district built within the dump sites hidden in the outskirts of Cairo, the arid capital. The streets, loaded with flies, gave off nauseating odors emanating from piles of cardboard, plastic, clothes, rotten organic material. She added: *A hot wind blew nonstop and literally everything is covered by the gray sand of the desert: streets, buildings, furniture.*

My imagination about Egypt, from readings and movies, conflicted with that image which lacked traces of the extraordinary genesis of the nation, the God Ra, the papyrus, the sacred ceremonies, the divine architects who built the Great Pyramid, protected by silence and the secrets of the Sphinx, the greatest initiation temple of the old world, where the Truth and Wisdom were revealed to the Pharaohs. Escaping from Egypt with the Hebrews, Moses parted the Red Sea with a single command. The Sacred Family took refuge in Egypt to escape Herod, marking its sands and the history of humanity with celestial steps and miracles.

I thought of rejecting this comment of the selfless server. The word *wonderful* clearly contradicted the description she gave me of the trashed city. But I decided to focus inwardly, and the response began to appear in the quote of the Egyptian writer Naguib Mahfouz, Nobel Prize winner:

It is clearly more important to treat your neighbor well, than to keep praying, fasting and touching your head on a prayer mat.

It was night when, leaving the airport for the hotel in the district of As Shoubra, the seven missionaries crossed the gigantic sand-colored city embedded in the desert on the fertile banks of the Nile River. Cairo is known as *the mother of all cities and also as the city of the one-thousand minarets*. From these thin towers with balconies, rings the sound of five daily calls to prayer in the country where 90% of the population are Muslims. The van moved among car horns and guttural melancholic lament of the music played on the radio. It left crowded avenues and entered streets and alleys loaded with vehicles pulled by animals, which suffered from the heavy weight of compacted trash. It avoided pedestrians and trash: *The amount of garbage is frightening, the dirty streets packed with people, external elevators taking trash up and down, balconies and garages filled full with bags of trash. Often it has no running water or electricity. Dogs and goats live inside the buildings and on the streets, surviving on the garbage. And very close to there, we went past a very chic neighborhood,* continues the missionary.

They arrived at the hotel, in awe of the unusual neighborhood full of huge bags of garbage. Clerks welcomed them and a waiter soon brought a colored tray with green, yellow, white and red juice, as a sign of welcome. What a pleasant surprise for the exhausted group! Because they needed phone chips and to exchange money that evening, the hotel manager made it a point to accompany them. He wanted to know where they would go the next day: *We will work in the house of the Sisters of Mother Teresa of Calcutta.* He took note of the address and, after leaving them at the hotel, went there. The next morning, he escorted them, rang the bell, waited for the Sister to arrive to receive them, informed her that they were staying at his hotel and please ask someone to bring them back when the activity was over, even if that was only a mere three-minute walk. Arab hospitality was also continued on the other days.

Once again, they join the Missionaries of Charity, who, in previous phone contacts, were aloof, but always received them as old acquaintances,

A nursery in Mokattam, and a home for
the elderly in As Shubra. Cairo, Egypt, 2018

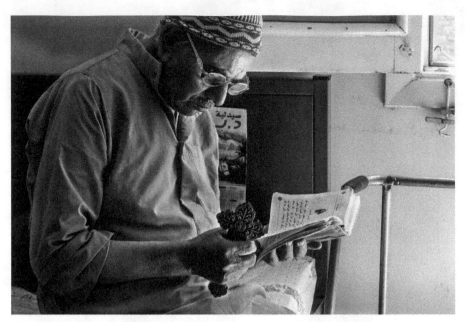

Home for the elderly in As Shubra. Cairo, Egypt, 2018

a missionary says: *On the first day, the sisters already placed their trust in the group. From then on, we worked in an integrated way.* They have two houses in Cairo, the most populated city in Africa and in the Middle-East.

In the home for the elderly in As Shubra, supported by twelve Missionaries of Charity, they asked the group to split between the women and the men's floor, and to pay special attention to each elderly person, usually having physical problems. The FIHM began to interact: games, haircut, nail-trimming, helping to give showers, serving meals, nursing duties, painting of seven beds.

A missionary nurse connected on a soul level to the pain of a man who would have his leg amputated in a few hours. She accompanied the doctor before his hospitalization and admired the unshakable serenity of the patient. Soon after, while she put a bandage on him, he began to pray. She closed her eyes in communion and plunged into a level of peace.

There was a time in Egypt when creative forces of the sacred sound were well known. The Egyptian Book of the Dead teaches that, first, God visualizes in His mind what He will create, and it begins to exist when He pronounces the name of the thing to be manifested.

Aware of the mystical power of music and of how much its vibration harmonizes and transforms, the missionaries arrived bringing their guitar and songs, flooding the patients with joy. The patients clapped their hands, swinging shoulders, arms, legs. They danced. And on the next day, the elderly reciprocated, singing their favorite songs.

Four days later, the representatives of peace drove nine miles to the base of Mokattam Hill, to give motherly attention to forty-three babies ages two months to three years. They were picked up by their mothers at the end of the day. The babies' fathers collected garbage in Cairo while their mothers and siblings, aged seven and up, sort before selling the material to recycling industries, which sustains the community. They are considered the best recyclers in the world, the ones who manage the best to make use of almost all the discarded material. In a few years, babies to whom missionaries gave bottles, changed diapers and warmly cherished on their lap, will continue the same work.

Residents of the so-called Garbage City are about 30,000 Copts, a minority in the country. The Egyptian Coptic Orthodox Christianity flourished shortly after the death of Jesus. Always persecuted and killed for their religious beliefs, they survive and protect themselves in a settlement on the outskirts of Cairo. Whereas in Cairo 99% are Muslim and 1% is Christian, in that district 10% are Muslim and 90% are Christian. This is why so many images of Our Lady, Jesus and saints decorate shops and balconies in the slum.

The missionaries found the babies in the nursery crying and very agitated. There was loud music in the room they cherish. To uplift their energy, the next day they sang soothing songs, watching them relax under the harmonious sounds. *We did everything; changed diapers, gave them bottles and soup and, on the other floor, played with children three years old and up.*

Fraternal love overflowed from the seven men and women, strangers coming from far-away lands. Looking in the eyes of their fellow beings, the missionaries became close to the elderly, children and their parents, the Sisters, workers and volunteers who occasionally showed up to help. Shen, the coordinator of the Mission, recalls: *We felt so much innocence, hospitality and purity in the Egyptians! Despite the material deprivations, limitations, they are extremely loving. Affection among human beings transcends cultures and beliefs, it is well above cultural and language barriers.*

Two sectors of the FIHF worked in parallel to each other, the Egypt Mission and the Pilgrimage of Peace. They were dedicated for two months prayerful meetings in Germany, Poland, Portugal and Switzerland.

Service from heart to heart has invisible results to the eyes. The missionaries don't seek results. They throw living seeds of love without looking where they will germinate. They cried out to the Angel of Cairo to do an acupuncture of peace in the so-called *mother of all cities*, which felt inner relief.

At their farewell, there was sheer gratitude. They went from one house to another smiling and hugging. The Missionaries of Charity offered them a song and gifts to each member of the mission, a medal of Mother Teresa of Calcutta and a key-chain with a mini-Bible. On that last day, the hotel manager asked to take a photo of the group to hang in the hotel lounge.

When their plane was about to land in Egypt, someone announced: *The Pyramids!* The seven rushed towards the airplane windows. Majestic, shrouded in old mysteries lost in the mists of the times. They had never visited colossal monuments surrounded by tourists. Material patrimony is fragile, subject to rot, they disappear, and are desacrated. On the other hand, steps climbed in the inner world are infinite.

The contrast between the ancient Nile and the current Egypt is striking. In ancient times, in the Pyramids, initiations took place, i.e., progressive expansions of consciousness signaling degrees in the long path of return to the Origin. Nowadays, initiations no longer happen in physical temples, but in the Inner Temple of those who consciously search evolutionary laws, which includes service, finding one's best in the other.

I finally understood. In the activities they experienced in Cairo, the Fire that is never put out enlightened the essence of the seven peace-makers. Touched by occult chemistry, the missionary had explained the days spent among Egyptian children and elderly: *Wonderful!*

Roraima Permanent Mission

Today, world tension consists of the fact that physical force and etheric energy are confronting each other... etheric force is intimately related with the highest spiritual aspect... this conflict will produce a re-orientation of humanity and of the individual towards the truest values.
Glamour: A World Problem, by Alice A. Bailey

In a house with an undisclosed address, the most vulnerable migrants are safeguarded. Granted free leasing since mid-2018 for the Fraternidade to protect Venezuelans who cannot be in the shelters, the House of Welcome receives no more than forty people at one time. They underwent abuse in squares, in streets. Feeling hopeless and angry for different reasons, they are frustrated and restless when they arrive. Women who suffered violence. Even with children, they are threatened by husbands. The house also relieves the despair of LGBTI—lesbians, gays, bisexuals, transsexuals and inter-sexual people.

Taking turns, coordinators of the fifth treatment unit of Fraternidade in Roraima explain to the temporary residents that they have come there to give love and, with simplicity, encourage them to heal intimate wounds during their stay in a safe daily routine, in which three daily meals relieve them from the torture of hunger. The servers develop the power of constant observation to seek to understand the needs of each refugee, and the heart of God smiles.

As they continuously recall their biological families, missionaries remember them: *Each human being is unique and is part of the great universal family.* At the new home, they learn to give fraternal help, attention to one another. *If a little child cries because her mother is giving birth at the hospital, who will take care of her? We will. We have to hug the three year old boy that asks, "Don't leave me alone."* Mutual respect, human diversity and the best of each one is valued. Gradually, residents exchange their kindheartedness, comb the hair of the epileptic youth, listen to the transvestite with a short skirt and green nail polish telling her story.

They celebrate birthday parties with cakes and balloons, bring together adult and children choirs, receive altruistic groups for joint activities. In the darkest hours for the group, clarity arises to deal with unpredicted obstacles. Knowing that words are not enough, the coordinators invite all of them to be in a circle holding hands, and emphasizes group strength: *Do not fear, do not run away. United, we have more power than any negative force. Let's pray!* Immediately, the group turns to the Heavens in silence and, without thoughts, opens to higher energies.

Their missionary teaching goes on: *We need to forgive. It is not easy, but we can do it little by little.* Forgiving with merciful love, what a difficult gift! There was a sixty five year old lady that had been abused. A missionary understood her pain and encouraged her, entrusting her with household chores. In two months, the lady had cheered up, was dressing up, applying lipstick. And she was told: *Oh, you look gorgeous!* With the UNHCR, they obtained a work record booklet for her. She felt reinvigorated, stepping out of the dark abyss in which she had plunged, and began to forgive the one who was abusive to her. At the farewell moment, before the missionaries returned to Minas Gerais, the lady sought words of truth hidden in her heart: *May God bless your generosity and, through us, may other people receive what you passed on to us.*

In the House of Welcome, the most fragile people can rest, but they know everyone will soon leave. Many will never see each other again, but they take a precious lesson with them: *Every morning we must begin again. With hope, bring goodness to each little action, to each new encounter. Always building a bridge to the Heavens, let us continue!*

 ## Educational Project The Common Good

In April 2018, a young missionary man made the draft of a project for two hundred children of the Pintolândia Shelter. The project was implemented in one classroom inside a container, which accommodates twenty children, and two classrooms in the former sports court.

Then, the UNICEF started to support the initiative. With financial funds, the project *O Bem Comum*—The Common Good—expanded to the shelters of Pacaraima and to the Nova Canaã, each one with its peculiarity and number of classrooms. A new schedule was established, along

Classes of *O Bem Comum* Project. Boa Vista, Roraima, Brazil, 2018

with more discipline. Since the project turned out to be very successful, the *UNICEF* extended it to ten shelters. Thousands of children are assisted by one hundred Brazilian and indigenous and non-indigenous Venezuelan educators. The main objective of *O Bem Comum* are two-fold. Leading confused children to current reality in a playful, healthy way, without traumas, so they can understand what is happening. The project also aims at preparing children to be introduced into the public educational system, whether of Roraima, or in the state of destination of their parents. Children begin to understand Portuguese, and the geographic size, and population of the city where they will soon live.

The relocation of Venezuelan refugees and migrants from Roraima to other parts of Brazil is implemented by the Armed Forces and the UNHCR and has grown in an organized and conscious way. *The Armed Forces set up an amazing structure in Pacaraima and Boa Vista. If they left, it would be chaos,* says the Boa Vista Fraternidade coordinator. In the Triage Center of the border, Venezuelans are vaccinated and receive documents. Out of hundreds of people who enter daily, some return to Venezuela. Others go to places in Brazil where they are already being awaited. However, 300 to 400 of them need to be directed to a shelter or be sent to another Brazilian state. Every week, one or two flights of the Brazilian Air Force transport at least 200 Venezuelans. Occasional news report that they are well, working and have a place of residence.

Para cada criança, o direito de aprender e brincar.

Little Canaries of Amazonia Choir

They live on the music that is grateful for life. Every day, sixty children and teenagers walk in the streets of Pacaraima to sing. They are poor, extremely poor. They leave hiding places where they live with families that survive on odd jobs. And they are hungry.

Míriam Blos sees them arrive with the eyes of her heart. She waits for them with the long table carefully set, colored tablecloth, flowers in the middle. While mothers cook in big pans, their sons and daughters sit, the choir conductor is at the end of the table. On top of the hill, the yard fills with giggles, kindness, reading of texts in Portuguese. The young singers only take part in the rehearsal after they are fed. The conductor and the Venezuelan instrument players instruct and attune the children's voices, which sing like angels a repertoire of classical pieces, popular rhythms, Brazilian and Venezuelan anthems, the song *Canarinhos Embaixadores da Paz*, composed by the conductor herself.

For seven years, the House of Music has survived on constant miracles. They are given musical instruments. If there is no gas or if the rent of musician's homes is delayed for months, money suddenly shows up in the bank accounts: if they lack food, bags of rice appear.

Visitors get charmed by the music and enchanted by the arduous surrender of the specialist in Amazonian sounds, undergraduate in Music, Education and Theology. *We get together to cooperate with the work that will give shape, with dignity, to the seeds of tomorrow,* Míriam Blos points out.

From September 2018, the Canaries of Amazonas Cultural Association has established three partnerships. The UNHCR finances the project. The Fraternidade gives it operational support in the rendering of accounts and in purchases. The army helps with a large part of the food and food supplements.

The objective is not only to give musical education to singers, but to create *more humane human beings*. In the overcoming of great challenges, emotions and thoughts of migrant adults and children become orderly. Solidarity harmonizes spaces of the Venezuelan consciousness.

Canarinhos da Amazônia Choir at the Federal University; trademark and Project *O Bem Comum*, a partnership between the Fraternidade and the UNICEF. Boa Vista, Roraima, Brazil, 2018

Colombia Humanitarian Mission

Things have a life of their own.
Everything is a matter of awakening your soul...
The truth is that the first changes are so slow
they are hardly noticed, and we keep looking
inside in the way we have always been, but
from the outside, the others notice them.
Gabriel Garcia Marquez

Two years after bringing love to Venezuelans in the north of Brazil, the Fraternidade was called to set up permanently in the Colombia-Venezuela border. They began to provide material or non-material assistance to the severe migratory crisis of Venezuelans escaping their country's social collapse, and also of Colombia's internal migrants, five million—the largest number of migrants in the world inside one owns country. For half a century, they try to escape collective violence.

With vibrant appreciation for life and each human being, and feeling grateful for the opportunity to serve them, seven missionaries met in the Northeast Colombia, in Cúcuta, the capital of the North Department of Santander, with 800,000 inhabitants. For five days, they began a first acknowledgment of the nation's complex mass migration. In recent years, the rural exodus has increased due to the number of Colombians displaced from cities, due to death threats from drug-trafficking groups.

In the presence of this gigantic human wave, missionary actions may seem minimal, but they are treasures. Gestures of collaboration have a symbolic value, as an instructor says: *The Love of God flowing through human hearts permeates entire nations. In silence, It embraces souls and more hearts with It's Grace, although this is invisible to the eyes.*

Humanitarian Colombia Mission is made up of the Colombian Light-Network and Youth Campaign for Peace members, missionaries and members of the monasteries. They aspire to generate unity and peace among human beings and nations. With light-handedness, servers and the people who are being served are warmed by the fire of benevolent gestures.

Venezuelan migrants receive support during the walk of more than 300 miles.
Andes, Colombia, 2018

There are three international bridges between the Venezuelan town of San Antonio de Tachira and Cúcuta. Early in the mornings, over thirty thousand people, mainly Venezuelans, begin to crowd the old bridge Simon Bolivar. Most return home after finding food and other relief, but about three thousand people exile daily. A part of those remain in Colombia: another part prefers to try life in other countries. According to official data, Colombia has received almost one million neighbors. Moreover, since the beginning of the crisis, Colombians who, in the past, had escaped to Venezuela under the terror of being forced to enlist in one of the outlaw gangs, have been returning with their Venezuelan wife and children.

One day Venezuelan and Colombian residents in Venezuela decide to leave, having lost hope in the land they love so much. They put backpacks or suitcases on their shoulders and go. Many carry big cardboard boxes or plastic bags full of objects. With no money for bus tickets, they walk hundreds of miles. A dream leads them: to settle down where they can get a job, save and send money to help hungry relatives left behind. In general, most migrants dedicate themselves to working hard to prosper, which benefits the societies welcoming them.

The exodus also increases through about two hundred and fifty *trochas*, clandestine muddy footpaths along the border. It is hard to calculate the extent of such human mobility, which is much greater and more complex than that of the Brazilian border with Venezuela. Men, women and children risk their life to escape hunger, unemployment, hyperinflation, police and political violence and persecution. Refugees and migrants move along jungle trails, cross the Tachira river, climb mountains. They come across drug-dealers, bandits, prostitutes and also armed paramilitary recruiting Venezuelans for the *bacrim*, Colombian gangs dedicated to trafficking, smuggling and extortion. These groups operate around the peripheries of about two hundred cities. Drug trafficking factions perpetuate fights for control of the cultivation of coca leaves in lands surrounding Cúcuta. Occupied by guerrillas, even the government has no access to it.

Missionaries study the history of the countries where they will work. Bathed by the Caribbean Sea and the Pacific Ocean, the Republic of Colombia, a country of fifty million inhabitants, the third largest population in Latin America, is Andean, Caribbean. Half of its territory is within the Amazonian forest, inhabited by multicolored birds. With historical social inequality, the elite of the country is white, but its people is mostly *criollo*, descendants of Spaniards born on the American continent, mixed with natives and Africans, just as in Venezuela.

At the beginning of the sixteenth century, Spanish settlers arrived on the Caribbean coast. They were not interested in exchanging knowledge with the native people who had inhabited the immense territory for more than 10,000 years. They ignored the developed Tairona civilization, whose Andean capital, the Lost City, was found in the 1970s.

Numerous indigenous Muiscas groups lived at 10,000 ft high, near where Bogota is today. They planted corn and potatoes and exploited salt, coal, copper and gold mines. Muiscas revered the Guatavita lake, heart of Colombia and symbol of the Great Mother. Spiritual ceremonies conducted on the lake gave origin to the El Dorado legend. The *zipa*, Muisca Chief, represented the male principle, the Sun God. He greased his body with honey and vegetable resin, sprinkling gold powder over it. Then, with four priests, softly navigated in a raft made of reed to the center of the circular lake, the representative of the female principle. Under the full moon light, his golden body shone, mirrored in the silver waters. Drums and chants accompanied the *zipa* from the shore making silence as the offering began. Gold ornaments created by the community were thrown on the waters. The sacred ritual celebrated the cosmic communion between the Sun God and the Great Goddess.

The priests possibly knew about the inter-dimensional passages in the clear lakes, which connect times and levels of consciousness. The surface of Guatavita reflects the skies like a mirror, and captures subtle supra-terrestrial communications. Lakes can receive archetypes of foods sent from other planets to be introduced on Earth. This information is condensed and then materialized. Just like the corn, coming from Venus, that Muiscas cultivated. Desecrated for centuries, today Guatavita is again surrounded by exuberant vegetation. Recently, in this park, the Council of the Muisca people has been given a great circular house. In the lake, it practices sacred rituals again, which return to the waters the silence and purity of the Great Mother.

But the Spanish conquerors wanted nothing to do with this. They coveted to plunder metals and precious stones, shipping the results of their pillage to Spain. Interested in indigenous labor, they subdued the Taironas and Muiscas easily. Only a few managed to escape isolating themselves in the back of the Amazonian forest, where they preserve their lifestyle. The others were quickly enslaved or decimated by the weapons and diseases brought from Europe—measles and smallpox—against which the natives did not have any antibodies. To the survivors, they imposed Catholicism and the Spanish language, forbidding them to communicate in the Chibcha language, which is still spoken by descendants in Colombia, Nicaragua, Honduras and Costa Rica.

After exhausting the indigenous people forced to work in mines, they resorted to African slavery. Colombian history differs little from the Latin American one with regard to the exploitation of human beings and of Nature, in the process of demographic and economic growth, in the colony's Independence, in political formation, under the influence of the Catholic Church. However, in Colombia, civil wars and brutal gangs have been generating fear and terror. Decades of mass murders, prejudice against minorities, unspeakable atrocities, corruption and exploitation of labor permeate the collective unconscious of the nation.

Along with the Venezuelan crowd entering the country after 2015, are the one million Colombian families displaced throughout the last half a century due to armed conflicts that left around 260,000 dead. Peasants and small rural land owners were the main victims. Sometimes drug dealers, or gun dealers, sometimes paramilitary forces or guerrillas expel them from places considered strategic by the guerrillas or extermination groups. They are forced to work transporting or selling drugs and the ones who refuse, are killed mercilessly. Besides, aiming at expanding their coffee monocultures or cattle raising, large farmers burned peasant houses and expelled them from their cultivated lands. Whole rural communities migrated as illegal squatters came to areas in the outskirts of urban centers. Most of them build precarious shacks on hills, forming *comunas*, like slums. Around Cúcuta there are areas occupied by guerrillas, to whom the government has no access, and where drug factions perpetuate struggles for control of land for coca planting.

Step by step, three to four hundred Venezuelans climb on foot the Colombian Andes every day. They leave from Cúcuta, at 1,000 ft of altitude, and reach 14,000 ft before beginning the descent from the mountains to the capital, Bogota, 370 miles away. At dawn and in freezing weather, they sleep exhausted by the side of the road. Downhearted, these people hardly notice the splendid green peaks and endless silent valleys.

They eat what charitable people give them. Among the ones who see the other's pain are the Fraternidade Missionaries. To relieve the walkers, they traveled 50 miles in a van, watching groups climb in a queue. They still did not know whom to help until they saw sixty migrants sitting by the road. They were suffering. The missionaries parked and approached smiling. They brought hot soup and harmony to the Latin-American brothers and sisters, whose pilgrimage had barely begun. The inadequate shoes caused blisters, the missionaries opened first-aids kits and humbly knelt before the swollen feet to put bandages on their wounds. Friar José de Arimateia says: *Through their reports, we learned about cases of hypothermia and altitude sickness. Some were suffering from physical-muscular fatigue.*

They extended their hands and opened merciful ears to listen to each one's story. *The warm-hearted encounter comforted them beyond words. They walk aimlessly, with no money, with no food, obviously extremely*

Fraternidade offers hot soup, affection and bandages on the feet of Venezuelans on their way to the capital or to other countries. Colombia, 2018

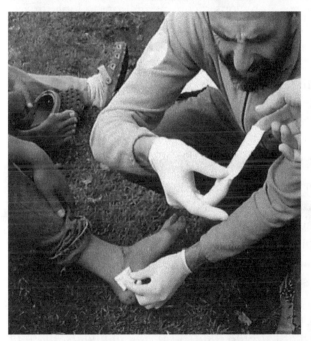

affected about leaving their homeland. We tried to encourage them to continue renewed with courage, states Imer.

When the missionaries waved good-bye, the Venezuelans had gained a breath of hope. They answered giving back what they had, bright smiles and warm farewells, which filled the missionaries with joy. Such simple fraternal connections are called heroic in the spiritual world, for their effect spreads subtle whirls of goodness for long distances.

Different humanitarian organizations are installed in Cúcuta to welcome, feed, and include the needy in society: churches and citizens open hostels, the UNHCR, the Red Cross International Committee. Upon their arrival, the Fraternidade got a precious recommendation: to look for Father Francesco Bortignon, the most important reference in care provided to the displaced, to immigrants without documents, to refugees, to deported adults and children. Active since the 1970s, the Father has free transit among all, including members of factions. Loved and respected, he enters where no one else goes to provide help for needy people, without distinction. He belongs to the Scalabrinian missionaries, followers of the motto: *If the migrant is not your brother or sister, God is not your Father.*

Soon, fifteen missionaries joined the teaching institution of the Scalabrinian Pilot Center, in the district of Camilo Daza, which assists 4,500 low-income students. Among them are 300 children of Venezuelan migrants or Colombians returning from Venezuela, besides 800 people who are displaced within Colombia. From Monday to Friday, the missionaries offered them their knowledge and experience, emotional support and instruction in subjects such as mathematics, languages, sciences. They also coordinated physical, manual, recreational and educational activities, mostly stimulating each student to perceive evolutionary impulses within themselves: *We talk with the children, trying to understand and inspire them to seek something beyond where they are, however little it may be. They perceive that we are there with our hearts, to share, to help, and quickly begin to trust us. A silent mysterious work based on love is gradually built.*

Teaching institution of the Scalabrinian Pilot Center.
Cúcuta, Colombia, 2018

Anchored on a philosophic, spiritual and ethical basis, the Fraternidade missions not only provide for the material level offering food, education and activities but they also work for the rescue of the dignity that each human being must minimally have. Besides that, the missionaries express examples of the standards for positive behavior—harmony, respect, confraternity, humbleness, silence, obedience, gratitude.

Exhausted from historic conflict, Colombians are taking important steps towards peace in order to open doors for citizens to seek the love that heals all pain. Some guerrilla groups surrender their weapons and commit to abandon armed fights. The government provides compensation for the victims.

Married to a Colombian, a Brazilian wife describes: *Colombians are gentle, joyful, hospitable, quite devout, concerned with spending money wisely, pacific and have strong family ties.* Although the hordes of Venezuelan migrants have created a phobia of fear of strangers, the Colombians are hospitable. They develop the *echado para adelante* characteristic, an expression that refers to those who look ahead without regretting the past.

New generations must learn to reconcile, to forgive neighbors, the enemy and the past that has wounded the soul of the nation. Colombia is being called to expand its consciousness of cooperation and to seek peace. Each citizen can bring forward the hidden spark within. The first ones to shine will radiate values to those who are still in the dark.

The devout Colombians chose the Lady of Chiquiquira as their patroness and queen. They feel supported by Her and by the Mother of Guatavita, who holds the key to healing and to communion between the Creation and the Creator.

Muiscas descendants of El Dorado reveal in a plaque written at the lake entrance: *Quartz is a doctor. When our heart is calm, holding no judgments nor anything negative, there is no evil that can do us harm, for we become doctors of ourselves. If our mind is as tranquil as the hills where each life form is sacred and respected as it is, our thought will be like an emerald. Gold is the sweat of the sun. Our body must reflect the good we have inside. This will give us the golden shine, for our actions will be from the quartz-heart, from emerald-thought, and thus we will be golden knowledge.*

An unfinished book

Serve! Serve your brothers and sisters, and the light will
turn on. You will see service not only among you, in the
mutual and fraternal help, but even in the Creation of
the Father. Service implies total detachment from the
egocentric petty self, it means a totally detached
surrender, united to love manifested in each act and work.
Patterns of Behavior for a New Humanity
by Trigueirinho

The book continues, without a full stop, as Fraternidade is a work in progress.

Dear reader, and what about the future? What potential missions will exist in the coming times? Would you take part in them?

On continents and in oceans, critical situations show typical end of times scenarios, such as the plastic micro-particles invisible to the naked eye that affect not only marine life that eats them but they end up in a person's meal. These particles begin to degenerate the genetic code. They alter the testosterone of men's sperm, reducing male fertility. Scientists project a drastic loss in fertility in the next forty to sixty years, that is, to our grand-children or great-grand-children. What can a mission do to minimize such wrongdoing?

Today, two permanent missions are active in Brazil: in Carmo da Cachoeira, Minas Gerais, and the Roraima Mission, with its high degree of complexity, which involves smaller missions. Abroad, the Humanitarian Colombia Mission was implemented. In Portugal, a house waits for the arrival of primary missionaries to be opened. As for the works of the Missionary Base of Greece, they are temporarily suspended.

In view of the growing humanitarian, social and natural emergencies, and the diversity of Fraternidade work guidelines, it has become essential to multiply the number of primary missionaries, those who coordinate the activities. They have learned the art of loving and of giving love throughout the battle, trying to do their best in each moment, in each mission. Importantly, they have gained strength throughout the Roraima Mission.

To meet multiple demands, the Missionary Academy Project was created. It aims to expand the Fraternidade services, training other primary missionaries to coordinate international missions. The Missionary Academy will train managers capable of organizing catastrophes and refugee camps. They must be able to communicate in two or more languages, manage people and finances, have knowledge about international relations and law.

Ricardo explains: *The training process will have introductory, basic and intermediate, besides specialization units. Active missionaries must also participate in the course, to improve and update their knowledge. It will eventually replace the current work of the Missionary Practices, a model of information learned by 6,000 people in five years, that gives participants some experience, but nothing in-depth.*

For further studies after building a foundation, each student chooses the area in which they are talented. In one unit there will be training for those who prefer to collaborate in emergencies—rescue from heights, water rescue, first-aid. Another unit will prepare those who are skilled in communicating and talking with institutions about working in partnership and will include studying geopolitics, international relations, inter-agencies relationship. One unit will cover administrative and financial aspects of the missions. Another, on health care, in which doctors, dentists, therapists, psychologists, nurses will participate. One unit will prepare graphic artist and sound editors to create beautiful mission documentaries. Specialists will be trained in legislation for protection of children from aggressions. A pedagogical unit will cover education, manual work, craftsmanship.

Practical learning walks side by side with inner transformation of those devoted to helping others. The main goal is to be an expression of the soul, to lead the server beyond the prison of human defects.

The opportunity for maturing is immense. Face to face with adversities, volunteers exercise being tranquil and silent, a healthy attitude in every situation. They gradually develop the invaluable quality of not getting emotionally involved with those in need. They discover how to treat situations they come across with the heart, trusting that the Universe manifests the essential, according to the karma of the individual or of the nation, and that not all depends on the effort of the missionary. They realize to what extent the feeling of pity for a family that was ill-treated by destiny blocks the server's spiritual energy and wears him out, without solving the issue.

On the other hand, active servers experience the impulse as if in war: *Let's go until we die.* Involved by daily life enthusiasm, they often do not perceive when they need to get help, nor do they give signs to their companions that a red light has turned on in them. The students need to deepen their self-analysis, be attentive to asking for help before they reach a point of weakness which opens doors and may lead them to an illness.

The FIHM remain in their primary task, strengthening the inner side of its members with prayers and instructions to raise their consciousness. Reminding them of our cosmic origin, our responsibility and role in the evolutionary chain, not expecting anything in return, to love, to serve, and be a spiritual energy transmitter to the Kingdoms of Nature. Members face challenges and perceive mundane life forces trying to destabilize them, learn to reconcile with them without losing the courage to persevere.

In face of our Planet's agony, idealistic people are attracted by missionaries' practices. Feeling the lack of something that goes beyond the ecological, cultural, philosophical, ideological or vegetarian level, these idealistic people have the courage to change for deeper experiences in surrender. They approach the work and begin to awaken to the unfathomable quest of the still unknown human being.

A flashing vision emerged in the mind of a young missionary during her training process. She was ignited by the splendor of a prophetic future: *I was in the future. I was there, and came back. I saw the sunset followed by a dark night. When the sun rose, it was as if a hurricane of bad things has gone away. I was walking slowly on well-patterned paths of polished, shining stones. The fresh dawn was colored by a golden light, and I felt a powerful peace.*

Everything passes. Missions and the current times of violent agitation will face a close. At last, when peace finally rules life, men and women will walk in the most beautiful fraternal pathways.

List of Fraternidade Humanitarian Missions

1st Mission: Nepal
October 20 to November 4, 2011: 18 volunteers

2nd Mission: Nicaragua
July 27 to 30, 2012: 10 volunteers

3rd Mission: Ethiopia
November 2 to 18, 2012: 15 volunteers

4th Mission: Ethiopia
February 4 to 22, 2013: 16 volunteers

5th Mission: Ethiopia and Kenya
April 23 to May 28, 2013: 10 volunteers

6th Mission: Permanent Carmo da Cachoeira Mission, Minas Gerais, Brazil
Since January 2014

7th Mission: Alagoas, Brazil
November 2 to 13, 2014: 15 volunteers

8th Mission: Rwanda
April 10 to 17, 2015: 14 volunteers

9th Mission: Uganda
April 17 to 25, 2015: 14 volunteers

10th Mission: Democratic Republic of the Congo
April 25 to May 3, 2015: 14 volunteers

11th Mission: Mariana, Minas Gerais, Brazil
November 25 to 28, 2015: 17 volunteers

Group of missionaries that served in Nepal, in Argentinian Chaco, in Rwanda, in Ethiopia, in Turkey and on the first Roraima Mission, in Brazil.

12th Mission: Turkey
January 19 to February 27, 2016: 14 volunteers

13th Mission: Chaco, Argentina
January 26 to February 10, 2016: 21 volunteers

14th Mission: Dolores, Uruguay
May 2 to June 8, 2016: 8 volunteers

15th Mission: Paraguay
June 20 to July 7, 2016: 17 volunteers

16th Mission: Greece Permanent Mission
September 2016 to June 2018

17th Mission: Roraima Permanent Mission, Brazil
Since November 3, 2016

18th Mission: Emergency Chile
February 7 to 24, 2017: 14 volunteers

19th Mission: Zona da Mata, Minas Gerais, Brazil
December 30, 2017 to January 8, 2018: 10 volunteers

20th Mission: Confraternizar Mission, Salta, Argentina
February 12 to 26, 2018: 17 volunteers

21st Mission: Egypt, Africa
June 14 to 23, 2018: 7 volunteers

22nd Mission: Lebanon/Angola
May 24 to June 23, 2019: 10 volunteers

23st Mission: Permanent Humanitarian Colombia Mission
Since August 2018

Light-Network Missions

Recurrent Regional Backcountry Mission, Alagoas, Brazil
Five communities of Palmeiras dos Índios and surroundings: twice a year, since
December 2014. About 25 volunteers from Northeastern states in each mission.

Recurrent Regional Chaco Mission, Argentina
Six indigenous communities of Resistencia and surroundings: four times a year,
since May 2016. About 120 volunteers altogether, with 30–40 at each mission.

Recurrent Regional and International Paraguay Mission
Seven indigenous communities of Ciudad del Este and Presidente Franco: three
times a year, since June 2016. About 20 volunteers at each mission.

Missionaries in transit,
wait at international airports

Eyes, the mirror of the soul. What story is there behind Eriannys' eyes, the seven year old girl on the cover?

Eriannys, born at a hospital in Tucupita, in Venezuela, was breastfed. At the age of four, she began to move around with her family. From the border city Santa Elena de Uairén, she went to an indigenous shelter in Pacaraima, Brazil, and from there to another one in Boa Vista.

She takes a pencil to her mother and asks her how to write, but the mother does not know. At the shelter's school, she finds hope. She likes to play with other children and, if she gets in a fight, she learned with her mother not to hit the person back. Her parents never took her to have contact with trees, flowers, rivers. She has now four brothers and sisters, but lost the other four, one of them because of measles. Her father, 36, her mother, 33, and her older brother, 12, are part of the current seven-member family. Being a good girl, she helps her mother look after the baby.

Eriannys and the hundred million children in the world who are in a similar situation are sheer grace and energy. May they persist and keep love blazing beyond every pain. Someday they will see the triumph of fraternity and of peace.

Ana Regina Nogueira

She was born in Belo Horizonte, Brazil, in 1948. Author of four books published by Irdin Editora, she is a photographer. In a voluntary way, she wrote the text, selected the photos, created the page layout.

The author donates her copyrights to Irdin Editora

CPSIA information can be obtained
at www.ICGtesting.com
Printed in the USA
LVHW080320120920
665566LV00001B/1